International Law: Examples and Explanations

International Law: Examples and Explanations

Edited by Silas Kearns

MURPHY & MOORE
www.murphy-moorepublishing.com

Murphy & Moore Publishing,
1 Rockefeller Plaza,
New York City, NY 10020, USA

ISBN: 978-1-63987-326-5

Cataloging-in-Publication Data

International law : examples and explanations / edited by Silas Kearns.
p. cm.
Includes bibliographical references and index.
ISBN 978-1-63987-326-5
1. International law. 2. International law--Interpretation and construction.
3. Law. I. Kearns, Silas.

KZ3410 .I58 2021
341--dc23

For information on all Murphy & Moore Publications
visit our website at www.murphy-moorepublishing.com

MURPHY & MOORE

Contents

Preface

This book was inspired by the evolution of our times; to answer the curiosity of inquisitive minds. Many developments have occurred across the globe in the recent past which has transformed the progress in the field.

International law refers to the set of standards, rules and norms which establish a common framework and normative guidelines which are used to guide states on a wide variety of subjects such as diplomacy, war, human rights and trade. The key objective of international law is to stabilize international relations. Some of the common sources of international law are treaties, international customs, international organizations, and law of the sea. States which do not abide by the international law can be met with coercive actions which can range from diplomatic and economic pressures to military interventions. This book provides significant information of this discipline to help develop a good understanding of international law and related fields. It presents the complex subject of international law in the most comprehensible and easy to understand language. Coherent flow of topics, student-friendly language and extensive use of examples make this book an invaluable source of knowledge.

This book was developed from a mere concept to drafts to chapters and finally compiled together as a complete text to benefit the readers across all nations. To ensure the quality of the content we instilled two significant steps in our procedure. The first was to appoint an editorial team that would verify the data and statistics provided in the book and also select the most appropriate and valuable contributions from the plentiful contributions we received from authors worldwide. The next step was to appoint an expert of the topic as the Editor-in-Chief, who would head the project and finally make the necessary amendments and modifications to make the text reader-friendly. I was then commissioned to examine all the material to present the topics in the most comprehensible and productive format.

I would like to take this opportunity to thank all the contributing authors who were supportive enough to contribute their time and knowledge to this project. I also wish to convey my regards to my family who have been extremely supportive during the entire project.

Editor

1

INTERNATIONAL ECONOMIC LAW IN SOUTH AFRICA

*Engela C Schlemmer**

1 International economic law in South Africa

The South African government has been actively involved in the negotiation and signature of international agreements relating for example to the field of international economic law ever since it became a union in 1910.[1] The first, but not necessarily related to international economic law, was the involvement of General Smuts in the drafting of the Covenant of the League of Nations.[2] And not long after that were the negotiations that led to the signing and ratification of the Articles of Agreement of the International Monetary Fund which came into force in 1945.[3]

Although the signatories of this agreement undertook to give effect to it in their domestic legal systems, the South African government chose not to do so and until today, the Articles of Agreement of the International Monetary Fund has not been incorporated into South African law.[4]

* Professor of law at the University of the Witwatersrand, Johannesburg, South Africa. This contribution will focus mainly on the WTO agreements. This work is based on research supported in part by financial contributions by the State Secretariat for Economic Affairs SECO of the Swiss Confederation, the World Trade Institute in Berne, Switzerland and the National Research Foundation of South Africa (UID nr 80820).

1 As a result of the UK South Africa Act, 1909 which created the Union of South Africa.

2 One of the big proponents of the League of Nations was Jan Christian Smuts (see C Howard-Ellis (ed) *The origin, structure & working of the League of Nations* (2003) 80ff).

3 International Monetary Fund and International Bank for Reconstruction and Development *Inaugural meeting of boards of governors, provisional list of members of the delegations officers of the Secretariat* (1946); and for some of South Africa's initial involvement see *Proceedings and documents of the United Nations Monetary and Financial Conference Bretton Woods, New Hampshire July 1-22, 1944 Vol I and II* (1948). Articles of Agreement of the International Monetary Fund (22 July 1944).

4 It needs to be mentioned that the article which has caused the most litigation or which has been cited most in litigation in many other jurisdictions, art VIII(2)(b), has never been the subject of litigation in South Africa and as such the domestic legal status of the IMF's articles of agreement has never been addressed by the South African courts.

In these early years of South Africa, there was no constitution that contained any provision regarding the treatment of international treaties in its domestic law. The legal status of international treaties in South Africa was governed by the common law which was considered to be more or less the same as English law and South Africa thus never followed an entirely monistic approach. The approach was rather more dualistic and thus in order for a treaty to have domestic effect, it had to be incorporated by legislation into South African law (→ De Wet/Introduction).[5]

2 Implementation of international economic law

2.1 The legal effect of treaties

A treaty is described in the Vienna Convention on the Law of Treaties as an international agreement between two states governed by international law.[6] Although South Africa is not a signatory to this treaty, it is quite clear that South Africa considers itself bound by the principles contained in the treaty and also applies it to its treaty practice.[7] This is not an uncommon phenomenon since the Convention codifies customary international law and South Africa has to a large extent always respected customary international law and the general principles of customary international law forms part of South African law (→ De Wet/Introduction).[8]

It is, however, trite law that a state is only bound by a treaty if it bound itself to it and if that treaty came into operation.[9] The mere fact that a treaty is in existence does not have any legal effect on non-signatories. It also does not form a source of international law for non-parties. The only exception to this rule is found in those instances where customary international law had been codified as is the case with the Vienna Convention on the Law of Treaties. The difference thus lies in the fact that in this instance, a state gives credence to customary international law

5 This is called the principle or doctrine of incorporation. See H Booysen *Volkereg en sy verhouding tot die Suid Afrikaanse Reg* (1989) 33; J Dugard *International Law: A South African perspective* (4th edn 2011) 42ff.

6 Vienna Convention on the Law of Treaties (the Vienna Convention) (23 May 1969, 1155 UNTS 331) art 2(1)(*a*).

7 See Booysen (n 5 above) 34.

8 The Constitution of the Republic of South Africa, 1996 sec 232. For the historical approach to customary international law in South Africa see *Nduli v Minister of Justice* 1978 (1) SA 893 (A) 906C - E, 'It was conceded by counsel for appellants that according to our law only such rules of customary international law are to be regarded as part of our law as are either universally recognised or have received the assent of this country. I think that this concession was rightly made'. See also the discussions by Dugard (n 5 above) 48 - 51; J Dugard 'International law is part of our law' (1971) 13 *South African Law Journal* 15; Booysen (n 5 above); AA Lamprecht 'Nullum crimen sine lege (iure) and jurisdiction in the adjudication of international crimes in national jurisdictions' unpublished LLD thesis, UNISA, 2010 475 - 479; and the sources they refer to.

9 Vienna Convention on the Law of Treaties (n 6 above) art 1(1)(g).

principles to which it is bound whereas in the other instance, a state is not bound by any obligations of treaty law that it did not agree to (you can only be bound by obligations that you had agreed to). The normal principles of *pacta sunt servanda* are thus applicable: without concensus, a state is not bound by international law obligations. And at the local level, citizens may only rely on treaties binding their government if those treaties are incorporated into South African law.

2.2 The legal status of the General Agreement on Tariffs and Trade 1947 in South African law

As indicated, South Africa participated in international law-making since the early years of the twentieth century and as such was one of the contracting parties to the General Agreement on Tariffs and Trade 1947. This agreement was incorporated into South African domestic law through the promulgation of the Geneva General Agreement on Tariffs and Trade Act in 1948.[10] The long title of this act stated its aim as 'to approve of the General Agreement on Tariffs and Trade concluded at Geneva on the thirtieth day of October, 1947; to make provision for the carrying out of the said agreement, and for matters incidental thereto'.[11]

The state law advisors interpreted the wording of section 3 of the act,[12] to mean that the application of the agreement (as part of South African law) was dependant on the (additional) actions of the governor-general, which required the publication of relevant proclamations.[13] Since no proclamations were ever published, the agreement thus never became part of the domestic law and the citizens of the country could also not rely on it in any litigation.[14] This is apparently also the information provided to the secretariat of the General Agreement on Tariffs and Trade; in South Africa's trade policy review of 1993 the following statement is found: 'it [South Africa] has observer status in the Government Procurement, Subsidies and Anti-Dumping Codes![15]The General Agreement [on Tariffs and Trade] has been approved by Parliament *but cannot be invoked before*

10 Geneva General Agreement on Tariffs and Trade Act 29 of 1948. It came into force on 9 April 1948.

11 n 10 above, long title. The General Agreement on Tariffs and Trade (GATT 1947) (30 October 1947, 55 UNTS 194) was primarily a customs matter and all the repealed sections of the act dealt with customs valuations, ie operational provisions.

12 'The agreement shall, in relation to the territories the governments of which are referred to in section two, be applied, either provisionally or definitively as the Governor-general may determine by proclamation in the *Gazette*, with effect from a date specified in such proclamations.'

13 See GS Eisenberg 'The GATT and the WTO agreements: comments on their legal applicability to the Republic of South Africa' (1993/1994) 19 *South African Yearbook of International Law* 132.

14 This act never formed the subject matter of any reported case.

15 South Africa never signed these codes.

national courts'.[16] The government's submission to the secretariat also makes no mention of the relevant act[17] and its implication for South Africa's trade policy. Eisenberg, without giving any cogent authority, is of the opinion that the act is still in operation and shall remain as such until South Africa withdraws from the agreement.[18] However, the only section remaining in the act, merely refers to the approval of the agreement which had been published in the *Government Gazette* in 1947.[19]

References to a number of other agreements that formed part of the tariff rounds of the General Agreement on Tariffs and Trade are to be found in other pieces of legislation, yet none of these agreements were ever incorporated into South African law. Notwithstanding references to treaty provisions found in legislation, such as section 74A of the Customs and Excise Act,[20] the particular international law documents were not incorporated and it is thus only the General Agreement on Tariffs and Trade of 1947 which was formally incorporated into South African domestic law.

Section 74A of the Customs and Excise Act as amended by Act 101 of 1985 provides as follows:

> (1) The interpretation of sections 65, 66 and 67 shall be subject to the agreement concluded at Geneva on 12 April 1979 and known as the Agreement on Implementation of Article VII of the General Agreement on Tariffs and Trade, the Interpretative Notes thereto, the Advisory Opinions, Commentaries and Explanatory Notes, Case Studies and Studies issued under the said Agreement on Implementation of Article VII of the General Agreement on Tariffs and Trade.[21]
>
> (2)(a) The Commissioner shall obtain and keep in his office two copies of such Agreement, Interpretative Notes, Advisory Opinions, Commentaries and Explanatory Notes, Case Studies and Studies and shall effect thereto any amendment thereof of which he is notified by the Secretariat of the Customs Co-operation Council, Brussels.
>
> (b) Whenever in any legal proceedings any question arises as to the contents of the said Agreement, or any such Interpretative Note, Advisory Opinion, Commentary, Explanatory Note, Case Study or Study (hereinafter in this paragraph referred to as the relevant document), or as to the date upon which any amendment thereof was effected thereto in terms of paragraph (a), a copy of the relevant document, or if amended as contemplated in paragraph (a), a

16 Emphasis added. GATT Secretariat 'Trade Policy Review Mechanism the Republic of South Africa' C/RM/S/37A 3 May 1993 vii http://www.wto.org/gatt_docs/English/SULPDF/91700080.pdf (accessed 30 April 2015).

17 Geneva General Agreement on Tariffs and Trade Act (n 10 above).

18 n 13 above, 133. See the discussion to follow on the validity and duration of the GATT 1947.

19 GN 2421 *GG* 3896 of 18 Nov 1947.

20 Customs and Excise Act 91 of 1964.

21 This refers to the Customs Valuation Agreement (Customs Valuation: Agreement on Implementation of Article VII of the General Agreement on Tariffs and Trade (Document code LT/TR/A/2), one of the Tokyo round codes).

> copy of the relevant document as so amended, shall, unless the contrary is proved, be accepted as sufficient evidence of the contents thereof or of the effective date of any amendment thereof, as the case may be.

This provision requires the use of the Agreement on Implementation of Article VII of the General Agreement on Tariffs and Trade (the customs valuation agreement or code), for purposes of interpretation. However, the mere requirement of using the international treaty for purposes of interpretation does not suddenly make it (that is, the treaty) part of South African law.[22] It is true that the interpretation along the lines of the international instrument does have an influence on the application of the particular provision in the domestic law but that still does not mean that the agreement itself became part of South African law.[23] It does not comply with the requirements stated in the *Pan American Airways* case as quoted below and neither does it comply with the constitutional requirements as enacted in both 1993 and 1996.[24] Treaties that are not properly incorporated do not form part of domestic law and treaties or provisions of treaties merely referred to in passing cannot be considered to be incorporated treaties or even to be considered to be incorporated by reference[25] and be given direct application in the domestic law.With the acceptance of the Agreement establishing the World Trade Organisation, the position regarding the GATT 1947 changed due to the fact that the GATT 1994 effectively replaced the GATT 1947 and as a result, the GATT 1947 is no longer a legally binding instrument which means that even though the act remains on the statute books and was not repealed, it

22 This seems to be confirmed by the latter part of the section that clearly states that the copy of the agreement would be considered evidence of its contents. One does not provide evidence of the law of a country before its own courts. The new Customs Duty Act 30 of 2014 (the date of commencement still has to be proclaimed) did not change this position (see secs 97 & 98). What has been changed however, is that is now clearly provided that the tariff classification of goods for customs purposes must be done in accordance with particular international instruments but if there are any inconsistencies between the international instrument and the act, the act would prevail (secs 96 and 97). Similar provisions are to be found concerning the valuation of imported goods (secs 113 & 114) etc.

23 See also C Roodt 'National law and treaties: An overview' (1987-1988) 13 *South African Yearbook of International Law* 72 92: 'It is important to note that a mere general or vague allusion to the treaty in a statute is not sufficient to constitute the necessary legislative implementation'; and A Sanders 'Transformation of treaties' (1974) *Tydskrif vir die Hedendaagse Romeins- Hollandse Reg* 364 369.

24 Prior to the 1993 and 1996 Constitutions, there was no obligation on courts to consider international law when interpreting legislation and it seems as if the government of the time wanted to ensure that specifically with regard to trade matters, an interpretation be followed that would take international law for this particular purpose into account. These provisions did not, however, incorporate the respective international law documents or treaties into South African law. The introduction of the constitution and sec 233, did not change this; sec 231 in essence codified the requirements set out in the *Pan American Airways v SA Fire and Accident Insurance Co Ltd* 1965 (3) SA 150 (A) case which requires an act of incorporation and until it is repealed, the requirements of s 231 cannot be ignored. In the case of GATT 1947 (n 11 above), the position was governed by the pre-constitutional era and as such provisions similar to sec 233 were not part of South African law.

25 The private law doctrine of 'incorporation by reference' also no longer finds application in South African law – see *Moses v Abinader* 1951 (4) SA 537 (A) 552D.

no longer has any legal significance. If an international instrument is repealed, there are no international obligations that need to be complied with and if the only remaining part of the domestic legislation, as is the case under discussion, merely refers to the initial GATT 1947 treaty – the act in essence has been abrogated by disuse.

The same should be applicable to instances where reference is made to international treaties and documents which should have been used for purposes of interpretation of actions if those treaties are no longer in effect. The law also does not work in such a manner that if a treaty is replaced by something new, that it would automatically follow that in municipal law, a new act of incorporation or an amendment of an existing legislative provision is not required.

2.3 The legal status of the Agreement establishing the World Trade Organisation in South African law

The South African government signed the Agreement establishing the World Trade Organisation on 15 April 1994.[26] The agreement was ratified by the South African parliament on 6 April 1995.[27] With its signature and the consequent ratification, the South African government gave its approval of the Agreement as required by the Final Act.[28] The approval given by the South African parliament did not include an incorporation act and neither did parliament expressly provide[29] that the agreement would form part of the law of the Republic.[30] And as Botha puts it:

26 'Results of the Uruguay Round Signing Ceremony on April 15th, 1994 in Marrakesh, Morocco' NUR086 18 April 1994 http://www.wto.org/gatt_docs/English/SULPDF/91770139.pdf (31.10.2014); see Eisenberg (n 13 above) 135 who wrongly states the date as 14 April 1994).

27 *Debates of the National Assembly (Hansard) Second Session – First Parliament* 23 Jan-11 Oct 1995 col 642 – 653; EC Schlemmer 'Ontwikkelende of ontwikkelde lidland: Suid-Afrika en die Wêreldhandelsorganisasie' (2007) *Tydskrif vir die Suid-Afrikaanse Reg* 786 - 799 and the sources referred to.

28 Final Act Embodying the Results of the Uruguay Round of Multilateral Trade Negotiations (http://www.wto.org/english/docs_e/legal_e/legal_e.htm#finalact (accessed 30 April 2015)); see also EC Schlemmer 'South Africa and the WTO ten years into democracy' (2004) 29 *South African Yearbook of International Law* 125; Schlemmer (n 27 above) 786ff.

29 Botha states that 'There was some difference in opinion in academic circles on exactly how Parliament was 'expressly so to provide'. In practice, however, this was effected by endorsement of the treaty and a declaration to this effect at the time of promulgation.' (NJ Botha 'International law' in Joubert (ed) 11(2ed) *LAWSA* para 444 and the sources he refers to.)

30 It had been argued elsewhere that due to the fact that the negotiations that took place leading to the signing of the agreement already started in September 1986 ('The Final Act of the Uruguay Round Press Summary' *NUR*084 5 April 1994 http://www.wto.org/gatt_docs/English/SULPDF/91770054.pdf (accessed 30 April 2015)), the whole process was governed by the pre-1993 Constitutional dispensation (which came into operation on 27 April 1994) and even though the 1993 Constitution contained a provision that deviated from the earlier legal position regarding the incorporation of treaties into domestic law before the treaty can have effect at a domestic level (sec 231(3) 'Where Parliament agrees to the ratification of or accession

> In assessing the municipal effect of treaties, therefore, it must be borne in mind that during the 'interregnum' between 27 April 1994 (the date on which the interim Constitution came into operation) and 4 February 1997 (the date on which the Constitution of the Republic of South Africa came into operation) a unique method was employed to accord treaties municipal application.[31]

It remains clear that no matter which format had to be followed, the result is thus that the WTO agreements do not form part of the South African domestic law. The coming into operation of the Constitution of the Republic of South Africa, 1996 did not change this legal position.[32]

In the period prior to the coming into operation of the interim constitution, the application of treaties in domestic law was treated as follows, as enunciated by the then Appellate Division[33] in *Pan American World Airways Incorporated v SA Fire and Accident Insurance Co Ltd*:[34]

> [T]he conclusion of a treaty, convention or agreement by the South African Government with any other Government is an executive and not a legislative act. As a general rule, the provisions of an international instrument so concluded, are *not embodied in our municipal law except by legislative process* ... In the absence of any enactment giving [its] relevant provisions the force of law, [it] cannot affect the rights of the subject.[35]

The Agreement establishing the World Trade Organisation and the covered agreements such as the General Agreement on Tariffs and Trade (1994) were never incorporated into South African law and thus can never

to an international agreement under subsection (2), such international agreement shall be binding on the Republic and shall form part of the law of the Republic, provided Parliament expressly so provides and such agreement is not inconsistent with this Constitution.'), that irrespective of the actions taken in parliament, the agreements do not form part of South African domestic law.

31 n 29 above, para 445.

32 See also in detail DJ Devine 'Some problems relating to treaties in the Interim South African Constitution and some suggestions for the definitive constitution' (1995) 20 *South African Yearbook of International Law* 1.

33 The name of the appellate division was changed to the supreme court of appeal by the Constitution of the Republic of South Africa, 1996 (item 16(3)(a) schedule 6)) with effect from 4 February 1997 when the Constitution came into operation. The supreme court of appeal (and prior to the name change, the appellate division) was the highest court in the Republic until 22 August 2013; the Constitutional Court was made the highest court of the Republic *in all matters* and not only limited to constitutional matters any longer with effect from 23 August 2013 (see sec 167 of the Constitution of the Republic of South Africa, 1996 as amended by the Constitution Seventeenth Amendment Act of 2012).

34 n 24 above.

35 n 24 above, 161 C-D – emphasis added. See also *S v Eliasov* 1967 (4) SA 583 (A) 591; H Booysen 'Judicial control of the prerogative in foreign affairs' (1977) *South African Yearbook of International Law* 216; M Olivier 'The status of international law in South African municipal law: section 231 of the 1993 constitution' (1993/4) 19 *South African Yearbook of International Law* 1 6; *Nduli v Minister of Justice* 1978 (1) SA 893 (A); *Maluleke v Minister of Internal Affairs* 1981 (1) SA 707 (BSC); *S v Petane* 1988 (3) SA 51 (C); C Roodt 'National law and treaties: an overview' (1987-88) *South African Yearbook of International Law* 72 - 94.

be the source of any rights for South African legal subjects. This has been confirmed by the Supreme Court of Appeal in *Progress Office Machines v SARS.*[36]

On numerous occasions, the South African courts have confirmed that a South African legal subject cannot rely on international law in order to circumvent the application of a rule of South African law.[37] The opposite should also be true, namely that any reliance on an international law principle that does not form part of South African law may not be sanctioned by South African courts and treated as a source of South African law. South African legal subjects do not derive any interests or rights worthy of legal protection from such international law provisions and as such these are not justiciable before a South African court.

Treaties that are not properly incorporated do not form part of domestic law, also, treaties or provisions merely referred to in passing cannot be considered to be incorporated and one can also not consider them to be incorporated by reference and in such a manner be given indirect application almost as if they had been incorporated.[38] The same should apply to reports of *inter alia* the international trade administration commission which all contain a statement indicating that the report is done 'in accordance with the International Trade Administration Commission Act ... the Anti-Dumping Agreement ... and the ... Anti-

36 *Progress Office Machines CC v South African Revenue Service & Others* 2008 (2) SA 13 (SCA) 17E-F. Also see *Glenister v President of the Republic of South Africa and Others* 2011 (3) SA 347 (CC) per Ngcobo CJ 'An international agreement that has been ratified by resolution of Parliament is binding on South Africa on the international plane. And failure to observe the provisions of this agreement may result in South Africa incurring responsibility towards other signatory States. An international agreement that has been ratified by Parliament under s 231(2), however, does not become part of our law, until and unless it is incorporated into our law by national legislation. An international agreement that has not been incorporated in our law cannot be a source of rights and obligations' (374G-375A). And see *Azanian Peoples Organization (AZAPO) v President of the Republic of South Africa* 1996 (4) SA 671 (CC) 'International conventions do not become part of the municipal law of our country, enforceable at the instance of private individuals in our courts, until and unless they are incorporated into the municipal law by legislative enactment' (per Mahomed DP (688C) with reference to *R v Secretary of State for the Home Department, Ex parte Brind* 1991 (1) AC 696 (HL) 761G-762D; *Pan American World Airways* (n 24 above); *Maluleke* (n 35 above) 712G-H; *Binga v Cabinet for South West Africa* 1988 (3) SA 155 (A) 184H-185D; *S v Petane* 1988 (3) SA 51 (C) 56F-G; HR Hahlo & E Kahn *The South African legal system and its background* (3rd edn 1968) 114; J Dugard *International Law: A South African perspective* (1994) 339-46. See however MD Stubbs 'Three-level games: Thoughts on *Glenister, Scaw* and international law' (2011) 4 *Constitutional Court Review* 138 who accepts (wrongly and without consideration of authority) that 'the GATT and WTO agreement (*sic*) had been incorporated into domestic law' (145) and '*Scaw* was a win for the state because it held a win-set. It had tentative agreement to, and ratification of, the GATT and the WTO agreement, coupled with full domestic ratification in the form of the ITA Act' (161). See also *Association of Meat Importers and Exporters v International Trade Administration Commission* 2013 (4) All SA 253 (SCA) para 58.

37 See *Binga v Administrator-General SWA* 1984 (3) SA 949 (SWA) 967; Booysen (n 5 above) 78; also see *Inter-Science Research & Development Services (Pty) Ltd v Republica Popular de Mocambique* 1980 (2) SA 111 (T) 124.

38 Legal subjects would still not be entitled to rely on any of the obligations that the government might not be complying with in such an instance.

Dumping Regulations[39]'.[40] This statement by the statutory commission cannot result in an indirect application of the treaty in South African domestic law. The mere fact that one might be relying on an international treaty for purposes of interpretation does not mean that interpretation *per se* or the interpretative tool can create rights which can be relied upon in a court of law.

The acceptance and coming into operation of the Agreement establishing the World Trade Organisation in Marrakesh in 1994, introduced a new era for international trade. The General Agreement on Tariffs and Trade of 1947 was replaced with the General Agreement on Tariffs and Trade of 1994 and although the 1947 Agreement is an annex to the Marrakesh agreement, it is replaced by the new agreement.

The procedure for the orderly termination of the 1947 agreement is contained in the concomitant decision of the preparatory committee for the World Trade Organisation entitled *Transitional Co-Existence of the GATT 1947 and the WTO Agreement*[41] and was adopted at the sixth special session held on 8 December 1994.[42] The decision provides that

> The legal instruments through which the contracting parties apply the GATT 1947 are herewith terminated one year after the date of entry into force of the WTO Agreement. In the light of unforeseen circumstances, the CONTRACTING PARTIES may decide to postpone the date of termination by no more than one year.[43]

After this period, the rights and duties by reason of the 1947 agreement do not continue any longer – the period of co-existence between GATT 1947 and the WTO Agreement is limited to one year with a possible extension of one year. The fact that the GATT 1947 is one of the annexes of the WTO agreement does not mean that it creates new rights and duties but that the rights and duties created after its termination arise out of GATT 1994 and the WTO agreement.

Thus, after December 1997 all of the international law rights and obligations that existed in terms of the 1947 agreement were terminated and replaced with new rights and obligations in terms of GATT 1994. As a result the Geneva General Agreement on Tariffs and Trade Act does not have any role to play and can almost be regarded as *pro non scripto*. If no

39 GN 3197 in *GG* 25684 of 14 November 2003.

40 See for example *Report No. 332 Investigation into the alleged dumping of staple polyester fibre in or imported from the People's Republic of China (PRC): final determination* 1.04.2010 http://www.itac.org.za/docs/Report%20332.pdf (accessed 31October 2014).

41 *Transitional co-existence of the GATT 1947 and the WTO Agreement* PC/W/17-6SS/W/3 of 7 Dec 1994 http://www.wto.org/gatt_docs/English/SULPDF/91840033.pdf (accessed 30 April 2015).

42 6SS/SR/1 http://www.wto.org/gatt_docs/English/SULPDF/91840166.pdf (accessed 30 April 2015).

43 *Transitional co-existence of the GATT 1947* (n 41 above) para 3.

rights and obligations exist at the international law level, it is also not possible to derive any rights or obligations at the domestic level that an individual may rely on. The fact that the act remained on the statute book[44] does not change the legal position.

It is true, however, that some important changes were made to South African legislation, especially regarding trade remedies and intellectual property, that were clearly aimed at giving effect to South Africa's international law obligations arising from the WTO agreements. However, it seems as if the Constitutional Court has on occasion applied the WTO agreements directly even though they do not form part of South African law.

3 The role of courts in applying and developing international economic law

3.1 Using the WTO agreements for purposes of interpretation

In terms of the Constitition of the Republic of South Africa, 1996, the Republic is bound by treaties that were binding on it prior to the Constitution[45] and it is also clear that customary international law forms part of South African law if it is not in violation of the Constitution or legislation.[46] The Constitution also provides that in interpreting the Bill of Rights the courts must consider international law.[47] Furthermore, when it comes to the interpretation of legislation, 'every court must prefer any reasonable interpretation of the legislation that is consistent with international law over any alternative interpretation that is inconsistent with international law' (→ De Wet/International Decisions; Chenwi).[48]

The Constitutional Court has already on a number of occasions stated that using international law as an interpretative assistant 'is to respect the careful way in which the Constitution itself creates concordance and unity between the Republic's external obligations under international law, and their domestic legal impact'.[49] It has also stated that:

44 With only one section still in place which merely confirms the incorporation of GATT 1947.

45 n 8 above, sec 231(5) 'The Republic is bound by international agreements which were binding on the Republic when this Constitution took effect'.

46 n 8 above, sec 232 'Customary international law is law in the Republic unless it is inconsistent with the Constitution or an Act of Parliament'.

47 This places a positive obligation on the courts to look at international law and thus treaties when they interpret the rights in terms of the bill of rights (see the Constitution (n 8 above) sec 39(1)(a)).

48 The Constitution (n 8 above) sec 233.

49 *Glenister* (n 36 above) 410F - G per Moseneke DCJ and Cameron J discussing the interrelationship between s 39(2) and s 7(2) of the Constitution.

> A further provision of the Constitution that integrates international law into our law reinforces this conclusion. It is s 233, which, as we have already noted, demands any reasonable interpretation that is consistent with international law when legislation is being interpreted. There is, thus, no escape from the manifest constitutional injunction to integrate, in a way the Constitution permits, international law obligations into our domestic law. We do so willingly and in compliance with our constitutional duty.[50]

However, Ngcobo CJ held in the same case that:

> [T]reating international conventions as interpretive aids does not entail giving them the status of domestic law in the Republic. To treat them as creating domestic rights and obligations is tantamount to 'incorporat[ing] the provisions of the unincorporated convention into our municipal law by the back door.[51]

At this point of the discussion, one has to differentiate the approach of the Constitutional Court with that of the Supreme Court of Appeal when it comes to the Agreement establishing the World Trade Organisation.

3.2 The approach of the Constitutional Court

In March 2010 the Constitutional Court gave a far reaching judgment in *International Trade Administration Commission v SCAW South Africa (Pty) Ltd.*[52] The applicant in this case was the international trade administration commission, a statutory body created in terms of section 7 of the International Trade Administration Act.[53] The purpose of the commission is *inter alia* to deal with applications for anti-dumping investigations and matters related to it. The commission should investigate and evaluate allegations of dumping in or to the Republic or the Common Customs Area created by the Southern African Customs Union (SACU) Agreement.[54] After investigating and evaluating an anti-dumping allegation/application, the commission makes a recommendation to the

50 *Glenister* (n 36 above) 410G - I.

51 *Glenister* (n 36 above) 376H.

52 *International Trade Administration Commission v SCAW South Africa (Pty) Ltd* 2012 (4) SA 618 (CC). The following discussion is based on EC Schlemmer 'Die grondwetlike hof en die Ooreenkoms ter Vestiging van die Wêreldhandelsorganisasie' (2010) *Tydskrif vir die Suid-Afrikaanse Reg* 749.

53 International Trade Administration Act 71 of 2002; it came into operation on 1 June 2003.

54 Southern African Customs Union (SACU) Agreement (2002 SACU Agreement) (21 October 2002).This international agreement has presumably been incorporated into South African law in terms of the schedule 1 of the International Trade Administration Act (n 53 above). The addition of the schedule to the act has however not been done yet since it seems as if this will only be done once all the relevant institutions have been created. It does however raise an interesting question, one which I do not attempt to address in this contribution, since the 2002 SACU agreement has already been incorporated into South African law by means of schedule 10 of the Customs and Excise Act (n 20 above). See the comments of Nugent JA in the *Association of Meat Importers and Exporters* (n 36 above) case that the Customs Union Agreement has not yet become law in the Republic (par 14).

minister of trade and industry[55] who in turn will request the minister of finance to promulgate anti-dumping duties in the *Government Gazette*.[56]

The respondent in this case was SCAW South Africa (Pty) Ltd, a South African company who was complaining about the dumping of steel products by Bridon International Limited (UK), a British company. This complaint was investigated by the Board on Tariffs and Trade (the predecessor of the commission) and as a result of the investigation and recommendation, the minister promulgated an anti-dumping duty of 42,1 per cent in February 2002,[57] thus before the enactment of the ITA Act. In August 2006 Bridon requested a review based on changed circumstances; the commission found in May 2007 that the anti-dumping duties should continue in force.[58]

On 19 February 2007, SCAW applied to the commission for a sunset review with the intention of having the duties maintained beyond the five-year period.[59] The anti-dumping regulations do provide that any investigations and reviews undertaken after its promulgation should be done in terms of the regulations. The first time these regulations could play a role, was thus in August 2006 when Bridon requested the review due to changed circumstances.[60]

The commission initiated a sunset review in August 2007 and in October 2008 recommended to the minister that the anti-dumping duties be terminated. As a result of this recommendation SCAW sought an urgent interim interdict to prevent the minister(s) from acting on the recommendations while the judicial review of the commission's investigation was ongoing. The interdicts were granted thus effectively extending the period of the anti-dumping duties for a period longer than five years. The commission then approached the Constitutional Court for

55 Once the SACU Tariff Board is created in terms of the 2002 SACU agreement (n 54 above), the recommendation will be made to this Board.

56 Customs and Excise Act (n 20 above) sec 55(2) & 56. The new Customs Duty Act 30 of 2014 which has not come into operation yet, clearly defines customs duties for purposes of the 2002 SACU agreement (sec 16).

57 And thus subject to the 1969 SACU (11 December 1969) agreement which provided that all SACU members were bound by the duties imposed by South Africa for purposes of goods entering the common customs area.

58 *SCAW South Africa* (n 52 above) 626F - 627A.

59 See *SCAW South Africa* (n 52 above) 627C - E for the details. It is however important to point out that the court refers to the anti-dumping regulations as authority whereas at the point in time when the anti-dumping duties were imposed, the regulations were not in force (they only came into force in November 2003) and they were also not promulgated with retrospective effect. The duties under discussion were thus imposed in terms of the Board on Tariffs and Trade Act 107 of 1986.

60 This discussion will only focus on the Constitutional Court's approach to the WTO agreements and the role of international law in South African domestic law and not on the detail of the anti-dumping law-related issues. For more detail and a discussion of some of the issues not dealt with in this discussion, see GF Brink '*International Trade Administration Commission v SCAW South Africa (Pty) Ltd* Case CCT 59/09 [2010] ZACC 6' (2010) *De Jure* 380.

leave to appeal, contending that the order was contrary to domestic law as well as to South Africa's international law obligations.[61]

In its judgment, the Constitutional Court frequently refers to the Anti-Dumping Agreement in order to determine the duration of the anti-dumping duties as well as the duration of the anti-dumping duties in the event of a sunset review. Little reference is made to the relevant domestic law provision. This is problematic since the treaty that the Court uses as yard stick, does not form part of South African domestic law and the relevant domestic law provision contains a much stricter requirement (which is more beneficial to the party paying the anti-dumping duties)[62] than that contained in the Anti-Dumping Agreement.[63] The Court also does not make reference to the South African Customs Union Agreement that does form part of South African domestic law. The importance of these two statements will be seen shortly.

3.2.1 The Southern African Customs Union Agreement

In its judgment, the Court places huge emphasis on the obligations of the ministers of trade and industry and finance that arise from national legislation. However, justice Moseneke did not take into account that, for the time being, the two ministers are, when it comes to dumping investigations and the recommendation and promulgation of anti-dumping duties, acting on behalf of the Southern African Customs Union and its Council of Ministers and not primarily as mandatories of South African legal subjects.[64] The fact that these local ministers are acting in a

61 Another important issue was whether the order given by the High Court 'trenches on separation of roles and powers between the national executive and the courts. This issue has been dealt with more extensively in Schlemmer (n 52 above).

62 See Ngcobo CJ's statement in the *Glenister* case (n 36 above) 378C: 'insofar as provisions in the international agreement give rise to rights and obligations under domestic law, these rights and *obligations flow from, and are limited by,* the extent to which the domestic legislation incorporating the agreement includes those provisions' (emphasis added).

63 See the more detailed discussion of this aspect in Schlemmer (n 52 above) 750 where it is argued that even if anti-dumping duties were to have remained in place for a period of seven years due to the intervening sunset review investigation an interpretation of art 11 of the Anti-Dumping Agreement would have led to the conclusion that it would not have amounted to a breach of the WTO obligations. In the case under discussion, however, the South African regulations are *stricter* than the suggested rules in the Anti-Dumping Agreement thus requiring the investigations to be completed quicker than in the Anti-Dumping Agreement, but the Court chose to focus primarily on an international law instrument which is not prescribing that countries enact legislation complying with it. Furthermore, the Court places a lot of emphasis upon the fact that the application for judicial review causes the anti-dumping duties to remain in effect for longer and loosing out of sight the fact that it is a requirement for members of the WTO who impose anti-dumping duties to make provision for their actions to be taken on review.

64 See the wording of the 1969 SACU Agreement (n 57 above) which was incorporated into South African law (GN 3914 *GG* 2584 of 12 Dec 1969); the 1969 Agreement was terminated from 15 July 2004 on the coming into operation of the 2002 SACU Agreement (R 800 *GG* 26537 of 2 July 2004) subject to the transitional provisions contained in art 50 which *inter alia* relates to dumping investigations etc.

representative capacity, puts the whole issue *in casu* most probably outside the ambit of the Constitutional Court's jurisdiction.[65]

Moseneke DCJ said the following:

> Constitutional issues
>
> The litigants are at one that the application for leave to appeal involves constitutional matters. That is indeed so. First, the order of the High Court restrains two members of Cabinet from exercising executive powers conferred upon them by the Constitution and national legislation. It is plain from section 85(2)(a), (b) and (e) of the Constitution, that the two Ministers exercise executive authority by "implementing national legislation"; by "developing and implementing national policy"; and by "performing any other executive function" provided for in national legislation. As we have seen, the Act and the BTT Act variously require the two Ministers to formulate and implement national policy and to perform specified executive functions related to exports and imports of goods and other international trade activities. More pertinently, they are required to impose, change or remove anti-dumping duties in order to realise the primary economic and developmental objects of the statutes (636E-637B).

It seems as if the justice approached the matter from the wrong angle. The application that was before the North Gauteng Court was for relief to prevent or restrain a minister from making a decision before the review of the process on which the recommendation to the minister would have been based. The legislation requires complainants to adhere to particular time periods and this matter could have been dealt with more expeditiously if the commission had reacted *immediately* on the request for a sunset review and had not delayed with its commencement. *In casu* the commission waited for almost six months before it commenced the review.[66] It would have been more appropriate had the parties rather applied for a *mandamus* at an earlier stage. In such an instance the commission would have been obliged to comply with its statutory duty. Cognisance should have been taken of the commission's bad track record to deal with investigations speedily and effectively.[67]

It is true that 'the setting, changing or removal of an anti-dumping duty is a policy-laden executive decision that flows from the power to formulate and implement domestic and international trade policy', as formulated by the justice.[68] However, the issue before the North Gauteng High Court was whether there was reason to grant an interdict so that the process leading to this executive decision could be taken on review. Allowing parties the capacity to request that these decisions and recommendations

65 See the discussion on the relationship between the commission and the SACU below.
66 *SCAW South Africa* (n 52 above) 627D - E The application was brought on 19 February 2007 and the commission only complied with the request on 17 August 2007.
67 See G Brink 'Proposed amendments to the anti-dumping regulations: Are the amendments in order?' (2006) *Tralac Working Paper No 21* 16.
68 *SCAW South Africa* (n 52 above) 637E.

be taken on review, is also one of the international law obligations that the government has to comply with and is contained in the anti-dumping regulations.[69] The justice does not mention this and it seems as if more emphasis is placed on some international law obligations than others; the treaty itself does not contain any order of priority or importance when it comes to the different obligations related to trade remedies.

In the same paragraph, justice Moseneke states that:

> That power [the power to impose anti-dumping duties] resides in the heartland of national executive authority. Separation of powers and the closely allied question whether courts should observe any level of 'deference' in making orders that perpetuate anti-dumping duties beyond their normal lifespan is a constitutional matter of considerable importance.[70]

This pronouncement is evidently wrong. For the time being, and until the Tariff Board of the Southern African Customs Union is formed, the commission undertakes the anti-dumping[71] investigations not only for South Africa but as a matter of fact for the whole of the Customs Union and the imposition of *inter alia* anti-dumping duties, is done on behalf of the Council of Ministers of the Southern African Customs Union.[72] It is thus of (regional) international importance and not merely a 'constitutional matter'. The formula used for the distribution of the income in the customs union gives a clear indication that the other members (Botswana, Lesotho, Namibia and Swaziland) of the customs union have a substantially greater financial interest than South Africa in the magnitude of the anti-dumping (and other) duties imposed, even though the South African domestic market would be influenced much more than the broader customs union market. This fact alone is indicative that the vested interests that are entitled to be legally protected are not in the first place purely that of the South African industry, the South African treasury and the South African economy, or of the two South African ministers and thus only governed by the South African Constitution and entitled to be protected by the Constitutional Court and the other South African courts. This would open the door for the conclusion that also any other member of the customs union may, in the same matter, approach their highest courts for a finding that may potentially be in conflict with another member's courts' finding on an anti-dumping matter between the same parties – this is not a situation that can be tolerated by any legal system.

69 And also contained in the Agreement on Implementation of Article VI of the General Agreement on Tariffs and Trade (Anti-Dumping Agreement) (15 April 1994).
70 *SCAW South Africa* (n 52 above) 637E - 638A.
71 All trade remedy investigations.
72 See the 1969 SACU agreement (n 57 above) arts 4 & 5 and the 2002 SACU agreement (n 54 above) art 50 and 51. A customs duty in this context includes anti-dumping duty, countervailing and safeguard duty – see the Customs and Excise (n 21 above) secss 1(1) & 55 and Cronje *Customs and Excise Service* (Oct 2014 SI 37) part IV 6 - 1.

The situation outlined above[73] with regard to the imposition of anti-dumping duties already existed prior to the coming into operation of the Southern African Customs Union agreement in 2002.[74] Article 50 of the 2002 agreement deals with the transition measures that are to remain in place until the relevant structures are created within the customs union itself as well as in the individual member states.[75] Article 50 provides as follows:

> A commission, technical liaison committee or *any other institution, obligation or arrangement of SACU which exists immediately before the entry into force of this Agreement shall,* to the extent that it is not inconsistent with the provisions of this Agreement, *continue to subsist, operate* or bind Member States of SACU as if it were established or undertaken under this Agreement, until the Council determines otherwise.[76]

This treaty was enacted into South African law in schedule 10 of the Customs and Excise Act[77] and came into operation on 15 July 2004[78] and thus forms part of the South African domestic law even though the Constitutional Court does not refer to it and also does not reckon with its implications.

3.2.2 The WTO Agreements

The Constitutional Court stated the matters that it had to consider in the *SCAW* case as follows:

> I think it is in the interests of justice for this Court to pronounce on: (a) the lawful extent of the legislatively prescribed lifespan of an anti-dumping duty; (b) whether the interdict had the effect of extending the lifespan of the existing anti-dumping duty; and if so, (c) whether the order trenches on separation of roles and powers between the national executive and the courts; (d) *whether the judicial extension of the anti-dumping duties threatens South Africa's trade relations and other obligations under international law*; (e) whether the matters to be determined by this Court on appeal will come up for decision in the final review before the High Court and therefore will not require this Court to prejudge the outcome of the review; and lastly, (f) whether there are reasonable prospects that this Court may find that whilst it may have been competent for the High Court to make the order it did, it was not constitutionally permissible or appropriate for it to do so.[79]

73 Regarding the investigations relating to trade remedies etc.
74 See n 72.
75 Currently only South Africa has a national body that can investigate trade remedy allegations and the Tariff Board for SACU has not been created; neither has the SACU tribunal been formed. Also refer to sec 2(1) of the transitional provisions in schedule 2 of the International Trade Administration Act (n 53 above).
76 Emphasis added.
77 *GG* 26537 of 02.07.2004.
78 It should also be added as schedule 1 of the International Trade Administration Act (n 53 above).
79 n 52 above, 643G - 644A. Emphasis added.

It is particularly the emphasised part that is relevant and the focus here will be on the Court's handling of international law and how it deals with South Africa's obligations in terms of our membership of the World Trade Organisation. Due to the Court's approach to South Africa's international obligations, it touches upon more aspects than would have been the case had the point of departure been different (and perhaps more correct).

In footnote 1 of the judgment, justice Moseneke makes the following statement:

> As a member of the WTO, South Africa is also a signatory to the General Agreement on Tariffs and Trade (GATT). *This agreement was approved by the South African Parliament through the Geneva General Agreement on Tariffs and Trade Act 29 of 1948.* The international rules relating to dumping are contained in article VI of the GATT and the Anti-Dumping Agreement.[80]

This statement is a clear indication that the justice lost sight of the fact that the General Agreement on Tariffs and Trade that was signed in 1947 and incorporated into South African law in 1948 is technically speaking not the same agreement as the General Agreement on Tariffs and Trade that is an annexe to the Agreement establishing the World Trade Organisation. The Agreement establishing the World Trade Organisation replaced the General Agreement on Tariffs and Trade of 1947 with that of 1994 'which is a new and legally distinct agreement'. Article II.4 of the agreement provides as follows:

> The General Agreement on Tariffs and Trade 1994 as specified in Annex 1A (hereinafter referred to as 'GATT 1994') *is legally distinct from the General Agreement on Tariffs and Trade, dated 30 October 1947*, annexed to the Final Act Adopted at the Conclusion of the Second Session of the Preparatory Committee of the United Nations Conference on Trade and Employment, as subsequently rectified, amended or modified (hereinafter referred to as 'GATT 1947').[81]

The agreement that was incorporated into South African law no longer has any legal force and effect at the international level and neither at the domestic level; one cannot argue that it can 'rule from the grave' and in such a manner import the WTO agreements into South African law.[82]

The fact that justice Moseneke in footnote 1 of the judgment refers to this act as supposed authority for the WTO agreements to form part of

80 Emphasis added. In the light of the fact that the case under discussion deals with dumping, it must be emphasised that South Africa was not a signatory to the socalled anti-dumping code and as such was not bound by it (see *Chairman of the Board v Brenco* 2001 (4) SA 511 (SCA) 528G - H).

81 Emphasis added. The legal position regarding this agreement is more correctly stated in *Association of Meat Importers and Exporters* (n 36 above) par 18.

82 See the discussion above. The WTO agreements were also signed as a 'package' in 1994 and not as separate agreements. The statement by the justice is thus not correct.

South African law, is alarming. For purposes of the legal issue at hand the reliance on that piece of legislation is wrong and unpersuasive.

After the signing of the Marrakesh agreement no legislative act can be traced in terms of which any of the agreements were enacted in full into South African law. Since none exist, these agreements do not form part of South African law and no individual (legal subject) may rely on any rights or legal protection contained in the agreements.[83] And yet is seems as if the Constitutional Court applies these agreements directly as if they form part of South African law.

WTO agreements used as an interpretative tool

The question to be considered is whether these agreements may not in any event, be used for purposes of the interpretation of legislation. In English law the presumption exists that in instances of ambiguity, it is *prima facie* presumed that the intention of the legislature was not to act in violation of its international law obligations. This is the case also in those instances where the treaty is not incorporated into domestic law.[84] The provisions of a treaty can thus be used advantageously in interpreting other legislative provisions.

The interpretation of legislation in instances of ambiguity, however, is something much different from considering the actions or inactions of a statutory body or an organ of state that may/has lead to the violation of a state's international law obligations. Lord Diplock said in the *Salomon* case that unambiguous legislation enacted after the conclusion of a treaty 'must be given effect to, whether or not they carry out Her Majesty's treaty

83 This has been confirmed in *Progress Office Machines* (n 36 above) 17E-F and also referred to by the Constitutional Court in its judgment.

84 See *Salomon v Commissioners of Customs and Excise* [1967] 2 QB 116 CA 143F; [1966] 3 All ER 871; *Theophile v Solicitor-General* [1950] AC 186 PC; C Roodt 'National law and treaties: an overview' (1987-88) 13 *South African Yearbook of International Law* 72 83ff. See also *Rustomjee v R* [1876] 2 QB 69 73 where it was held that 'as in making the treaty, so in performing the treaty, she [the queen] is beyond control of municipal law, and her acts are not to be examined in her own courts'. This has also been confirmed in *Lonrho Exports Ltd v Export Credits Guarantee Department* [1996] 4 All ER 673: 'The courts will not adjudicate upon the transactions of or between sovereign states, and in all matters relating to foreign relations, judges should be circumspect and rarely should judges intervene where diplomats fear to tread (see *Maclaine Watson & Co Ltd* [1989] 3 All ER 523 at 544, [1990] 2 AC 418 at 499 per Lord Oliver and *R v Secretary of State for Foreign and Commonwealth Affairs, ex p Pirbhai* (1985) Times, 17 October (689)'.
A recent decision by the Zimbabwean High Court also held a similar point of view: 'On the pragmatic approach that has come to be adopted in international practice, neither legal system enjoys primacy over the other. In principle, they both hold sway and supremacy in their respective domains. ... The resultant divergence between the two systems is reconciled on the basis that the State incurs international responsibility for having violated its international obligations and must accordingly effect the requisite reparations in order to satisfy its international responsibility' (*Route Toute BV v Minister of National Security Responsible for Land, Land Reform and Resettlement* HH 128 (2009) 17-18 and confirmed in *Gramara (Private) Ltd v Government of the Republic of Zimbabwe* 2010 JOL 25340 (ZH) 5).

obligations, for the sovereign power of the Queen in Parliament extends to breaking treaties'.[85]

Prior to the new constitutional dispensation, it was accepted in South African law that courts were not allowed to test the compliance of subordinate legislation against the existence of international law obligations.[86] Currently the Constitutional Court may test any piece of legislation in order to determine whether it complies with the values contained in the Constitution. However, to read into this the capacity to find subordinate legislation invalid because it does not comply with South Africa's international law obligations is taking the matter too far.

The role of unincorporated treaties in the interpretation of legislation and especially also subordinate legislation has been the subject of much debate.[87] In the past the debate was around the existence (or absence) of a presumption that parliament shall not enact legislation that violates our international law obligations. The existence of such a presumption is not supported by South African authority.[88] The end of this debate seem to indicate that if a treaty does not form part of domestic law, it should not be used for purposes of interpretation unless it can be shown that the piece of legislation was enacted to give effect to the Republic's international law obligations.

In terms of the old constitutional dispensation, the courts could not test legislation against international law.[89] The new constitutional dispensation did not change much. If legislation violates the constitution or constitutional values, and the reason for the violation is found to be the violation of international law obligations, it would be possible to reach such a finding. However, apart from the explicit reference in section 39 and the interpretation of the Bill of Rights, there is nothing contained in the current Constitution that empowers the courts to test the validity of legislation against international law norms that do not form part of South African law.

When it comes to the interpretation of legislation, courts are enjoined to find an international law conforming interpretation. This does not mean, however that the Constitutional Court is suddenly endowed with

85 n 84 above, 143E & 875 respectively.
86 See the *Binga* cases (n 36 & 37 above) and Roodt (n 23 above) 74 & 87.
87 See J Dugard 'The revocation of the mandate for Namibia revisited' (1985) 1 *South Afrcan Journal of Human Rights* 154 - 159; G Erasmus 'Mandates, military service and multiple choice' (1985-6) *South African Yearbook of International Law* 115 - 137; J Dugard 'International law' (1984) *Annual Survey of South African Law* 80 - 81; P Schaffer 'The inter-relationship between public international law and the law of South Africa: An overview' (1983) 32 *ICLQ* 277 308; Roodt (n 23 above) 87ff and the sources referred to.
88 See Roodt (n 23 above) 88 - 89 and the sources referred to.
89 *Collco Dealings v Inland Revenue Commissioners* [1962] AC 1 (HL) 19; *Croft v Dunphjy* [1933] AC 156 (PC) 164; *Cheney v Conn* [1968] 1 All ER 779 780; *Alexander v Pfau* [1902] TS 155 159; and the *Binga* case (n 36 above) 964.

the capacity to test whether every piece of legislation complies with the principles of international law. This would fall outside its jurisdiction.The same applies to the power of the Court to reprimand a minister or government department for actions that may be considered in breach of an international law obligation. The capacity to exercise a policy decision lies with the relevant ministry. If another state is to complain about the actions of the South African executive it must be done in the correct *fora.* The South African courts do not have inherent jurisdiction to adjudicate matters of international law.

To my mind, the new constitutional dispensation did not change anything in this regard. Section 233 provides that:

> When interpreting any legislation, every court must prefer any reasonable interpretation of the legislation that is consistent with international law over any alternative interpretation that is inconsistent with international law.

The focus is on the *interpretation* of the legislation and not on the *application* or *execution* thereof. If the provisions of the relevant piece of legislation is clear and unambiguous, it is not necessary to look at any other means of interpretation. When one is dealing with the *application* or *execution* of legislation, one is dealing with elements of administrative law where other rules of law would rather apply. In this instance, the provision in the regulation is more friendly towards the person against whom the anti-dumping duties are levied than what is provided for in the treaty. In the judgment, justice Moseneke states that the recommendation of the commission was made in terms of national legislation that regulates the administration of international trade and 'seeks to give effect to the international obligations of the Republic' and that the Court is thus 'required by the Constitution to *interpret* domestic legislation governing the duration of anti-dumping duties consistently with these international obligations'.[90] Interestingly enough there is no reference in the judgment to anything in the legislation or the regulations that is in need of interpretation. No reference can be found to anything that is ambiguous or unclear. The problem that the Court is faced with is rather dealing with the *effect* that the action of the commission and the recommendation of the minister would have on the duration of the anti-dumping duties. In other words, the problem at hand deals with the *application* of the regulation and the *effect* of the actions of the commission. The Court does not pronounce on these issues at all.

If the legislature wanted to prevent South Africa from potentially breaching its international law obligations and thus not to impose anti-dumping duties with a duration of longer than five years, it should expressly have provided so. It should further have made express provision for the weall and woe of the anti-dumping duties in those instances where

90 *SCAW South Africa* (n 52 above) 637D - E emphasis added.

an undeceived importer (or exporter) wants to take the action of the commission on review. The relevant anti-dumping agreement contains an obligation that enjoins a WTO member to make proper provision for access to the courts so that the aggrieved parties affected by the actions of the government or government institutions are able to take these actions on review. This obligation is also contained in the regulations but the justice does not pronounce on this. It is thus submitted that even though the WTO agreements may be used as interpretative tools, it was not necessary for purposes of the regulation at stake.

The authority of the Constitutional Court to make a finding on the breach by South Africa of a WTO obligation

It is generally accepted that '[t]he public international law relationships between states are, because of the doctrine of sovereign immunity, outside the domain of municipal courts'.[91] In the House of Lords, Lord Templeman held[92] that '(i)nternational law regulates the relations between sovereign states and determines the validity, the interpretation and the enforcement of treaties'. In the same case, Lord Oliver of Aylmerton stated that:

> It is axiomatic that municipal courts have not and cannot have the competence to adjudicate on or to enforce the rights arising out of transactions entered into by independent sovereign States between themselves on the plane of international law.[93]

Thus, according to these arguments it is not possible for domestic courts to deal with disputes between states falling within the international law domain.

In the *SCAW* case, however, the Constitutional Court did not take the particular nature of international law obligations into account and it also did not consider which court has the authority or jurisdiction to make a determination whether one is dealing with a violation of international law or not. In terms of international law, a violation of international law will

91 H Booysen 'The administrative law implications of the "customary international law is part of South African law" doctrine' (1997) 22 *South African Yearbook of International Law* 46, 50 and the sources referred to; see also H Damian *Staatenimmunität und Gerichtszwang* (1985) 10ff; see also S Fatima *Using international law in domestic courts* (2005) 277; J Crawford *Brownlie's principles of public international law* (8th edn 2012) 63.

92 In *JH Rayner (Mincing Lane) Ltd v Department of Trade and Industry* 1990 2 AC 418 526j as quoted in *Swissborough Diamond Mines (Pty) Ltd v Government of the Republic of South Africa* 1999 (2) SA 279 (T) 328G.

93 *JH Rayner (Mincing Lane) Ltd* (n 92 above) at 544e. 'So far as individuals are concerned, it *is res inter alios acta* from which they cannot derive rights and by which they cannot be deprived of rights or subjected to obligations; and it is outside the purview of the Court not only because it is made in the conduct of foreign relations, which are a prerogative of the Crown, but also because, as a source of rights and obligations, it is irrelevant' (545a). This has also been quoted with approval in the *Swissborough* case (n 92 above) 328G - I.

only be an issue if the international law subject against whom the obligation is owed complains about the violation – the reason being because one is dealing with an international law relationship.

The position regarding the obligations in terms of the World Trade Organisation Agreements is the same: reciprocal duties and obligations are owed to other members of the WTO. Pauwelyn explains it as follows:

> WTO obligations are of the reciprocal type. They are not integral in nature. A breach of WTO obligations does not necessarily affect the rights of all other WTO members. More than one, and in some instances all, WTO members may be so affected. But if all WTO Members are, indeed, affected this is not *necessarily* so, based on the *nature* of the WTO obligation. It is a consequence rather of WTO obligations being trade-related and trade restrictions, in turn, being capable of affecting the economic interests (not necessarily the rights) of many WTO members.[94]

The concomitant result is that if a breach takes place, it is at a bilateral level.

> WTO dispute settlement does not, in the first place, tackle *breach*, but rather nullification of benefits *that accrue to a particular member.* Panel and Appellate Body proceedings only examine claims made by one WTO member against one other WTO member. Most importantly, in case the defendant loses and does not comply within a reasonable period of time, the winning state will be authorised to impose *state-to-state countermeasures against the losing state* (DSU Art. 22). This exclusively bilateral modality of enforcement of WTO rules is an important indication that most WTO obligations are reciprocal in nature.[95]

It is thus clear that the obligations arising out of the WTO agreements are reciprocal in nature and that a *member* has to complain about a violation or a breach and since it is a closed treaty system, only members of the WTO may approach the Dispute Settlement Body for eventual adjudication of a dispute.[96]

The parties *in casu* were not in an international law relationship and the party requesting the interdict is not another state complaining of a potential breach of international law, but a national of South Africa. In cases of dumping it is typically not states that are guilty of dumping products but primarily an exporter (a company like Bridon *in casu*) and it would be the exporter who would be guilty of dumping and it is also this

94 J Pauwelyn 'The nature of WTO Obligations' *Jean Monnet Working Paper* 1/02 (2002) 12ff; also see M Hahn *Die einseitige Aussetzung von GATT-Verpflichtungen als Repressalie* (1995) 396.

95 Pauwelyn (n 94 above) 17 - 18 – emphasis added.

96 *United States – Import prohibition of certain shrimp and shrimp products* WT/DS58/AB/R report of the appellate body of 12 Oct 1998 par 101; see also G Erasmus 'The incorporation of trade agreements and rules of origin: the extent of constitutional guidance' (2003) 28 *South African Yearbook of International Law* 157 165.

company's actions which are investigated by the relevant authorities. The imposition of anti-dumping duties is also not directed against a state but against particular products from particular manufacturers or exporters. The international dispute only arises after the exporter, Bridon, complains to its home state and the home state decides that it is worth its while to take up the matter at the international level.[97] The only body with the necessary capacity to adjudicate a potential breach of the WTO agreements, is the Dispute Settlement Body of the WTO.[98]

No domestic court has inherent jurisdiction to pronounce on an international law matter. The South African courts and also the Constitutional Court do not have the capacity to adjudicate whether an act by the South African government, a legislative provision or any action on the side of the commission *in casu* amounts to a violation of the WTO agreements and yet, this is the end effect of the Constitutional Court's judgment.

3.3 The approach of the Supreme Court of Appeal

In a more recent case, *Bridon International GmbH v International Trade Administration Commission,*[99] the Supreme Court of Appeal, without referring to the *SCAW* case, found that particular provisions of the ITA act were promulgated to give effect to South Africa's WTO obligations.[100]

Unlike in the *SCAW* case, the Court does not get confused between the GATT 1947 and 1994.[101] The Court correctly states that the WTO Agreement and the Agreement on Implementation of Article VI of GATT became binding on the Republic. Just as the Constitutional Court, the Court confuses the constitutional mechanism that had to be applied but correctly held that 'because they were not enacted into our municipal law

97 P Van den Bossche 'General introduction to WTO dispute settlement' in P Van den Bossche *The law and policy of the World Trade Organization* (2005) 172 202; Erasmus (n 96 above) 165. It is often also only at this stage that the deficiency of a particular legislative provision comes to the fore – see Cottier and Takenoshita 'The balance of power in WTO decision-making: towards weighted voting in legislative response' 2003 *Aussenwirtschaft* 169.

98 See R Bustamante 'The need for a GATT doctrine of *locus standi:* Why the United States cannot stand the European Community's banana import regime' (1997) 6 *Minnesota Journal of Global Trade* 533-583; WJ Davey 'Has the WTO dispute settlement system exceeded its authority?' (2001) 4 *Journal of International Economic Law* 95 97 - 99; and Pauwelyn (n 94 above) 23ff.

99 *Bridon International GmbH v International Trade Administration Commission* 2013 (3) SA 197 (SCA).

100 n 99 above, 202H - I 'These sections, together with the Anti-Dumping Regulations, promulgated by the minister in GN 3197 of 14 November 2003, were clearly intended to give effect to South Africa's obligations in terms of international instruments to protect confidential information in the course of anti-dumping proceedings.'

101 Although it must immediately be pointed out that there was no discussion of the issue.

by national legislation ... the provisions of these agreements did not in themselves become part of South African law'.[102]

The Court found that the WTO agreements do not form part of South African law but due to the fact that the relevant statutory provisions dealing with anti-dumping investigations and the disclosure and protection of confidential information were an attempt to give effect to South Africa's international law obligations, in interpreting the relevant sections of the act and regulations, an interpretation that is conforming with international law, should be followed – thus complying with the constitutional obligation in section 233. This is then also the way in which the Court further deals with the matter.[103]

It is of importance to note that the Court does not refer to the finding of the Constitutional Court in the *SCAW* case where it found, by implication, that the WTO agreements are part of South African law and in essence applied it directly. This is a clear indication that the Court must have considered that decision to be wrong. The decision by the Constitutional Court was given almost two years prior to the decision of the Supreme Court of Appeal and at that stage the Supreme Court of Appeal was still the highest court in South African concerning all matters other than constitutional matters and was thus not bound by the decision of the Constitutional Court.[104]

The decision of the Supreme Court of Appeal in *Association of Meat Importers and Exporters v The International Trade Administration Commission* is also a clear indication that South African courts normally do not apply unincorporated treaties in their decisions but that they will use the wording of a treaty when they have to deal with the interpretation of a domestic provision that is based on the wording of such a treaty. In this case the Court said the following with regard to the *Progress Office Machines* case which received a lot of criticism due to its end result:

> To give the regulation that meaning will not mean this country is in breach of its obligations under article 11.3 of the WTO Agreement. The meaning given to article 11.3 in *Progress Office Machines* is authoritative only so far as that article is applied domestically, but is immaterial so far as this country's relations with its WTO partners are concerned. Perhaps they might see things in the same way as this court did in *Progress Office Machines* – in which case the regulations no doubt call for amendment – but perhaps they might not – in which case all is well and good. *It is not for us to speculate on how the WTO members understand their agreement.*[105]

102 *Bridon International GmbH* (n 99 above) 202H - 203C.
103 See also *Association of Meat Importers and Exporters* (n 36 above) par 61.
104 This position changed with the enactment of the Constitution Seventeenth Amendment Act 72 of 2012 and the Superior Courts Act 10 of 2013 which made the Constitutional Court the highest court in all matters – this legislative (and Constitutional) amendment came into effect on 23 August 2013.
105 *Association of Meat Importers and Exporters* (n 36 above) para 82 – emphasis added.

The emphasised part is an affirmation of the legal position discussed above (→ 4.6) indicating the sense that international law matters are not justiciable in domestic courts.

There thus seems to be a clear distinction between the application of legal principles regarding the application of international economic law between the Constitutional Court and the Supreme Court of Appeal. The fact that the Constitutional Court sometimes states the law correctly, but then applies it incorrectly, is a matter of concern. The fact that it is now the court of last appeal in all matters and no longer only constitutional matters may be a matter for concern.

4 Conclusion

The Agreement establishing the World Trade Organisation and its covered agreements, as well as any other international treaty, need to be treated with circumspection when they have not been incorporated into a country's domestic law. The South African Constitutional Court in the *SCAW* matter dealt with the WTO agreements as if they formed part of South African law even though it first stated that such unincorporated treaties do not form part of domestic law. This position is also held by the Supreme Court of Appeal but different from the Constitutional Court; it has up until now, applied these principles correctly.

Just as much as it is within the power of the executive to decide which treaties to sign, it is also within their power to decide to renege on their obligations. Even though the executive does not necessarily intend to be bound to the letter to its international law obligations (whether it be the obligations in terms of the WTO agreements or others), it seems as if the Constitutional Court is of the opinion that, especially with regard to the WTO agreements, the executive should be so inclined. The Court's finding that the decision of the High Court results in a breach of South Africa's international law obligations in the *SCAW* case, in essence contains a value judgment concerning what the policy of the executive in this instance should be without any evidence to this effect being presented.

As to the Constitutional Court's finding in the *SCAW* case that in not keeping to the duration of the anti-dumping duties, there is a breach of the country's WTO obligations, the Constitutional Court embarked on the international law terrain and in particular the terrain of the WTO's Dispute Settlement Body. No domestic court has the jurisdiction or capacity to make such a finding.

The Supreme Court of Appeal on the other hand has dealt with the application and implication of the WTO agreements in South African law in a much more nuanced and pure manner and held that it is not within its authority or jurisdiction to pronounce on the meaning of such unincorporated agreements – thus that they are not justiciable. It is hoped that the precedents that were created by this Court would be followed in future and that the unsound argumentation of the Constitutional Court in this respect would be corrected.

All in all, South Africa and in particular the legislature has to a large extent tried to give effect to the international law obligations arising from the WTO agreements[106] there has however not been a uniform approach to the application of the relevant statutory provisions. The fact that the Constitutional Court has taken over the role as the court of final instance in all matters, might not be to the benefit of the trading community. The unfortunate decision in the *SCAW* case might not be of important precedential value, but it has given signals which are not necessarily in line with the development of international economic and trade law principles in South Africa and the approach regarding the justiciability of international law obligations is not in line with developments elsewhere.

106 '[The] passing of the International Trade Administration Act 71 of 2002 (ITAA) creating ITAC and the promulgation of the Anti-Dumping Regulations made under s 59 of ITAA are indicative of an intention to give effect to the provisions of the treaties binding on the Republic in international law' (*Progress Office Machines* (n 36 above) para 6 and also cited with approval in *Association of Meat Importers and Exporters* (n 36 above) para 60, 61).

BIBLIOGRAPHY

Booysen, H (2nd edn 1989) *Volkereg en sy verhouding tot die Suid Afrikaanse Reg* Juta & Co Ltd: Cape Town

Crawford, J (8th ed 2012) *Brownlie's principles of public international law* Oxford University Press: Oxford

Damian, H (1985) *Staatenimmunität und Gerichtszwang* Springer: Berlin/New York

Dugard, J (4th edn 2011) *International Law: A South African perspective* Juta & Co Ltd: Cape Town

Fatima, S (2005) *Using international law in domestic courts* Hart Publishing: Oxford

Hahn, M (1995) *Die einseitige Aussetzung von GATT-Verpflichtungen als Repressalie* Springer: Berlin/New York

Howard-Ellis, C (ed) (2003) *The origin, structure & working of the League of Nations* (original edition 1929) Reprinted by Lawbook Exchange Ltd: New York

Van den Bossche, P 'General introduction to WTO dispute settlement' in Van den Bossche, P (2005) *The law and policy of the World Trade Organization* Cambridge University Press: Cambridge

2

INTERNATIONAL ENVIRONMENTAL LAW IN GERMANY

*Wolfgang Durner**

1 Relevant international law obligations

1.1 The development of international environmental law

From its very beginning international law has covered certain aspects of environmental protection. Even the traditional freedom of fishing on the high seas, in a way, could be regarded as an international obligation governing the use of the environment. Nevertheless, throughout the 19th century the idea to protect the environment was not yet a central consideration in the making of international law and thus most relevant parts of international environmental law were created in the second half of the 20th century.[1] As the harmful impacts of industrialisation became more widespread and affected neighbour states, international courts and tribunals had to resolve bilateral conflicts on the sharing of common resources and transfrontier pollution. Due to the absence of applicable treaty law, this led to the establishment of important abstract rules. Particular important ones were the duty to prevent damage to the environment of other states and the principle of equitable utilisation of shared resources. Today both of these rules are universally accepted as part of customary international law (→ 1.2.2). When environmental threats grew in dimension and soon transcended bilateral constellations, environmental protection became one of the striking examples for the transformation of the international law of coexistence towards an international law of cooperation.[2] While rules on bilateral environmental

* Professor of Public Law at Bonn University, Germany and Director of the Bonn Institute for Water Law.

1 U Beyerlin & T Marauhn *International environmental law* (2011) 1; PH Sand 'The evolution of international environmental law' in D Bodansky et al (eds) *The Oxford handbook of international environmental law* (2007) 30; P Sands & J Peel *Principles of international environmental law* (3rd edn 2012) 22; D Tladi *Sustainable development in international law* (2007) 13.

2 W Friedmann *The changing structure of international law* (1964) 60.

conflicts still remain a cornerstone of international environmental law, much of modern treaty-making has shifted to address global environmental challenges.

The earliest attempts of the international community to establish cooperative environmental treaty law focused on the protection and management of species with an economic value such as birds useful for agriculture,[3] whales[4] and fish.[5] These regional approaches became even wider in scope after the creation of the United Nations.[6] In 1972, a crucial step was taken with the United Nations Conference on the Human Environment in Stockholm, which produced various environmental agreements such as the 1972 London Dumping Convention and the 1972 World Heritage Convention. Those agreements were complemented by two important soft law-documents, the Stockholm Declaration with 26 principles on the environment and development[7] and an Action Plan containing 109 recommendations. Twenty years later, the 1992 United Nations Conference on Environment and Development in Rio aimed to integrate environmental and developmental policy by promoting 'sustainable development'.[8] According to principle 4 of the Rio Declaration 'environmental protection shall constitute an integral part of the development process chain and cannot be considered in isolation from it'. Under this long-term approach, modern treaty law frequently seeks to launch a cooperative process rather than imposing immediate international obligations. This framework aims at the establishment of international organisations and enables the subsequent elaboration of substantive law.[9]

1.2 Sources of international environmental law

According to article 38 of the ICJ Statute the Court shall apply mainly international conventions, international custom and the general principles of law. While in an environmental context the role of general principles is rather neglectable,[10] treaty and customary law both play an important role. Moreover, certain aspects of international environmental policy are

3 Convention pour la protection des oiseaux utiles à l'agriculture (19 March 1902, 51 LNTS 221); Convention on Nature Protection and Wild Life Preservation in the Western Hemisphere (12 October 1940, 161 UNTS 193); M Bowman et al *Lyster's international wildlife law* (2nd edn 2010) 3.

4 International Convention for the Regulation of Whaling (2 December 1946, 161 UNTS 72).

5 International North Pacific Fisheries Convention (9 May 1952, 205 UNTS 79).

6 Sands & Peel (n 1 above) 26.

7 LB Sohn 'The Stockholm Declaration on the Human Environment' (1973) 14 *Harvard International Law Review* 423; P Birnie et al *International law and the environment* (3rd edn 2009) 48.

8 L Campiglio et al (eds) *The environment after Rio* (1994); Tladi (n 1 above) 22.

9 Beyerlin & Marauhn (n 1 above) 241; D Bodansky *The art and craft of international environmental law* (2010) 136; T Gehring 'Treaty making and treaty evolution' in Bodansky et al (n 1 above) 467.

10 Birnie et al (n 7 above) 26 - 28.

subject to non-binding norms which are usually labelled by the collective term of 'soft law' (→ 1.2.3).

1.2.1 International environmental treaties

Since 1972, international environmental treaties have become substantial in number and fairly comprehensive in scope. Two groups of agreements should be distinguished: On the one hand, global conventions seeking to address global environmental problems and fostering universal participation. On the other hand, regional conventions that either deal with resources or problems of a regional scope or seek to establish particular regional standards. Both groups of agreements are of significant relevance in the German context and some prime examples should be mentioned:

Global conventions

With respect to the protection of the global atmosphere the two key regimes are formed by the 1985 Vienna Convention for the Protection of the Ozone Layer and the 1992 UN Framework Convention on Climate Change (UNFCCC). Both were supplemented by important protocols, the 1987 Montreal Protocol on Substances that deplete the Ozone Layer and the 1997 Kyoto Protocol respectively.[11] While the former regime has resulted in a rather far-reaching ban on ozone depleting substances, progress in preventing climate change has been remarkably poor. In another area, international trade in hazardous wastes is regulated by the 1989 Basel Convention on the Control of Transboundary Movements of Hazardous Wastes and their Disposal,[12] which is based on a prior informed consent scheme for transfrontier movements and seeks to promote the reduction of hazardous waste generation as well as environmentally sound waste disposal.

For chemicals, a comparable regime is formed by the 1998 Rotterdam Convention on the Prior Informed Consent Procedure for Certain Hazardous Chemicals and Pesticides in International Trade (PIC-Convention) and the subsequent 2001 Stockholm Convention on Persistent Organic Pollutants (POP-Convention) that seeks to ban or reduce the production, trade and use of certain ultra-hazardous chemicals.[13] Other global conventions aim to protect the marine environment. The most important ones include the 1972 London Convention on the Prevention of Marine Pollution by Dumping of Wastes

11 D Bodansky et al *International climate change law* (forthcoming).
12 K Kummer *International management of hazardous wastes* (2nd edn 1999) 87; D Langlet *Prior informed consent and hazardous trade* (2nd edn 2009) 73.
13 M Pallemaerts *Toxics and transnational law* (2003) 419; DA Wirth 'Hazardous substances and activities' in Bodansky et al (n 1 above) 394; Langlet (n 12 above) 115.

and Other Matter (London Dumping Convention) and the 1973/1978 International Convention for the Prevention of Pollution from Ships (MARPOL Convention). These specific instruments are embedded into the wider context of the 1982 United Nations Convention on the Law of the Sea (UNCLOS) and its Part XII on the Protection and Preservation of the Marine Environment[14] (→ Vrancken, Proelß). Deficits in regulating land based sources of marine pollution are still a main weakness of this regime.[15] Freshwater protection is addressed by the 1997 UN Convention on the Law of Non-Navigational Uses of International Watercourses,[16] which has so far not received the 35 ratifications necessary to enter into force.

With respect to nature conservation, the most important agreements include the 1971 Ramsar Convention on Wetlands of International Importance, especially as Waterfowl Habitat,[17] the 1972 Convention Concerning the Protection of the World Cultural and Natural Heritage (World Heritage Convention)[18] and the 1979 Bonn Convention on the Conservation of Migratory Species of Wild Animals.[19] In contrast to the abovementioned conventions, the 1973 Convention on International Trade in Endangered Species of Wild Flora and Fauna (CITES) takes a different approach in regulating trade – for instance by completely abolishing trade in ivory – rather than protecting endangered species in situ.[20] All these agreements are supplemented by the quite over-ambitious 1992 Convention on Biological Diversity (CBD) that seeks to address almost every aspect of the protection of biological diversity.[21]

Regional treaties

Not all important environmental problems have so far been addressed by multilateral conventions. Partially the gaps are filled by regional agreements. Several significant legal instruments for environmental protection have been negotiated under the auspices of the United Nations Economic Commission for Europe (UNECE) and thus have mainly European parties. Transboundary air pollution in Europe is quite effectively regulated by the 1979 Geneva Convention on Long-Range

14 A Kirchner (ed) *International marine environmental law* (2003); D Freestone & SMA Salman 'Ocean and freshwater resources', in Bodansky et al (n 1 above) 337.

15 Pallemaerts (n 13 above) 35.

16 L Boisson de Chazournes *Fresh water in international law* (2013) 26; S McCaffrey *The law of international watercourses* (2nd edn 2007) 359.

17 Bowman et al (n 3 above) 403.

18 Bowman et al (n 3 above) 451.

19 Bowman et al (n 3 above) 535.

20 Bowman et al (n 3 above) 483; for the convention's most recent developments see J Scanlon 'CITES at its best: CoP16 as a 'watershed moment' for the world's wildlife' (2013) 22 *Review of European Community & International Environmental Law* 222.

21 Bowman et al (n 3 above) 587; AE Boyle 'The Rio Convention on Biological Diversity' in M Bowman & C Redgewell (eds) *International law and the conservation of biological diversity* (1996) 33.

Transboundary Air Pollution (LRTAP) and its protocols.[22] Regional European conventions aimed at protecting the marine environment with German participation include the 1992 Convention for the Protection of the Marine Environment of the North-East Atlantic (OSPAR Convention) and the 1992 Helsinki Convention on the Protection of the Marine Environment of the Baltic Sea Area.[23] On land they are *inter alia* complemented by the 1979 Bern Convention on the Conservation of European Wildlife and Natural Habitats[24] and the 1991 Convention on the Protection of the Alps and its various implementation protocols.[25]

Moreover, some important European conventions seek to establish stricter standards with respect to general issues of environmental protection: The 1991 Espoo Convention on Environmental Impact Assessment in a Transboundary Context and its 2003 Protocol on Strategic Environmental Assessment provide for a wide application of the instrument of environmental impact assessment including public participation.[26] Freshwater resources are governed by the 1991 Helsinki ECE-Convention on the Protection and Use of Transboundary Watercourses and International Lakes,[27] a framework treaty which is further regionalised by various bilateral or regional treaties on specified rivers and lakes, most important amongst them the 1999 Convention on the Protection of the Rhine.[28] The 1992 Helsinki Convention on the Transboundary Effects of Industrial Accidents promotes international cooperation to prevent and to manage industrial accidents.[29] The 1998 Aarhus Convention on Access to Information, Public Participation in Decision-making and Access to Justice in Environmental Matters sets ambitious standards for environmental participation and litigation.[30] Some of these regional conventions have created detailed standards that oblige state parties to introduce rather far-reaching administrative and judicial procedures into their national environmental legislation. Germany

22 Birnie et al (n 7 above) 342 ; L Gündling 'Multilateral cooperation of states under the ECE Convention on Long-range Transboundary Air Pollution' in C Flinterman et al (eds) *Transboundary air pollution* (1986) 19.
23 A Proelß *Meeresschutz im Völker- und Europarecht* (2004) 191; Sands & Peel (n 1 above) 409.
24 Bowman et al (n 3 above) 297; C Lasén Díaz 'The Bern Convention: 30 Years of nature conservation in Europe' (2010) 19 *Review of European Community & International Environmental Law* 185.
25 Bowman et al (n 3 above) 639.
26 Sands & Peel (n 1 above) 814; A Boyle 'Developments in the international law of environmental impact assessments and their relation to the Espoo Convention' (2011) 21 *Review of European Community & International Environmental Law* 227.
27 Boisson de Chazournes (n 16 above) 33.
28 Birnie et al (n 7 above) 573.
29 Sands & Peel (n 1 above) 623.
30 Sands & Peel (n 1 above) 858.

in particular had to face fairly significant obstacles to comply with some of the Aarhus Convention's obligations (→ 2.2.4 and 3.2).[31]

In terms of general importance, by far the most prominent regional treaty is the European Convention on Human Rights (→ Wenzel). According to the German Constitutional Court's *Görgülü* decision, German law, especially the constitutional human rights of the basic law, must be interpreted in harmony with the convention's requirements (→ Herdegen).[32] While neither the European Convention nor its protocols guarantee a specific right to a healthy environment, the European Court of Human Rights has held repeatedly that environmental aspects may affect the right to life (article 2), the right to privacy (article 8) and the right to the peaceful enjoyment of one's possessions (article 1, protocol 1).[33] In 1994 for example, in its landmark-decision '*López Ostra v Spain*', the Court found that by not taking any measures to protect the plaintiff against smoke that originated from a waste treatment plant located a few meters from her home, Spain had violated the right to privacy and family life since it had failed to find an adequate balance between economic development and the plaintiff's rights.[34] In the light of this case law, the European Convention on Human Rights guarantees a minimum standard of environmental protection as a human right which compels European states to regulate environmental risks and to enact and enforce environmental laws.[35]

1.2.2 Customary environmental obligations

While an increasing number of aspects of international environmental protection are covered by specific treaty law, customary international obligations still remain relevant to fill legislative gaps, to guide non-parties to these agreements and to offer a conceptual framework for the further elaboration of treaty law.[36] However, opinions are divided as to what extent certain general rules of international environmental policy – such as the precautionary principle or the polluter pays principle – have become customary law; in particular, the status of the principle of 'sustainable

31 Some of these are listed in Germany's latest implementation report for the fifth Conference of Parties 2014: Bundesregierung *Nationaler Umsetzungsbericht der Aarhus-Konvention für Deutschland* (2013). The competing conceptual philosophies of German and supranational environmental law are emphasised by R Breuer (ed) *Umweltschutz im Widerstreit differierender Konzepte* (2000).

32 BVerfG Case 2 BvR 1481/04, (14 October 2004) (2005) 111 *Entscheidungen des Bundesverfassungsgerichts* 307; C Tomuschat 'The effects of the judgments of the European Court of Human Rights according to the German Constitutional Court' (2010) 11 *German Law Journal* 513.

33 Council of Europe (ed) *Manual on human rights and the environment* (2nd edn 2012).

34 ECHR Case *López Ostra v Spain* App no 16798/90 (9 December 1994) (1994) ECHR 46.

35 A Boyle 'Human rights and the environment: where next?' (2012) 23 *European Journal of International Law* 613 615 summarizing the case law of the European Court of Human Rights.

36 Birnie et al (n 7 above) 34 - 37; P-M Dupuy 'Formation of customary international law and general principles' in Bodansky et al (n 1 above) 450.

development' called for in principle 4 of the Rio Declaration (→ 1.1), has been discussed controversially.[37] In spite of this controversy, the ability of such principles to guide state behaviour may be quite independent of the question as to whether or not they are legally binding[38] (→ 2.3.3). Nevertheless, a limited but increasing number of environmental obligations exist that are almost universally recognised as customary international law.

Most important amongst these is a principle established in the Trail Smelter dispute in 1941 according to which no state is entitled to use its territory in a way that would cause harm by air pollution to another state's territory.[39] This 'no harm principle' was later integrated into principle 21 of the 1972 Stockholm Declaration of the United Nations Conference on the Human Environment. According to principle 21 states have

> the sovereign right to exploit their own resources pursuant to their own environmental policies, and the responsibility to ensure that activities within their jurisdiction or control do not cause damage to the environment of other states or of areas beyond the limits of national jurisdiction.

In its advisory opinion on the *Legality of the Threat or Use of Nuclear Weapons* in 1996 the ICJ found this general obligation of states 'to respect the environment of other States or of areas beyond national control' had become customary international law.[40] This principle has been invoked in dozens of international agreements and may be regarded as the backbone of modern international environmental law. In its modern formulation it constitutes a general duty to prevent and reduce environmental harm.[41]

This duty is essentially substantive, but also has a procedural dimension: In its very first decision in the 1949 *Corfu Channel case* (*UK v Albania*) the ICJ recognised an obligation to warn other states of imminent danger which was *inter alia* based by the Court on 'elementary considerations of humanity'.[42] This duty to notify other states has been affirmed in various environmental contexts, amongst others in article 198 of the UNCLOS with respect to the marine environment. The *Lac Lanoux*

37 For a detailed analysis see Tladi (n 1 above) 94 - 112; for differing views compare Sands & Peel (n 1 above) 208 on the one hand ('There can be little doubt that the concept of sustainable development has entered the corpus of customary international law'.) and Birnie et al (n 7 above) 125 - 127 on the other hand.

38 Bodansky (n 9 above) 191; more generally N de Sadeleer *Environmental principles: from political slogans to legal rules* (2002).

39 *Trail Smelter Arbitration (USA v Canada)* Arbitral Tribunal, 3 U.N. Rep. Int'l Arb. Awards 1905 (1941) see further on the impacts of this precedent RM Bratspies & RA Miller *Transboundary harm in international law: Lessons from the trail smelter arbitration* (2006).

40 *Legality of the Threat or Use of Nuclear Weapons Advisory Opinion* (8 July 1996) (1996) ICJ Reports 241 para 29.

41 Birnie et al (n 7 above) 137.

42 *Corfu Channel case (United Kingdom v Albania)* (15 December 1949) (1949) ICJ Reports 4 22.

arbitration of 16 November 1957 had to settle a dispute between France and Spain on the admissibility of a French project involving the diversion of the waters of *Lac Lanoux*, a lake situated on French territory whose waters eventually flow to Spain. The Tribunal, while finding that France had taken Spanish interests into sufficient consideration, stressed that

> according to the rules of good faith, the upstream State is under the obligation to take into consideration the various interests involved, to seek to give them every satisfaction compatible with the pursuit of its own interests, and to show that in this regard it is genuinely concerned to reconcile the interests of the other riparian state with its own.[43]

These obligations imply a duty of prior notification before carrying out projects potentially harmful to the environment of other states.[44] According to recent ICJ case law, a state has to give 'prior notice' of such activities and 'use its best endeavours to find common solutions' with neighbour states affected.[45] These standards have become even stricter where shared resources such as watercourses or wildlife stocks are affected. In its judgment of 25 September 1997 on the *'Case Concerning the Gabicikovo-Nagymaros Project'*, the Court endorsed the principle of equitable utilisation of a 'shared resource' and recognised that under international law each riparian state had the 'right to an equitable and reasonable share of the natural resources' of the Danube.[46] A further significant step in developing customary environmental obligations was the ICJ's decision of 20 April 2010 in the *Pulp Mills* case where the Court found that

> it may now be considered a requirement under general international law to undertake an environmental impact assessment where there is a risk that the proposed industrial activity may have a significant adverse impact in a transboundary context, in particular, on a shared resource.[47]

1.2.3 Soft law in the field of environmental protection

There is a large amount of soft law in the field of environmental protection which to a differing extent may be able to influence state behaviour.[48] The term 'soft law', however, refers to a hybrid group of norms: The Stockholm and the Rio Declarations have been mentioned as governmental declarations that proclaim certain general instruments and abstract

43 *Lac Lanoux Arbitration (France v Spain)* (1957) 24 International Law Reports (1957) 101 139.
44 FL Kirgis *Prior consultation in international law* (1983) 88 and 128.
45 *Certain Activities Carried out by Nicaragua in the Border Area (Nicaragua v Costa Rica) Order* (8 March 2011) (2011) ICJ Reports 26.
46 *Case Concerning the Gabcikovo Nagymaros Project (Hungary v Slovakia)* (25 September 1997) (1997) ICJ Reports 7 56
47 *Pulp Mills on the River Uruguay (Argentina v Uruguay)* (2010) ICJ Reports 14 83.
48 Beyerlin & Marauhn (n 1 above) 289; P-M Dupuy 'Soft law and the international law of the environment' (1991) 12 *Michigan Journal of International Law*, 420; SJ Toope 'Formality and informality' in Bodansky et al (n 1 above) 107.

principles on the environment and development some of which – such as the environmental impact assessment recommended in principle 17 of the Rio Declaration – subsequently became customary law (→ 1.2.2). Similar documents have been elaborated by NGOs; one of the most important ones is the International Union for Conservation of Nature (IUCN) which has submitted various soft law documents, amongst them drafts for the codification of international environmental law.[49]

On the other hand, certain more technical types of soft law may be very specific and detailed such as the United Nations' recommendations on classification and labelling of Chemicals[50] or UNEP's recommendations on best available techniques under the POP-Convention.[51] They may serve as a means to establish accepted interpretations of more general treaty obligations[52] and are able to become part of national law through legislative or judicial reception as will be shown by some examples (→ 2.3.3 and 3.1).

1.3 German participation in international environmental law making

Germany's participation in international environmental law making has been quite comprehensive. By the end of 2014, Germany was party to more than 60 multilateral and almost 70 bilateral treaties on environmental issues including fisheries.[53] All of the central conventions mentioned above (→ 1.2.1) have been ratified by Germany and are thus binding once they enter into force. These formal treaties are supplemented by dozens of technical or executive agreements, notes of understanding and informal environmental arrangements.[54] Increasingly, Germany has sought to influence negotiations for international environmental agreements and hosted conferences on environmental issues such as the UN negotiations for a binding global climate change agreement taking place in Bonn in June 2013. Germany's former capital Bonn has become seat of several international environmental institutions such as the Secretariat of the UNFCCC (→ 1.2.1), the Secretariat of the UN

49 International Union for Conservation of Nature (IUCN) 'International Convenant on Environment and Development' in H Bocken & D Ryckbost (eds) *Codification of environmental law* (1996) 183.
50 United Nations *Globally harmonized system of classification and labelling of chemicals (GHS)* (3rd edn 2009).
51 UNEP *Overview and summary of outcomes from the regional consultations on the draft guidelines on Best Available Techniques (BAT) and Best Environmental Practices (BEP) relevant to article 5 and Annex C of the Stockholm Convention on Persistent Organic Pollutants (POPs)* (2005).
52 Birnie et al (n 7 above) 148.
53 *Fundstellennachweis B. Völkerrechtliche Vereinbarungen*, Bundesgesetzblatt 2014 II, 1026.
54 For a detailed survey see WE Burhenne & PH Sand 'Internationale Umweltvereinbarungen' in K Hansmann & D Sellner (eds) *Grundzüge des Umweltrechts* (4th edn 2012) 1157 1161 - 1205.

Convention to Combat Desertification (UNCCD) and UNEP's Convention on Migratory Species of Wild Animals.

2 Incorporation of international environmental obligations into the German legal order

2.1 Germany's mitigated dualism

The German Basic Law, being based on the concept of dualism, allows international law to become part of the German legal order only once it is accepted as national law. However, the Basic Law's dualist concept is mitigated by certain clauses that incorporate international norms into the German legal order. This applies to customary international law through article 25 of the Basic Law and – to a lesser extent – to basic fundamental rights through article 1(2) of the Basic Law (→ Wolfrum/Vöneky, Herdegen).

2.1.1 Incorporation of customary international law through article 25 of the Basic Law

According to article 25 Basic Law, the 'general rules of international law' shall be an integral part of federal law and shall take precedence over parliamentary laws and directly create rights and duties for the inhabitants of the federal territory. While treaty law requires legislative transformation to become part of the national legal order, universally accepted customary environmental obligations are in principle able to be applied directly.[55]

In the field of environmental protection, however, most of the provisions of customary international law mentioned above are too general to create rights and duties for non-state actors. Moreover, even where customary obligations might be concrete enough to be applied by national courts, usually there are international treaties as well as European and domestic provisions which set out those principles in more specific terms. Thus, the general duty to protect the environment (→ 1.2.2) is confirmed in article 20a of the Basic Law (→ 2.3.1). The customary duty to carry out environmental impact assessments in a trans-border context (→ 1.2.2) is – in much more detail – part of the 1991 Espoo Convention (→ 1.2.1) and is further elaborated in Directive 2011/92/EU on the Assessment of the Effects of certain Public and Private Projects on the Environment and in the implementing German Environmental Impacts Assessment Act (*Gesetz über die Umweltverträglichkeitsprüfung*). Those European and national provisions may be interpreted in the light of their

55 R Geiger *Grundgesetz und Völkerrecht* (6th edn 2013) 153.

international origins (→ 3.1) but nevertheless leave very little scope for the application of article 25 of the Basic Law.

For all these reasons, there is hardly any domestic case law with respect to the customary environmental obligations and not a single case for customary environmental obligations taking precedence over domestic parliamentary laws. In 2008, the Federal Administrative Court referred to the customary no harm principle (→ 1.2.2) in order to support its before established doctrine that foreign plaintiffs have locus standi in German courts in order to challenge German permits that may have transboundary impacts (→ 3.3).[56] In 2013, on the other hand, the higher administrative Court of North-Rhine Westphalia refused to accept the existence of a customary international ban on nuclear weapons. Therefore, the plaintiff had no legal standing to claim the withdrawal of the US forces' nuclear arms from German territory.[57]

In the literature some bolder consequences have been suggested: It has been argued, for instance, that an allegedly self-executing customary 'human right to water' prohibits stopping the supply of drinking water even to those clients who violate their contract and refuse to pay their bills.[58] Such a human right – whose very existence is still rather uncertain – also played a prominent role in the Constitutional Court of South Africa's *Mazibuko* case[59] (→ Chamberlain/Murombo). In German courts, on the other hand, customary environmental law plays only a minor role. International environmental law, as a matter of principle, requires transformation to have significant domestic effects.

2.1.2 The need for transformation of international environmental treaties

According to article 59(2) of the Basic Law, treaties that regulate the political relations of the Federation or relate to subjects of federal legislation shall require the parliamentary consent in form of a federal law. Even if the content of this provision leaves scope for differing interpretations,[60] article 59 implies that environmental treaties require legislative transformation in order to become applicable in the domestic legal order unless they are directly applicable (→ Wolfrum/Vöneky). This

56 BVerwG Case 4 C 3/07 (16 October 2008) (2009) 132 *Entscheidungen des Bundesverwaltungsgerichts* 151 158.

57 OVG Münster Case 4 A 1913/11 (7 May 2013) (2013) 26 *Neue Zeitschrift für Verwaltungsrecht Rechtsprechungs-Report* 789.

58 SR Laskowski 'The (missing) implementation of the human right to water and sanitation in the Federal Republic of Germany' in H Smets (ed) *Le droit à l'eau potable et à l'assainissement, sa mise en oeuvre en Europe* (2012) 181 188 who restricts this claim to 20 liters per day.

59 Boisson de Chazournes (n 16 above) 157.

60 Geiger (n 55 above) 163; M Nettesheim 'Article 59' in M Herdegen et al (eds) *Maunz & Dürig, Grundgesetz, loose leaf commentary* (2009) paras 173 - 180.

transformation may be carried out through autonomous domestic legislation. The dominant model, however, relies to a large extent upon transformation through European Union law.

2.2 The dominant model: Transformation trough European Union legislation

Article 192(1) of the Treaty on the Functioning of the European Union (TFEU) empowers the European Parliament and the Council to take action – including legislative action – in order to achieve the environmental objectives referred to in article 191(1). As those objectives cover more or less any aspect of environmental protection – including the protection of human health and the promotion of measures at international level to deal with regional or worldwide environmental problems – the Union is given comprehensive legislative competence in the field of environmental protection.[61] According to the ECJ, these legislative powers include taking measures which relate to criminal law in order to ensure that the rules on environmental protection are fully effective.[62] According to article 192(2), provisions with a primarily fiscal nature or affecting urban and landscape planning and land use are included as well, even though they require unanimity in the Council. Moreover, provisions enacted under article 114(1) may also regulate environmental aspects if their main object is the establishment and functioning of the internal market.[63] With respect to its member states, the Union is thus entitled to transform virtually any international environmental obligation into Union Law which then either has direct effect in the member states or obliges them to implement the respective obligations in their domestic legislation (→ 2.2.4).

Furthermore, the Union's primary law – the treaties founding the Union – contains some substantive guidelines for the Union's environmental policy which may be regarded as an implementation of international law: According to article 191(2) of the TFEU the

> Union policy on the environment shall aim at a high level of protection taking into account the diversity of situations in the various regions of the Union. It shall be based on the precautionary principle and on the principles that preventive action should be taken, that environmental damage should as a priority be rectified at source and that the polluter should pay.

This provision, in fact, transforms some of the most prominent principles of international environmental policy into binding European constitutional law: The general duty to protect the environment, the

61 JH Jans & HHB Vedder *European environmental law* (4th edn 2012) 59 - 64.
62 Case C-176/03 *Commission v Council* [2005] ECR I-7879, paras 46ff.
63 Case C-300/89 *Commission v Council* [1991] ECR I-2878, para 11; Jans & Vedder (n 61 above) 74 - 79.

precautionary principle and the polluter pays principle – whether or not they may be regarded as formally binding customary international law (→ 1.2.1) – are thus binding for the European legislator and form a conceptual framework for the Union's secondary environmental law making.[64]

2.2.1 The Union's external competences in the field of environmental protection

Under article 216(1) of the TFEU the Union may conclude an agreement with one or more third countries or international organisations where this is necessary in order to achieve one of the objectives referred to in the Treaties. These objectives include the environmental policy set out in article 191(1) of the TFEU[65] (→ 2.2.1). Based on its external environmental competences, the Union has concluded more than 50 international treaties in the field of environmental protection which have been implemented by a similar number of acts of secondary legislation.[66]

2.2.2 Mixed agreements

In negotiating and concluding international environmental treaties the Union may be forced to adopt 'mixed agreements' which on the European side must be signed and ratified both by the European Union and its member states.[67] This is the case when neither the Union nor the member states have exclusive competence in the area covered by the treaty as is the case in the field of environmental protection according to article 191(1) of the TFEU. The legal standards defining the Union's external competences are complicated and depend on the extent the Union has exercised its internal legislative powers and adopted provisions.[68] In practice, however, and due to political rather than legal considerations most of the abovementioned treaties have been concluded as mixed agreements, sometimes even without any clarification of the respective competences of

64 A Epiney *Umweltrecht der Europäischen Union* (3rd edn 2013) 141; K Meßerschmidt *Europäisches Umweltrecht* (2011) 264.

65 S Breier 'Die Außenkompetenzen der Gemeinschaft und ihrer Mitgliedstaaten auf dem Gebiet des Umweltschutzes' in PC Müller-Graff et al (eds) *Die Europäische Gemeinschaft in der internationalen Umweltpolitik* (2006) 99; Jans & Vedder (n 61 above) 64 - 74.

66 Lists of those treaties are provided by W Heintschel von Heinegg 'Spektrum und Status der internationalen Umweltkonventionen – Der Beitrag der Europäischen Gemeinschaft zur fortschreitenden Entwicklung des völkervertraglichen Umweltschutzes' in Müller-Graff et al (n 65 above) 77 92 and by Meßerschmidt (n 64 above) 327.

67 C Hillion & P Koutrakos (eds) *Mixed agreements revisited. The EU and its member states in the world* (2010).

68 T C Hartley *The foundations of European Union Law* (7th edn 2010) 173.

Union and member states.[69] Nevertheless, under normal circumstances the Union and its member states will participate in international environmental conventions jointly and will develop common negotiating positions and seek to unite their negotiating powers.

On that basis, over the last two decades the European Union has become a major player in international environmental negotiations.[70] Increasingly the Commission and the European Court of Justice both seek to widen the Union's competences and to reduce member states' abilities to pursue a separate diplomatic strategy. In 2010 for instance the Court held that the Unions' member states are subject to special

> duties of action and abstention in a situation in which the Commission has submitted to the Council proposals that, although they have not been adopted by the Council, represent the point of departure for concerted Community action. [71]

Sweden therefore had infringed the 'duty of cooperation in good faith' by unilaterally proposing to list a substance in Annex A to the Stockholm POP-Convention (→ 1.2.1).

In the *Slovak Brown Bear* case the ECJ noted, that according to the 'declaration of competence' made in accordance with the signing of the Aarhus Convention (→ 1.2.1) the Community had stated that

> the legal instruments in force do not cover fully the implementation of the obligations resulting from article 9(3) of the Convention ... and that, consequently, its Member States are responsible for the performance of these obligations at the time of approval of the Convention by the European Community.

The Court, nevertheless, found that contrary to this official statement article 9(3) of the Aarhus Convention fell within the scope of Union law and that the Court had jurisdiction to interpret the provision.[72] The decision's underlying intention is apparently to enlarge the Union's negotiating powers[73] which is even more obvious since the 'declaration of

69 In its declaration of competence under the Climate Change Convention the Community stated to be competent 'alongside its Member States ... as determined by the Treaty establishing the European Economic Community.' (Climate Change Secretariat *United Nations Framework Convention on Climate Change Handbook* (2006) 45).

70 C Bretherton & J Vogler *The European Union as global actor* (2nd edn 2006) 85 ('global leader'); J Brunnée 'The United States and international environmental law: Living with an elephant' (2004) 15 *European Journal of International Law* 617 624; Müller-Graff et al (n 65 above); S Fröhlich *Die Europäische Union als globaler Akteur* (2007).

71 Case C-246/07 *European Commission v Sweden* [2010] ECR I-03317, paras 71ff.; P van Elsuwege 'Note to Commission v Sweden' (2011) 105 *American Journal of International Law* 307.

72 Case C-240/09 *Slovak Bear* [2011] ECR I-01255, paras 28 - 43.

73 C Eckes 'Environmental policy "outside-in": How the EU's engagement with international environmental law curtails national autonomy' (2012) 13 *German Law Journal* 1151 1165; Jans & Vedder (n 61 above) 72 - 74; D Krawczyk 'Case Note: The

competence' in question had been based on the Court's own former case law. Therefore, while mixed agreements are in practice still the predominant model for Germany's environmental diplomacy, the respective negotiating powers will increasingly be transferred to the European level.

2.2.3 Regulations, directives and decisions

Having entered into a mixed agreement, the European Union may either implement the treaty through European legislation or leave implementation to its member states. The Union's secondary law, as a matter of principle, is of tremendous importance for the German legal order (→ Hestermeyer). Normally, the Union will seek to harmonise implementation of environmental treaties to the fullest extent possible, provided that these measures find political support in the Council. In order to transform international obligations into European law, the Union will – under normal circumstances – enact either regulations or directives; in rare circumstances implementation will be restricted to mere decisions.[74]

Strengthening international obligations through Union implementation

Irrespective of the form chosen, nonetheless, the obligation in question for various reasons will substantially gain in relevance and enforceability due to its transformation:[75] European regulations have direct effect in the domestic legal order of the member states, and under certain conditions the same applies to directives. According to the principle of supremacy Union law takes precedence over domestic law in case of a conflict. Their execution is subject to the supervision of the Commission under article 17 of the Treaty on European Union as well as to the other enforcement mechanisms of European Union law (→ Hestermeyer). Reservations the member states may have formulated under article 19 of the Vienna Convention on the Law of Treaties when signing or ratifying a mixed agreement do not have any relevance with respect to Union law implementing this agreement.

Moreover, the European Court of Justice tends to give obligations a far stricter meaning than international courts and is quite willing to disregard the literal content of the text in order to promote the underlying objective of a European provision.[76] With regard to legislation meant to implement

Slovak Brown Bear case: The ECJ hunts for jurisdiction and environmental plaintiffs gain the trophy' (2012) 14 *Environmental Law Review* 53.

74 See generally HCH Hofmann et al *Administrative law and policy of the European Union* (2011) 91 - 94.

75 M Rossi 'Europäisiertes internationales Umweltverwaltungsrecht' in C Möllers et al (eds) *Internationales Verwaltungsrecht* (2007) 165 171.

76 Hartley (n 68 above) 72.

international obligations, this may – particularly with regard to procedural aspects – result in a strengthening of its environmental effectiveness.[77] A striking example for this is the interpretation of the provisions of Directive 2003/35/EC which implemented article 9(2) of the Aarhus Convention (→ 1.2.1): In the negotiation of the Convention Germany insisted on a wording of article 9(2) which it believed to allow the continuance of the concept of impairment of a subjective right as a precondition for judicial standing.[78] Subsequently, Germany insisted on this formulation being integrated into the implementing Directive 2003/35/EC. Nevertheless, the ECJ considering the overall environmental purposes of the directive, obligated member states to allow non-governmental organisations to invoke any 'rule flowing from EU environment law and intended to protect the environment' irrespective of whether that rule protects only the interests of the general public or the interests of individuals.[79] Transformation into Union Law has thus given article 9(2) of the Aarhus Convention a far reaching meaning which would have been rather unlikely according to the normal standards of interpretation of international law.

Regulations

The strictest option to implement international law at the Union level is by enacting regulations. According to article 288(2) of the TFEU, a regulation has general application, is binding in its entirety and directly applicable in all member states. Regulations do not require or even allow any formal transformation through the member states[80] (→ Hestermeyer) although supplementary national legislation may be necessary to set their provisions into action (→ 2.3.4). Nevertheless, in conformity with the principle of subsidiarity enshrined in article 5(3) of the Treaty on the European Union, regulations are comparatively rarely used in the area of environmental protection.[81] The main field of application for environmental regulations is where the free movement of goods and the functioning of the European Single Market are affected. Thus, the 1989 Basel Convention's provisions on the transboundary movements of hazardous wastes (→ 1.2.1) have been transformed into directly applicable European regulations on shipments of waste since 1994.[82] The same applies with respect to chemicals to the 1998 Rotterdam PIC-Convention (→ 1.2.1) which is

77 Y Shigeta 'The ECJ's 'hard' control over compliance with international environmental law' (2009) 11 *International Community Law Review* 251; for a practical example – EU legislation meant to implement CITES – see VGH Kassel Case 8 UE 3440/89 (20 October 1993) (1994) 47 *Neue Juristische Wochenschrift* 1427.

78 A Schwerdtfeger *Der deutsche Verwaltungsrechtsschutz unter dem Einfluss der Aarhus-Konvention* (2010) 126.

79 Case C-115/09 *Trianel* [2011] ECR I-03673, para 50.

80 Hartley (n 68 above) 216.

81 Meßerschmidt (n 64 above) 181.

82 Council Regulation (EEC) 259/93 of 1 February 1993 on the supervision and control of shipments of waste within, into and out of the European Community [1993] OJ L30/1; replaced by Regulation (EC) 1013/2006 of 14 June 2006 on shipments of waste [2006] OJ L 190/1.

implemented by a European Export-Import-Regulation,[83] and to the 1973 Convention on the International Trade in Endangered Species of Wild Flora and Fauna (→ 1.2.1), whose provisions are implemented uniformly in all EU member states by a set of European Regulations.[84]

Directives

The Union's standard approach however for transforming international environmental obligations is the enactment of implementing directives. A directive, according to article 288 (2) of the TFEU,

> shall be binding, as to the result to be achieved, upon each Member State to which it is addressed, but shall leave to the national authorities the choice of form and methods.

Thus, directives do require national implementation by member state legislation. Under normal circumstances, national authorities and national courts are expected to apply these national statutes rather than the directive, even though national courts are

> bound to interpret domestic law so far as possible, once the period for transposition has expired, in the light of the wording and the purpose of the directive concerned.[85]

Moreover, even directives can have direct effect when their provisions are unconditional and sufficiently clear and precise and have not been implemented after the expiry of the period for transposition (→ Hestermeyer).[86] As the Union's environmental directives have become extremely detailed over the years – detailed to an extent that the directives tend to be several times longer than the domestic German implementation acts – under normal conditions sufficient precision in the abovementioned sense is the rule rather than an exception.

All in all, there are more than 50 European directives that implement international obligations: Directive 2011/92/EU on the Assessment of the Effects of certain Public and Private Projects on the Environment and its predecessors transform both the customary duty to carry out environmental impact assessments in a transboundary context (→ 1.2.2)

83 Regulation (EC) 689/2008 of 17 June 2008 concerning the export and import of dangerous chemicals [2008] OJ L 204/1; Langlet (n 12 above) 133.

84 Council Regulation (EC) 338/97 of 9 December 1996 on the protection of species of wild fauna and flora by regulating trade therein [1997] OJ L61/1; Commission Regulation (EC) No 865/2006 of 4 May 2006 laying down detailed rules concerning the implementation of Council Regulation (EC) No 338/97 [2006] OJ L166/1; Commission Implementing Regulation (EU) No 792/2012 of 23 August 2012 laying down rules for the design of permits, certificates and other documents provided for in Council Regulation (EC) No 338/97 [2012] OJ L242/13.

85 Case C-212/04 *Konstantinos Adeneler and Others v Ellinikos Organismos Galaktos* [2006] ECR I-6057, para 108.

86 For references see Hartley (n 68 above) 219.

as well as the 1991 Espoo Convention (→ 1.2.1) into European Law. The 1979 Bern Convention on the Conservation of European Wildlife and Natural Habitats (→ 1.2.1) was implemented – and in many respects transcended – by the Habitats-Directive 92/43/EEC,[87] one of the Union's most important environmental achievements which established the European network *Natura 2000*.[88] The 1992 Helsinki Convention on Industrial Accidents (→ 1.2.2) has been transformed by various directives, the newest one being the 'Seveso III Directive' 2012/18/EU.[89] Some additional examples for European directives implementing international law will be presented in the context of their German implementation (→ 2.3.2).

A rather special case is the Union's implementation of the customary concept of equitable utilisation of shared water resources (→ 1.2.2) which forms the cornerstone both of the 1997 UN Watercourses-Convention and of the 1991 Helsinki ECE-Convention on Transboundary Watercourses (→ 1.2.1). Elements from all these sources have been transformed into European law by the Union's Water Framework Directive 2000/60/EC[90] which establishes an integrated transboundary river basin management for Europe and instruments such as the obligatory 'management plan' which still clearly show the directive's international origins.[91] In fact, in case of transboundary rivers the directive's implementation is coordinated by the 'river commissions' established by and acting under international law to manage the shared resource.[92] In the case of the river Maas, even a new international agreement was negotiated and set into force in order to implement directive 2000/60/EC.[93] Under this approach, international law, Union law and domestic provisions amalgamate into a hybrid comprehensive regime.[94]

Due to various reasons, *inter alia* the fact that the period for transposition is often unrealistically short, the ECJ has frequently found environmental directives to be directly effective.[95] This applied also to

87 Council Directive 92/43/EEC of 21 May 1992 on the conservation of natural habitats and of wild fauna and flora [1992] OJ L206/7.

88 M Gellermann *Natura 2000* (2nd edn 2003); R Slepcevic *Litigating for the environment* (2009) 59.

89 Directive 2012/18/EU of the European Parliament and of the Council of 4 July 2012 on the control of major-accident hazards involving dangerous substances [2012] OJ L197/1.

90 Directive 2000/60/EC of the European Parliament and of the Council establishing a framework for the Community action in the field of water policy [2000] OJ L327/1.

91 J Sohnle 'Les thèmes de la directive cadre sur l'eau dans le concert des normes internationales' (2008) 9 *ERA-Forum* 423.

92 Boisson de Chazournes (n 16 above) 176. This approach had been elaborated by A Epiney & A Felder *Überprüfung internationaler wasserwirtschaftlicher Übereinkommen im Hinblick auf die Implementierung der Wasserrahmenrichtlinie* (2002).

93 S Solf *Europäisches Flussgebietsmanagement und deutsche Wasserwirtschaftsverwaltung* (2006) 176

94 G Reichert *Der nachhaltige Schutz grenzüberschreitender Gewässer in Europa* (2005) 340.

95 L Krämer *Focus on European environmental law* (1992) 160; Meßerschmidt (n 64 above) 223.

various provisions of the Unions implementation directives, *inter alia* to the provisions of Directive 2003/35/EC implementing article 9(2) of the Aarhus Convention in the German based *Trianel* case[96] (→ 2.2.4). One of the more controversial cases[97] was the *Großkrotzenburg* decision in which the ECJ recognised the direct effect of the duty to carry out environmental impact assessments under the EIA Directive 865/377[98] which was later replaced by the abovementioned Directive 2011/92/EU. For several years, German courts – contrary to the point of view in all other member states – considered article 6 of the Habitats Directive to have certain pre-effects[99] which 'more or less acknowledged the direct effect of article 6'.[100]

Decisions

In some instances, the Union will enact neither regulations nor directives but restrict itself to simple implementation decisions. This was the case with respect to the Kyoto Protocol elaborated under the UN-Climate Change Convention (→ 1.2.1) which commits the Union to a collective greenhouse gas reduction target. The Protocol was adopted on behalf of the Community by Council Decision 2002/358/EC of 25 April 2002 which at the same time confirmed in its Annex II an internal 1998 'burden sharing agreement' that had been concluded amongst the member states in order to allocate differentiated emission levels to each of them. Basically, it is left to the member states to enact legislation in order to meet their individual reduction targets. Thus, the European implementation of the Climate Change Convention results in a complex multi-level governance system.[101]

2.3 National transformation of international environmental obligations

National transformation is required for the implementation of bilateral or multilateral (mixed) agreements which have not or not completely been transformed into European regulations or directives. Moreover, national implementation is also mandatory for international obligations which have been transformed into European directives.

96 n 79 above, para 59.
97 M Hedemann-Robinson *Enforcement of European Union environmental law* (2007) 232.
98 Case C-431/92 *Großkrotzenburg* [1995] ECR I-2189, paras 28 - 40.
99 BVerwG Case 4 VR 3.97 (21 January 1998) (1998) 17 *Neue Zeitschrift für Verwaltungsrecht* 616 622; BVerwG Case 4 A 9.97 (19 May 1998) (1998) 17 *Neue Zeitschrift für Verwaltungsrecht* 961 967; BVerwG Case 4 C 2.99, (27 January 2000) (2000) 115 *Deutsches Verwaltungsblatt* 814; BVerwG Case 4 A 28.01 (17 May 2002) (2002) 21 *Neue Zeitschrift für Verwaltungsrecht* 1243 1244.
100 JH Jans 'Case law analysis. The habitats directive' (2000) 12 *Journal of Environmental Law* 385 388.
101 W Durner 'The implementation of the climate change convention' (1999) 37 *Archiv des Völkerrechts* 357; M Schröder 'Klimaschutz durch die Europäische Union' (2006) 90 *Jahrbuch des Umwelt- und Technikrechts* 19.

2.3.1 Constitutional law

Some basic customary elements of international environmental law have been confirmed by the German Constitution: In 1994, under the influence of the Rio Conference, a new article 20a was introduced into Germany's Basic Law:

> Mindful also of its responsibility toward future generations, the state shall protect the natural foundations of life and animals by legislation and, in accordance with law and justice, by executive and judicial action, all within the framework of the constitutional order.

This provision confirms in clear language the general duty to protect the environment established in the Trail Smelter arbitration and formulated *inter alia* in principle 21 of the 1972 Stockholm Declaration (→ 1.2.2).[102] Moreover, the reference to the 'responsibility toward future generations' is generally understood to refer to the concept of 'sustainable development' adopted at the Rio Conference (→ 1.2.2).[103] Both principles, whether they are internationally binding or not, have thus become formal constitutional law in Germany. Moreover, the constitutions of all German states contain similar provisions.[104]

It should be noted, however, that in establishing objective duties article 20a falls short of recognising a basic human right to a healthy environment as had been demanded before by various political groups.[105] However, like in the case of the European Convention of Human Rights (→ 1.2.1), the German Constitutional Court has held that the right to life and physical integrity enshrined in article 2(2) of the Basic Law implies a duty of the German state to protect individuals against pollution.[106] Both article 20a of the Basic Law as well as the constitution's basic human rights

102 HG Dederer 'Grenzüberschreitender Umweltschutz' in J Isensee & P Kirchhof (eds) *Handbuch des Staatsrechts der Bundesrepublik Deutschland* vol XI (3rd edn 2013) 857 882 - 884 points out that article 20a extends to transboundary environmental affairs.

103 Dederer (n 102 above) 887; K Gärditz 'Article 20a GG' in M Beckmann et al (eds) *Landmann/Rohmer, Umweltrecht, Loose leaf commentary* (2013) paras 52 - 66; HJ Peters 'Art. 20a GG – Die neue Staatszielbestimmung des Grundgesetzes' (1995) 14 *Neue Zeitschrift für Verwaltungsrecht* 555; M Reese 'Leitbilder des Umweltrechts' (2010) 21 *Zeitschrift für Umweltrecht* 339 341; A Rest 'International environmental law in German Courts' in M Anderson & P Galizzi (eds) *International environmental law in national courts* (2002) 81 - 85.

104 M Kloepfer *Umweltrecht* (3rd edn 2004) 113.

105 Kloepfer (n 104 above) 117; R Steinberg *Der ökologische Verfassungsstaat* (1998) 76.

106 BVerfG Case 1 BvR 385/77 (20 December 1979) (1980) 53 *Entscheidungen des Bundesverfassungsgerichts* 30; Case 1 BvR 612/72 (14 January 1981) (1981) 56 *Entscheidungen des Bundesverfassungsgerichts* 54 73.

thus establish a minimum standard of individual protection which necessarily must be implemented at the level of statute law.[107]

2.3.2 Secondary legislation

Apart from these general concepts, most of the implementation of international environmental law takes place through secondary legislation. While in the field of environmental protection some minor legislative competences rest with the German states (*Länder*), most of the international obligations in question require implementation at the federal level.[108]

Autonomous implementation of international obligations – Implementation of directives

Parallel to the European Union's increasing activities in concluding and implementing international environmental agreements (→ 2.2.2), the autonomous domestic implementation of international obligations has lost parts of its original field of application. Nonetheless, in areas not as yet covered by Union legislation international environmental obligations require national implementation. Such implementation is normally carried out through federal statutes, in particular with respect to activities subject to German law (due to its flag-state jurisdiction) which take place outside of the Union's territory. Thus, sections 4 and 5 of the German High Seas Dumping Act (*Hohe-See-Einbringungsgesetz*) of 1998 prohibit all sorts of dumping with narrowly defined exceptions for dredged materials and sea funerals thereby implementing Germany's obligations under the London Dumping Convention (→ 1.2.1). The German Protocol on Environmental Protection Implementing Act (*Umweltschutzprotokoll-Ausführungsgesetz*) of 1994 transforms Germany's obligations under the 1991 Madrid Protocol on Environmental Protection to the Antarctic Treaty into federal law.

Where the treaty in question was signed as a mixed agreement both by the Union and by its member states (→ 2.2.2), the German legislator's task is normally defined by European implementation law, and member states will be responsible either to implement European directives or to supplement European regulations. With respect to the abovementioned examples (→ 2.2.4), the European Directive 2011/92/EU on the Assessment of the Effects of certain Public and Private Projects on the Environment is implemented by various implementation acts, the most important of which is the Federal Environmental Impacts Assessment Act (*Gesetz über die Umweltverträglichkeitsprüfung*). The European Habitats-Directive 92/43/EEC has been implemented both in the Federal Nature

107 Kloepfer (n 104 above) 134; Steinberg (n 105 above) 140 - 152.
108 Dederer (n 102 above) 868.

Conservation Act (*Bundesnaturschutzgesetz)* as well as in the 16 Nature Conservation Acts of the German states. The same applies to the Union's Water Framework Directive 2000/60/EC which required implementation both at the federal level through the Federal Water Act (*Wasserhaushaltsgesetz*) as well as at the state level by the 16 State Water Acts. In 2012, the Waste Framework Directive 2008/98/EC which implements both the 1972 London Dumping Convention as well as the 1989 Basel Convention's provisions on waste reduction and environmentally sound waste disposal (→ 1.2.1) has been transformed into domestic law by the new Federal Waste Management and Product Recycling Act (*Kreislaufwirtschaftsgesetz*).

Transformation techniques: Parliamentary statutes and administrative regulations

As mentioned above, international treaties, in order to become domestically applicable, normally require both legislative ratification as well as normative transformation into German law (→ 2.1 and 2.1.1). With respect to framework treaties, the standard model for federal environmental implementation statutes will be a parliamentary statute that sets out the basic obligations for the executive and at the same time, in order to allow for more flexible implementation of details, grants competence to issue administrative regulations either to the Federal Minister for the Environment or to another branch of the federal government according to article 80 of the Basic Law.[109] A typical and rather early example for this approach is article 2 of the MARPOL Implementation Act (*MARPOL-Umsetzungsgesetz*) of 1973[110] which empowers the Federal Ministry of Transport, Building and Housing to enact regulations in order to implement amendments to MARPOL or its Protocols (→ 1.2.1) provided that these amendments remain within the limits set out by the aims of MARPOL.[111] Similarly, decisions and standards elaborated under the OSPAR-Convention for the Protection of the North-East Atlantic (→ 1.2.1) are transformed into national law by administrative regulations enacted by the Federal Minister for the Environment.[112]

109 HD Treviranus 'Inkraftsetzen völkerrechtlicher Vereinbarungen durch Rechtsverordnungen' (1983) 36 *Neue Juristische Wochenschrift* 1948.

110 Gesetz zu dem Internationalen Übereinkommen von 2.11.1973 zur Verhütung der Meeresverschmutzung durch Schiffe und zu dem Protokoll von 1978 zu diesem Übereinkommen (MARPOL-Gesetz, Bundesgesetzblatt 1982 II 2) in der Fassung der Bekanntmachung vom 18.09.1998 (Bundesgesetzblatt 1998 II 2546).

111 For more details C Tietje *Internationalisiertes Verwaltungshandeln* (2001) 371.

112 Tietje (n 111 above) 377; see also Proelß (n 23 above) 346 on the absence of EU implementation.

Integration into the system of national environmental law or reference to international law?

Traditionally, international environmental obligations tend to be rather general in scope and leave wide discretion to the national legislator on how to achieve the objectives agreed upon. In these instances, it may be possible to conform to the international obligations by strictly applying existing domestic law. In most instances, therefore, the international origin of the domestic provisions is not visible for the reader.[113] Thus, the reduction targets fixed under the 1979 Geneva Convention on Transboundary Air Pollution and its protocols (→ 1.2.1) have been achieved by setting strict emission standards under the existing Federal Clean Air Act (*Bundes-Immissionsschutzgesetz).*[114] Similarly with respect to marine pollution, the emission standards fixed in the Federal Waste Water Regulation (*Abwasserverordnung*) ensure the fulfilment of the reduction targets elaborated under the OSPAR Convention and the Helsinki Convention (→ 1.2.1) with respect to marine pollution from land based sources.[115] Considering the wide scope of the 1992 Convention on Biological Diversity (→ 1.2.1), almost any German provision on nature and animal protection might be interpreted as implementing this programmatic treaty. Also, vast parts of German energy law, in a way, can be regarded as means of implementation of the Kyoto Protocol and therefore may be interpreted in the light of the Protocol's objectives (→ 3.1).[116]

Sometimes, however, national implementation legislation explicitly refers to international agreements and even to their concrete obligations. In order to transform the Aarhus Convention's provisions on access to justice in environmental matters (→ 1.2.1) into domestic law, parliament chose to create a new law, the Environmental Appeals Act (*Umwelt-Rechtsbehelfsgesetz)* which brought major changes to Germany's administrative procedural law.[117] A similar case is presented by the abovementioned Federal Environmental Impacts Assessment Act. A rather far reaching example for this technique of implementation are sections 5 and 6 of the German Seabed Mining Act (*Meeresbodenberg-baugesetz)* of 1995 which oblige all persons engaged in deep seabed mining to respect the applicable provisions both of UNCLOS as well as of its 1994 implementation agreement. These provisions with their umbrella reference to UNCLOS renounce any formal transformation and restrict themselves to setting the international provisions into force. This approach may be

113 W Durner 'Internationales Umweltverwaltungsrecht' in C Möllers et al (eds) *Internationales Verwaltungsrecht* (2007) 121 130.

114 J Salzwedel & W Preusker *The law and practice relating to pollution control in the Federal Republic of Germany* (1982) 24 - 78.

115 J Salzwedel & W Durner 'Wasserrecht' in Hansmann & Sellner (n 54 above) 593 622 & 663.

116 BVerwG Case 7 C 11.10 (10 October 2012) (2013) 32 *Neue Zeitschrift für Verwaltungs-recht* 592 594.

117 S Schlacke *Überindividueller Rechtsschutz* (2008) 232 - 311.

explained by the fact that several of the central provisions of UNCLOS are regarded as self-executing.[118] However, interpretative problems associated with the convention, are thereby drawn into the domestic law system (→ Proelß).

2.3.3 Legislative reception of international environmental soft law

National implementation of international environmental law is not confined to binding international obligations but may also include recommendations, declarations or other forms of international soft law (→ 1.2.3). Even the constitutional reception of the concept of 'sustainable development' in article 20a Basic Law (→ 2.3.1) may refer to a concept which – at least in 1994 – was at the international level still restricted to a soft law-status (→ 1.2.2). Similarly, various international recommendations, such as WHO standards, are formally transformed into domestic law through national or European legislation.

Normally, these recommendations will only be mentioned in the explanatory memorandum to the Act in question. The memorandum to the Federal Regulation concerning Drinking Water (*Trinkwasserverordnung*), for instance, stipulates that the regulation not only aims at implementing the European Directive 98/83/EC on the quality of water intended for human consumption but also refers to the 2004 WHO Guidelines for Drinking Water Quality.[119] On the other hand, section 25(1) of the German Plant Protection Act (*Pflanzenschutzgesetz*) explicitly provides that international agreements in particular the FAO's International Code of Conduct on the Distribution and Use of Pesticides[120] have to be taken into account when exporting pesticides. This provision renders international soft law legally binding.[121] Similar provisions exist at the EU-level: The 'Globally Harmonized System of Classification and Labeling of Chemicals',[122] formally a mere recommendation of several UN-institutions, is transformed into binding European law through Regulation (EC) No 1272/2008 of 16 December 2008 on classification, labeling and packaging of substances and mixtures.[123] All these obligations, while rooting in international soft law, may therefore influence human behavior rather effectively at the domestic level due to their legislative reception.

118 A Proelß 'The 'Erika III' Package: Progress or breach of international law?' in H-J Koch et al (eds) *Climate change and environmental hazards related to shipping* (2013) 129 139.
119 Bundesrats-Drucksache 530/10 of 2.9.2010, 51, 65, 75 & 90.
120 Food and Agriculture Organization of the United Nations (FAO) *International code of conduct on the distribution and use of pesticides* (2003).
121 Durner (n 113 above) 144 - 145 & 161.
122 United Nations *Globally harmonized system of classification and labelling of chemicals* (3rd edn 2009).
123 H Wahl 'Die EG-GHS-Verordnung' (2008) *Stoffrecht* 249.

2.3.4 *Transnational environmental management*

International environmental cooperation is not restricted to entering into and transforming legal obligations but also includes transnational collaboration at the administrative level. Some domestic provisions explicitly refer to international agreements in order to allocate the respective tasks to federal or state agencies. Section 13(1) of the German Waste Transportation Act (*Abfallverbringungsgesetz*), a national supplement to the abovementioned regulation 1013/2006 on Shipments of Waste (→ 2.2.4), provides that the Federal Environmental Agency (*Umweltbundesamt*) shall act as the 'competent authority' under article 2(6) of the 1989 Basel Convention on the Control of Transboundary Movements of Hazardous Wastes (→ 1.2.1). In a similar approach, sections 44-51 of the Federal Nature Conservation Act (*Bundesnaturschutzgesetz*) supplement the Union's regulations that implement the CITES-Convention (→ 1.2.1 and 2.2.4). In cooperating with the international Secretariats established under those treaties, domestic agencies become part of a global administrative network.[124]

The most important examples for international administrative cooperation, however, deal with the transnational environmental management of shared environmental resources. With respect to international rivers, the abovementioned river or basin commissions (→ 2.2.4) play an important role in such transboundary management. Germany is represented in several of these institutions.[125] The most prominent one is the International Commission for the Protection of the Rhine against Pollution which was established in 1950. Based in Koblenz, Germany, it operates under the 1999 Convention on the Protection of the Rhine (→ 1.2.1) and is widely considered to be amongst the most effective institutions to manage freshwater resources worldwide.[126] The Commission coordinates not only the implementation plans of the European Water Framework Directive 2000/60/EC (→ 2.2.4)[127] but also – under its 'Warning and alarm plan Rhine' – the riparian state's emergency action in case of pollution incidents[128] as well as their combined efforts to reduce floods.[129]

124 N Krisch & B Kingsbury 'Introduction: Global governance and global administrative law in the international legal order' (2006) 17 *European Journal of International Law* 1.

125 For references see M Niedobitek *Das Recht der grenzüberschreitenden Verträge* (2001) 73.

126 Birnie et al (n 7 above) 575; E Louka *International environmental law: Fairness, effectiveness, and world order* (2005) 231; Sands & Peel (n 1 above) 320.

127 International Commission for the Protection of the Rhine (ICPR) *Rhine 2020: Program on the sustainable development of the Rhine Conference of Rhine Ministers* (2001).

128 International Commission for the Protection of the Rhine (ICPR) *Warning and alarm plan Rhine: Reported incidents* (2010).

129 International Commission for the Protection of the Rhine (ICPR) *Report on the identification of potential significant flood risk areas in the international river basin district Rhine* (2013).

A less far reaching example for the internationalisation of common environmental resources is the transnational management of habitats, in particular with respect to transboundary national parks. Again, those parks are frequently established on the basis of bilateral administrative agreements or even formal international treaties which are concluded by the German states rather than by the Federation.[130] Up to now, no transnational agencies have been founded under these agreements, but administrative cooperation between national agencies is institutionalised. In some of the German states, on the other hand, environmental administrations may cooperate in such habitat protection even without any formal legal basis. This applies to the transfrontier '*Internationalpark Unteres Odertal*' which was established by two national regulations in Germany and in Poland on the basis of a common declaration of both Governments.[131]

3 The role of courts in applying and developing international environmental law

According to the German Constitutional Court, the German Basic Law is 'völkerrechtsfreundlich', intended to accommodate international law.[132] For German judges acting under the Basic Law's dualist concept this implies the duty to refer to international environmental law as an interpretative guideline, to apply and enforce self-executing international environmental law and generally to accommodate international law in order to meet Germany's international obligations.

3.1 International environmental law as an interpretative guideline

Both the ECJ as well as the German judiciary have frequently referred to the role of international environmental law as an interpretative guideline. According to the ECJ, when secondary EU legislation meant to implement international environmental obligations requires interpretation, the implemented treaty's objectives, principles and provisions must be taken

130 For references see Niedobitek (n 125 above) 80; for illustrative case studies K Abele *Grenzüberschreitende Ausweisungen von Natur- und Landschaftsschutzgebieten. Perspektiven der Zusammenarbeit zwischen Baden-Württemberg, Frankreich und der Schweiz am Beispiel Oberrhein* (1997).

131 E Gerbsch 'Grenzüberschreitende Zusammenarbeit im deutsch-polnischen (Inter-) Nationalpark "Unteres Odertal": Ein Projekt mit Vorbildfunktion?' in M Niedobitek & A Löwe (eds) *Grenzüberschreitende Zusammenarbeit in Europa* (2013) 227 232; for older references see B Scharinger *Rechtsgrundlagen für die Errichtung von Nationalparken* (1999) 93.

132 BVerfG Case 2 BvR 2365/09 (4 May 2011) (2011) 128 *Entscheidungen des Bundesverfassungsgerichts* 326; Geiger (n 55 above) 179; V Röben *Außenverfassungsrecht* (2007) 207.

into account.[133] German courts in interpreting national or European environmental legislation may also refer to its supranational origins although rather few judgments address those origins explicitly.[134] This is particularly the case where the provisions in question have explicitly been enacted in order to implement international obligations. The London Dumping Convention (→ 1.2.1) for instance is transformed into national law by the German High Seas Dumping Act (*Hohe-See-Einbringungsgesetz* → 2.3.2). In order to construe this national statute and its central term 'disposal', the Federal Administrative Court referred to the international convention and its protocols.[135] Similar references were made to MARPOL with respect to European and German MARPOL-implementation legislation,[136] to the 1979 Bern Convention (→ 1.2.1) in interpreting the Habitats-Directive 92/43/EEC[137] and the Federal Nature Conservation Act (*Bundesnaturschutzgesetz*),[138] to article 6 of the Aarhus Convention with respect to section 3(2) of the Federal Building Code (*Baugesetzbuch*),[139] to CITES in interpreting the former German implementation act[140] or even generally to 'international and regional conventions' protecting certain species in order to prove that they are being threatened.[141]

Even international environmental soft law may be applied as an interpretative guideline to construe national statutes and may thus have a domestic effect without any formal legislative reception (→ 2.3.3). Consequently, German courts have frequently referred to WHO-recommendations in order to interpret national provisions that fix

133 Case C-154/02 *Jan Nilsson* [2003] ECR I-12733, para 39 (CITES); Case C-308/06 *International Association of Independent Tanker Owners (Intertanko) and Others* [2008] ECR I-4057, para 52 (MARPOL); C Zengerling *Greening International Jurisprudence* (2013) 68.

134 Rest (n 103 above) 79.

135 BVerwG Case 7 C 7.10 (14 July 2011) (2011) 22 *Zeitschrift für Umweltrecht* 538 540.

136 BGH, Case III ZR 358/03 (2 December 2004) (2006) 19 *Neue Zeitschrift für Verwaltungsrecht Rechtsprechungs-Report* 28 30.

137 BVerwG Case 9 A 64/07 (12 August 2009) (2010) 134 *Entscheidungen des Bundesverwaltungsgerichts* 308 325.

138 OVG Schleswig Case 1 L 321/91 (2 July 1993) (1993) 15 *Natur und Recht* 97 98.

139 BVerwG Case 4 CN 3/12 (18 July 2013) (2013) 32 *Neue Zeitschrift für Verwaltungsrecht* 1413 1415.

140 Amtsgericht Nürnberg, Case 67 Gs 442/81 (12 June 1981) (1982) 35 *Neue Juristische Wochenschrift* 535;VGH Mannheim Case 10 S 1891/89 (15 September 1989) (1989) 10 *Neue Zeitschrift für Verwaltungsrecht* 84ff; VGH Kassel Case 3 TG 3273/95 (29 November 1995) (1995) 9 *Neue Zeitschrift für Verwaltungsrecht Rechtsprechungs-Report* 432 433.

141 VGH München Case 22 B 10.1875 (24 May 2011) (2011) 22 *Zeitschrift für Umweltrecht* 486.

142 Eg BVerwG Case 1 C 102.76 (17 February 1978) (1978) 55 *Entscheidungen des Bundeswaltungsgerichts* 250 259; VGH Mannheim Case 3 S 590/02 (19 April 2002) (2002) 16 *Neue Zeitschrift für Verwaltungsrecht Rechtsprechungs-Report* 27ff; for more general observations on the reception of European and international standards see E Albrecht 'Standards and Thresholds in German Environmental Law' in M Schmidt et al (eds) *Standards and Thresholds for Impact Assessment* (2008) 19ff.

standards of human harm[142] or to resolutions of the non-governmental International Union for Conservation of Nature (→ 1.2.3) with respect to construing national wildlife law.[143] All in all, the important role of international environmental law as an interpretative guideline is undisputed. This role has been strengthened in the context of the ECJ's *Brown Bear* case, even though some of the German court decisions in the aftermath of the ECJ's ruling may raise the question of where to draw the boundaries of proper judicial interpretation (→ 3.3).

3.2 Self-executing international environmental law

Self-executing international environmental law as part of European Union law

International agreements which are binding for the Union become an integral part of the Unions legal order[144] and have legal effects in the Union's internal law and in the member states. To the extent that their provisions are self-executing and establish 'a clear, precise and unconditional obligation which is not subject, in its implementation or effects, to the adoption of any subsequent measure', they are regarded as directly applicable (→ Wolfrum/Vöneky).[145] However, since environmental agreements are frequently formulated in a rather broad and political language[146] and therefore usually not self-executing[147] there have been only few cases where the ECJ applied this doctrine in an environmental context.[148] In 2004, for instance, the Court found that article 6(3) of the Protocol and article 6(1) of the amended Athens Protocol for the Protection of the Mediterranean Sea against Pollution from Land-based Sources had direct effect.[149]

143 OVG Lüneburg Case 3 K 2630/98 (22 February 1999) (1999) 20 *Natur und Recht* 470 471ff; BVerwG Case 6 BN 1/99 (10 September 1999) (1999) 19 *Neue Zeitschrift für Verwaltungsrecht* 198 200; OVG Koblenz Case 1 A 10200/09 (28 October 2009) (2009) 23 *Neue Zeitschrift für Verwaltungsrecht Rechtsprechungs-Report* 310 311.

144 Case C-344/04 *International Air Transport Association (IATA) and European Low Fares Airline Association (ELFAA) v Department for Transport* [2006] ECR I-403, para 36; Case C-459/03 *Commission v Ireland* [2006] ECR I-4635, para 82; Epiney (n 64 above) 61.

145 Case C-300/98 *Dior* [2000] ECR I-11307, para 42; R Uerpmann-Wittzack 'The constitutional role of public international law' in A v Bogdandy & J Bast (eds) *Principles of european constitutional law* (2nd edn 2010) 131 139.

146 Rest (n 103 above) 80.

147 Zengerling (n 133 above) 56. According to D Bodansky 'International environmental law in United States courts' (1998) 7 *Review of European, Comparative & International Environmental Law* 57 58 US courts up to 1998 had only ruled on the self-executing status of two environmental treaties – CITES and the Basel-Convention – finding both of them non self-executing.

148 Zengerling (n 133 above) 69; for further suggestions see Epiney (n 64 above) 65.

149 Case C-213/03 *Pêcheurs de l'étang de Berre* [2004] ECR I-3757, paras 39 - 46.

Self-executing international environmental law in the domestic legal order

Even under the Basic Law's mitigated dualism, German courts have always accepted the principle that self-executing international obligations have direct effect in the domestic order and must be obeyed by public authorities.[150] However, for the reasons stated above, only very few cases of self-executing environmental obligations have been accepted. In the field of nature protection the Federal Administrative Court will take into consideration whether or not a wetland affected by a project is protected by the 1971 Ramsar Convention (→ 1.2.1) even though there are no specific national provisions on wetlands.[151] While these decisions do not explicitly mention the concept of self-executing international law, they suggest that article 3(1) of the Ramsar Convention is regarded as being self-executing.[152] Nevertheless, until very recently self-executing environmental obligations played only a fairly limited role in domestic litigation (→ 2.1.1). Conventions, whose direct applicability has explicitly been denied by German courts include the Kyoto-Protocol[153] and the UNCLOS provisions on marine pollution.[154]

An illustrating decision for the limited immediate relevance of international environmental obligations in domestic litigation is the *Waldschlösschenbrücke* case in which the plaintiff, challenging the permit for a bridge on the river Elbe, argued that the project violated the UNESCO-World Heritage Convention (→ 1.2.1). In 2007 the Higher Administrative Court of Saxony rejected this claim arguing that the convention would not strictly prohibit the building of the bridge. Additionally, however, the Court noted that the convention had not been transformed into national law upon its ratification due to the legislator's assumption that German law would be in accordance with the obligations of the treaty. Thus, the Convention, even though binding for Germany, had not become part of domestic law and its impact was confined to influencing the interpretation

150 BVerwG Case 1 C 52.87 (6 October 1988) (1989) 80 *Entscheidungen des Bundesverwaltungsgerichts* 233 235ff.

151 BVerwG, Case 4 A 15.01 (17 December 2002) (2002) 23 *Natur und Recht* 539 543; see also OVG Lüneburg, Case 7 MS 91/05 (12 December 2005) (2006) 17 *Zeitschrift für Umweltrecht* 94 96.

152 W Durner 'Naturschutzrechtliche Anforderungen' in J Ziekow (ed) *Handbuch des Fachplanungsrechts* (2nd edn 2014) sec 7 at 2.

153 BVerwG Case 4 C 4/02 (13 March 2003) (2003) 22 *Neue Zeitschrift für Verwaltungsrecht* 738 740.

154 OVG Hamburg Case 1 Bf 162/04 (15 September 2004) (2004) 16 *Zeitschrift für Umweltrecht* 208 209.

of the applicable national provisions.[155] This reasoning has been approved by the German Constitutional Court.[156]

3.3 Tendencies to accommodate and to promote international law

The ECJ's *Slovak Brown Bear* case: Semi self-executing international environmental law?

The ECJ, however, strengthened the relevance of international obligations considerably in the *Slovak Brown Bear* case where it had to decide on the direct applicability of article 9(3) of the Aarhus Convention. According to this provision:

> [E]ach Party shall ensure that, where they meet the criteria, if any, laid down in its national law, members of the public have access to administrative or judicial procedures to challenge acts and omissions by private persons and public authorities which contravene provisions of its national law relating to the environment.

The reader should be reminded that the then European Community, when ratifying the Aarhus Convention, had stated that its member states were responsible for the implementation of article 9(3) of the Convention (→ 2.2.2) and that Germany had insisted on language that was believed to allow the continuance of its own rather narrow concept of judicial standing in environmental matters (→ 2.2.3).

After finding that article 9(3) of the Aarhus Convention – contrary to the Union's declaration of competence – fell within the scope of European Union law and its own jurisdiction (→ 2.2.2) – the Court stated that the provision did not meet the abovementioned standards for self-executing norms and therefore did not have any direct effect in the Union (→ 3.2). Quite surprisingly, the Court then declared:

> It is, however, for the referring court to interpret, to the fullest extent possible, the procedural rules relating to the conditions to be met in order to bring administrative or judicial proceedings in accordance with the objectives of article 9(3) of that convention and the objective of effective judicial protection of the rights conferred by European Union law, in order to enable an environmental protection organization ... to challenge before a court a

155 OVG Bautzen Case 4 BS 216/06 (9 March 2007) (2007) 17 *Landes- und Kommunalverwaltung* 520 522; A v Bogdandy & D Zacharias 'Zum Status der Weltkulturerbekonvention im deutschen Rechtsraum – Ein Beitrag zum internationalen Verwaltungsrecht' (2007) 26 *Neue Zeitschrift für Verwaltungsrecht* 527 531; Dederer (n 102 above) 880.

156 BVerfG Case 2 BvR 695/07 (29 May 2007) (2007) 26 *Neue Zeitschrift für Verwaltungsrecht* 1176 1177.

decision taken following administrative proceedings liable to be contrary to European Union environmental law.[157]

In Germany, this rather sibylline passage gave rise to a controversial discussion on its impact on the domestic legal order with dozens of papers suggesting completely different solutions on how to implement the objectives of article 9(3) of the Aarhus-Convention by means of judicial interpretation.[158] Some courts, such as the Higher Administrative Court of Rhineland-Palatinate have denied the possibility to derive legal standing from article 9(3) of the Aarhus Convention,[159] other courts, including the Federal Administrative Court, have been more creative[160] and some courts even went so far as to suggest that article 9(2 and 3) – in fact contrary to the ECJ's interpretation – both had direct effect simply due to its ratification.[161] At the time being, one has to conclude that the ECJ's vague reasoning in the *Brown Bear* case, at least in Germany, has resulted in absolute confusion to such an extent that it has become almost impossible to foresee the legal solution German courts will eventually follow. In giving a non-self-executing treaty provision an effect that comes extremely close to transforming it into national law by means of mere judicial interpretation, the *Slovak Brown Bear* case has promoted international law to an extent that raises delicate questions of democratic legitimacy (→ Schlemmer).

The *Emsland* case: Promoting international cooperation beyond international obligations

Some decisions of German courts have also promoted international law in a way that goes well beyond using international treaties as a mere interpretative guideline for national statutes. Historically, the most important of these may be the *Emsland* decision. In the *Emsland* case the

157 *Slovak Bear* (n 72 above) paras 44 - 52.

158 See for instance J Berkemann 'Der slowakische Braunbär im deutschen Prozessrecht' (2013) 128 *Deutsches Verwaltungsblatt* 1137; F Ekardt 'Das Umweltrechtsbehelfsgesetz vor dem EuGH und dem BVerwG' (2012) 31 *Neue Zeitschrift für Verwaltungsrecht* 530; K Gärditz 'Verwaltungsgerichtlicher Rechtsschutz im Umweltrecht' (2014) 33 *Neue Zeitschrift für Verwaltungsrecht* 1 5; A Schink 'Der slowakische Braunbär und der deutsche Verwaltungsprozess' (2012) 65 *Die öffentliche Verwaltung* 622; S Schlacke 'Zur fortschreitenden Europäisierung des (Umwelt-)Rechtsschutzes' (2014) 33 *Neue Zeitschrift für Verwaltungsrecht* 11; M Seibert 'Verbandsklagen im Umweltrecht' (2013) 32 *Neue Zeitschrift für Verwaltungsrecht* 1040.

159 OVG Koblenz Case 8 B 10254/13 (27 February 2013) (2013) 32 *Neue Zeitschrift für Verwaltungsrecht* 881 882; similar VGH Kassel Case 2 B 1716/12 (20 March 2013) (2013) 127 *Deutsches Verwaltungsblatt* 731; OVG Schleswig Case 12 MN 300/12 (30 July 2013) (2013) 26 *Neue Zeitschrift für Verwaltungsrecht Rechtsprechungs-Report* 917 918.

160 BVerwG, Case 7 C 21.12 (5 September 2013) (2014) 33 *Neue Zeitschrift für Verwaltungsrecht* 64; M Lau 'Das Urteil des BVerwG vom 5.9.2013 oder vom Versuch, den "slowakischen Braunbären" zu zähmen?' (2013) 33 *Neue Zeitschrift für Verwaltungsrecht* 637.

161 VGH Kassel Case 9 B 1916/11 (19 March 2012) 25 *Neue Zeitschrift für Verwaltungsrecht Rechtsprechungs-Report* 544 545; OVG Münster Case 8 D 38/08.AK (12 June 2012) (2012) 34 *Natur und Recht* 722 728.

Federal Administrative Court had to decide on the lawsuit of a Dutch citizen residing in the Netherlands who asked for judicial review of a permit to construct and operate a nuclear power plant issued by a German authority under the German Atomic Energy Act (Atomgesetz). The question was whether or not the plaintiff had locus standi to apply to a German administrative court. Until then, most European courts had been reluctant to accept environmental lawsuits by non-residents.[162] While the Administrative Court of Oldenburg had argued that the German permit had no legal effect in the Netherlands and therefore the plaintiff had no legal standing in Germany, the Federal Administrative Court in its judgment of 17 December 1986 stressed that the principle of territoriality did not prohibit national courts to grant legal standing to foreigners. Moreover, the Court argued that the provisions of the *Atomgesetz* on the protection against the harmful effects of ionising radiation were not limited to the protection of the environment in Germany but also intended to implement Germany's 'international obligations'. On the basis of these considerations, the Court concluded that section 7(2) AtG in the light of its international purpose granted locus standi to the Dutch plaintiff.[163]

While the Court did not refer to specific international norms, the most fundamental of these 'international obligations' is obviously the abovementioned no harm principle (→ 1.2.2). In 2008, indeed, the Federal Administrative Court referred directly to the no harm principle and clarified that granting locus standi to foreign plaintiffs contributed to fulfil Germany's customary obligation not to cause harm to another state's environment.[164]

The *Emsland* case turned out to be a landmark decision that became a precedent for many other fields of environmental protection. Since 1986, German courts, as a matter of principle, have granted locus standi in environmental matters irrespective of the plaintiff's citizenship, nationality or domicile.[165] The Federal Administrative Court's reasoning is even more remarkable since the principle of equal access to national remedies, which has become binding for Germany under article 3(9) of the 1998 Aarhus Convention (→ 1.2.1) and may since then have become regional

162 For details see M Bothe et al (eds) *Rechtsfragen grenzüberschreitender Umweltbelastungen* (1982).

163 BVerwG Case 7 C 29/85 (17 December 1986) (1987) 75 *Entscheidungen des Bundesverwaltungsgerichts* 285; for a thorough case-analysis in English see Rest (n 103 above) 97 - 99.

164 BVerwG Case 4 C 3/07 (16 October 2008) (2008) 132 *Entscheidungen des Bundesverwaltungsgerichts* 151 158.

165 OVG Saarlouis, Case 8 Q 4/93 (25 March 1994) (1995) 14 *Neue Zeitschrift für Verwaltungsrecht* 97; OVG Saarlouis Case 8 M 10/93 (23 September 1997) (1998) 27 *Amtliche Sammlung von Entscheidungen der Oberverwaltungsgerichte Rheinland-Pfalz und Saarland* 60ff; OVG Münster, Case 20 D 118/03.AK *inter alia*, (3 January 2006) (2006) 17 *Zeitschrift für Umweltrecht* 375ff; OVG Lüneburg, Case 7 ME 263/02 (29 December 2006) (2007) 18 *Zeitschrift für Umweltrecht* 154 155ff; Rest (n 103 above) 100; J Menzel *Internationales Öffentliches Recht* (2011) 750.

customary law,[166] was not as yet part of public international law in 1986 when the principle was applied only amongst the member states of the Nordic Council.[167] Thus, while the *Emsland* decision was inspired by international law, this body of law did not yet require the consequences drawn by the Court.

4 Assessment, achievements and challenges

German environmental law was already quite advanced and detailed when international environmental law began to emerge in the 1970s.[168] Therefore, for a long time, international influences on German environmental law were rather limited as Germany was able to meet most of its international obligations on the basis of existing domestic law. Overall, the impact of international environmental law on the German legal order has been appreciable but restricted.

Since the mid-1980s, however, some new elements were introduced into German law such as the environmental impact assessment. Most of these innovations had European origins, and as a matter of principle the international influences have to some extent been overshadowed by the process of European integration. In particular, the 1998 Aarhus Convention (→ 1.2.1) introduced far-reaching standards on participation and litigation that modify the traditional German law of administrative procedure quite fundamentally.[169] In many instances, these developments helped to modernise German environmental law.[170] On the other hand, as the *Brown Bear* case illustrates, this development may cause some collateral damage as well (→ 3.3). Judicial reception of vague international concepts that have not been transformed by the democratic legislator compromises legal certainty and shifts political power from parliament to the courts. For Germany, the main challenge of the future reception of international environmental law may therefore well be to open its domestic law to international developments without compromising the existing balance of powers.

166 As suggested by Dederer (n 102 above) 891.
167 Birnie et al (n 7 above) 306.
168 Kloepfer (n 104 above) 94 - 103.
169 Kloepfer (n 104 above) 105; Schwerdtfeger (n 78 above).
170 See generally N Wiesinger *Innovation im Verwaltungsrecht durch Internationalisierung* (2013) 15.

BIBLIOGRAPHY

Abele, K (1997) *Grenzüberschreitende Ausweisungen von Natur- und Landschaftsschutzgebieten. Perspektiven der Zusammenarbeit zwischen Baden-Württemberg, Frankreich und der Schweiz am Beispiel Oberrhein* Nomos: Baden-Baden

Albrecht, E 'Standards and thresholds in German environmental law' in Schmidt, M; Glasson, J; Emmelin, L & Helbron, H (eds) *Standards and thresholds for impact assessment* (2008) Springer: Berlin

Beyerlin, U & Marauhn, T (2011) *International environmental law* Hart Publishing: Oxford

Birnie, P; Boyle, A & Redgwell, C (3rd ed 2009) *International law and the environment* Oxford University Press: New York

Bodansky, D (2010) *The art and craft of international environmental law* Harvard University Press: Cambridge

Bodansky, D; Brunnée, J & Rajamani, L (forthcoming) *International climate change law* Oxford University Press

Boisson de Chazournes, L (2013) *Fresh water in international law* Oxford University Press: Oxford

Bothe, M; Prieur, M & Ress, G (eds) (1982) *Rechtsfragen grenzüberschreitender Umweltbelastungen* Springer: Berlin

Bowman, M; Davies, P & Redgwell, C (2nd edn 2010) *Lyster's International wildlife law* Cambridge University Press: New York

Boyle, AE 'The Rio Convention on Biological Diversity' in Bowman, M & Redgewell, C (eds) (1996) *International law and the conservation of biological diversity* Kluwer Law International: London

Bratspies, RM & Miller, RA (2006) *Transboundary harm in international law: Lessons from the trail smelter arbitration* Cambridge University Press: New York

Breier, S 'Die Außenkompetenzen der Gemeinschaft und ihrer Mitgliedstaaten auf dem Gebiet des Umweltschutzes' in Scheuing DH (ed) (2006) *Die Europäische Gemeinschaft in der internationalen Umweltpolitik* Nomos: Baden-Baden

Bretherton, C & Vogler, J (2nd edn 2006) *The European Union as global actor* Routledge: Abingdon

Burhenne, WE & Sand, PH (4th ed 2012) 'Internationale Umweltvereinbarungen' in Hansmann, K & Sellner, D (eds) *Grundzüge des Umweltrechts* Erich Schmidt Verlag: Berlin

Campiglio, L; Pineschi, L & Siniscalco, D (eds) (1994) *The environment after Rio: International law and Politics* Graham & Trotman/Martinus Nijhoff: London

UN Climate Change Secretariat (2006) *United Nations Framework Convention on Climate Change Handbook* Climate Change Secretariat: Bonn

Council of Europe (ed) (2nd ed 2012) *Manual on human rights and the environment* Council of Europe: Strasbourg

Dederer, HG 'Grenzüberschreitender Umweltschutz' in Isensee, J & Kirchhof, P (eds) (3rd ed 2013) *Handbuch des Staatsrechts der Bundesrepublik Deutschland* CF Müller: Heidelberg

De Sadeleer, N (2002) *Environmental principles: from political slogans to legal rules* Oxford University Press: Oxford/ New York

Dupuy, PM 'Formation of customary international law and general principles' in Bodansky, D; Brunnée, J & Hey, E (2007) (eds) *Oxford handbook on international environmental law* Oxford University Press: Oxford/ New York

Durner, W 'Internationales Umweltverwaltungsrecht' in Möllers, C; Voßkuhle, A & Walters, C (eds) (2007) *Internationales Verwaltungsrecht* Mohr Siebeck: Tübingen

Durner, W 'Naturschutzrechtliche Anforderungen' in Ziekow, J (ed) (2nd edn 2014) *Handbuch des Fachplanungsrechts* CH Beck: Munich

Epiney, A & Felder, A (2002) *Überprüfung internationaler wasserwirtschaftlicher Übereinkommen im Hinblick auf die Implementierung der Wasserrahmenrichtlinie* Umweltbundesamt: Berlin

Epiney, A (3rd ed 2013) *Umweltrecht der Europäischen Union* Heymann: Cologne/ Munich

Freestone, D & Salman, SMA 'Ocean and freshwater resources' in Bodansky, D; Brunnée, J & Hey, E (2007) (eds) *Oxford handbook on international environmental law* Oxford University Press: Oxford/New York

Friedmann, W (1964) *The changing structure of international l*aw Columbia University Press: New York

Fröhlich, S (2007) *Die Europäische Union als globaler Akteur* VS Verlag für Sozialwissenschaften/Springer: Wiesbaden

Gärditz, K 'Article 20a GG' in Beckmann, M; Durner, W; Mann, T & Röckinghausen, M (eds) (2013) *Landmann/Rohmer, Umweltrecht, Loose leaf commentary* CH Beck: Munich

Gehring, T 'Treaty making and treaty evolution' in Bodansky, D; Brunnée, J & Hey, E (2007) (eds) *Oxford handbook on international environmental law* Oxford University Press: Oxford/New York

Geiger, R (6th edn 2013) *Grundgesetz und Völkerrecht* CH Beck: Munich

Gellermann, M (2nd edn 2003) *Natura 2000* Blackwell Wissenschaft: Berlin

Gerbsch, E 'Grenzüberschreitende Zusammenarbeit im deutsch-polnischen (Inter) Nationalpark "Unteres Odertal": Ein Projekt mit Vorbildfunktion?' in Niedobitek, M & Löwe, A (eds) (2013) *Grenzüberschreitende Zusammenarbeit in Europa* Sachs Universitätsverlag der TU Chemnitz: Chemnitz

Gündling, L 'Multilateral cooperation of states under the ECE Convention on Long-range Transboundary Air Pollution' in Flinterman, C; Kwiatkowska, B & Lammers, JG (eds) (1986) *Transboundary air pollution: International legal aspects of the co-operation of states* Martinus Nijhoff: Dordrecht/Boston

Hartley, TC (7th edn 2010) *The foundations of European Union Law: An introduction to the constitutional and administrative law of the European Union* Oxford University Press: Oxford/New York

Hedemann-Robinson, M (2007) *Enforcement of European Union environmental law: Legal issues and challenges* Routledge-Cavendish: London/New York

Hillion, C & Koutrakos, P (eds) (2010) *Mixed agreements revisited. The EU and its member states in the world* Hart: Oxford/Portland

Hofmann, HCH; Rowe, GC & Türk, A (2011) *Administrative law and policy of the European Union* Oxford University Press: Oxford/New York

International Union for Conservation of Nature (IUCN) 'International Convenant on Environment and Development' in Bocken, H & Ryckbost, D (eds) (1996) *Codification of environmental law* Kluwer Law International: The Hague/Boston

Jans, JH & Vedder, HHB (4th ed 2012) *European environmental law* Kluwer Law International: The Hague/Boston

Kirchner, A (ed) (2003) *International marine environmental law* Kluwer Law International: The Hague/New York

Krämer, L (1992) *Focus on European environmental law* Sweet & Maxwell: London

Kummer, K (2nd ed 1999) *International management of hazardous wastes: The Basel Convention and related legal rules* Clarendon Press/ Oxford University Press: Oxford/New York

Langlet, D (2nd ed 2009) *Prior informed consent and hazardous trade: Regulating trade in hazardous goods at the intersection of sovereignty, free trade and environmental protection* Kluwer Law International: Alphen aan den Rijn

Laskowski, SR 'The (missing) implementation of the human right to water and sanitation in the Federal Republic of Germany' in Smets, H (ed) (2012) *Le droit à l'eau potable et à l'assainissement, sa mise en oeuvre en Europe* Académie de l'Eau: Marseilles

Louka, E (2005) *International environmental law: Fairness, effectiveness, and world order* Cambridge University Press: Cambridge/New York

McCaffrey, S (2nd edn 2007) *The law of international watercourses* Oxford University Press: Oxford/ New York

Menzel, J (2011) *Internationales Öffentliches Recht* Mohr Siebeck: Tübingen

Meßerschmidt, K (2011) *Europäisches Umweltrecht* CH Beck: Munich

Nettesheim, M 'Article 59' in Herdegen, M ; Klein, HH ; Herzog, R & Scholz, R (eds) (2009) *Maunz & Dürig, Grundgesetz Kommentar, loose leaf commentary* CH Beck : Munich

Niedobitek, M (2001) *Das Recht der grenzüberschreitenden Verträge* Mohr Siebeck: Tübingen

Pallemaerts, M (2003) *Toxics and transnational law: International and European regulation of toxic substances as legal symbolism* Hart Publishing: Oxford/Portland

Proelss, A (2004) *Meeresschutz im Völker- und Europarecht* Duncker & Humblot: Berlin

Proelss, A 'The "Erika III" package: Progress or breach of international law?' in Koch, H-J; König, D; Sanden, J & Verheyen, R (eds) (2013) *Climate change and environmental hazards related to shipping* Martinus Nijhoff: Leiden/Boston

Reichert, G (2005) *Der nachhaltige Schutz grenzüberschreitender Gewässer in Europa* Duncker & Humblot: Berlin

Rest, A 'International environmental law in German Courts' in Anderson, M & Galizzi, P (eds) (2002) *International environmental law in national courts* BIICL: London

Rossi, M 'Europäisiertes internationales Umweltverwaltungsrecht' in Möllers, C; Voßkuhle, A & Walters, C (eds) (2007) *Internationales Verwaltungsrecht* Mohr Siebeck: Tübingen

Salzwedel, J & Durner, W 'Wasserrecht' in Hansmann, K & Sellner, D (eds) *Grundzüge des Umweltrechts* Erich Schmidt Verlag: Berlin

Salzwedel, J & Preusker, W (1982) *The law and practice relating to pollution control in the Federal Republic of Germany* Graham & Trotman: London

Sands, P & Peel, J (3rd ed 2012) *Principles of international environmental law* Cambridge University Press: New York

Sands, PH 'The evolution of international environmental law' in Bodansky, D; Brunnée, J & Hey, E (eds) (2007) *The Oxford handbook of international environmental law* Oxford University Press: Oxford/New York

Scharinger, B (1999) *Rechtsgrundlagen für die Errichtung von Nationalparken* Nomos: Baden-Baden

Schlacke, S (2008) *Überindividueller Rechtsschutz: Phänomenologie und Systematik überindividueller Klagebefugnisse im Verwaltungs- und Gemeinschaftsrecht, insbesondere am Beispiel des Umweltrechts* Mohr Siebeck: Tübingen

Schwerdtfeger, A (2010) *Der deutsche Verwaltungsrechtsschutz unter dem Einfluss der Aarhus-Konvention* Mohr Siebeck: Tübingen

Slepcevic, R (2009) *Litigating for the environment: EU law, national courts and socio-legal reality* Verlag für Sozialwissenschaften: Wiesbaden

Solf, S (2006) *Europäisches Flussgebietsmanagement und deutsche Wasserwirtschafts-verwaltung* Erich Schmidt: Berlin

Steinberg, R (1998) *Der ökologische Verfassungsstaat* Suhrkamp: Frankfurt am Main

Tietje, C (2001) *Internationalisiertes Verwaltungshandeln* Duncker & Humblot: Berlin

Tladi, D (2007) *Sustainable development in international law* Pretoria University Law Press: Pretoria

Toope, SJ 'Formality and informality' Bodansky, D; Brunnée, J & Hey, E (2007) (eds) *Oxford handbook on international environmental law* Oxford University Press: Oxford/New York

Uerpmann-Wittzack, R 'The constitutional role of public international law' in van Bogdandy, A & Bast J (eds) (2nd edn 2010) *Principles of european constitutional law* Hart/ CH Beck: Oxford/Munich

United Nations (3rd ed 2009) *Globally harmonized system of classification and labelling of chemicals* United Nations: New York/Geneva

Wiesinger, N (2013) *Innovation im Verwaltungsrecht durch Internationalisierung* Mohr Siebeck: Tübingen

Wirth, DA 'Hazardous substances and activities' in Bodansky, D; Brunnée, J & Hey, E (2007) (eds) *Oxford handbook on international environmental law* Oxford University Press: Oxford/New York

3

THE RECEPTION OF INTERNATIONAL LAW IN THE GERMAN LEGAL ORDER

Rüdiger Wolfrum, Holger Hestermeyer** & Silja Vöneky****

1 Background[1]

1.1 International law

International law – treaty law as well as customary international law – regulates or at least influences national regulations of an increasing number of issues that were traditionally considered to belong to the internal affairs of states. Accordingly, the number of international treaties that states conclude, bilateral as well as multilateral ones, has increased significantly: For example, Germany is a party to more than 3000 (bilateral and multilateral) international treaties.[2] Indubitably, the international legal order has reached a density and complexity not anticipated in the middle of the 20th century.[3]

In light of these developments it is particularly important to assess the relationship between international law and national law. In this regard, it is mandatory to clearly distinguish between, on the one hand, the binding

* Director emeritus of the Max Planck Institute for Comparative Public Law and International Law, Heidelberg, Germany and Co-Director of the Max Planck Foundation for International Peace and the Rule of Law. He is also a judge and former president of the International Tribunal for the Law of the Sea and a member of the Institut de Droit international.

** Reader at the Dickson Poon School of Law at Kings College London, United Kingdom.

*** Co-Director of the Institute for Public Law and Professor of Public International Law and Ethics of Law at the University of Freiburg, Germany.

1 We are grateful to Mrs Mirka Möldner, Mr Daniel Wisehart and Mr Jakob Jürgensen for their support and valuable input.

2 See S Vöneky 'Verfassungsrecht und völkerrechtliche Verträge' in J Isensee & P Kirchhof (eds) *Handbuch des Staatsrechts* vol XI (3rd edn 2013) sec 236 para 2.

3 R Wolfrum 'Kontrolle der auswärtigen Gewalt' (1997) 56 *Veröffentlichungen der Vereinigung der Deutschen Staatsrechtslehrer* 38 42; W Fiedler 'Quantitative und qualitative Aspekte der Einordnung der Bundesrepublik Deutschland in völkerrechtliche Verträge' in R Geiger (ed) *Völkerrechtlicher Vertrag und staatliches Recht vor dem Hintergrund zunehmender Verdichtung der internationalen Beziehungen* (2000) 11ff.

force of commitments on the international level, whether they derive from international treaties, customary international law, binding decisions of international organisations or general principles of law, and, on the other hand, the legal applicability of such international commitments at the national law level. It is quite possible that the two – for one reason or another – do not match, that is, that even though a state is bound by a rule of international law, that same rule cannot be applied as binding law by organs of that state. Since a state, in general, cannot invoke national law as a justification for its failure to implement an international commitment,[4] it violates international law in such a situation unless it changes its national law.

As a rule – and with the exception in particular of some treaties – international law does not establish how states are to implement their international obligations at the national level. The applicable mechanism is determined by the approach towards the relationship between national law and international law of the respective national system. Traditionally, one distinguishes between two different approaches – monism and dualism. The former assumes that there is only one body of law and, accordingly, international law is 'the law of the land'.[5] Dualism, in contrast, assumes that international law and national law are entirely separate branches of law and that, accordingly, a mechanism must exist through which international law may be invoked and made applicable at the national level.[6] Such a view avoids any question of supremacy of one legal system over the other. There are several variations to these two basic approaches.[7] The practical relevance of these theories is disputable. The practice of states differs widely in this respect and does not follow either of the theories in its pure form.

1.2 The German legal system

The German State can trace its ancestry back to the Holy Roman Empire that grew out of the Eastern part of the empire of Charlemagne, divided in the treaty of Verdun in 843, and that was dissolved in 1806. Even though in the decades after the dissolution there was no German state, it was during this time – in 1849 – that Germany's first modern constitution was drafted as a brainchild of the revolutionary movement of 1848 (*Paulskirchenverfassung*). While tremendously influential in later times, the

4 This principle is well established in international law and codified by the Vienna Convention on the Law of Treaties (23 May 1969, 1155 UNTS 331) art 27.

5 US Constitution art VI clause 2 ('This Constitution, and the laws of the United States which shall be made in Pursuance thereof; and all treaties made, or which shall be made, under the authority of the United States, shall be the supreme law of the land ...').

6 O Oppenheim, R Jennings & A Watts (eds) *Oppenheim's international law* (9th edn 1992) 53.

7 Compare eg J Crawford *Brownlie's principles of public international law* (8th edn 2012) 48ff.

constitution never came into force. It was not until the proclamation of the German Empire in 1871 that Germany was reunited as a state. 1871 also saw the entry into force of the constitution of the German Empire, on which Bismarck exercised a significant influence. After World War I Germany obtained a democratic constitution with the foundation of the Weimar Republic in 1919. That constitution proved unable to prevent the rise to power of the national socialists in 1933, under which Germany not only brought a disastrous war upon the world, but also committed some of the worst atrocities in history. Germany's post World War II constitution – the *Grundgesetz* (Basic Law) from 1949 – is heavily influenced by the failure of the Weimar Republic and the crimes committed by Germany during the Third Reich.

Germany's legal system is, in principle, a civil law one with its roots both in Germanic law and in the reception of Roman law.[8]

Today, the Federal Republic of Germany is a federal country composed of 16 states referred to as '*Länder*'. As a general principle the Federation is only competent where it says so in the Basic Law. In practice, though, the Federation is exercising the most significant powers with the exception of the cultural field. The federal structure also has repercussions for the German Parliament. It consists of two houses that participate in legislative affaires: the *Bundestag*, directly elected by the German population and responsible for electing the Chancellor who is the head of the Government and proposes the ministers, and the *Bundesrat*, which consists of members of the governments of the *Länder* and through which the *Länder* participate in the legislation and administration of the Federation and in matters concerning the European Union (article 50 of the Basic Law).

1.3 The Basic Law and international law

One of the consequences that the drafters of the German Basic Law drew from German history was a conscious decision for what has been referred to as an 'internationally open' constitution.[9] This principle of openness can already be identified in the Preamble of the Basic Law[10] and has been used by the Federal Constitutional Court (*Bundesverfassungsgericht*) also when dealing with the relationships between German national law and

8 See eg G Köbler *Deutsche Rechtsgeschichte* (6th edn 2005).

9 The term goes back to K Vogel *Die Verfassungsentscheidung des Grundgesetzes für eine internationale Zusammenarbeit* (1964). See in depth also C Tomuschat 'Staatsrechtliche Entscheidung für die internationale Offenheit' in J Isensee & P Kirchhof (eds) *Handbuch des Staatsrechts* vol XI (3rd edn 2013) 3.

10 It reads: 'Conscious of their responsibility before God and man, inspired by the determination to promote world peace as an equal partner in a united Europe, the German people in the exercise of their constituent power, have adopted this Basic Law …'.

international law (applied to that context it is known as *Völkerrechts-freundlichkeit*).[11] It should be noted, however, that while the German Constitution was, for the time in which it was drafted, maybe exceptionally open towards international law, that openness is perhaps not as pronounced as in some more recent constitutions such as South Africa's.

The openness of the Basic Law towards the international system is reflected in numerous of its provisions. Two pillars of this openness should be mentioned in this contribution: first of all the Basic Law envisages international cooperation. We have already mentioned the Preamble of the Basic Law, which states that the *pouvoir contituant* was 'inspired by the determination to promote world peace as an equal partner in a united Europe'. The desire for cooperation is further expressed in articles 23 and 24 of the Basic Law. The former addresses cooperation in the context of establishing a united Europe (→ Hestermeyer). The latter concerns cooperation in the context of international organisations, to which the Federation may transfer sovereign powers according to article 24(1) of the Basic Law, in the context of systems of mutual collective security (article 24(2)) and of compulsory international arbitration (article 24(3)). It should be mentioned that the Basic Law does not – and in this respect it differs from the examples of several other states – entrust the conduct of foreign relations only to the executive. Instead the executive and the legislature have to co-operate in this respect.[12]

The second pillar of openness of the Constitution that deserves mention – and which is the main topic of this contribution – is the role that the Basic Law ascribes to international law. The German Constitution does not impose either monism or dualism in its pure form. Whereas in respect of international treaties article 59 of the Basic Law[13] follows dualism, general rules of international law (which includes customary international law and general principles of law) are, according to article 25 of the Basic Law, considered to be part of the German legal system.[14] Binding decisions of international organisations, courts and tribunals do not fit easily into this dichotomy. As many other constitutions the Basic Law does not contain provisions concerning the national implementation of binding decisions of international organisations or of international

11 See on this M Herdegen 'Article 25' in M Herdegen et al (eds) (2013) *Maunz & Dürig, Grundgesetz Kommentar*, paras 6ff with further reference to the jurisprudence of the Federal Constitutional Court and doctrinal works.

12 M Nettesheim 'Article 59' in Herdegen et al (n 11 above) para 7.

13 Art 59(2) of the Basic Law reads: 'Treaties that regulate the political relations of the Federation or relate to subjects of federal legislation shall require the consent or participation, in the form of a federal law, of the bodies responsible in such a case for the enactment of federal law. In the case of executive agreements the provisions concerning the federal administration shall apply mutatis mutandis.'

14 Art 25 of the Basic Law reads: 'The general rules of international law shall be an integral part of federal law. They shall take precedence over the laws and directly create rights and duties for inhabitants of the federal territory.'

courts and tribunals (→ Herdegen). As far as binding decisions of the Security Council are concerned – this is particularly important for individual sanctions – they are implemented on the national level either through a governmental decree, a regulation of the European Union, or both (→ Payandeh).[15]

In light of Germany's past the drafters of the Constitution could not and did not content themselves with merely making customary international law part of German law when it came to the law governing the waging of a war of aggression.[16] According to article 26 of the Basic Law:

> (1) Acts tendering to and undertaken with the intent to disturb the peaceful relations between nations, especially to prepare for a war of aggression, shall be unconstitutional. They shall be made a criminal offence.
>
> (2) Weapons designed for warfare may be manufactured, transported or marketed only with the permission of the Federal Government. Details shall be regulated by a federal law.

This provision, too, is given meaning by its historical background.[17] It does not exclude Germany from participating in international efforts under Chapter of the UN Charter to preserve or restore international peace or security or to participate in activities under the mandate of NATO. Equally it does not restrict Germany in respect to self-defence as provided for by the UN Charter (→ Schmalenbach).

Finally, after the horrible crimes committed by Germany during the Nazi era, human rights was another area that the framers of the Basic Law paid much attention to. Even though international human rights law was still in its infancy when the Basic Law was drafted, article 1(2) of the Basic Law already shows signs of constitutional 'openness' by providing: 'The German people therefore acknowledge inviolable and inalienable human rights as the basis of every community, of peace and of justice in the world.' According to the Constitutional Court the provision grants special protection to core international human rights standards, entailing an obligation (which is also based on article 59(2) of the Basic Law) to take

15 See also the German *Außenwirtschaftsgesetz* sec 4 (Foreign Trade and Payments Act, a working translation is available at http://www.bmwi.de/BMWi/Redaktion/PDF/A/awg-englisch,property=pdf,bereich =bmwi2012,sprache=de,rwb=true.pdf (accessed 8 June 2015).

16 See in this respect the Charter of the United Nations (the UN Charter) (26 June 1945, 1 UNTS XVI) art 2(4) and the Rome Statute of the International Criminal Court (the Rome Statute) (17 July 1998) art 8 *bis* as amended in Kampala. At the time of writing this article the amendment has been ratified by 23 States including Germany but excluding South Africa.

17 R Streinz 'Article 26' in M Sachs (ed) *Grundgesetz Kommentar* (6th edn 2011) para 1.

the European Convention on Human Rights into account when applying the fundamental rights of the Basic Law (→ Wenzel).[18]

However, the role of international treaties or customary law in German national law does not fully describe the role that the Basic Law ascribes to international law. Account also has to be taken of the law of the European Union that is to some extent part of the national legal system and to some extent heavily influences that system. European Union law may equally transport international legal standards into national law (→ Hestermeyer). This is particularly true for international environmental law and international economic law (→ Durner, Hensgen), but partially true for many if not most fields of law, as can be seen, for example, in the field of the law of the sea (→ Proelss).

Finally, it is appropriate to mention that there are more informal forms of receiving international law. For example, the human rights chapter of the Basic Law was developed with an early draft of the Universal Declaration of Human Rights in mind (→ Wenzel).[19] This is only one of many examples of how national law may be influenced by international law. The interrelationship works both ways, however. International law is also being influenced by national law. The prime example since the 1970s has been international environmental law.

The following sections will explain in more detail how international law is implemented into national law in Germany. It will start by setting out the status of international treaties in the German legal order and will then describe the role of rules of general international law, before arriving at a short conclusion. It should be mentioned that this chapter will *not* describe how treaties signed by the European Union become part of German law. That aspect of the complex puzzle piece of the German and European multi-level system will be discussed in this volume in the chapter on regional integration (→ Hestermeyer).

2 The status of treaties in the domestic legal order

Firstly, we will discuss the reception of international treaties in the German legal system. The Basic Law does not specify what it regards as an international treaty. The Federal Constitutional Court has held that for the definition of the notion of 'international treaty' in article 59 of the Basic Law the definition of the term under international law is decisive: all agreements between two or more subjects of international law which are

18 BVerfG Case 2 BvR 1481/04 (14 October 2004) (2005) 111 *Entscheidungen des Bundesverfassungsgerichts* 307.

19 See D Eberhardt 'Der Einfluss der Allgemeinen Erklärung der Menschenrechte auf die Grundrechtsberatungen des Grundgesetzes im Parlamentarischen Rat' (2009) 14 *Menschenrechtsmagazin* 162; H Dreier 'Kontexte des Grundgesetzes' (1999) 114 *Deutsches Verwaltungsblatt* 667 772ff.

meant to change the legal situation between the parties.[20] Although article 32(1) mentions only relations with foreign states and article 59 only speaks of foreign states, it is generally accepted that treaties with international organisations are also covered, however, treaties with the Holy See are not.

Before we can address the issue of how treaties concluded by the German Federation are transposed into national law, however, we will have to discuss two preliminary issues, namely – firstly – the *competence* of the Federation to conclude treaties, given that Germany is both a federal state and a member state of the European Union and that hence there are three entities that can theoretically conclude treaties: the EU, the Federal Republic of Germany and the German *Länder*, and – secondly – the procedure for concluding treaties by the Federation.

2.1 Competence for the conclusion of treaties in a multi-level system

The first question one has to ask when discussing the implementation of international agreements in Germany is the question who concludes such international agreements. All three state entities of the multi-level system of governance of Germany may, in principle, conclude treaties: the European Union, the Federal Republic of Germany and the *Länder*.

The power of the European Union to conclude treaties is defined in the Treaty on the Functioning of the European Union (TFEU), which provides in its article 216(1) that the

> Union may conclude an agreement with one or more third countries or international organisations where the Treaties so provide or where the conclusion of an agreement is necessary in order to achieve ... one of the objectives referred to in the Treaties, or is provided for in a legally binding Union act or is likely to affect common rules or alter their scope.

In the areas listed in article 3 of the TFEU that competence for the conclusion of international agreements is exclusive. These areas include the common commercial policy, instances in which the conclusion of an international agreement is provided for in a legislative act of the Union, or is necessary to enable the Union to exercise its internal competence, or in so far as the conclusion may affect common rules or alter their scope. In other fields EU member states retain the capacity to conclude treaties. In light of the division of competences it is possible that both the European Union and Germany become parties to the same treaty. Even where the European Union alone acts, however, German institutions, including the German Parliament, remain involved.[21] More details on treaties of the

20 BVerfG Case 2 BvE 3/92 *inter alia* (12 July 1994) (1994) 90 *Entscheidungen des Bundesverfassungsgerichts* 286 359.

21 See the Basic Law art 23.

European Union are provided in the chapter on regional integration in this volume.

The division of competences to conclude treaties between the federal level and the *Länder* is the topic of article 32 of the Basic Law, which provides:

> (1) Relations with foreign states shall be conducted by the Federation.
>
> (2) Before the conclusion of a treaty affecting the special circumstances of a Land, that Land shall be consulted in timely fashion.
>
> (3) Insofar as the Länder have power to legislate, they may conclude treaties with foreign states with the consent of the Federal Government.

It is, thus, in principle the Federation that concludes treaties, even though there is an obligation of consultation with a *Land* where treaties affect the special circumstances of that *Land*. The *Länder* may also conclude treaties, but only insofar as they have power to legislate and only with the consent of the Federal Government.

If taken literally, the general competence of the Federation to conclude treaties creates problems in particular where the *Länder* have an exclusive power to legislate. We have already pointed out (and will discuss in more detail in this section) that Germany follows a dualistic model with respect to treaties, that treaties thus have to be transposed into national law to become applicable law. If the Federation can conclude treaties in matters of exclusive competence of the *Länder*, however, it would have to be the *Länder* that have to pass laws transposing the treaty. The resulting problems have led to much debate whether the Federation really can conclude treaties in such cases. In practice, the Federation and the *Länder* have reached an agreement about the matter,[22] which provides, amongst others, that the Federation shall reach agreement with the *Länder* before concluding agreements in areas of exclusive competence of the *Länder*.[23]

2.2 Treaty conclusion by the Federation

While article 32 of the Basic Law determines which entity – Federation or *Länder* – may conclude treaties, it is article 59 that stipulates which organ is competent to conclude international treaties or, in other words, has the competence to represent Germany externally. Article 59 of the Basic Law reads:

> (1) The Federal President shall represent the Federation for the purposes of international law. He shall conclude treaties with foreign states on behalf of the Federation. He shall accredit and receive envoys.

22 The so-called 'Lindauer Absprache' dated 14 November 1957.
23 For details see R Geiger *Grundgesetz und Völkerrecht* (5th edn 2010) 117 - 113.

> (2) Treaties that regulate the political relations of the Federation or relate to subjects of federal legislation shall require the consent or participation, in the form of a federal law, of the bodies responsible in such a case for the enactment of federal law. In the case of executive agreements the provisions concerning federal administration shall apply mutatis mutandis.

Article 59(1) of the Basic Law thus establishes that the competence to formally represent Germany in international relations rests, in principle, with the Federal President. It is worth noting that the government is not even mentioned in this context. However, this does not mean that the Federal President has the power to take the necessary decisions. This is the prerogative of the government and predominantly the Chancellor and the minister of Foreign Affairs.[24] It is thus the government that directs the foreign policy.

Article 59(2) of the Basic Law goes on to require, for certain categories of treaties, the 'consent or participation, in the form of a federal law, of the bodies responsible in such a case for the enactment of federal law', that is, the approval of Parliament, which means, as indicated above, that for those categories the executive and the legislature have to co-operate.[25] Article 59(2) of the Basic Law thus requires a distinction between international treaties requiring parliamentary approval and treaties not requiring such approval and, for the latter, sets up a two-step process distinguishing between the negotiation of an international treaty and its approval by Parliament. In both cases, the negotiation of international treaties is the prerogative of the executive. The preparation of such negotiations takes place on the level of the executive. The delegation undertaking the negotiations is composed of members of various ministries. However, on several occasions members of Parliament have been included in the delegation of Germany. It is – in principle – also the prerogative of the executive to decide whether the approval by Parliament of a particular treaty is to be sought. However, approval by Parliament is a right of the Parliament and if the executive does not seek approval where it is required by the Constitution, the Government can be sued in the Federal Constitutional Court.[26] We will address the two categories of treaties requiring and treaties not requiring approval by Parliament in turn.

2.2.1 International treaties requiring approval by Parliament

Article 59(2) of the Basic Law refers to two different categories of international treaties, whose conclusion requires the consent of

24 Nettesheim (n 12 above) paras 34 & 53.

25 C Calliess in Isensee & Kirchhof (n 9 above) sec 83 para 52.

26 See the admissible claims in BVerfG Case 2 BvE 2/07 (3 July 2007) (2008) 118 *Entscheidungen des Bundesverfassungsgerichts* 244, even though the Court held no rights to be violated in that case.

Parliament: those that 'regulate the political relations of the Federation' and those that 'relate to subjects of federal legislation'.

As far as the first category is concerned, it is evident that the notion of 'regulate the political relations' is open to interpretation. It is clear from the wording that all highly political treaties are included in this category, such as treaties concerning the territorial integrity of Germany, treaties dealing with its independence or treaties through which Germany accepts significant financial commitments. However, the category also includes international treaties whose primary objective is not as far reaching but which have a significant political side effect.[27] The Federal Constitutional Court decided that whether an international treaty regulates political relations does not only depend upon the subject area to which the international treaty concerned belongs, but also upon the circumstances of the particular case at hand. The Court came to the conclusion that even a traditional commercial treaty could be considered as regulating political relations depending on those circumstances.[28] It is to be noted in this context that the Federal Constitutional Court does not accept a political question doctrine.[29] Also, human rights treaties may be considered as international treaties affecting political relations,[30] although they may also be considered as belonging to the second category of treaties referred to in article 59 of the Basic Law. The objective of requiring consent by Parliament for treaties belonging to the first category of treaties mentioned in article 59(2) of the Basic Law is to ensure that the executive does not take actions that are of significant relevance for the international relations of Germany without having involved Parliament previously.

The second category of international treaties that requires consent by Parliament, according to article 59(2) of the Basic Law, is treaties that 'relate to subjects of federal legislation'. This category covers all treaties that have to be implemented through legislation.[31] The objective of this clause is quite evident. It constitutes a guarantee that the executive does not enter into international commitments which might be contrary to existing legislation or which might infringe upon future legislation. In fact, the necessity to seek approval by Parliament for this type of international treaty reflects a significant principle in German constitutional law, namely that important decisions require such approval (so-called *Wesentlichkeitstheorie*).[32]

27 Vöneky (n 2 above) para 16.
28 BVerfG Case 2 BvE 2/51 (29 July 1952) (1952) 1 *Entscheidungen des Bundesverfassungsgerichts* 372 382ff.
29 Compare eg N Achterberg 'Deutschland 30 Jahre nach dem Grundgesetz' in (1980) 38 *Veröffentlichungen der Vereinigung Deutscher Staatsrechtslehrer* 78.
30 Vöneky (n 2 above) para 17.
31 BVerfG Case 2 BvE 2/51 (n 28 above) 388ff.
32 See on this fundamental principle BVerfG Case 2 BvL 8/77 (8 August 1978) (1979) 49 *Entscheidungen des Bundesverfassungsgerichts* 89 126; compare also HH Klein 'Stellung und Aufgaben des Bundestags' in *Handbuch des Staatsrechts* vol III (3rd edn 2005) sec 50 paras 23ff.

As a consequence of a progressive interpretation of the two clauses, the number of international treaties requiring Parliament's consent has increased. Whereas, for example, in the beginning the executive alone accepted the statutes of international organisations, at least for universal ones, now this is being done with the consent of Parliament.

But it is not only the conclusion of the treaty itself that requires approval by Parliament. Where a treaty was the subject of approval by Parliament, amendments to the treaty, too, need such approval. Only under certain circumstances is such approval not necessary for amendments, namely if the previous act of Parliament already embraced the amendments or if the amendments are purely of a drafting nature, such as correcting typos.

Despite Parliament's power to accept or refuse the approval of international agreements falling into the two mentioned categories, the influence of Parliament on the content of international treaties is, in reality, limited. Certainly there may be a discussion in Parliament, but Parliament considers a treaty only after the international negotiations have concluded. Thus, the only options that remain for Parliament are to approve or not to approve an international treaty. Where a treaty permits its ratification only in parts or where public international law allows the formulation of a reservation Parliament may also grant approval only for relevant parts of the agreement or on condition of the formulation of a reservation.[33] But it is not only these limited options that restrict the impact of Parliament. Parliament also has a rather limited impact on the content of treaties for practical political reasons: As we stated, the German Chancellor, who proposes the ministers and is the head of government, is elected by the *Bundestag* and hence government is based upon the majority of the *Bundestag*. The rejection of an international treaty by Parliament that the government wants to be accepted is hence rather unlikely.

One *caveat* has to be made in this respect, however. There is the possibility that the *Bundesrat*, which, as the house representing the *Länder*, may have a different majority than the *Bundestag*, may take a more critical position on a treaty proposed by the Government. However, only a limited number of international treaties require the approval of the *Bundesrat*.

Reflecting on the procedure set up for treaties requiring approval by Parliament, one may critically say that the material scope of international treaties and in particular the relevance they have for individuals and the reality of their democratic legitimisation does not match. This is even truer if one takes into account that international treaties, particularly the ones establishing international organisations, may change gradually through

33 Geiger (n 23 above) 118.

practice.[34] The German Parliament is not necessarily aware of such developments and, in particular, has no means to influence them. The Federal Constitutional Court has considered this phenomenon in respect to NATO, for example,[35] without in practice really strengthening the position of Parliament too much.[36] It may be said, in this regard, that international law has an increasing problem concerning its national democratic legitimisation.

2.2.2 International treaties not requiring approval by Parliament

All international treaties that do not require approval by Parliament are, according to article 59(2) of the Basic Law, so-called 'executive agreements'. Such treaties mostly refer to administrative issues within the competence of the Federal Government as compared to the competence of the *Länder*.

2.2.3 Unilateral acts

Another category of acts of international law should be mentioned in this context: unilateral acts. Unilateral acts are declarations by a state or international organisation causing legal consequences under international law – without the need for a second act as would be the case for a treaty requiring reciprocal declarations by at least two states.[37] Examples of such acts are protests, waivers, renunciations or withdrawal. The German Government does not need approval by Parliament to undertake such acts.

2.3 Incorporation of treaties into national law

The main issue concerning the relationship between international treaties and national law is to make sure that an international treaty internationally in force becomes effectively applicable at the national level. This includes that it may be invoked before national courts.

In a legal system such as the one of Germany, which follows the dualistic approach as far as international treaties are concerned, such applicability requires a decision under national law ordering the international treaty in question to be applicable nationally. Again, we have to distinguish between the two categories of treaties created by article 59(2)

34 See E Klein & S Schmahl 'Die Internationalen und die Supranationalen Organisationen' in W Graf Vitzthum & A Proelß (eds) *Völkerrecht* (6th edn 2013) 237 256ff.

35 BVerfG Case 2 BvE 6/99 (22 November 2001) (2002) 104 *Entscheidungen des Bundesverfassungsgerichts* 151; BVerfG Case 2 BvE 2/07 (n 26 above).

36 Strengthening the role of Parliament see BVerfG Case 2 BvR 2194/92 *inter alia* (12 October 1993) (1994) 89 *Entscheidungen des Bundesverfassungsgerichts* 155 188; BVerfG Case 2 BvE 6/99 (n 35 above) 195.

37 See G Dahm et al *Völkerrecht* vol I/3 (2nd edn 2002) 764.

of the Basic Law, namely treaties requiring approval by Parliament and treaties not requiring such approval.

2.3.1 International treaties requiring approval by Parliament

As we have shown, all treaties that require a law for their implementation (as well as treaties that regulate the political relations of the Federation) need to be approved by Parliament before they can be concluded by the executive. The consent by Parliament provided for in article 59(2) of the Basic Law, which needs to be given 'in the form of a federal law', has a triple function: It mandates the executive to ratify the international treaty in question as already indicated, it orders the applicability of that treaty on the national level in Germany and it establishes the rank of that treaty in the German legal system. These functions also explain why the consent has to be expressed in the form of a federal law. Treaties requiring approval by Parliament are thus (with a *caveat* that we will come to later) introduced into the national legal system by the law expressing the approval.

It is a matter of dispute, however, what the 'order of applicability' of the international treaty actually means. According to one line of thought, the law passed by Parliament incorporates the international treaty in question in the national legal system as German law; it is 'transformed' into national law.[38] Other authors takes the position that the law ordering the national applicability of an international treaty is exactly that, namely an order to apply the treaty, which leaves its status as an international treaty unchanged.[39] This is not a purely academic question. If the word 'transformation' is taken literally it would mean that the national legislature could change the international treaty later (which none of the authors proposing a 'transformation' actually suggest), that the national rules on interpretation rather than those of public international law apply and that the German translation of the treaty in question rather than the authentic languages would be decisive. It appears that even most proponents of the theory shy away from its consequences, and rightly so, as they seem to be contrary to articles 31 to 33 of the Vienna Convention on the Law of Treaties. This also no longer reflects the reality of the German jurisprudence. At least the federal courts, when interpreting international treaties, have clearly respected the relevant international rules on interpretation and have pointed out discrepancies between

38 H Triepel *Völkerrecht und Landesrecht* (1899) 112, 258; compare also the critical assessment by W Rudolf *Völkerrecht und Deutsches Recht: Theoretische und dogmatische Untersuchungen* (1967) 158ff & 205ff.

39 KJ Partsch 'Die Anwendung des Völkerrechts im innerstaatlichen Recht' (1964) 6 *Berichte der Deutschen Gesellschaft für Völkerrecht* 20ff; B Kempen 'Article 59' in H von Mangoldt et al (eds) *Kommentar zum Grundgesetz* vol 2 (6th edn 2010) paras 89ff.

authentic and merely translated texts.[40] Thus, the theory suggesting that the statute approving the treaty merely orders its application is preferable.

The introduction of the treaty into German law by a statute expressing the consent of Parliament does not mean that all provisions can equally be applied in proceedings. To be directly applicable in proceedings a treaty provision not only has to be part of German law (which it becomes through approval by Parliament), it also has to be self-executing, that is, sufficiently precise and not requiring a further implementing act.[41] Whether the provision is self-executing and whether it grants individual rights is, ultimately, a matter of interpretation.[42]

Finally, we should address the *caveat* we made at the beginning of the section when we stated that treaties requiring approval by Parliament are – with a *caveat* – introduced into the national legal system by the law expressing the approval. The one exception concerns treaties concluded by the federation in areas for which the *Länder* have exclusive legislative competence. In those cases it is not clear to what extent the approval by (federal) Parliament can order the applicability of the treaty, as under the Basic Law any normal law in the area would have to be passed by the *Länder*, not by the Federation. In practice this does not seem to have caused significant problems, as the *Länder* are included in the treaty-making process according to the Agreement between them and the Federation described above and have either passed the relevant laws or applied the relevant Conventions. However, recently some courts held that the federal statute expressing consent to the UN Convention on the Rights of Persons with Disabilities cannot order the applicability of the Convention in areas of exclusive legislative competence of the states and they accordingly did not apply the Convention.[43] The ruling surprised many as none of the major human rights conventions appear to have been implemented by state law (→ Wenzel).[44]

Another salient question concerns the status or rank of international treaties in the German legal system. Since the treaties that are the topic of this section have been adopted by Parliament in form of a federal law, their status is that of a federal act of Parliament. Due to their origin in public

40 BVerwG Case 2 C 38/81 (25 November 1982) (1983) 98 *Deutsches Verwaltungsblatt* 507 508; BGH Case II ZR 94/74 (7 November 1974) 63 *Entscheidungen des Bundesgerichtshofes in Zivilsachen* 228 230.

41 BVerfG Case 2 BvR 2115/01 *inter alia* (19 September 2006) (2007) 60 *Neue Juristische Wochenschrift* 499.

42 Geiger (n 23 above) 158f.

43 See in detail Hessischer VGH Case 7 B 2763/09 (12 November 2009); Niedersächsisches OVG Case 2 ME 278/10 (16 September 2010); see also BVerfG Case 6 B 52.09 (18 January 2010).

44 See *Stellungnahme der Monitoring-Stelle zur UN-Behintertenrechtskonvention zur Stellung der UN-Behindertenrechtskonvention innerhalb der deutschen Rechtsordnung* http://www.institut-fuer-menschenrechte.de/presse/stellungnahmen/stellungnahme-der-monitoring-stelle-zur-un-behindertenrechtskonvention.html (accessed 3 March 2015).

international law, however, some particularities apply. The interpretation of prior or subsequent national law has to take the relevant international treaty into account, which has become part of national law; there is an obligation to interpret German national law with a view to harmonising it with the international commitments Germany has entered into.[45] However, the *lex-posterior* principle applies and later legislation can hence contradict the treaty, even though this case – in which Germany violates international law and is under an obligation to change the law – is limited to instances where an interpretation of the later law in conformity with the treaty is not possible and the treaty cannot be regarded as *lex specialis*.[46]

Given the rank of treaties as federal law, they have to conform to the Basic Law. If they do not, they do, of course, remain internationally valid, but cannot be applied internally without an amendment to the Constitution. It is for the Federal Government to resolve the legal conflict. In application of the regular courses of action, the Federal Constitutional Court may review whether an international treaty or the act of Parliament approving it is in violation of the Constitution. It may do so even before Parliament's approval of the treaty by a provisional measure.[47]

2.3.2 International treaties not requiring approval by Parliament

Administrative agreements do not require approval by Parliament and hence are not integrated into national law through such approval. According to their very definition, they do not require implementation by legislation either. They are instead integrated into national law by acts of the executive such as regulations by ministers[48] and enjoy the rank of the relevant act in the German legal order.

International treaties increasingly set up international organisations that themselves take binding decisions requiring implementation in national law.[49] These can be implemented under already existing laws, or require an act of implementation by the organs that are competent.[50] At times, much like administrative agreements, they are rendered applicable by regulation of the competent federal minister. Whether this will be done under article 59 of the Basic Law currently remains open to discussion.

45 Compare on this issue C Tomuschat 'Die staatsrechtliche Entscheidung für die internationale Offenheit' in J Isensee & P Kirchhoff (eds) *Handbuch des Staatsrechts* vol VII (1st edn 1992) sec 172 paras 27ff.
46 Vöneky (n 2 above) para 26.
47 Compare in that regard the jurisprudence of the Federal Constitutional Court on the European Stability Mechanism (ESM), order of 12 September 2012, 2 BvR 1390/12, an English translation can be accessed at: https://www.bundesverfassungsgericht.de/entscheidungen/ rs20120912_2bvr139012en.html (accessed 3 March 2015).
48 See Geiger (n 23 above) 160.
49 Eg resolutions under Chapter VII of the UN Charter or the Rules issued by the International Seabed Authority.
50 Geiger (n 23 above) 161.

2.4 Denunciation and withdrawal from a treaty

The denunciation of or withdrawal from an international treaty is a prerogative of the executive even if the international treaty in question has received parliamentary approval.[51]

3 The status of general rules of international law in the domestic legal order

As already indicated, general rules of international law benefit from a different regime of incorporation. Article 25 of the Basic Law provides:

> The general rules of international law shall be an integral part of federal law. They shall take precedence over the laws and directly create rights and duties for inhabitants of the federal territory.

The Basic Law does not specify what is meant by 'general rules of international law'. However, it is evident that these words only include those rules that are applicable universally, excluding regional international law.

The majority view is that article 25 of the Basic Law refers to customary international law as well as to general principles of law as referred to in article 38 of the Statute of the International Court of Justice, but not to international treaties.[52] The latter is due to the fact that international treaties are dealt with specifically in article 59 of the Basic Law and that they cannot be qualified as 'general rules'. To the extent that an international treaty codifies customary international law, the rule is covered by article 25 – in spite of the fact that it is also contained in an international treaty. For example, the rules of interpretation of the Vienna Convention on the Law of Treaties have attained the status of customary international law and hence are covered by article 25 of the Basic Law. Important principles such as the principle of *pacta sunt servanda,* large parts of the Draft Articles on State Responsibility[53] as well as – and this is evident – *ius cogens* are covered by article 25 of the Basic Law, too.[54]

It is to be noted that customary international law as well as general principles of law are developing progressively. In that respect the reference in article 25 is a dynamic one. In the case of a legal dispute, those general rules of international law are applicable that were in force at the time the relevant activity giving rise to the dispute was undertaken.

51 Critical R Wolfrum 'Kontrolle der auswärtigen Gewalt' in (1997) 56 *Veröffentlichungen der Vereinigung der Deutschen Staatsrechtslehrer* 38ff & 50.
52 Herdegen (n 11 above) para 1.
53 GAOR 56th Sess Suppl 10, Doc A/56/10 43ff.
54 Herdegen (n 11 above) paras 23ff only speaks of universal customary law.

As far as the customary international law covered by article 25 of the Basic Law is concerned, its applicability does not depend on Germany belonging to the promoters of such customary international law. It is sufficient that Germany did not object thereto.

Where a rule falls under article 25 of the Basic Law, all German institutions have to protect and uphold it. Article 25 makes it quite clear that individuals may directly invoke such general rules of international law before courts. If courts have doubts about whether or not such a general rule of international law exists, they are obliged to submit that question to the Federal Constitutional Court (see article 100(2) of the Basic Law). Failure to have recourse to the Federal Constitutional Court is considered a violation of due process.[55] The case law of the Federal Constitutional Court that stems from this procedure shows that general rules of international law do indeed have practical relevance in the German system. Practice focuses on several areas, such as sovereignty, powers of the state and immunity (including state immunity), state responsibility, rights of aliens and the prohibition of the use of force.[56]

As to the rank of the general rules of international law article 25 states that '[t]hey shall take precedence over the laws'. The precise rank is in dispute. Some authors argue that general rules hold the same rank as the Basic Law or even that they rank above it. However, the majority view – and the view of the Federal Constitutional Court – is that they rank between federal law and the Basic Law.[57]

Article 25 of the Basic Law is maybe the clearest expression of the international openness of the German Constitution. It was designed against the background of the total rejection and the gross and comprehensive violation of international law under the Nazi-regime. The idea of the drafters of the Basic Law was to establish an open door allowing general principles of international law to automatically influence German law. As we have stated that open door is, indeed, relevant. However, maybe it proved to be less relevant in practice than originally expected and is losing further relevance. This is due to several developments. International treaty law has developed rapidly after World War II and Germany has become a party to most universal international treaties. When international treaties are applied, especially after having been approved by the German Parliament, recourse to the – far less explicit and more difficult to determine – general rules of international law is less attractive. Nevertheless, article 25 still occupies a central role in respect of

55 G Sturm & S Detterbeck 'Article 100' in M Sachs (ed) *Grundgesetz Kommentar* (6th edn 2011) para 27.
56 For an overview see H-J Cremer 'Allgemeine Regeln des Völkerrechts' in Isensee & Kirchhof (n 9 above) sec 235 paras 34 - 40.
57 See Herdegen (n 11 above) para 42; BVerfG Case 2 BvL 52/71 (29 May 1974) (1975) 37 *Entscheidungen des Bundesverfassungsgerichts* 271.

the relationship between international law and German national law, demonstrating the openness of the Basic Law.

4 The role of the judiciary in the interpretation and application of international law

The role of the German judiciary in interpreting and applying international law is largely determined by the German Constitutional Court, which has – since the very beginning of its jurisprudence – granted a considerable role to international law, thus implementing the Basic Law's 'openness' to international law.[58]

Thus, the Court has read the Basic Law as containing an obligation to interpret municipal law in accordance with international law – a principle reminiscent of the US 'Charming Betsy' doctrine,[59] that is referred to in German as *völkerrechtsfreundliche Auslegung*. The obligation is not imposed explicitly in the Basic Law, but results from a comprehensive reading of its provisions relating to international law.[60] To further reinforce this doctrine the Court has adopted a generous reading of its own competences in constitutional complaints. In these proceedings the Court is limited to enforcing constitutional law, but has read its competences to include the prevention of a violation of international law:

> as part of its jurisdiction the Constitutional Court has to pay special attention to preventing or remediating, to the extent possible, violations of international law, which result from the erroneous application or inobservance of provisions of international law by German courts and cause the responsibility of the Federal Republic of Germany under international law. In individual cases this can require comprehensive scrutiny.[61]

The scope of the obligation to interpret municipal law in conformity with international law is defined by the concepts of municipal and international law.

With regard to municipal law the obligation of interpretation in conformity with international law clearly relates to legislation: to the extent possible, legislation has to be interpreted in conformity with international law. Where such an interpretation is not possible, that is, where legislation explicitly contradicts international law, the normative hierarchy of the German system imposes different solutions depending on

58 See F Schorkopf 'Völkerrechtsfreundlichkeit und Völkerrechtsskepsis in der Rechtsprechung des Bundesverfassungsgerichts' in T Giegerich (ed) *Der 'offene Verfassungsstaat' des Grundgesetzes nach 60 Jahren* (2010) 131ff.
59 *Murray v The Schooner Charming Betsy* 6 US 64.
60 Tomuschat (n 9 above) paras 36ff.
61 BVerfG Case 2 BvR 1107/77 *inter alia* (23 June 1981) (1982) 58 *Entscheidungen des Bundesverfassungsgerichts* 1 34 (translation by the authors, internal citations deleted).

the nature of the rule of international law. General rules of international law prevail over national legislation according to article 25 of the Basic Law. Where the pertinent rule of international law is one of treaty law, however, the principle of *lex posterior* applies (unless the treaty rule can be regarded as *lex specialis*) and later municipal law prevails, resulting in a violation of international law. However, such cases are exceedingly rare. Only the field of tax law seems to have given rise to a statistically relevant number of cases in which courts have assumed a conflict between international and municipal law that could not be resolved by interpretation.[62] In contrast, when it comes to interpreting the Basic Law the Constitutional Court has been much more reluctant to proceed with an interpretation that is in accordance with international law. While such an interpretation is possible with respect to general rules of international law under article 25 of the Basic Law, treaties in general do not have an impact on the interpretation of the Constitution. The European Convention is an exception to this rule. The Court has explicitly held that

> as to constitutional law the text of the Convention and the case law of the European Court of Human Rights serve as aids for the determination of content and scope of the fundamental rights and the principles of the rule of law of the Basic Law, to the extent that this does not limit the protection of fundamental rights of the Basic Law ...[63] (→ Wenzel).

With regard to international law the previous paragraph shows that the scope of the obligation of interpretation in conformity with international law depends on whether the provision of international law falls under article 25 of the Basic Law or is one of treaty law. In some instances German courts have even used non-binding international documents as an aid to the interpretation of municipal law. Thus, the highest German civil court (*Bundesgerichtshof*) regarded a contract concerning the sale of cultural property as contrary to public policy and hence void under the German civil code as it violated the interest of mankind in the protection of cultural property, even though a relevant convention at the time was not yet in force for Germany and customary international law did not prohibit the sale either.[64] However, the relevance of such non-binding documents often referred to as 'soft law' has to be established on a case-by-case basis. Finally, it should be mentioned that provisions of European Union law benefit from what has developed into a *sui generis* regime. In particular, the supremacy of European Union law has largely been recognised by the German legal system (→ Hestermeyer).

62 Tomuschat (n 9 above) para 44.
63 BVerfG Case 2 BvR 1481/04 (n 18 above) (translation by the authors). See Tomuschat (n 9 above) paras 37ff.
64 BGH Case II ZR 113/70 (22 June 1972) 59 *Entscheidungen des Bundesgerichtshofes in Zivilsachen* 82. See A Bleckmann 'Sittenwidrigkeit wegen Verstoßes gegen ordre public international' (1974) 34 *Zeitschrift für ausländisches öffentliches Recht und Völkerrecht* 112.

5 Conclusion

With respect to international treaties the German system seems, at first sight, to be complex, which could be considered a disadvantage. As demonstrated, the Basic Law provides for an intricate system of competences concerning the conduct of foreign relations and the implementation of obligations incurred. It distinguishes between the competence to represent Germany internationally and the competence to decide on the foreign policy. Furthermore, article 59 of the Basic Law provides for the co-operation of the executive and the legislature with respect to the conclusion of more significant treaties. Certain international treaties may also be concluded by the *Länder*, which means that the system foresees a horizontal as well as a vertical distribution of competences. Finally, with respect to the implementation, the legislative competences of the Federation and *Länder* also have to be born in mind. However, what appears at first sight to be complex demands, in practice boils down to the establishment of cooperative relationships between the relevant entities in the conclusion of treaties, which enhances the chance of their effective implementation. With respect to general rules of international law, article 25 of the Basic Law demonstrates the openness of the German legal system with respect to international law.

The rules of the Basic Law are not complete; gaps have had to be filled for example by the jurisprudence of the Federal Constitutional Court. Whether the rules are still adequate considering the changes in international law is an open question; alternatives are, however, difficult to develop.

BIBLIOGRAPHY

Calliess, C 'Auswärtige Gewalt' in Isensee, J & Kirchhof, P (eds) (vol IV, 3rd edn 2013) *Handbuch des Staatsrechts* CF Müller: Heidelberg

Crawford, J (8th edn 2012) *Brownlie's principles of public international law* Oxford University Press: Oxford/New York

Cremer, H-J 'Allgemeine Regeln des Völkerrechts' in Isensee, J & Kirchhof, P (eds) (3rd edn 2013) *Handbuch des Staatsrecht* CF Müller: Heidelberg

Dahm, G; Delbrück, J & Wolfrum, R (vol I/3, 2nd edn 2002) *Völkerrecht* de Gruyter: Berlin

Fiedler, W 'Quantitative und qualitative Aspekte der Einordnung der Bundesrepublik Deutschland in völkerrechtliche Verträge' in Geiger, R (ed) (2000) *Völkerrechtlicher Vertrag und staatliches Recht vor dem Hintergrund zunehmender Verdichtung der internationalen Beziehungen* Nomos: Baden-Baden

Geiger, R (5th edn 2010) *Grundgesetz und Völkerrecht* CH Beck: Munich

Herdegen, M 'Article 25' in Herdegen, M; Klein, HH; Herzog, R & Scholz, R (eds) (2013) *Maunz & Dürig, Grundgesetz Kommentar* CH Beck: Munich

Kempen, B 'Article 59' in von Mangoldt, H; Klein, F & Stark, C (eds) (vol 2, 6th edn 2010) *Kommentar zum Grundgesetz* Franz Vahlen:Munich

Klein, E & Schmahl, S 'Die Internationalen und die Supranationalen Organisationen' in Graf Vitzthum, W & Proelß, A (eds) (6th edn 2013) *Völkerrecht* de Gruyter: Berlin

Köbler, G (6th edn 2005) *Deutsche Rechtsgeschichte* Vahlen: Munich

Nettesheim, M 'Article 59' in Herdegen, M; Klein, HH; Herzog, R & Scholz, R (eds) (2013) *Maunz & Dürig, Grundgesetz Kommentar* CH Beck: Munich

Oppenheim, O; Jennings, R & Watts, A (eds) (9th edn 1992) *Oppenheim's international law* Longmans: London

Rudolf, W (1967) *Völkerrecht und Deutsches Recht: Theoretische und dogmatische Untersuchungen* Mohr: Tübingen

Schorkopf, F 'Völkerrechtsfreundlichkeit und Völkerrechtsskepsis in der Recht-sprechung des Bundesverfassungsgerichts' in Giegerich, T (ed) (2010) *Der 'offene Verfassungsstaat' des Grundgesetzes nach 60 Jahren* Duncker & Humblot: Berlin

Streinz, R 'Article 26' in Sachs, M (ed) (6th edn 2011) *Grundgesetz Kommentar* CH Beck: Munich

Sturm, G & Detterbeckm S 'Article 100' in Sachs, M (ed) (6th edn 2011) *Grundgesetz Kommentar* CH Beck: Munich

Tomuschat, C 'Die staatsrechtliche Entscheidung für die internationale Offenheit' in Isensee, J & Kirchhoff, P (eds) (vol VII, 1992) *Handbuch des Staatsrechts* CF Müller: Heidelberg

Triepel, H (1899) *Völkerrecht und Landesrecht* Hirschfeld: Leipzig

Vogel, K (1964) *Die Verfassungsentscheidung des Grundgesetzes für eine internationale Zusammenarbeit* Mohr: Tübingen

Vöneky, S 'Verfassungsrecht und völkerrechtliche Verträge' in Isensee, J & Kirchhof, P (eds) (vol XI, 3rd edn 2013) *Handbuch des Staatsrechts* CF Müller: Heidelberg

4

INTERNATIONAL ENVIRONMENTAL LAW IN SOUTH AFRICA

*Lisa Chamberlain (CALS)**
*Tumai Murombo (Mandela Institute)***

1 Introduction

Environmental law in South Africa is a recent field of law and regulation; however it has emerged as one of the most actively regulated areas where the state and regulators are churning out legislation, norms and standards, and other policy instruments expeditiously. Prior to 1994 before South Africa transitioned to the democratic dispensation, the environment was regulated through fragmented and often conflicting national and sectoral laws that often were not informed by modern principles of environmental management. The advent of the Constitution of the Republic of South Africa, 1996 meant that all laws had to be aligned to the principles and rights that underlie the Constitution. Amongst these is the principle of sustainable development enshrined in the environmental rights provision, section 24. Nevertheless, given the global and transboundary nature of most environmental challenges, even before 1996 international environmental law heavily influenced South African environmental law. The trend of infusing domestic environmental law with international hard and soft law principles continued after 1996 with South Africa openly joining international bodies that had hitherto shunned it during apartheid. This chapter explores the role that international environmental law has played in shaping and directing domestic environmental law in South Africa, analysing the strengths and weaknesses of this internationalisation approach. The interface between international environmental law and domestic environmental law is demonstrated through selected illustrative fields of environmental regulation, without intending an exhaustive study of all environmental sectors.

* Deputy Director, Centre for Applied Legal Studies (CALS) and Senior Lecturer, School of Law, University of the Witwatersrand (Wits), Johannesburg, South Africa.
** Director and Associate Professor of Law, Mandela Institute, School of Law, University of the Witwatersrand, Johannesburg, South Africa.

Beginning with the regional context and sources of environmental law, the chapter proceeds with an exposition of the changing role played by South Africa in international environmental law and diplomacy. The last part analyses how the judiciary has incorporated international environmental law. This chapter is embedded with an analysis of how South Africa has transformed or incorporated international environmental law principles.

1.1 Relevant international law obligations

The chapter discussing international environmental law in Germany has dealt with the development of international environmental law and sources of international environmental law (→ Durner). In this chapter, we supplement this only with a brief outline of the regional instruments relevant to the African continent.

1.2 Regional sources of international law

There are a number of regional instruments relevant to environmental regulation in South Africa. The most significant of these are outlined below.[1] The approach of the African regional instruments to environmental regulation is a distinctly anthropocentric one that focuses on equitable allocation of natural resource benefits and participation in environmental decision-making. The dominant themes are reliance on a human rights framework, access to resources, fair distribution of benefits, special consideration for vulnerable groups and protection of resources for Africa's children.

The 1968 African Convention on the Conservation of Nature and Natural Resources[2] represents the first comprehensive environmental management treaty in Africa. It addresses the management of natural resources including wildlife and endangered species. A revised version of the Convention was adopted in 2003.[3] It is interesting to note that the first

1 Please note that the instruments discussed below are by no means the complete list. In addition, the treaties discussed are complemented by a wide range of African soft law mechanisms such as the African Common Position on the African Environment and Development and the African Strategies for the Implementation of Agenda 21. For a more detailed discussion see H Strydom & N King (eds) *Fuggle & Rabie's environmental management in South Africa* (2nd edn 2009) 182 - 188.

2 African Convention on the Conservation of Nature and Natural Resources (15 September 1968); see detailed analysis in M Bowman et al *Lyster's international wildlife law* (2nd edn 2010) 262.

3 B Erinosho 'The Revised African Convention on the Conservation of Nature and Natural Resources: Prospects for a comprehensive treaty for the management of Africa's natural resources' *African Journal of International and Comparative Law* (2013) 21 378; M Van der Linde 'Review of the African Convention on Nature and Natural Resources (1969 - 2001)' (2002) 2 *African Human Rights Law Journal* 33; note however that neither version has been ratified by South Africa.

version of this Convention predates the Stockholm Conference of 1972, indicating that Africa was taking steps to implement a more co-ordinated approach to environmental governance ahead of what are typically considered as the watershed moments in the development of international environmental law on the global stage in the early 1970s (→ Durner).[4]

At the sub-regional level, South Africa is also influenced by the Southern African Development Community (SADC) Protocols, a number of which are relevant to environmental regulation.[5]

1.2.1 The use of a human rights framework

From an early stage, African regulation of the environment has been premised on a rights-based approach.[6] This is notwithstanding the uncertainty around the relationship between human rights law and environmental law in the international arena at the time.[7] The African approach is evident in the 1981 African Charter on Human and People's Rights (the Banjul Charter),[8] which includes a right to a satisfactory environment favourable to the development of the rights-holder.[9]

This 'right to a satisfactory environment' has been interpreted by the African Commission on Human and Peoples' Rights to encompass substantive obligations such as pollution prevention, the promotion of conservation and ensuring ecological sustainable development and the use of natural resources. This wording is repeated almost identically in section 24(b) of the Constitution of South Africa, which enshrines an environmental right. The African Commission has further indicated that the right to a satisfactory environment also includes what might be termed 'procedural protections' in the form of access to information to affected communities involved and the opportunity to participate in the development process.[10]

4 M van der Linde 'Regional environmental law under the auspices of the African Union' in Strydom & King (n 1 above) 166.

5 All the SADC Protocols discussed below have been ratified by South Africa, see http://www.sadc.int/documents-publications/protocols (accessed 20 April 2015).

6 For which see generally AE Boyle & MR Anderson (eds) *Human rights approaches to environmental protection* (1998).

7 For instance Boyle argues that the failure of the Rio Declaration to recognise environmental rights is indicative of the continuing uncertainty of the role of human rights in environmental law at the time. AE Boyle 'The role of international human rights law in the protection of the environment' in Boyle & Anderson (n 6 above) 43.

8 African Charter on Human and Peoples' Rights (the Banjul Charter) (27 June 1981, CAB/LEG/67/3 rev. 5, 21 I.L.M. 58). Ratified by South Africa in 1996.

9 n 8 above, art 24. Prior to this the environmental right had been included only in international soft law instruments. See Strydom & King (n 1 above) 177.

10 Communication 155/96 *Social and Economic Rights Action Centre & the Centre for Economic and Social Rights v Nigeria*. This decision has been criticised for not clearly stating which international law instruments it took into account and for failing to consider contemporary developments in Africa such as the revised African Convention on the Conservation of Nature and Natural Resources; see Strydom & King (n 1 above) 179 - 180.

1.2.2 Equity and balancing environmental and developmental imperatives

Equitable allocations of resources, and the relationship between natural resources and development, are themes that underpin Africa's regional law mechanisms. Included in the Banjul Charter (→ 1.2.1) is the right to free disposal of wealth and natural resources.[11] Of particular interest is that this right also calls on state parties to 'eliminate all forms of foreign exploitation particularly that practised by international monopolies so as to enable their peoples to fully benefit from the advantages derived from their national resources'.[12]

The need to balance exploitation of natural resources and development initiatives is reflected also in the SADC Protocol on Mining which contains a provision on environmental protection which enjoins member states to promote sustainable development by balancing mineral development and environmental protection.[13]

1.2.3 Links between natural resources, conflict and governance mechanisms

In Africa, natural resources have been associated with conflict for centuries[14] and the regional instruments acknowledge this. The African Charter on Democracy, Elections and Governance[15] reflects the African understanding of the link between natural resources, environmental protection, good governance and peace and security. Article 9 requires state parties to design and implement social and economic policies and programmes that promote sustainable development and human security. This Charter further calls on state parties to institutionalise good economic and corporate governance through, amongst other things, equitable allocation of the nation's wealth and natural resources,[16] and compels the pursuit of sustainable development and human security through achievement of New Partnership for Africa's Development (NEPAD) objectives and the United Nations Millennium Development Goals (MDGs).[17]

11 n 8 above, art 21.
12 As above.
13 SADC Protocol on Mining (8 September 1997) art 8.
14 PA Mwanika 'Natural resources conflict management processes and strategies in Africa' (2006) 216 *Institute for Security Studies (ISS) Paper* 2 http://www.issafrica.org/uploads/216.pdf (accessed 4 May 2015).
15 African Charter on Democracy, Elections and Governance (30 January 2007).
16 African Charter on Democracy, Elections and Governance (n 15 above) art 33.
17 African Charter on Democracy, Elections and Governance (n 15 above) art 37.

1.2.4 Intergenerational equity

Several of the relevant regional instruments include references to the need for environmental protection in order to ensure intergenerational equity and to manage the resources of the continent in such a way as to do justice to the interests of the next generation. These include the African Charter on Democracy, Elections and Governance, which compels states to implement policies and strategies to protect the environment to achieve sustainable development for the benefit of, not only present, but also future generations.[18]

The SADC Protocol on Forestry further acknowledges that many people in the region depend on forests for their livelihood and that sustainable forest management is essential to the alleviation of poverty.[19] It aims to promote the development, conservation, sustainable management and utilisation of all types of trees, to achieve effective protection of the environment, and again to safeguard the interests of both the present and future generations.

1.2.5 Environmental health

After the Basel Convention,[20] which aims to protect human health and the environment against the adverse effects of hazardous wastes, came into force (→ Durner), it became evident that many developed countries were continuing to export their toxic waste to developing countries in general and Africa in particular.[21] In response to this reality, and to article 11 of the Basel Convention which encourages parties to enter into bilateral, multilateral and regional agreements on hazardous waste to help achieve the objectives of the Convention, a group of African countries entered into the 1991 Convention on the Ban on the Import into Africa and the Control of Transboundary Movement and Management of Hazardous Wastes within Africa (Bamako Convention). The Bamako Convention came into force in 1998 and prohibits import of hazardous waste into less developed countries.[22] The Bamako Convention mirrors the Basel Convention

18 n 15 above, art 42. Note however the disappointing omission of any direct references to the environment in the 1990 African Charter on the Rights and Welfare of the Child (African Children's Charter) (11 July 1990, CAB/LEG/24.9/49) which was ratified by South Africa in 2000.

19 SADC Protocol on Forestry (3 August 2002).

20 Basel Convention on the Control of Transboundary Movements of Hazardous Wastes and their Disposal (the Basel Convention) (22 March 1989).

21 See for example the Nigeria-Italy Waste Trade incident (the *Koko* case) in Nigeria and the Probo Koala incident in Ivory Coast, see also EC Eguh 'Regulations of transboundary movement of hazardous wastes: Lessons from Koko' (1997) 9 *African Journal of International and Comparative Law* 130 - 155 for an analysis of the *Koko* case.

22 South Africa has not yet ratified the Bamako Convention; see generally K Kummer *International management of hazardous waste* (1999).

except that it goes further in prohibiting all imports of hazardous waste, without provision of exceptions to be made.[23]

The SADC Protocol on Health calls on state parties to collaborate, co-operate and assist in a cross-sectional approach to address regional environmental health issues, including toxic waste, waste management, pollution of air, land and water and the degradation of natural resources.[24] These instruments are useful in giving content to the South African environmental right that includes the right to an environmental that is not harmful to health.

1.2.6 Special protection for marginalised and vulnerable groups

Another strong theme which emerges from an analysis of the relevant regional instruments is how many of them recognise that existing vulnerable groups stand to be further marginalised and disempowered by decisions around the exploitation of natural resources and distribution of their associated benefits. The Protocol on the Rights of Women in Africa[25] recognises the crucial link between environmental protection and the rights of women and contains a number of provisions that speak to this connection.[26]

Article 18 enshrines women's rights to a healthy and sustainable environment. It further calls on state parties to adopt an approach that facilitates women's access to energy sources and their inclusion in environmental governance. Special mention is also made of the need to protect and enable the development of women's indigenous knowledge systems. This acknowledgement of the role of women in maintaining and enriching indigenous knowledge systems is particularly commendable given the deep understanding of ecosystems possessed by rural African women.[27] Article 19 develops these ideas further by providing for women's right to enjoy their right to sustainable development. This, in turn, requires state parties to approach development planning in a gender-sensitive way which recognises the disproportionate impact of environmental harm on women, promotes their inclusion in decision-making, and facilitates their access to natural resources.[28] Other examples are articles 30 and 31 of the African Charter on Democracy, Elections and Governance that speak to

23 D Tladi 'The quest to ban hazardous waste import into Africa: First Bamako and now Basel' (2000) 33 *Comparative and International Law Journal of Southern Africa* 210.

24 SADC Protocol on Health (18 August 1999) art 23.

25 Protocol to the African Charter on Human and People's Rights on the Rights of Women in Africa (Maputo Protocol) (11 July 2003).

26 Ratified by South Africa in 2004.

27 M Van der Linde & E Basson 'Environment' in S Woolman & M Bishop (eds) *Constitutional Law of South Africa* (2nd edn 2014) 50 - 57.

28 In addition, art 15 provides a right to food security in terms of which women must be provided with access to clean drinking water, sources of domestic fuel, land, and the means of producing nutritious food; art 16 provides for a right to adequate housing, which is envisaged as a right to acceptable living conditions in a healthy environment.

citizen participation and the participation of vulnerable groups in development processes.

In addition, the SADC Protocol on Gender and Development requires state parties, by 2015, to review all of their policies and laws that determine, access to, control over and benefit from productive resources by women in order to end discrimination against women with regard to land and water rights.[29]

1.2.7 Ecosystem approach and regional cooperation

At a regional level, the 1991 Treaty Establishing the African Economic Community (Abuja Treaty) aims to promote social, economic and cultural development using an integrated and co-ordinated approach in the region. Chapter of the Abuja Convention requires member states to harmonise their policies on energy and natural resources.

At a sub-regional level, the SADC Protocol on Shared Watercourses[30] is premised on another of the regional themes, which is the need to adopt an ecosystem approach to the management of natural resources. This Protocol recognises that many watercourses in the region are shared amongst several member states hence necessitating that these watercourses be developed in an environmentally sound manner. To this end, SADC passed an initial Protocol on Shared Watercourses in 1995, which was revised in 2000. The Protocol aims to foster closer cooperation for protection, management, and use of shared watercourses in the region. Member states agree to cooperate on projects and exchange information on shared watercourses, consulting with each other and collaborating on initiatives that balance development of watercourses with conservation of the environment.

The SADC Protocol on Energy also requires regional cooperation. It enshrines the principle of ensuring that the development and use of energy is environmentally sound[31] and addresses cooperation between SADC countries in the development of renewable energy capacity. The SADC Protocol on Wildlife Conservation and Law Enforcement recognises that wildlife resources in Southern Africa have the potential to affect the region's economic development and environmental protection and thus seeks to establish a common framework for conservation and sustainable use of wildlife in the region. Member states agree to collaborate with one another on common approaches for achieving the goals of international agreements on wildlife. The Protocol advocates that member states harmonise legal instruments for wildlife, establish management

29 SADC Protocol on Gender and Development (16 August 2008) art 18. This Protocol has not yet come into force.
30 SADC Protocol on Shared Watercourses (7 August 2000).
31 SADC Protocol on Energy (24 August 1996) art 2(8).

programmes for wildlife, and create a regional database of wildlife status and management.

1.2.8 Reflections and assessment

It is therefore clear that a lot of work has been done in Africa to implement good practices in environmental regulation. In fact, Van der Linde highlights that approximately one third of all treaties developed by the African Union are relevant to the environment in some way.[32] As seen from the instruments outlined above, in Africa, these practices include: the use of a human rights framework; constructing environmental regulation against the backdrop of sustainable development discourse; acknowledging the pervasive link between control of natural resources and peace and stability in Africa; managing resources with the interests of future generations in mind; addressing environmental health concerns as part of environmental regulation; providing special protection for vulnerable groups, particularly women; and adopting an ecosystem approach based on regional cooperation.

Nevertheless the African challenge remains one of implementation. Despite a progressive system on paper, sometimes leading the way in the international arena, environmental regulation in Africa remains disjointed. In addition, it has thus far failed to address the persistent problem of the disproportionate impact of environmental degradation on the most marginalised and vulnerable members of society. Furthermore, South Africa has not yet ratified a number of the key regional instruments revealing a disappointing level of commitment to regional norms and cooperation.

2 South African participation in international environmental law making

South Africa prides itself as a powerhouse in Africa not only economically but also in terms of regional foreign policy and how Africa interacts with the global political economy.[33] South Africa sitting at the UN Security Council and as a member of the BRICS group, is closely watched as its policy positions and decisions may be crucial reflections of how Africa, especially Southern Africa thinks on particular issues. This could be

32 n 1 above, 168.

33 Recent reports indicates that Nigeria has just eclipsed South Africa in this economic leadership position: C Bisseker '"Wake-up call" for SA as Nigeria's economy takes top spot' *Business Day* (7 April 2014). JO Agoi 'Nigeria all set to overtake SA as Africa's largest economy' *Mail & Guardian* (6 April 2014).

misleading given the diversity of African country positions on many issues and the geopolitical dynamics and age-old allegiances.[34] Nevertheless, what is beyond doubt is that South Africa has proved herself a leader in terms of developing a modern environmental regulatory framework that is, relative to other African countries, more in sync with international aspirations and efforts to manage global environmental challenges.[35] This participation in global efforts begun even before democracy in 1994, and culminated in South Africa hosting the 2002 World Summit on Sustainable Develop (WSSD)[36] as well as recently the Conference of the Parties (COP17) to the UNFCCC in 2011.[37]

This outward assessment of South Africa's progress is often a contrast to some internal criticism that the country is not doing enough to prepare for climate change, transition to renewable energy or take the lead in promoting sustainability and poverty alleviation. Generally, therefore the perception of Africa as a dormant receiver of international law[38] is fast changing to an understanding that Africa can contribute to the development of international law including environmental law.[39] In the next section we explain how international environmental treaties become law in South Africa and note the innovation that the courts have also developed to incorporate the spirit of some soft law declarations that are not yet considered as binding at the international level.

2.1 Incorporation of treaty-based international environmental law

The South African Constitution defines how international treaties become part of municipal law (→ De Wet/Introduction). However, unlike some European countries and like other African countries, South Africa's Constitution provides for a dualist system whereby international treaties

34 The National Development Plan (2011) 239 observes that: 'Apart from the perception of South Africa as a regional bully, there is also the view that policy makers [in South Africa] have a weak grasp of African geopolitics.'

35 This is a separate question from the question of implementation and enforcement.

36 Outcomes of the 2000 WSSD include the Johannesburg Declaration on Sustainable Development (September 2002, A/CONF.199/20) the Plan of Implementation of the World Summit on Sustainable Development (September 2002, A/CONF.199/20) and Johannesburg Principles on the Role of Law and Sustainable Development (2002).

37 Held in Durban in 2011; sec 26 of the National Environmental Management Act 107 of 1998 (NEMA) now formally entreats Minister to be engaged in regional and international environmental treaty negotiation.

38 AP Mutharika 'The role of international law in the 21st century: An African perspective' (1995) 18 *Fordham International Law Journal* 1706 1719; A Boyle 'Relationship between international environmental law and other branches of international law' in D Bodansky et al (eds) *Oxford handbook on international environmental law* (2007) 125 - 126 – contrast J Glazewski *Environmental law in South Africa* Service Issue 1 (2013) 2 - 4 arguing that international environmental law has become a branch of international law in its own right, a view which the authors share.

39 RF Oppong 'Re-imagining international law: An examination of recent trends in the reception of international law into national legal systems in Africa' (2007) 30 *Fordham International Law Journal* 296 318.

do not generally become law at the municipal level unless expressly incorporated[40] by domestic legislation.[41] We say generally, because the South African Constitution in fact provides for exceptions to this general dualist model (→ De Wet/Introduction above). Thus for example in *Glenister,* despite ruling that treaties must be constitutionally incorporated into domestic law in order to be applicable, the Constitutional Court immediately cited an Australian case on the status of the UN Convention on the Rights of the Child under Australian law, and a Canadian and other commonwealth cases to support its ruling.[42] This was regardless the status of these treaties in South Africa itself.

The general legal framework for this domestication of international treaties and exceptions to the rules has extensively been explored elsewhere (→ De Wet/Introduction). In the context of environmental law these Constitutional provisions enable courts interpreting section 24 of the Constitution to rely on international law, foreign law and customary international law as well. All this must be done to promote the spirit of the Bill of Rights. The duty to consider 'the spirit' of the Bill of Rights can, in the hands of a proactive judiciary and policy makers, be used effectively to ensure that South Africa's domestic laws and regulations are aligned to relevant international environmental law developments.[43] For example, before the recent regulations that explicitly incorporate the Convention on the International Trade in Endangered Species (CITES),[44] there were Provincial nature conservation ordinances[45] that in effect regulated hunting and trade in endangered species. The interpretation of section 24(b)(ii) of the Constitution regarding the duty to 'promote conservation' is likely to become a contested issue once further steps are taken to look at options to stamp out rhino poaching. Some of the proposed option such as

40 JH Jackson 'Statue of treaties in domestic legal systems: a policy analysis' (1992) 86 *American Journal of International Law* 310 argues that the terms 'incorporation', 'transformation,' 'adoption,' 'reception', have all been used interchangeably to refer to the process by which a country enacts municipal legislation to implement its obligations under a treaty. He states that there is no agreed definition of the concept of 'transformation'.

41 *Glenister v President of the Republic of South Africa and Others* 2011 (3) SA 347 (CC) para 92; The Constitution of the Republic of South Africa, 1996 sec 231(2).

42 n 41 above, para 93.

43 This is cemented by sec 233 of the Constitution (n 41 above), which provides that 'when interpreting any legislation, every court must prefer any reasonable interpretation of the legislation that is consistent with international law over any alternative interpretation that is inconsistent with international law'.

44 Convention on International Trade in Endangered Species (CITES) Regulations *General Notice* R.173 in *Government Gazette* 33002 (5 March 2010) as amended by *Government Notice* R575 *Government Gazette* 34452 (11 July 2011) made under sec 97(1)(b)(iv) of the National Environmental Management: Biodiversity Act 10 of 2004.

45 Provincial ordinances include the Nature and Environmental Conservation Ordinance 19 of 1974 as amended by proclamation 3 of 2011 (23 September 2011) (Eastern Cape Province), Nature Conservation Ordinance 8 of 1969 (Free State Province), Nature Conservation Ordinance 12 of 1983 as amended by Gauteng General Law Amendment Act 4 of 2005 (Gauteng province), and the Nature Conservation Ordinance 12 of 1983 (Mpumalanga). These invariably deal with hunting, harvesting, fishing, permitting and conservation of natural resources.

legalising trade[46] in Rhino horn directly conflict with the status of the Rhino under CITES. Similarly, before the incorporation of the Convention on Biological Diversity (CBD) through the National Environmental Management: Biodiversity Act in 2004,[47] the treaty was indirectly implemented by provincial nature conservation ordinances. No matter how ineffective such incidental incorporation of the underlying principles was; in reality the ordinances implemented some of the country's obligations in term of the CBD and CITES.[48]

In other instances, municipal legislation or regulations existed prior to a treaty whose effect was to implement procedures and strategies later agreed on in a treaty. The environmental impact assessment (EIA) process was first formally implemented in South Africa through the Environment Conservation Act 73 of 1989[49] before the Rio Declaration of 1992 and popularisation of the concept at the international level. It had been practised in South Africa since the 1970s.[50] The development of an EIA regime drew more from the USA National Environmental Policy Act (NEPA) 1968,[51] than international environmental law.[52] This is unsurprising given that international environmental agreements are also mostly informed by state and regional communities' practices.[53]

The South African constitutional system has always provided for the express incorporation of international environmental treaties. What emerged in 1996 was a further streamlining of the dualist legal system by the addition of faster and indirect, if somewhat ambiguous, processes for

46 A Taylor et al 'The viability of legalising trade in rhino horn in South Africa' Department of Environmental Affairs and Tourism, South Africa (2014)

47 National Environmental Management: Biodiversity Act 10 of 2004 (NEMBA) specifically provides in section 5 that it was enacted to '[give] effect to ratified international agreements affecting biodiversity to which South Africa is a party, and which bind the Republic'.

48 Convention on Biological Diversity (CBD) (5 June 1992, 1760 UNTS 79). The hunting restrictions and controlled taking provisions essentially promoted the concept of sustainable use of biodiversity, which is amongst the objects of the CBD. In addition, legislation creating national parks enacted before the CBD convention directly promoted *in situ* conservation as now required by the treaty.

49 See generally M Kidd & F Retief 'Environmental assessment' in Strydom & King (n 1 above) 970 973 & 976 on the history of EIAs in South Africa.

50 Glazewski (n 38 above) 10 - 13; while the Rio Declaration is soft law, its principles have fundamentally shaped domestic developments on matters that may still not be legally provided for in international law. Thus the EIA process, while not enshrined in any general treaty, can be found in treaties focused on specific issues such as the Convention on Biological Diversity (n 48 above) art 14, and the United Nations Framework Convention on Climate Change (UNFCCC) (9 May 1992, 1771 UNTS 107) art 4 (1)(f).

51 Kidd & Retief (n 49 above) 975 - 977.

52 It is only recently in the *Pulp Mills on the River Uruguay (Argentina v. Uruguay)* ICJ (20 April 2010) (2010) ICJ Reports 14 that international law directly addressed EIA as a potential legally binding general principle.

53 Development of the precautionary principle, public participation Aarhus Convention, and polluter pays principle; see for instance JB Wiener 'Precaution' in Bodansky (n 38 above) 597, 599 on development of the precautionary principle; see also N de Sadeleer *Environmental principles: From political slogans to legal rules* (2002) 23.

the judiciary to rely on international environmental treaties when interpreting environmental rights.[54]

Apart from the Constitutional framework for incorporation of international (environmental) law, in environmental law, the National Environmental Management Act (NEMA) provides for a process in terms of which the Minister of Environmental Affairs is required to monitor that treaties to which the South Africa is a part are incorporated or transformed and implemented and also recommend the ratification of treaties to which the country is not yet a part. One of the fundamental principles of environmental management in the NEMA is that '[g]lobal and international responsibilities relating to the environment must be discharged in the national interest'.[55] This is elaborately expressed in section 25[56] of the NEMA. This empowerment provision is potent in the hands of a Minister who is proactive in promoting the ratification and incorporation of relevant international environmental law treaties. This is crucial given the need to ensure that domestic regulation of environmental issues that often have international implications or that are inevitably shaped by international developments. This is a unique feature of environmental regulation. The commitment by South Africa to incorporating international environmental treaties into its domestic law whenever necessary and consistent with our Constitution and environmental laws is crucial. To date several treaties have been transformed into domestic law[57] while other principles of international environmental law have also found their way into our law through court decisions – whether or not the relevant treaty has been ratified.[58]

54 See *Fuel Retailers Association of Southern Africa v Director-General: Environmental Management, Department of Agriculture, Conservation and Environment, Mpumalanga Province and Others* 2007 (10) BCLR 1059 (CC); 2007 (6) SA 4 (CC) and *Director: Mineral Development, Gauteng Region and Another v Save the Vaal Environment and Others* 1999 (2) All SA 381 (A) cases analysed below.

55 n 37 above, sec 2(4) (n).

56 n 37 above, sec 25 '(1) Where the Republic is not yet bound by an international environmental instrument, the Minister may make a recommendation to…Parliament regarding accession to and ratification of an international environmental instrument, which may deal with the following: (a) available resources to ensure implementation, (b) views of interested and affected parties, (c) benefits to the Republic, (d) disadvantages to the Republic, … (h) the respective responsibilities of all national departments involved, (i) the potential impact of accession on national parties, (j) reservations to be made, if any, and (k) any other matter which in the opinion of the Minister is relevant. (2) Where the Republic is a party to an international environmental instrument the Minister, after compliance with the provisions of sec 231 (2) and (3) of the Constitution, may publish the provisions of the international environmental instrument in the Gazette and any amendment or addition to such instrument. (3) The Minister may introduce legislation in Parliament or make such regulations as may be necessary for giving effect to an international environmental instrument to which the Republic is a party'.

57 Glazewski (n 38 above) 2 - 20, see list of ratified treaties in M van der Linde & L Feris (eds) *Compendium of South African environmental legislation* (2010) 678ff http://www.pulp.up.ac.za/pdf/2010_01/2010_01.pdf (accessed 20 April 2015).

58 See case analysis below.

Furthermore South Africa has taken a clear lead in Southern Africa in ensuring that domestic environmental regulation promotes the objectives of global regulation. This is confirmed by the efforts that South African courts and policy makers have made to incorporate and give legislative content even to emerging soft international law norms which, in some cases, are regarded as unsettled at the international level.[59]

2.2 Incorporation of customary international environmental law (→ De Wet/Introduction)

As a source of international environmental law, customary law principles are directly applicable in South African law by virtue of section 232 of the Constitution. The section provides that '[c]ustomary international law is law in the Republic unless it is inconsistent with the Constitution or an Act of Parliament'. The real paradox in this constitutional provision is the determination of when a principle of customary international environmental law is inconsistent with the Constitution or domestic legislation. Anyway is customary international law evocable by individual citizens? The constitutional provision incorporating customary international clearly shows that this source of international environmental law is automatically a source of law in South Africa without more. An interesting example is the case of *Fuel Retailers*, dealt with in detail in part 4 below where the Constitutional Court went to great lengths to interpret the principle of sustainable development, which in our view clearly has approximated the status of customary international law and is indeed included in many treaties in different variants.[60]

Contestation of how, at the municipal level, states actually implement sustainable development is a separate matter as long as the countries agree that, as a matter of practice, it is desirable for them to promote sustainable development. Even if sustainable development has not met the criteria for customary international law, several international treaties in fact use this

59 P Sands *Principles of international environmental law* (2nd edn 2003) 266, these includes principles and concepts like sustainable development, the precautionary principle (approach), polluter pays principle etcetera made law by the NEMA (n 37 above) sec 2(4) and the Constitution (n 41 above) sec 24.

60 P Sands (n 59 above) 254 argues that: 'There can be little doubt that the concept of 'sustainable development' has entered the corpus of international customary law, requiring different streams of international law to be treated in an integrated manner.' But other authorities doubt this proposition, see V Lowe 'Sustainable development and unsustainable arguments' in A Boyle & D Freestone (eds) *International law and sustainable development: past achievements and future challenges* (1999) 30 who vehemently disputes any legal status for sustainable development, noting that it is 'hard to see that the concept of sustainable development can be regarded as having sufficient identifiable normative meaning to be capable of generating a self-contained norm of customary international law, no matter what its utility as a description of policy goals in international treaties might be. It lacks, in my view, a fundamentally norm creating character. The argument that sustainable development is a norm of customary international law, binding on and directing the conduct of states, and which can be applied by tribunals, is not sustainable'.

principle to inform the obligations that state parties undertook.[61] For instance the UN Convention on Biological Diversity refers to the notion of 'sustainable use' of biological resources.[62] Likewise the UN Framework Convention on Climate Change binds state parties to

> protect the climate system for *the benefit of present and future generations of humankind*, on the basis of equity and in accordance with their common but differentiated responsibilities and respective capabilities.[63] (emphasis added).

The phrase highlighted in this article lies at the core of the definition of the principle of sustainable development. Article 3(4) expressly provides that: '[t]he Parties have a right to, and should, promote *sustainable development'* thus creating a legal right. Magraw and Hakwe support that 'sustainable development' may be a legal principle depending on where it occurs in a treaty.[64] Either way therefore we argue that the principle of sustainable development is now a fundamental underpinning legal norm for international environmental law as manifested in many environmental treaties.[65] Nevertheless, there remains considerable debate on the exact scope of the concept, which leads some to contest this view. However, frustration with the difficulty of achieving and measuring sustainability is giving way to other ways of thinking such as resilience theory[66] and adaptive management.[67]

In the *Advisory Opinion on the Legality of the Treaty on Nuclear Weapons*, Weeramantry J (in the minority) again opined that several principles of international environmental law have achieved the status of customary international law. These included the precautionary principle,[68] public trustee doctrine, intergenerational equity, preventative principle, public

61 United Nations Convention to Combat Desertification in those Countries Experiencing Serious Drought and/or Desertification, Particularly in Africa (Desertification Convention) (14 October 1994) art 5(d), of the Convention on Biological Diversity (n 48 above) arts 1, 8, 11, 12, 16, 17 & 18; UNFCCC (n 50 above) art 3(4); Convention for the Protection of the Marine Environment of the North-East Atlantic (22 September 1992, 2354 UNTS 67) art 1.

62 Convention on Biological Diversity (n 48 above) art 10 read with art 2 which defines 'Sustainable use' as 'the use of components of biological diversity in a way and at a rate that does not lead to the long-term decline of biological diversity, thereby maintaining its potential to meet the needs and aspirations of present and future generations' http://www.cbd.int/convention/text (accessed 20 April 2015).

63 n 50 above, art 3(1); *Fuel Retailers* (n 54 above) para 47.

64 n 38 above, 623.

65 For an extensive analysis of this trend and treaties that directly or indirectly use the principle, see Sands (n 59 above) 253 & 269.

66 See generally CS Holling 'Resilience and stability of ecological systems' (1973) 4 *Annual Review of Ecology and Systematics* 1, 17.

67 C Arnold & L Gunderson 'Adaptive law and resilience' (2013) 43 *Environmental Law Reporter* 10426; RK Craig & MH Benson 'Replacing sustainability' (2013) 4 *Akron Law Review* 84.

68 UNFCCC (n 50 above) art 3(3); see also A Boyle 'Relationship between international environmental law and other branches of international law' in Bodansky (n 38 above) 127 arguing that 'environmental impact assessment, transboundary risk management and the precautionary principle or approach' are now customary international law norms.

participation, common heritage of mankind and the polluter pays principle. The judge stated that:

> [T]hese principles of environmental law thus do not depend for their validity on treaty provisions. They are part of customary international law. They are part of the sine qua non for human survival. Practical recognitions of the principle that they are an integral part of customary international law are not difficult to find in the international arena.[69]

All these principles now form part of binding South African environmental law, having been directly incorporated in section 2(4) of the NEMA.[70] To the extent that we argue that sustainable development may be customary international law, it has therefore shaped domestic developments in South Africa especially in the sphere of land use planning and EIA. Separately, other principles such as sovereignty over natural resources, freedom of the high seas[71] and state responsibility[72] have also informed the development of domestic marine law in South Africa (→ Vrancken).

What is clear from the practice in South Africa is that, given that customary principles of international law often apply between states, the country has relied on these principles to develop and shape domestic legislation governing transboundary and marine resources.

2.3 Soft law in international environmental law

While international 'hard' environmental law has influenced South African environmental law, a unique feature of environmental law is the significant role played by soft law instruments,[73] in the domestic development of environmental law. Soft law norms have influenced municipal law in the field of environmental law far more than any other field of international law. Given the complexity and controversy of most global environmental challenges, it was never going to be easy for the community of nations to conclude definitive legally binding international

69 *Nuclear Weapons Advisory Opinion* (1996) 35 ILM 809, as reported by E Heinze & M Fitzmaurice (eds) *Landmark cases in international law* (1998) 1339.

70 The principles in NEMA (n 37 above) sec 2(4) are also incorporated by reference in other environmental management legislation, for which see NEMBA (n 47 above) sec 7, Protected Areas Act 57 of 2003 sec 5(1) (a), Minerals and Petroleum Resources Development Act 28 of 2002 sec 37(1), Air Quality Act 39 of 2004 sec 5(2), Integrated Coastal Management Act 24 of 2008 sec 5(1).

71 International Convention for the Prevention of Pollution from Ships Act 66 of 1996; International Convention Relating to Intervention on the High Seas in Cases of Oil Pollution Casualties Act 64 of 1987; South African Maritime Safety Authority Act 5 of 1998.

72 *Trail Smelter Arbitration case (United States v Canada)* Arbitral Tribunal, 3 UN Rep. International Arbitration Awards 1905 (1941), *Corfu Channel case (United Kingdom v Albania)* ICJ (15 December 1949) (1949) ICJ Reports (duty to warn of environmental hazards).

73 P Dupuy 'Formation of customary international law and general principles' in Bodansky et al (n 38 above) 458; Lowe (n 60 above) 30 argues that there is a very thin line between 'hard' and 'soft' law.

environmental treaties. Hence many controversial issues are left to the vicissitudes of non-binding soft law declarations and resolutions.

A number of international environmental treaties are ambiguous and subject to various interpretations and exceptions to the extent that their Achilles heel has been the difficulty of giving content and scope to the obligations assumed by state parties.[74] The on-going negotiations of a successor to the Kyoto Protocol is testimony enough of the difficulty of giving specific content to state obligations in environmental treaties. Partly because of this, states have found it comforting to sign onto soft law declarations and action plans that per se are not legally binding, as part of a lowest hanging fruit approach. South Africa has incorporated many soft law principles into its municipal environmental law both legislatively and through judicial interpretation (→ 4).[75]

What is interesting in most cases where the courts have referred to the soft law principles is that despite the express constitutional provision for sustainable development and further elaboration in section 2(4) of the NEMA and other legislation, the courts insist on drawing on soft law instruments to give meaning and perspective to the principle of sustainable development and its effect on environmental regulation in the country (→ 4).[76] This certainly comports with the constitutional mandate for courts to take into account international law and customary law not inconsistent with the constitution in interpreting the bill of rights including sec 24 environmental rights.

2.4 The need for transformation of international environmental treaties

One cannot overemphasise the necessity of transformation or incorporation of international environmental law into municipal law. By their nature environmental problems not only transcend political boundaries, but more importantly the effects of contemporary global environmental law problems require multilateral concerted efforts in order to be effective. For instance, while small country measures to reduce greenhouse gas emissions and mitigate the impacts of climate change are important, by themselves these are insignificant. If measures to mitigate climate change are reported to be effective only in time periods of the order of fifty years one can understand this insignificance. The regulation of genetically modified organisms (GMOs) in a globalised world economy where agricultural produce and genetic material move seamlessly from one

74 A number of concepts morph from one status to another (general principle, normative concept, custom, legal obligations or rights) across treaties, declarations and cases.

75 Glazewski (n 38 above) 2 - 8ff; see also the use of soft law principles in *Fuel Retailers* (n 54 above).

76 *Fuel Retailers* and *Save the Vaal* cases (n 54 above).

country to another is ineffective without harmonisation of standards and biosafety laws and policies at a regional and international level.[77]

Synergy, integration, harmonisation and the prevention of pollution-haven shopping,[78] all call for the transformation of international environmental law principles, norms and standards across nations. It is difficult to universalise some legal norms. This challenge should not prevent the universal adoption of principles aimed at promoting sustainable livelihoods, and saving the human race from ecological disasters without raising false alarms or promoting inequitable access to natural resources among countries. Harmonisation and regulatory integration is important in the Southern African and African context given the increasing importance of Foreign Direct Investment (FDI) for development as well as the resurgence of the scramble for Africa especially from the East.[79] The threat of environmental degradation and insatiable unsustainable extraction of natural resources for profits, that are often shipped abroad, requires regional communities to agree on effective environmental regulation while allowing needed but sustainable economic and social development activity.

International and regional legal mechanisms have a particular relevance to the regulation of natural resources because these resources and the environmental problems associated with their use or misuse, do not observe political boundaries drawn by people. Ecosystems[80] need to be understood holistically because a disruption in the natural equilibrium at one point in the ecosystem can have impact in an entirely different place. Some natural resources (like minerals) remain in one place but many others (such as air, water, mammals and birds) are a lot more fluid in their movement. So for example, pollution of the Limpopo River, which forms the boundary between South Africa and Zimbabwe, may have significant consequences for the downstream users of that river in Mozambique. In addition, humans often use natural landmarks, such as rivers and mountain ranges, to define political boundaries in a way, which does not make sense from an ecosystem management point of view. A river is typically located at the very centre of an ecosystem so using a river as a

77 South Africa has created a framework in the Genetically Modified Organisms Act for the use of GMO technology while most of her neighbours in the SADC region expressly prohibit the importation of genetically modified organisms.

78 A strategy where industry especially multinational corporations chose to do business in countries where environmental and pollution control regulations and standards are low and poorly enforced.

79 ME Margulis et al 'Land grabbing and global governance: critical perspectives' (2013) 10 *Globalizations* 1, 3 'Land grabbing is an important site of new transnational political struggles for authority and control over resources and governance. These struggles go beyond who should control the land, and are contests largely about what should be grown on it, how, by whom, for what markets, hence the future of global agriculture'.

80 For the historical development of the 'ecosystem concept' see D Tarlock 'Ecosystems' in Bodansky et al (n 38 above) 578. The ecosystem approach now permeates most biodiversity conservation treaties and domestic laws and policies such the CBD and the Biodiversity Act.

national border effectively carves up the ecosystem in a very artificial way. Legal instruments that cut across national boundaries are therefore particularly important in the environmental context.[81] These have been developed but appear to face challenge sin terms of compliance and enforcement against violations by riparian states.

2.5 National transformation of international environmental obligations

2.5.1 General principles of environmental law

The creation of a right that is not harmful to health and well-being in the South African Constitution in 1996 opened the doors to the domestication of international environmental law treaties that are aimed at promoting sustainable development and sustainable use of natural resources. The constitutional provision mandates the state to take legislative measures to promote the rights and to prevent pollution and promote conservation while allowing justifiable socio-economic development to take place. In implementing its constitutional obligation South Africa enacted the NEMA, the Mineral and Petroleum Resources Development Act (MPRDA), the National Water Act and other sectoral environmental legislation. What is unique about the NEMA is that as framework legislation it incorporates several principles of international environmental law, whether embedded in a treaty, customary principle or soft law declarations.[82]

These general principles of environmental management in section 2 of the NEMA incorporate some principles which are still contested in international law. Subsequent media specific legislation discussed below continues this process, underpinned by adherence to the ecosystem approach[83] and integrated environmental management.[84] The NEMA, read together with the Specific Environmental Management Acts (SEMAs),[85] the National Water Act and the Minerals and MPRDA represent an integrated natural resources regulatory system. This system is heavily informed by the principles in section 2(4) of the NEMA which, as

81 These include the UN Convention on the Law of Non-Navigational Uses of International Watercourses (21 May 1997) and the SADC Protocol on Shared Watercourses (n 30 above).

82 *Fuel Retailers* (n 54 above) para 59.

83 Secretariat of the CBD convention defines this approach as 'a strategy for the integrated management of land, water and living resources that promotes conservation and sustainable use in an equitable way … It recognizes that humans, with their cultural diversity, are an integral component of ecosystems' http://www.cbd.int/ecosystem (accessed 20 April 2015).

84 Defined in sec 23 of the NEMA (n 37 above) but largely borrowed from environmental management sciences where managing natural resources is supposed to be informed by an understanding that a holistic approach is necessary given the connectedness or integration of nature.

85 Listed in n 70 above.

discussed above, borrow heavily from hard and soft international law. Yet despite this apparently neat system, areas of fragmentation, inconsistency and regulatory conflict remain that impede the effective implementation of this domestic regime.[86]

2.5.2 Biodiversity and nature conservation

Various statutes have been enacted to implement South Africa's obligations under biodiversity conservation and sustainable use international treaties. These statutes include general enactments and legislation aimed at conservation of specific species. The general legislation includes the National Environmental Management: Biodiversity Act[87] and the National Environmental Management: Protected Areas Act,[88] National Forests Act, National Heritage Resources Act,[89] the Marine Living Resources Act,[90] and the Antarctic Treaties Act.[91] Arguably the Biodiversity Act incorporates several international obligations as mandated in section 5 of the Act. These include the CBD, CITES, and the 1971 Ramsar Convention on Convention on Wetlands of International Importance especially as Waterfowl Habitat.

The Biodiversity Act is one of the clearest cases of transformation on international environmental law into domestic law. The concepts, definitions, principles, objectives and strategies adopted in the domestic legislation are directly transposed from the CBD convention.[92] Similarly, the National Heritage Resources Act is heavily informed and implements the Convention Concerning the Protection of the World Cultural and Natural Heritage.

2.5.3 Air quality, climate change and pollution control

While there are regional treaties on transboundary air pollution and

86 N Rossouw & K Wiseman 'Learning from the implementation of environmental public policy instruments after the first ten years of democracy in South Africa' (2004) 22 *Impact Assessment and Project Appraisal* 131 138.

87 n 47 above.

88 National Environmental Management: Protected Areas Act 57 of 2003 implementing protected area treaties and soft law instruments especially those developed by the IUCN on Protected Area classification and management strategies.

89 National Forests Act 84 of 1998, National Heritage Resources Act 25 of 1999 incorporating the Convention Concerning the Protection of the World Cultural and Natural Heritage (16 November 1972) http://whc.unesco.org/archive/convention-en.pdf (accessed 20 April 2015).

90 The Marine Living Resources Act 18 of 1998.

91 Antarctic Treaties Act 60 of 1996 implementing the Convention on the Conservation of Antarctic Marine Living Resources (1980) and the Agreed Measures for the Conservation of Antarctic Fauna and Flora (1964).

92 NEMBA (n 47 above) sec 2 (b) expressly provides that it was enacted, among other objects, 'to give effect *to ratified international agreements* relating to biodiversity which are binding on the Republic'. (emphasis).

multilateral treaties governing the effects of air pollution,[93] South Africa decided to enact a single piece of legislation that implements the country's obligations regarding air quality. The National Environmental Management: Air Quality Act is an omnibus Act at once regulating air quality and controlling air pollution. In 2011 regulations were proposed to regulate ozone-depleting substances in line with the Montreal Protocol.[94] An amendment bill to the Air Quality Act proposes to amend the Act to include a provision in sec 53 giving the Minister powers to make regulations

> that are not in conflict with [the] Act, regarding (a) any matter necessary to give effect to the Republic's obligations in terms of an international agreement relating to air quality and climate change.

While this builds on section 25 of the NEMA, the inclusion of 'greenhouse gas' and 'ozone-depleting substances' in the Act can easily be used by the Minister to implement the country's international climate change obligations using the Air Quality Act and without specific climate change or ozone related legislation.[95] In addition section 50 regulates transboundary air pollution.

It is clear therefore that the Air Quality Act implements treaty obligations under some atmospheric, air quality and pollution control treaties.[96] South Africa, without specific climate change legislation, has already put in place statutory and policy measures to partly address the sources of greenhouse gases that cause climate change. These include the Long Term Mitigation Strategy,[97] National Climate Change Response White Paper 2011, proposed Carbon Tax Policy 2011, and the National Development Plan: Vision 2030. In addition the country has already been

93 The Convention on Long-range Transboundary Air Pollution (Geneva Convention on Transboundary Air Pollution) (13 November 1979, 1302 UNTS 217).

94 Proposed regulations regarding the phasing-out and management of ozone depleting substances in the Republic of South Africa *Government Notice* 12 in *Government Gazette* No. 33925 (14 January 2011).

95 The preamble of the National Environmental Management: Air Quality Act 39 of 2004 says that 'whereas atmospheric emissions of ozone-depleting substances, greenhouse gases and other substances have deleterious effects on the environment both locally and globally' confirming that the Act was enacted in the context of these international environmental challenges.

96 These include the Vienna Convention for the Protection of the Ozone Layer (22 March 1985) and the respective Montreal Protocol on Substances that Deplete the Ozone Layer (16 September 1987, 1522 UNTS 3), the UNFCCC (n 50 above) and its Kyoto Protocol to the United Nations Framework Convention on Climate Change (Kyoto Protocol) (11 December 1997, UN Doc FCCC/CP/1997/7/Add.1).

97 Scenario Building Team *Long Term Mitigation Scenarios: Scenario Document* (Department of Environment Affairs and Tourism, Pretoria, October 2007) http://www.erc.uct.ac.za/Research/publications/07Scenario_team-LTMS_Scenarios.pdf (accessed 20 April 2015).

sending country reports required under the FCCC the last of which was submitted in 2011.[98]

There are other policies in the agricultural sector, waste management and energy that, read together with the Air Quality Act, all aim to either mitigate of, or promote adaptation to climate change impacts or the reporting and monitoring of state obligations under the FCCC. Whilst not comprehensive these laws and policies must be applauded as measures implementing the country obligations under the FCCC in circumstances where national social and economic imperatives are imposing enormous pressure on natural capital.

2.5.4 Water resources

While it has been more straightforward to incorporate international obligations on matters governing biodiversity, waste and air pollution, the international regulation of water resources and shared watercourses is far more complex and polycentric. The Constitution of South Africa enshrines the internationally recognised right of access to water.[99] The main water legislation the National Water Act was, amongst other things, enacted to create a new regime of water rights, dispensing with private water rights and promote equitable access.[100] It was also enacted to implement South Africa's international undertakings[101] on integrated water resources management.[102] In particular Chapter[103] of the National Water Act provides for international water management.[104]

The Water Services Act also plays a fundamental role in the transformation of international norms and standards of water quality and access to water without express reference to such international norms and standards. Together with the National Water Act, this Act provides for the

98 Department of Environmental Affairs *South Africa's Second National Communication under the United Nations Framework Convention on Climate Change* (2011). The first report was submitted in 2000.

99 The Constitution (n 41 above) sec 27 (1)(b); UN Committee on Economic, Social and Cultural Rights (CESCR) *General Comment No. 15: The Right to Water (arts. 11 and 12 of the Covenant)* (20 January 2003, E/C.12/2002/1), art 12(1); Convention on the Elimination of All Forms of Discrimination Against Women (18 December 1979, 1249 UNTS 13) art 14(2) (h); Convention on the Rights of the Child (CRC) (20 November 1989, 1577 UNTS 3) art 24(2)(c).

100 National Water Act 36 of 1998 sec 2 (a) - (f).

101 Including regional obligations eg SADC Protocol on Shared Watercourse Systems (1995).

102 National Water Act (n 100 above) sec 2 (1); Department of Water Affairs and Forestry (DWAF) *Blueprint for survival: National Water Resources Strategy for South Africa* (2004).

103 n 100 above, sec 102 - 108.

104 n 100 above, sec 102 indirectly informed by the 1997 United Nations Convention on the Law of the Non-Navigational Uses of International Watercourses (n 81 above) in matters concerning transboundary and shared watercourses.

right of access to water and sanitation, all of which promotes the general standard of health recognised in international law.[105] South Africa is a water scarce country and has to take extra measures to ensure the sustainable management and use of water resources, as well as prevent water pollution and wastage. The fulfilment of the objects of the Water Services Act and the national Act are inextricably tied to an environmental not harmful to health and well-being in section 24 of the Constitution.[106] While adopting a modern system under the National Water Act was noble, the implementation of this international system of classification and management of water resources has proved a challenge for the government.[107]

3 Application of international environmental law by the courts

Complementing the more formal incorporation of international environmental law in South Africa, the courts have been proactive in interpreting and applying environmental law in a way that embeds international environmental law principles and concepts. While insisting that an international treaty does not become law unless expressly incorporated as prescribed by the Constitution, South African courts have concomitantly applied the call in the Constitution to interpret the Bill of Rights in a manner consistent with international law and by referring to both international and foreign law where necessary to give meaning and content to novel concepts.

As mentioned above, section 233 of the Constitution provides that when interpreting legislation, the court *must* prefer any reasonable interpretation that is consistent with international law to any alternative interpretations, which are inconsistent with international law. In addition, when interpreting the Bill of Rights in particular, a court must consider international law and may consider foreign law.[108] As will be demonstrated below, the South African Constitutional Court regards the

105 Implementing the right to water in art 11 & 12 of the International Covenant on Economic, Social and Cultural Rights (CESCR) (16 December 1966, 993 UNTS 3) even before South Africa had ratified the convention; see further discussion of the *Mazibuko* case below for the court's reliance on international water and environmental jurisprudence.

106 n 41 above, sec 24 provides of 'rights to an environment not harmful' and 'well-being' – quite broad concepts that encompass access to water and food, hence sec 2 (a) WSA refers to the sec 24 environmental right expressly.

107 See discussion of water rights related cases below. It is impossible to distinguish the access to water jurisprudence form environmental sustainability law, as General Comment No 15 *The right to water* (arts 11 & 12 of the International Covenant on Economic, Social and Cultural Rights) E/C.12/2002/11 (20 January 2003) clearly shows the connection between the right to the highest standard of health, right to food and right of access to water at the international level.

108 n 41 above, sec 39(2).

interpretation clauses to refer to binding as well as non-binding international instruments.

However, despite the existence of a constitutionally enshrined environmental right in South Africa, there has been relatively little litigation on the environmental right (in comparison to other rights in the Bill of Rights). This may be due to a number of factors including the way in which access to justice challenges play out in this sector, the technical subject matter of cases and the need for scientific experts, the fractured nature of the South African environmental regulatory system, the risk of being subjected to vexatious and frivolous litigation (so called SLAPP suits)[109] and the absence of quick, effective legal remedies for environmental harm.[110]

Nevertheless, in the litigation that has taken place, the area in which the South African courts have relied most on international environmental law as an interpretive aid, is in relation to sustainable development. A brief discussion of the use of international environmental law in relation to access to water is also included below.

3.1 Sustainable development

Perhaps the most important South African case from an international environmental law perspective is the Constitutional Court decision in *Fuel Retailers v DG Environmental Management, Mpumalanga*.[111] The case concerns the nature and scope of the obligations of environmental authorities when they make decisions that may affect the environment,

109 Strategic Litigation Against Public Participation (commonly referred to as a SLAPP suit) is a phenomena, which traces its origin primarily to the United States but has reared its head in South Africa in the environmental sector. Essentially, SLAPP suits are an abuse of litigation used by powerful and well-resourced parties in order to silence inconvenient criticism. Typically they take the form of allegations of defamation against environmental activists although large corporates are showing increasing creativity in their use of the threat of litigation. Although our courts have been highly critical of such abuse, a court judgment often provides little reassurance to activists faced with personalised and often quite vicious, attack. For a more detailed discussion see T Murombo & H Valentine 'SLAPP Suits: an emerging obstacle to public interest environmental litigation in South Africa' (2011) 27 *South African Journal on Human Rights* 82.

110 See Further J Dugard & A Alcaro 'Let's Work Together: environmental and socio-economic rights in the courts' (2013) 29 *South African Journal on Human Rights* 14; T Humby 'Reflections on the Biowatch Dispute - reviewing the fundamental rules on costs in the light of the needs of constitutional and/or public interest litigation' (2009) 1 *Potchefstroom Electronic Law Journal* 95; M Kidd 'Public interest environmental litigation: recent cases raise possible obstacles' (2010) 13 *Potchefstroom Electronic Law Journal* 27.

111 *Fuel Retailers* (n 54 above)

and, in particular, the interaction between socio-economic development and the protection of the environment.[112]

3.1.1 Drawing from customary international environmental law

Much of the majority judgment in *Fuel Retailers*, written by Ngcobo J, is devoted to exploring the development of the concept of sustainable development in international law, its application in South African law and finally its import and consequence for the case concerned.[113] Ultimately the Court confirms that the definition of sustainable development contained in the NEMA incorporates two of the internationally recognised elements of the concept of sustainable development – namely the principle of integration of environmental protection and socio-economic development and the principle of inter-generational equity.[114]

The Court summarises the evolving elements of the concept of sustainable development which have emerged in international environmental law as including

> the integration of environmental protection and economic development (the principle of integration); sustainable utilisation of natural resources (the principle of sustainable use and exploitation of natural resources); the right to development; the pursuit of equity in the use and allocation of natural resources (the principle of intra-generational equity); the need to preserve natural resources for the benefit of present and future generations (the principle of inter-generational and intra-generational equity); and the need to interpret and apply rules of international law in an integrated systematic manner.[115]

The Court emphasises that it is in the light of the developments in the international law of environment and sustainable development that the concept of sustainable development must be construed and understood in South African law.[116]

In addition to the NEMA definition of sustainable development, the Court goes on to affirm that the principles of NEMA (which provide the general framework within which environmental management and

112 The case involved an application to the environmental authorities for authorisation to develop a filling station in Mpumalanga. The proposed development was objected to on various grounds, including that the construction of the filling station would have an adverse impact on the environment. The environmental authorities granted authorisation for the construction of the filling station despite the objections to it.

113 L Ferris 'Sustainable development in practice: *Fuel Retailers Association of Southern Africa v Director-General Environmental Management, Department of Agriculture, Conservation and Environment, Mpumalanga Province*' (2008) 1 *Constitutional Court Review* 235.

114 *Fuel Retailers* (n 54 above) para 59.

115 *Fuel Retailers* (n 54 above) para 51.

116 *Fuel Retailers* (n 54 above) para 56.

implementation decisions must be formulated) are also drawn from international experience.[117]

The Constitutional Court appears to adopt the position that the principle of sustainable development has attained the status of customary international law. The Court refers with seeming approval to the opinion of Vice-President Weeramantry in *Gabeíkovo-Nagymaros Project (Hungary/ Slovakia),* which adopts this stance.[118] Note that the principle of sustainable development has already been incorporated into section 24 of the South African Constitution, as well as NEMA and other environmental legislation. The Court's reference to the customary international law principle of sustainable development is therefore as an interpretive guide, and in order to elaborate on the origin of the principle so as to highlight its significance in domestic EIA processes.[119]

3.1.2 Reference to soft law

In *Fuel Retailers,* the Court also looks to international soft law in deconstructing the meaning of 'economic and social development', which appears in the text of the environmental right in section 24 of the Constitution. Here the Court refers to the *Declaration on the Right to Development*[120] to explain that economic and social development is essential to the well-being of human beings.[121]

The Court also quotes from the Brundtland Report[122] to explain the relationship between development and the environment. The Brundtland Report states that economics and ecology should be integrated in decision making and law-making processes not only to protect the environment, but also to protect and promote development.[123] The Court picks up this theme when it holds that the environment and development are inexorably linked as unlimited development is detrimental to the environment and the destruction of the environment is detrimental to development. The facilitation of development thus requires the protection of the

117 *Fuel Retailers* (n 54 above) para 59.
118 *Fuel Retailers* (n 54 above) para 54 citing his Separate Opinion at 207.
119 *Fuel Retailers* (n 54 above) para 46 - 50.
120 Declaration on the Right to Development adopted by General Assembly Resolution 41/128 (4 December 1986) http://www.un.org/documents/ga/res/41/a41r128.htm (accessed 4 May 2015). Article 1 asserts '[t]he right to development is an inalienable human right'. The Preamble describes development as 'a comprehensive economic, social, cultural and political process, which aims at the constant improvement of the well-being of the entire population'.
121 *Fuel Retailers* (n 54 above) para 44.
122 Our Common Future: Report of the World Commission on Environment and Development (Brundtland Report) (1987) http://www.un-documents.net/our-common-future.pdf (accessed 20 April 2015).
123 n 122 above, *Fuel Retailers* (n 54 above) para 42 & 44.

environment, which cannot happen unless developmental decision-making pays attention to the costs of environmental destruction.[124]

The articulation of sustainable development in the Brundtland Report was later applied to the issuing of mining licenses by the South African Supreme Court of Appeal in *Director: Mineral Development, Gauteng Region and Another v Save the Vaal Environment and Others*[125] when the Court held that in an application for a mining licence, the decision-maker must promote development which meets present needs without compromising the ability of future generations to meet their own needs.[126]

Further reference to international soft law by the Constitutional Court in *Fuel Retailers* comes in the form of judicial reference to the Stockholm Declaration of the United Nations Conference on the Human Environment[127] (as the origin of the concept of sustainable development in international law), the Rio Declaration on Environment and Development[128] (as support for the proposition that the international community has reached a real consensus on sustainable development as a core principle of environmental protection) and the Johannesburg Declaration on Sustainable Development[129] (where sustainable development was reaffirmed as a world priority).

3.1.3 Taking guidance from international jurisprudence

Moreover the South African Constitutional Court also evidences its openness to drawing from the wisdom of international jurisprudence when, in *Fuel Retailers*, it refers to the decision of the International Court of Justice in the *Gabeíkovo-Nagymaros Project (Hungary/Slovakia)* case[130] in affirming the importance of a sustainable development approach.[131]

124 *Fuel Retailers* (n 54 above) para 44.
125 *Save the Vaal* (n 54 above).
126 This case has been interpreted as establishing a precedent whereby, through analogy, principles of international environmental soft law can be directly legally enforceable in South Africa; see Fuggle & Rabie (n 1 above) 183.
127 The Declaration of the United Nations Conference on the Human Environment (the Stockholm Declaration) (16 June 1972, U.N. Doc. A/Conf.48/14/Rev.1) http://www.unep.org/Documents/Default.asp?DocumentID=97&ArticleID=1503 (accessed 20 April 2015), *Fuel Retailers* (n 54 above) para 46.
128 The United Nations Conference on Environment and Development was held in Rio de Janeiro, Brazil on 3 - 14 June 1992, http://www.un.org/documents/ga/conf151/aconf15126-1annex1.htm (accessed 20 April 2015). This Conference adopted among other instruments, the Rio Declaration on Environment and Development (the Rio Declaration) (14 June 1992, UN Doc. A/CONF.151/26 (vol. I)); *Fuel Retailers* (n 54 above) para 49 - 50.
129 United Nations Department of Economic and Social Affairs-Division for Sustainable Development Johannesburg Declaration on Sustainable Development 2002 para 5, http://www.joburg.org.za/pdfs/johannesburgdeclaration.pdf (accessed 20 April 2015); n 54 above, para 53.
130 *Gabèikovo-Nagymaros Project (Hungary/Slovakia)* ICJ (25 September 1997) (1998) ICJ Reports 88.
131 *Fuel Retailers* (n 54 above) para 54.

3.2 Access to water

Recourse to international law is again found in *Mazibuko and Others v City of Johannesburg and Others*,[132] a case about the correct interpretation of section 27(1)(b) of the South African Constitution, which provides that everyone has the right of access to sufficient water. South African constitutionalism adopts an approach in terms of which the rights in the Bill of Rights should be viewed as connected and interdependent. Within this context, the right of access to water and the environmental right enjoy a particularly close relationship given the anthropocentric formulation and interpretation of the scope of environmental law in South Africa. The courts have often characterised the environmental right as a socio-economic right. Similarly the fulfilment of the right of access to water is directly dependent on the available, and sustainable management and use of water resources. The sustainable use of water resources is also impacted by infrastructure and development planning in terms of environmental and planning legislation such as the requirements for EIA.

In *Mazibuko*, the Court refers to article 2(1) of the International Covenant on Economic, Social and Cultural Rights[133] to buttress the approach of the South African Constitution to socio-economic rights, which is to characterise the state's obligation as one of 'progressive realisation' of such rights.[134] In a discussion of the notion of a minimum core of socio-economic rights, in which the Court confirms its rejection of this approach, the Court also refers to General Comment 3 of the United Nations Committee on Economic, Social and Cultural Rights[135] as the origin of the notion of minimum core.[136]

3.3 Tendencies to accommodate and promote international standards and technologies beyond law

In the environmental context, recourse to practices and experience outside of national borders occurs not only with regard to the law, but also in relation to science. South Africa frequently looks to technologies, emission

132 *Mazibuko and Others v City of Johannesburg and Others* 2010 (3) BCLR 239 (CC); 2010 (4) SA 1 (CC).
133 International Covenant on Economic, Social and Cultural Rights (16 December 1966, 993 UNTS 3) art 2(1).
134 n 132 above, para 40.
135 General Comment 3 'The nature of States Parties' obligations (art 2(1))' Fifth Session, 1990, UN Doc E/1991/23.
136 *Mazibuko* (n 132 above) para 52. In General Comment 3, the United Nations Committee on Economic, Social and Cultural Rights stated in para 10 that: '[it] is of the view that a minimum core obligation to ensure the satisfaction of, at the very least, minimum essential levels of each of the rights is incumbent upon every State party'. Thus, for example, a State party in which any significant number of individuals is deprived of essential foodstuffs, of essential primary health care, of basic shelter and housing, or of the most basic forms of education, is prima facie, failing to discharge its obligations under the Covenant.

standards, environmental models and practical guidelines used elsewhere. For example in the *Fuel Retailers* case, the Court notes that the Gauteng Guidelines[137] that regulate the space between fuel stations (requiring a distance of three kilometres in urban areas and 25 kilometres in rural areas) was based on a review of international approaches.[138] A full discussion of the range of international models used in environmental management in South Africa is beyond the ambit of this chapter, but it is worth noting that South Africa looks for guidance beyond our borders in respect of more than just legal instruments and their interpretation.

4 Conclusion

Environmental law is a field where multilateralism is a prerequisite for effective global efforts to deal with transboundary and global challenges such as climate change, wildlife poaching, and the use of biotechnology. While South Africa has taken the lead in Africa in terms of developing a robust environmental regulatory regime, challenges still remain with implementation of the elaborate system. South Africa has ratified most of the key international environmental treaties and her constitution allows for transformation of international environmental law as well as direct application of customary international law. Environmental law and rights is one of the areas where South Africa has complied most with its international treaty obligations in terms of legislative transformation. The country has gone beyond formal transformation of international treaties by enacting legislation that incorporates soft law principles from declarations, decisions and resolutions of international bodies. The result is that even some environmental law norms and concepts, whose legal status is still questioned in international law such as sustainable development, have been given legal status in South Africa. In addition to legislative transformation South African courts have been proactive in using the Constitutional mandate to use international, foreign and customary law as interpretive beacons in deciding environmental cases. This willingness by the courts to use international environmental law is further supported by a preparedness to use soft law principles and norms.

137 Gauteng Provincial Government, Agriculture, Conservation, Environmental and Land Affairs EIA Administrative Guideline *Guideline for the Construction and Upgrade of Filling Stations and Associated Tank Installations* (2002).

138 n 54 above, para 74, the Guidelines indicate, for example, that in Dublin guidelines have been published which indicate that new petrol stations will generally not be permitted on national roads or adjoining residential areas and will only be considered in rural areas if they are in the immediate environs of rural villages; in Singapore existing filling stations located within one kilometre of an interchange are considered to be inappropriately located; in Germany filling stations should only be erected on rural roads where there is a clear need and there should be 25 kilometres between filling stations; and in Denmark drivers requiring high octane petrol will have access to a filling station within 30 kilometres.

The progressive stance taken by South Africa towards international environmental law however, masks domestic contradictions that sometimes affect the effectiveness of the environmental regulatory system. South Africa's social, economic and political context often requires the country to prioritise and focus on socio-economic development, poverty alleviation, and job creation – priorities that inevitably require the country to downplay or ignore sustainable land use planning and environmental regulation principles to which it has subscribed and legislated in domestic laws. Some of the environmental principles are often (misguidedly) seen as obstructions to the developmental agenda of the country and hence the poor compliance and enforcement record.

The ambiguity, lack of precision and vagueness of concepts borrowed from international environmental law have created problems in terms of giving these concepts content and scope that can guide environmental decision-makers and courts. However, relative to other African countries South Africa has advanced far ahead in terms of developing a system of environmental regulation that reflects and aligns with international developments.

BIBLIOGRAPHY

Bowman, M; Davies, P & Redgwell, C (2nd edn 2010) *Lyster's International wildlife law* Cambridge University Press: New York/Cambridge

Boyle, A 'Relationship between international environmental law and other branches of international law' in Bodansky, D; Brunnée, J & Hey, E (2007) (eds) *Oxford handbook on international environmental law* Oxford University Press: Oxford/Cambridge

Boyle, AE & Anderson, MR (eds) (1998) *Human rights approaches to environmental protection* Clarendon Press: Oxford

De Sadeleer, N (2002) *Environmental principles: From political slogans to legal rules* Oxford University Press: Oxford/New York

Dupuy, P 'Formation of customary international law and general principles' in Bodansky, D; Brunnée, J & Hey, E (2007) (eds) *Oxford handbook on international environmental law* Oxford University Press: Oxford/New York

Heinze, E & Fitzmaurice, M (eds) (1998) *Landmark cases in international law* Kluwer Law International: London

Kidd, M & Retief, F 'Environmental assessment' in Strydom, H & King, N (eds) (2nd edn 2009) *Fuggle & Rabie's environmental management in South Africa* Juta Law: Cape Town

Kummer, K *International management of hazardous waste* (1999) Oxford University Press: Oxford/New York

Lowe, V 'Sustainable development and unsustainable arguments' in Boyle, A & Freestone, D (eds) (1999) *International law and sustainable development: Past achievements and future challenges* Oxford University Press: Oxford

Sands, P (2nd edn 2003) *Principles of international environmental law* Cambridge University Press: Cambridge

Strydom, H & King, N (eds) (2nd edn 2009) *Fuggle & Rabie's Environmental management in South Africa* Juta Law: Cape Town

Tarlock, D 'Ecosystems' in Bodansky, D; Brunnée, J & Hey, E (2007) (eds) *Oxford handbook on international environmental law* Oxford University Press: Oxford/New York

Van der Linde, M & Basson, E 'Environment' in Woolman, S & Bishop, M (eds) (2nd edn 2014) *Constitutional Law of South Africa* Juta Law: Cape Town

Van der Linde, M & Feris, L (eds) (2010) *Compendium of South African environmental legislation* Pretoria University Law Press: Pretoria

Van der Linde, M 'Regional environmental law under the auspices of the African Union' in Strydom, H & King, N (eds) (2nd edn 2009) *Fuggle & Rabie's Environmental management in South Africa* Juta Law: Cape Town

Wiener, JB 'Precaution' in Bodansky, D; Brunnée, J & Hey, E (2007) (eds) *Oxford handbook on international environmental law* Oxford University Press: Oxford/New York

5

THE RECEPTION OF INTERNATIONAL LAW IN THE SOUTH AFRICAN LEGAL ORDER

*Erika de Wet**

1 Background

The Republic of South Africa is a unitary state with a common law tradition. Its common law is a blend of Anglo-American and Roman-Dutch Law. The latter refers to the legal system that applied in Holland during the seventeenth and eighteenth centuries. It comprised a mixture of medieval Dutch law and the Roman law of Justinian as received in Holland.[1] Roman-Dutch law was transported to the Cape when the Dutch settled there in 1652. Subsequently the principles of Roman-Dutch law were strongly influenced by English law, following the British occupation of South Africa in the early nineteenth century.[2]

Although South Africa became a republic (thereby rejecting the British Queen as head of state) only in 1961, it has been self-governing since 1910. Moreover, it was recognised as a sovereign state under international law already during the 1930s, a fact formalised *inter alia* by the Status of the Union Act 69 of 1934. Apartheid became the official state policy after the victory of the National Party in 1948. Between 1948 and the country's first democratic elections in 1994, the country's apartheid policies lead to its international isolation. During this time South Africa refused to become a party to many multilateral treaties, particularly in the field of African organisation, human rights, and humanitarian law.[3] However, this position changed significantly after the first multi-racial elections on

* The contribution is based on E de Wet 'South Africa' in D Shelton (ed) *International law and domestic legal systems: Incorporation, transformation and persuasion* (2011) 567 - 593. The research undertaken for this chapter constituted part of a research sojourn as fellow of the Stellenbosch Institute for Advanced Study (STIAS) in September 2013.

1 J Dugard 'South Africa' in D Sloss (ed) *The role of domestic courts in treaty enforcement* (2009) 449.

2 As above.

3 J Dugard 'South Africa' in D Sloss (n 1 above) 448.

27 April 1994 and the subsequent enactments of the interim Constitution in 1994 and the so-called final Constitution of 1996.[4]

Under the final Constitution, executive power is vested in a President, who is both the chief of state and head of government. Legislative authority is granted to a bicameral legislature consisting of the National Assembly, which elects the President; and the National Council of Provinces, which has special powers to protect regional interests, including the cultural and linguistic traditions of ethnic minorities. The judicial system is based on a combination of Roman-Dutch law and English common law. The Constitutional Court is the highest court for interpreting and deciding constitutional issues, while the Supreme Court of Appeal is the highest court for non-constitutional matters.

Following the 1994 elections, most sanctions imposed by the international community in opposition to the system of apartheid were lifted. South Africa rejoined the Commonwealth (which it left in 1961) on 1 June 1994 and was accepted by the UN General Assembly on 23 June 1994. South Africa also subsequently became a member of the Southern African Development Community (SADC) and served as the African Union's (AU) first president from July 2003 to July 2004.

The subsequent sections will illuminate in more detail the relationship between international law and domestic law since the introduction of the new constitutional dispensation. The analysis will first introduce the constitutional provisions and statutory references pertaining to international law. Thereafter it will explore the status of treaties in the domestic legal order, with references *inter alia* to the different categories of treaties and the extent to which they need to be incorporated by Parliament in order to have effect within the Republic. Subsequently, the chapter examines the limited role that customary international law has thus far played in the domestic order, before outlining the role of the judiciary in interpreting and applying international law.

As subsequent chapters will give an in-depth analysis of the current status of various sub-areas of international law in the Republic, the aim of this chapter is limited to introducing the general principles governing the

4 For the text of the Constitution of the Republic of South Africa, 1996, see http://www.gov.za/documents/constitution-republic-south-africa-1996 (accessed 20 April 2015). For the Interim Constitution of the Republic of South Africa, 1993 see http://www.constitutionalcourt.org.za/site/constitution/english-web/interim/ (accessed 20 April 2015). See also T Maluwa 'International human rights norms and the South African Interim Constitution' (1994) 19 *South African Yearbook of Human Rights* 29; DJ Devine 'The relationship between international law and municipal law in the light of the Interim South African Constitution 1993' (1995) 44 *International and Comparative Law Quarterly* 1; R Keightly 'Public international law and the final Constitution' (1996) 12 *South African Journal on Human Rights* 406; J Dugard 'International law and the South African Constitution' (1997) 8 *European Journal of International Law* 77.

relationship between international and domestic law, thereby providing a contextual background for the subsequent chapters.

1.1 Constitutional provisions pertaining to international law

Unlike the earlier constitutions of 1910, 1961, and 1983, the interim Constitution expressly recognised international law and the role it had to play in municipal law. The provisions in the interim Constitution that specifically dealt with international law covered the signature and ratification of international agreements and their application in domestic law,[5] the status of customary international law in South African domestic law,[6] as well as the interpretive role of international law.[7] The final Constitution of 1996 envisaged only minor changes with respect to these provisions.[8] Of particular importance are sections 231-233 of the Constitution, as well as section 39, which constitutes a part of the Bill of Rights.

Section 231 regulates the signing, ratification, and implementation of international agreements (treaties):

> (1) The negotiating and signing of all international agreements is the responsibility of the national executive.
>
> (2) An international agreement binds the Republic only after it has been approved by resolution in both the National Assembly and the National Council of Provinces, unless it is an agreement referred to in subsection (3).
>
> (3) An international agreement of a technical, administrative or executive nature, or an agreement which does not require either ratification or accession, entered into by the national executive, binds the Republic without approval by the National Assembly and the National Council of Provinces, but must be tabled in the Assembly and the Council within a reasonable time.
>
> (4) Any international agreement becomes law in the Republic when it is enacted into law by national legislation; but a self-executing provision of an agreement that has been approved by Parliament is law in the Republic unless it is inconsistent with the Constitution or an Act of Parliament.
>
> (5) The Republic is bound by international agreements which were binding on the Republic when this Constitution took effect.

Section 232 concerns customary international law and determines that 'Customary international law is law in the Republic unless it is inconsistent with the Constitution or an Act of Parliament'.

5 Interim Constitution (n 4 above) chapter VI sec 82(1)(i), chapter XV sections 231(2) & (3).
6 Interim Constitution (n 4 above) chapter XV sec 231(4).
7 Interim Constitution (n 4 above) chapter III sec 35(1), chapter XIV sec 227(2)(d), (e) (concerning the National Defence Force). Keightly (n 4 above) 406.
8 n 4 above, chapter XIV secs 231 - 233.

Section 233 requires an international law friendly interpretation of legislation: 'When interpreting any legislation, every court must prefer any reasonable interpretation of the legislation that is consistent with international law over any alternative interpretation that is inconsistent with international law.'

Of particular importance in the practice of courts is section 39 concerning the interpretation of the constitutional Bill of Rights:

> (1) When interpreting the Bill of Rights, a court, tribunal or forum:
> (a) must promote the values that underlie an open and democratic society based on human dignity, equality and freedom;
> (b) must consider international law; and
> (c) may consider foreign law.
>
> (2) When interpreting any legislation, and when developing the common law or customary law, every court, tribunal or forum must promote the spirit, purport and objects of the Bill of Rights.

Reference should also be made to section 200(2) of the Constitution, which regulates the Defence Force:

> The primary object of the defence force is to defend and protect the Republic, its territorial integrity and its people in accordance with the Constitution and the principles of international law regulating the use of force.

These provisions marked a formal turning point in the country's approach towards international law, especially regarding the use of international human rights law as a guideline for interpreting the Constitution. Although South Africa's common law tradition implies that decisions of foreign courts have been influential since its inception, until 1994 this influence was largely restricted to areas of private and commercial law.[9] Before 1994 no reference was made to decisions of international monitoring bodies in the human rights field because South Africa was not party to any human rights treaties and many of its policies were directly at odds with the principles embodied in international human rights law. However, since the adoption of the interim and final Constitutions, decisions of international human rights bodies and of foreign courts pertaining to international law are frequently invoked (→ 4).[10]

1.2 Statutory references to international law

It is also worth noting that various statutes refer expressly to international law, in accordance with section 233 of the Constitution, which requires

9 Dugard (n 1 above) 466.
10 As above.

ordinary legislation to be interpreted in accordance with international law.[11] In some instances the legislation makes clear that it is to be interpreted in accordance with international law. In other instances the statute incorporates language that resembles that contained in international instruments, including ones that are not binding on South Africa. This enhances the ability of the executive and the courts to interpret the legislation in accordance with present and future developments in relation to the relevant area of international law.[12]

An example of a statute that explicitly requires interpretation consistent with international law is the Promotion of Equality and Prevention of Unfair Discrimination Act. This provides that any person interpreting the Act may be mindful of international law.[13] Similarly, the Implementation of the Rome Statute of the International Criminal Court Act provides that a court applying the Act must consider conventional and customary international law.[14] In addition, the Labour Relations Act states that one of the primary objects of the Act is to give effect to obligations incurred by the Republic as a member state of the International Labour Organization (ILO) and requires the Act to be interpreted in compliance with the public international law obligations of the Republic.[15]

2 The status of treaties in the domestic legal order

2.1 The definition and classification of treaties

The term 'international agreement' in the Constitution is synonymous with the term 'treaty' as defined in article 2(1) in the Vienna Convention on the Law of Treaties 1969 (Vienna Convention).[16] This meaning has developed in the practice of the Office of the Chief State Legal Adviser in the absence of a definition of 'international agreement' in the Constitution and despite the fact that South Africa is not a party to the Vienna Convention. The term 'international agreement' in section 231 is therefore to be understood as referring to written agreements between subjects of international law that embody legally enforceable rights and obligations.[17]

11 Dugard (n 1 above) 463.
12 E Couzens 'The incorporation of international environmental law (and multilateral environmental agreements) into South African domestic law' (2005) 30 *South African Yearbook of International Law* 138.
13 Promotion of Equality and Prevention of Unfair Discrimination Act 4 of 2000 sec 3(2)(a).
14 Implementation of the Rome Statute of the International Criminal Court Act 27 of 2002 sec 2.
15 Labour Relations Act 66 of 1995 secs 1& 3. Dugard (n 1 above) 463.
16 Vienna Convention of the Law of Treaties (the Vienna Convention) (23 May 1969, 1155 UNTS 331).
17 Vienna Convention (n 16 above) art 2(1) determines that: 'a "treaty" means an international agreement concluded between states in written form and governed by international law, whether embodied in a single instrument or in two or more related

This view also seems to have been endorsed by the Constitutional Court in *Harksen v President of South Africa*,[18] which concerned the attempt by Jürgen Harksen to prevent his extradition to Germany where he was charged with fraud.[19] One of the issues central to the dispute was whether ad hoc extradition under section 3(2) of the Extradition Act 67 of 1962[20] (where South Africa had not concluded an extradition agreement with the requesting state) should also comply with the constitutional prerequisites for an international agreement. The question was whether the signature (consent) of the South African President to a statement that permitted the extradition of Harksen to Germany constituted an international agreement.[21] The Constitutional Court determined that presidential consent in terms of section 3(2) of the Extradition Act was a domestic act, implying that in accordance with South African domestic law Harksen could be brought before a magistrate's court in order to initiate the extradition proceedings.[22] It did not amount to an 'international agreement' in terms of section 231 of the Constitution, as it was not an instrument that intended to create international legal rights and obligations between state parties.[23]

No provision is made for oral agreements or for unilateral acts in either the Constitution or in the Manual on Executive Acts of the Office of the President of South Africa (Manual), which serves as a guide to the practice of the Office of the Chief State Legal Advisor.[24] As far as the written agreements are concerned, section 231 of the Constitution distinguishes between two types of agreements. The first requires parliamentary approval in terms of section 231(2), meaning that both houses of Parliament (the National Assembly and the National Council of Provinces) sitting separately have to give approval, before the Executive may give its consent to bind the Republic on the international level.[25]

instruments and whatever its particular designation.' See also J Schneeberger 'A labyrinth of tautology: The meaning of the term 'international agreement' and its significance for South African law and treaty making practice' (2001) 26 *South African Yearbook of International Law* 3; Dugard (n 1 above) 457.

18 *Harksen v President of South Africa & Others* 2000 (2) SA 825 (CC).

19 As above.

20 Extradition Act 67 of 1962 sec 3(2) deals with extradition to countries with which South Africa has not concluded an extradition agreement.

21 *Harksen* (n 18 above) para 13.

22 *Harksen* (n 18 above) para 21.

23 Schneeberger (n 17 above) 30.

24 N Botha 'Treaty making in South Africa: A reassessment' (2000) 25 *South African Yearbook of International Law* 72; *2006 Manual on Executive Acts of the Office of the President of South Africa* (hereinafter the Manual), chapter 5 www.dfa.gov.za/foreign/bilateral/conclusion_agreement0316.pdf (accessed 15 April 2015); Schneeberger (n 17 above) 38. The Constitutional Court did not elaborate on the criteria to be considered when determining the intention of the parties where this was not stated clearly. In practice the Office of the Chief State Legal Adviser has developed guidelines similar to those of the US Department of State. These include the significance of the arrangement and the substantive provisions used; the specificity or generality of the language used; the form of the arrangement; the absence of familiar treaty clauses such as entry into force; amendment and termination provisions; and the name of the agreement.

25 Botha (n 24 above) 79.

The second concerns technical, administrative or executive agreements that can, in accordance with section 231(3), be concluded by the national executive alone.[26] Although Parliament has to be notified about these agreements, they are exempt from the sometimes lengthy parliamentary approval procedure. The Constitution does not give any indication of which agreements would qualify as technical, administrative or executive.[27] The internal practice that has developed within the Office of the Chief State Legal Adviser is to consider as 'technical' those agreements that do not have major political significance; do not require additional budgetary allocation from Parliament over and above the budget provided by a particular government department; and agreements that do not impact domestic law.[28] They are often of a bilateral nature and concern routine agreements for which a single government department is responsible for implementation. This encompasses the vast majority of agreements that South Africa has concluded since 1994.[29]

The procedure foreseen for 'technical' agreements in section 231(3) requires an average of three months. Despite being of an expedited nature, the procedure is not always fast enough to accommodate the requirements of modern-day international relations. In such circumstances the executive prefers informal agreements because of their simplicity, swiftness, flexibility, and confidentiality. However, they do not create reciprocal rights and duties under international law, even though they are almost always honoured in practice.[30] Since they are of a non-binding nature, they are also exempt from the procedures prescribed in section 231 of the Constitution.[31]

The frequent use of technical agreements and informal agreements implies that a large number of agreements are excluded from the democratic verification process. The situation is particularly acute in relation to informal agreements. Whereas Parliament is at least notified about the conclusion of technical agreements in accordance with section 231(3), no such notification occurs in relation to informal agreements.[32] Although these expedited procedures are necessary for the conduct of efficient international relations in the twenty-first century, it can be problematic from the perspective of democratic accountability that lies at

26 In practice only ministers sign international agreements. The Manual (n 24 above) 5.1.5; Schneeberger (n 17 above) 3. See also *Hugh Glenister v the President of the RSA*, 2011 (3) SA 347 (CC) para 89.

27 In practice the terms 'technical, administrative and executive agreements' in sec 231(3) of the Constitution form a single category and are interchangeable; The Manual (n 24 above) 5.5; Botha (n 24 above) 76.

28 The Manual (n 24 above) 5.5; Schneeberger (n 17 above) 4.

29 Schneeberger (n 17 above) 4 - 5; Botha (n 24 above) 76.

30 Schneeberger (n 17 above) 7.

31 Scheeberger (n 17 above) 28.

32 Schneeberger (n 17 above) 7.

the heart of section 231(2).[33] However, at the time of writing there has not yet been any case before a South African court challenging a particular classification of an agreement by the executive as 'technical', nor of the validity of informal agreements.

The role of Parliament in the ratification process also has implications for reservations to treaties. In those instances where treaties are subject to the parliamentary process foreseen in section 231(2), Parliament will have the opportunity to scrutinise the reservation attached by the executive.[34] In addition, Parliament may also insist on additional reservations. The issue of reservations does not, however, seem to play a prominent role in South African treaty-making and the domestic courts have not yet been confronted with interpretation issues pertaining to reservations, such as their legality or scope.

2.2 Treaty conclusion and implementation

2.2.1 The need for incorporation

In accordance with section 231(1) of the Constitution the negotiation and signature of treaties is the exclusive competence of the executive; Parliament has no role to play at this level. Moreover, the Manual indicates that the provinces may not enter into agreements governed by international law, except as agents of the national executive. The individual concerned would therefore have to require specific authorisation to this effect by way of Presidential Minute together with credentials issued by the Department of International Relations and Co-operation.[35]

Section 231(2) and (3) of the Constitution exclusively regulates the conditions under which the Republic would be bound by international agreements on the international level. In order for treaties to apply domestically, section 231(4) prescribes that these agreements must first be enacted into domestic law by means of legislation, unless their provisions

33 The democratisation of the treaty-making process as foreseen in section 231(2) of the Constitution does not encompass the negotiation and signature of treaties. In accordance with section 231(1) of the Constitution, those functions vest solely in the hand of the executive. See Botha (n 24 above) 77, 80.

34 The Manual (n 24 above) 5.11; Botha (n 24 above) 84.

35 The Manual (n 24 above) 5.25; *Glenister* case (n 26 above) para 89; Botha (n 24 above) 956. Theoretically the possibility also exists that unauthorised agreements concluded between the provinces and foreign entities enjoying treaty-making capacity could receive the subsequent approval of the national executive in accordance with article 8 of the VCLT. Such an agreement would still be subject to parliamentary approval in terms of section 231(2) of the Constitution, unless it qualifies as a section 231(3) agreement.

are self-executing. This approach was confirmed by the Constitutional Court in the *AZAPO* and *Glenister* cases,[36] as well as the Supreme Court of Appeal in the *Progress Office Machines* case.[37] The *Azapo* case concerned the 1949 Geneva Conventions on the Laws of War, while the *Glenister* case pertained to various international and regional treaties combating corruption. The *Progress Office Machines* case for its part concerned the World Trade Organization (WTO) Agreement and the Agreement on Implementation of Article VI of the General Agreement on Tariffs and Trade. The *Progress Office Machines* and *Azapo* cases will be explored in more detail in (→ 2.2.2 and → 3). Although the issue of self-executing treaties will also be illuminated below, this concept has thus far remained a dead letter in the practice of South African courts.[38]

Four principle methods are employed to transform treaties into municipal law. The first and most simple technique of incorporation is considering the pre-existing legislation sufficient to give effect to subsequent treaty obligations. An example is the Convention on International Trade in Endangered Species of Wild Fauna and Flora (CITES) 1973, which South Africa ratified in 1975.[39] Second, the provisions of a treaty may be embodied in the text of an Act of Parliament. This, for example, was the case with the Implementation of the Rome Statute of the International Criminal Court Act, which implemented South Africa's obligations under the Rome Statute of the International Criminal Court 1998, which South Africa ratified in 2000.[40] Third, the treaty may be included as a schedule to a statute. One example of such wholesale importation is the World Heritage Convention Act 49 of 1999. By way of a schedule, the Act incorporates into South African law the entire Convention concerning the Protection of the World Cultural and Natural Heritage of 1972.[41]

Sometimes incorporations of this kind delegate particular powers related to the enforcement of the international agreement to the relevant cabinet minister. For example, the Marine Pollution (Prevention of Pollution from Ships) Act 2 of 1986 (MARPOL Act) incorporates the International Convention for the Prevention of Pollution from Ships 1973 through a schedule. Section 3 of the MARPOL Act provides that the

36 *Azanian Peoples Organisation (AZAPO) v President of the RSA* 1996 (4) SA 671 (CC). On 17 March 2011 the Constitutional Court once again confirmed this approach in the *Glenister* case (n 26 above) para 92.

37 *Progress Office Machines CC v SARS* 2008 (2) SA 13 (SCA). In essence, this reaffirms the dualist approach which was also endorsed by the highest court (the Appellate Division of the Supreme Court) in South Africa before 1994. *Pan American World Airways Inc v SA Fire and Accident Insurance Co Ltd* 1965 (3) SA 150 (A).

38 Dugard (n 1 above) 455.

39 Couzens (n 12 above) 143.

40 M du Plessis, 'International criminal courts, the International Criminal Court, and South Africa's implementation of the Rome Statute' in J Dugard *International Law: A South African perspective* (2011) 197.

41 Couzens (n 12 above) 130.

Minister of Transport may make regulations relating to carrying out the provisions of the Convention.[42]

Finally, an enabling Act of Parliament may grant the executive the power to bring a treaty into effect in municipal law by means of proclamation or notice in the Government Gazette.[43] A pertinent example in this regard is the Extradition Act (last amended in 1996). It constitutes a framework Act that deals with a specific class of international agreements, namely those pertaining to extradition. Section 2(1)(a) of the Act provides that the President may enter into agreements with foreign states to provide for the surrender, on a reciprocal basis, of persons accused or convicted of the commission of extraditable offences.[44] Once ratified by Parliament,[45] the Minister gives notice of the agreement in the Government Gazette.[46] This proclamation effectively amounts to a simplified incorporation procedure for a large number of similar agreements. The Constitutional Court in the *Quagliani* case unfortunately overlooked the role of the proclamation in the Government Gazette as an element of the incorporation process. The case concerned the validity and enforceability of an extradition agreement concluded in 1999 between the United States and South Africa. Sachs J, on behalf of the Court, correctly noted that the nature and number of the extradition agreements makes it desirable that they be implemented in an effective manner.[47] However, he then confused matters by stating:

> [The Agreement] either became law in South Africa as a result of the prior existence of the Act which constitutes the anticipatory enactment of the Agreement for the purpose of section 231(4) of the Constitution. Or the Agreement has not become law in the Republic as contemplated by section 231(4) but the provisions of the Act are all that is required to give domestic effects to the international obligation that the Agreement creates.[48]

Not only is it difficult to follow the meaning of this contradictory statement,[49] but it would seem to overlook the fact that one is in fact dealing with a simplified incorporation procedure. The Extradition Act is indeed anticipatory in as far as it provides a simplified procedure for a class of agreements that still have to be concluded. However, that does not change the fact that they are dependent on incorporation into municipal

42 Couzens (n 12 above) 133.
43 Dugard (n 1 above) 453; *Glenister* case (n 26 above) para 99.
44 n 20 above, sec 2(1)(a). *President of the RSA v Nello Quagliani; President of the RSA v Stephen Mark van Rooyen;* and *Steven William Goodwin v D-G, Department of Justice and Constitutional Development* 2009 (4) 345 (CC) para 42.
45 Ratification is explicitly required in the Extradition Act (n 20 above) sec 3(a).
46 Extradition Act (n 20 above) sec 3(a).
47 *Quagliani* (n 44 above) para 45.
48 *Quagliani* (n 44 above) para 47.
49 For criticism, see N Botha 'Rewriting the Constitution: the "strange alchemy" of Justice Sachs indeed!' (2009) 34 *South African Yearbook of International Law* 253.

law, in the form of ministerial proclamation, as foreseen by Parliament in the Extradition Act.

Another area where the issue of expedited implementation through secondary legislation is of significance concerns the implementation of Security Council decisions adopted under Chapter of the United Nations Charter 1945. As it stands, South Africa has no general legislation in place that would facilitate expedited implementation of such decisions. Instead, it relies on issue specific legislation, which can result in a fragmented (or even conflicting) approach to enforcement. It also carries the risk that in areas where no issue specific legislation exists, Security Council decisions will not be implemented on the domestic level or only implemented with great delay (→ Tladi).[50]

Once implemented, it seems that the courts broadly follow the international law rules of treaty interpretation contained in article 32 of the Vienna Convention, when interpreting the incorporated version.[51] Although this is not directed by the Constitution or statute, it follows from the fact that the South African rules of statutory interpretation conform to a large extent with those contained in the Vienna Convention. South African law also recognises the textual, intent, and purposive approaches to statutory interpretation that constitute the core principles of interpretation in the Vienna Convention.[52]

Finally, it is important to underscore that a treaty enacted into law will have the same status in domestic law as the Act through which it is incorporated.[53] This implies that enacted treaties do not merely rank below the Constitution which is the supreme law of South Africa,[54] but can also rank below a Parliamentary Act – depending on the manner of its incorporation. While a treaty enacted into law by an Act of Parliament will enjoy the same status as other Parliamentary Acts, a treaty enacted into law through subordinate legislation (for example, a ministerial proclamation in the Government Gazette), will be on par with other subordinate legislation.[55]

50 See also H Strydom & T Huarka 'South Africa' in V Gowlland-Debbas (ed) *National implementation of United Nations sanctions: A comparative study* (2004) 430 432.

51 Dugard (n 1 above) 464.

52 Courts have also on occasion invoked the preparatory works of incorporated treaties in their process of interpretation, as permitted by article 32 of the Vienna Convention (n 16 above). In *Portion 20 of Plot 15 Athol (Pty) Ltd v Rodriguez* 2001 (1) SA 1285 (W) 1293, the High Court considered the preparatory works of the International Law Commission when interpreting the Vienna Convention of Diplomatic Relations 1961, which is incorporated into South African Law. Dugard (n 1 above) 464 - 665.

53 *Glenister* case (n 26 above) para 100; Dugard (n 1 above) 463.

54 As above.

55 An example would be the extradition agreements referred to above in connection with *Quagliani* (n 44 above); Dugard (n 1 above) 463.

2.2.2 Self-executing treaties

As has been indicated above, the second part of section 231(4) provides that a self-executing provision of an agreement that has been approved by Parliament is law in the Republic unless it is inconsistent with the Constitution or an Act of Parliament. At first sight this phrase seems to imply that a clause in a treaty will only be self-executing when the language of the treaty so indicates and when existing municipal law, either common law or statute, is adequate in the sense that it fails to place any obstacle in the way of treaty application.[56] In concrete terms this would mean that the nature and content of the relevant treaty provision is such that it is capable of judicial enforcement in the absence of any further measures for implementation (that is, self-executing).[57] In addition, the direct enforcement should not result in a conflict with existing domestic law.

However, whether this interpretation will persevere in practice remains to be seen. No South African court has thus far been willing to engage in the meaning of self-execution, let alone hold a provision of a multilateral treaty, which has not been expressly incorporated by Parliament, to be self-executing.[58] In the *Grootboom* case (concerning the constitutional right to housing), the Constitutional Court merely noted in passing that where a relevant principle of international law binds South Africa, it may be directly applicable.[59] In the *Quagliani* case the Constitutional Court skirted the issue by stating that it was not necessary to consider the question of the self-executing nature of the agreement.[60]

More recently the Western Cape High Court rejected the self-execution of the International Covenant on Civil and Political Rights 1966 (ICCPR) as a whole in the *Claassen* case.[61] Although the ICCPR was

56 Dugard (n 1 above) 455.
57 This is the practice that has been followed by courts in the Netherlands, where all substantive rights in the European Convention of Human Rights have over time been recognized as self-executing. E de Wet 'The reception process in The Netherlands and Belgium' in H Keller & A Stone Sweet (eds) *A Europe of rights: The impact of the ECHR on national legal systems* (2008) 229.
58 M Killander 'Judicial immunity, compensation for unlawful detention and the elusive self-executing treaty provision: *Claassen v Minister of Justice and Constitutional Development* 2010 (6) SA 399 (WCC)' (2010) 26 *South African Journal on Human Rights* 386. *Claassen v Minister of Justice and Constitutional Development* 2010 (6) SA 399 (WCC).
59 *The Government of the Republic of South Africa & Others v Grootboom & Others* 2000 (11) BCLR 1169 (CC) para 26.
60 n 44 above, para 36. Given the fact that the Extradition Act provided for simplified incorporation of extradition agreements, it was indeed not necessary to decide on the issue of their self-execution. However, the Court's convoluted reasoning reignited the doctrinal debate. See G Ferreira & W Scholz, 'Has the Constitutional Court found the lost ball in the high weeds? The interpretation of section 231 of the South African Constitution' (2009) XLII *Comparative & International Law Journal of Southern Africa* 269 271. They argued that the Court's judgment amounted to an implicit acceptance of the self-executing nature of the extradition agreement. In reaching this conclusion they overlooked the incorporating effect of the ministerial proclamation in the Government Gazette.
61 n 58 above, para 36.

ratified by South Africa in 1998, it has not yet been incorporated into domestic law.[62] In this instance the appellant claimed damages, based on delict, arising out of alleged unlawful detention. The action was brought, *inter alia*, against the magistrate in his personal capacity. Of particular relevance was whether the unlawful committal of the appellant to prison in breach of the right to freedom and security of the person in section 12(1) of the Constitution,[63] or of the breach of the right to compensation for unlawful detention in article 9(5) of the ICCPR,[64] affected the judicial immunity that would otherwise protect the magistrate from liability under domestic law.[65] In reaching the conclusion that this was not the case, the Court noted that the ICCPR is not a self-executing legal instrument. The formal adoption of its provisions did not, of itself, amend the established domestic law.[66]

Not only does this statement seem to be based on the (highly inaccurate) assumption that the ICCPR as a whole is in conflict with existing domestic law, but it also ignores the fact that the Constitution requires a 'provision-by-provision' approach to self-execution. Section 231(4) of the Constitution refers to a 'self-executing provision of an agreement' and not 'self-executing agreement'. The Court should therefore first have examined whether article 9(5) of the ICCPR is clear and precise enough to be directly applicable (self-executing), whereafter it should have considered whether it indeed conflicts with existing domestic law.

The flipside of the de facto irrelevance of self-execution in South African treaty law is that treaties do generally serve as a direct basis for litigation between private parties. The basis for legal standing is to be sought in domestic law on the basis of constitutional, statutory, or common law.

However, it is important to note that an unincorporated treaty can be used to challenge and invalidate subordinate legislation. This was confirmed by the Supreme Court of Appeal, in the *Progress Office Machines* case.[67] The question concerned whether an anti-dumping duty period, contained in secondary legislation issued by the Ministry of Finance, violated article 11(3) of the World Trade Organization Agreement on the

62 Dugard (n 1 above) 454.

63 Section 12(1) of the Constitution determines that: (1) Everyone has the right to freedom and security of the person, which includes the right - (a) not to be deprived of freedom arbitrarily or without just cause; (b) not to be detained without trial; (c) to be free from all forms of violence from either public or private sources; (d) not to be tortured in any way; and (e) not to be treated or punished in a cruel, inhuman or degrading way.

64 International Covenant on Civil and Political Rights (ICCPR) (16 December 1966, UNTS 999 171) art 9(5) determines that: 'Anyone who has been the victim of unlawful arrest or detention shall have an enforceable right to compensation.' http://www2.ohchr.org/english/law/ccpr.htm (accessed 20 September 2013).

65 *Claassen* (n 58 above) para 5, 24.

66 *Claassen* (n 58 above) para 36.

67 *Progress Office Machines* (n 37 above) para 11.

Implementation of Article VI of the General Agreement on Tariffs and Trade. The Supreme Court of Appeal stated that although South Africa has ratified the WTO Agreement in 1995 it has not yet been enacted into municipal law, nor has the Agreement on Implementation of Article VI of the General Agreement on Tariffs and Trade. No rights are therefore derived from these international agreements. However, the International Trade Administration Act 71 of 2002 had to be interpreted in accordance with international law, where reasonable, as required by section 233 of the Constitution.[68]

The Supreme Court of Appeal continued by stating that subordinate legislation (such as the notice by the Minister of Finance imposing an anti-dumping duty) must be reasonable and that a court may insist that the subordinate legislation be in compliance with a state's international obligations in order to be valid.[69] This meant that subordinate legislation that violated international obligations would as such be unreasonable and to that extent invalid.[70] In line with this reasoning the Supreme Court of Appeal invalidated an anti-dumping duty that exceeded the period provided for by the international agreements.[71]

2.2.3 Treaty termination

The issue of treaty termination is not regulated in the Constitution or by statute. However, in practice it seems that where a decision to terminate a treaty is taken, this will be done in accordance with international law practice, including the provisions of the VCLT.[72] Although the decision to terminate a treaty vests in the executive, it is arguable that the spirit of section 231(2) would require parliamentary involvement in the same manner as foreseen for ratification. This would imply the consent to termination of both Houses of Parliament in relation to all 'non-technical' treaties.[73] Where a treaty has been incorporated into municipal law in terms of section 231(4) of the Constitution, the implementing will also have to be repealed by the legislature. As long as the legislation is in place, the treaty obligations will de facto still be in force in the Republic, despite the fact that South Africa would not be bound formally by them on the international level.[74]

68 *Progress Office Machines* (n 37 above) para 6.
69 *Progress Office Machines* (n 37 above) para 12, 6.
70 *Progress Office Machines* (n 37 above) para 12.
71 *Progress Office Machines* (n 37 above) para 12, 20.
72 n 16 above, art 3. The general principle concerning termination is contained in article 54 VCLT, 'The termination of a treaty or the withdrawal of a party may take place: (a) in conformity with the provisions of the treaty; or (b) at any time by consent of all the parties after consultation with the other contracting States.'
73 Botha (n 24 above) 85.
74 As above.

It is also noteworthy that treaties are not published systematically on paper in South Africa.[75] However, interested parties can obtain information, including copies of the treaty in question, from the Treaty Section of the Office of the Chief State Legal Adviser. This section serves as the national record-keeping authority and also makes available treaties online.[76]

3 The status of customary international law in the domestic legal order

As indicated at the outset, section 232 of the Constitution determines that customary international law is law in the Republic unless it is inconsistent with the Constitution or an Act of Parliament. This means that South Africa has a monist approach towards customary international law and that in the domestic legal order it constitutes a particular species of the common law.[77]

However, customary international law does not feature prominently in court practice. Where reference is made, it tends to be short and to inform the reasoning or interpretation already decided on by the court, rather than being the basis of the decision. This scant treatment of customary international law in court practice forms a strong contrast with the extensive references to international human rights instruments in court practice, as will be illuminated (→ 4.1). This is most likely a result of the fact that most litigators and judges are not yet well versed in public international law beyond the area of human rights, despite the fact that 20 years have gone by since the adoption of the new constitutional dispensation. Also, the vague nature of many customary international law obligations reduces their utility as a guideline for interpretation.

The references to customary law have however featured in cases pertaining to treaty law, international humanitarian law and jurisdiction. In the *Harksen* decision the Cape High Court accepted that the definition of a treaty in article 2(1)(a) of the Vienna Convention was a codification of customary international law.[78] Subsequently on appeal the Constitutional Court was reluctant to accept the customary law status of article 46 of the Vienna Convention, according to which a state may not invoke the fact that its consent to be bound by a treaty has been expressed in violation of

75 Botha (n 24 above) 87.

76 See Department of International Relations and Cooperation; Office of the Chief State Law Advisor Treaty Section http://www.dfa.gov.za/chiefstatelawadvicer/treatysection.html (accessed 20 April 2015).

77 Dugard (n 1 above) 474.

78 *Harksen v President of the RSA* 1998 (2) SA 1011 (C); N Botha 'Extradition on the basis of a treaty: section 5 of the Extradition Act 67 of 1962 considered' (2000) 25 *South African Yearbook of International Law* 249.

a provision of its national law.[79] The Court noted that the extent to which the Vienna Convention reflects customary international law was by no means settled. However, it did not attempt to draw a distinction between those obligations in the Vienna Convention that were generally accepted as customary international law and those that were more contentious.[80]

The customary international law status of international humanitarian law has thus far also received only superficial attention. The most prominent example remains the *AZAPO* case, which was one of the very first cases that the Constitutional Court had to decide when taking up its work in 1995.[81] In addition to its historic importance in the South African context, it also reflects the Constitutional Court's willingness to give precedence to the clear language of the Constitution, if such language were to result in a conflict with customary international law. The *AZAPO* case concerned the constitutionality of the Truth and Reconciliation Commission, which was set up to deal with crimes committed during the era of apartheid. In its terms of reference it was awarded the power to grant amnesty under certain conditions to individuals responsible for violations of human rights.[82] Some of the members of families who had lost persons close to them as a result of the death and torture squads of the apartheid regime challenged the constitutionality of the so-called Reconciliation Act, which established the Truth and Reconciliation Commission.[83]

The Constitutional Court essentially decided that the so-called post-amble to the interim Constitution (which was in force at the time), required that amnesty be granted to persons who had violated the law in the course of the conflicts of the past and allowed for the modalities to be established by national legislation.[84] Essentially, the constitutional terms were conclusive of the matter to the extent that they presupposed full amnesty to be given.[85] The Constitutional Court doubted whether the Geneva Conventions 1949 were relevant, since the Court regarded the obligation to prosecute those guilty of grave breaches of the Geneva Conventions applicable only to international armed conflict.[86] The Court also submitted that neither of the two Additional Protocols 1977 to these Conventions were applicable, since they were not signed or ratified by

79 Vienna Convention (n 16 above) art 46(1) determines that: 'A State may not invoke the fact that its consent to be bound by a treaty has been expressed in violation of a provision of its internal law regarding competence to conclude treaties as invalidating its consent unless that violation was manifest and concerned a rule of its internal law of fundamental importance.'

80 *Harksen* (n 18 above) para 26.

81 n 36 above; AM Gross 'The Constitution, reconciliation and transitional justice: Lessons from South Africa and Israel' (2004) 40 *Stanford Journal of International Law* 47, 69 - 77.

82 The Promotion of National Unity and Reconciliation Amendment Act 87 of 1995.

83 *AZAPO* (n 36 above) para 6.

84 *AZAPO* (n 36 above) para 7.

85 *AZAPO* (n 36 above) para 9.

86 *AZAPO* (n 36 above) para 30.

South Africa at the relevant time.[87] Consequently, there was nothing in the Promotion of National Unity and Reconciliation Act that constituted a breach of the obligations of South Africa in terms of the instruments of international law, as relied on by the applicants.[88]

Implicit in the Court's decision was also the assumption that the potential customary international law norms relevant to the question before it were too imprecise to overcome the strong language of the amnesty.[89] The language of amnesty indicated that in order to reveal the truth, effect closure, and protect the new democratic government from huge economic liability for the crimes of the previous government, there should be indemnity both from civil and criminal liability for the perpetrators of apartheid crimes.[90]

Had the Court in the *AZAPO* case engaged in a more extensive survey of the relevant international practice in the area, it would have found additional support for its conclusion and not (as was implicitly feared), opposition to its views. For example, according to the Appeals Chamber of the International Criminal Tribunal for the Former Yugoslavia (ICTY) in the *Tadić* case,[91] the Geneva Conventions clearly indicate that acts that must be prosecuted by states under the rubric of 'grave breaches' are only classified as such if such acts occur against persons or property protected by the Conventions (that is, in international armed conflicts).[92] This is a restrictive definition and does not include persons participating in, or civilians affected by, an internal conflict.[93] The Court could have backed its conclusion by the *Tadić* decision, but refrained from doing so.

87 *AZAPO* (n 36 above) para 29. The Geneva Conventions and two additional protocols were finally enacted into South African domestic law by the Implementation of the Geneva Conventions Act 8 of 2012 which entered into force on 1 December 2012.

88 Presentation by former Justice of the Constitutional Court of South Africa, A Sachs, at a seminar in Amsterdam on 7 March 2003 (speaking notes at seminar; on file with the author).

89 *AZAPO* (n 36 above) para 34.

90 Sachs (n 88 above).

91 *Prosecutor v Tadić (Jurisdiction)* (1996) 35 International Legal Materials 32.

92 n 91 above, para 81; eg, Geneva Convention for the Amelioration of the Condition of the Wounded and Sick in Armed Forces in the Field (Geneva I) (12 August 1949, 75 UNTS 31) art 50 ('Grave breaches to which the [Convention] relates shall be those involving any of the following acts, if committed against persons or property protected by the Convention: willful killing, torture or inhuman treatment, including biological experiments, willfully causing great suffering or serious injury to body or health, and extensive destruction and appropriation of property, not justified by military necessity and carried out unlawfully and wantonly'). Geneva Convention for the Amelioration of the Condition of Wounded, Sick and Shipwrecked Members of Armed Forces (Geneva II) (12 August 1949, 75 UNTS 85) art 51; Geneva Convention relative to the Treatment of Prisoners of War (Geneva III) (12 August 1949, 75 UNTS 135) art 130; Geneva Convention Relative to the Protection of Civilian Persons in Time of War (Geneva IV) (12 August 1949, 75 UNTS 287) art 147.

93 C Greenwood 'International humanitarian law and the *Tadić* case' (1996) 7 *European Journal of International Law* 265, 275 - 276. The Appeals Chamber considered the concept of grave breaches under the Convention inseparable from the concept of

In addition, the *Tadić* decision provided support for the fact that an obligation to prosecute for acts committed at the time in question could not easily be derived from customary law as codified by Common Article 3 of the Geneva Conventions.[94] While the ICTY affirmed that Common Article 3 governed internal strife and had acquired customary law status,[95] violations of Common Article 3 had, nonetheless, at that point in time, never been treated as crimes under international law.[96] Although violations of Common Article 3 could exist as international offences subject to universal jurisdiction, they did not yet implicate the mandatory type of jurisdiction envisioned by the Geneva Conventions.[97] The same consideration applied to Additional Protocol II to the Geneva Conventions.[98] The ICTY further submitted that 'many' of Additional Protocol II's provisions would also enjoy some degree of customary character.[99] However, the ICTY's reference in this regard is rather vague and Additional Protocol II has not generally been regarded as declaratory of customary international law.[100]

A similar conclusion could have been drawn from an inquiry into whether other principles of customary international law relating to torture, war crimes, and crimes against humanity required prosecution of offenders. On the one hand, apartheid has been labelled as a crime against

protected persons and property, and believed that neither concept featured in Common Article 3, the only provision in the Conventions applicable to internal armed conflicts. *Tadić* decision (n 91 above) para 81.

94 n 92 above, art 3; Common Article 3 determines, *inter alia*, that the following acts are and shall remain prohibited with respect to civilians: (a) violence to life and person, in particular murder of all kinds, mutilation, cruel treatment and torture; (b) taking of hostages; (c) outrages upon personal dignity, in particular humiliating and degrading treatment; (d) the passing of sentences and the carrying out of executions without previous judgment pronounced by a regularly constituted court, affording all the judicial guarantees which are recognized as indispensable by civilized peoples.

95 *Tadić* decision (n 91 above) paras 98, 103, 109, 116, 134; UN Security Council, *Report of the Secretary-General Pursuant to Paragraph 2 of Security Council Resolution 808* (1993) S/25704 [Contains text of the Statute of the International Tribunal for the Prosecution of Persons Responsible for Serious Violations of International Humanitarian Law Committed in the Territory of the Former Yugoslavia since 1991]; UNSC Resolution 820 (1993) Adopted by the Security Council at its 3200th meeting, on 17 April 1993, S/RES/820 (1993).

96 Greenwood (n 93 above) 279 - 280; *Tadić* decision (n 91 above) paras 83, 134 ('All of these factors confirm that customary international law imposes criminal liability for serious violations of Common Article 3, as supplemented by other general principles and rules on the protection of victims of internal armed conflict, and for breaching certain fundamental principles and rules regarding means and methods of combat in civil strife.')

97 *Tadić* decision (n 91 above) para 81.

98 Protocol Additional to the Geneva Conventions of 12 August 1949, and Relating to the Protection of Victims of Non-International Armed Conflicts (Protocol II) (8 June 1977, 1125 UNTS 609).

99 *Tadić* decision (n 91 above) para 117.

100 Greenwood (n 93 above) 278; *Tadić* decision (n 91 above) paras 107, 110.

humanity by the General Assembly[101] and the Apartheid Convention.[102] This may suggest a customary international law obligation to prosecute those who committed the crime of apartheid, particularly with respect to systematic murder, torture, and disappearances, which were all crimes under South African law before 1990. However, a survey of state practice at the time would probably have revealed that state practice was still too uncertain and unsettled to support such a rule.[103]

In essence, therefore, a proper interpretation of the amnesty clause in light of South Africa's international customary obligations would have added authority to the position asserted by the Constitutional Court. In addition to the unfamiliarity of the judges with international humanitarian law, the Constitutional Court's failure to engage in such a process was also due to time constraints.[104] Although several months had already passed since the establishment of the Truth and Reconciliation Commission,[105] it could not start functioning until there was a ruling on the legality of the amnesty. Moreover, the language of the interim Constitution was explicit, resulting in the Constitutional Court's inclination towards giving preference to it, even if this could potentially lead to a violation of customary international law obligations.[106]

The *Basson* case also concerned the issue of extra-judicial killings committed during the apartheid era, but in this instance on Namibian soil, at a time when the country was still de facto administered by South Africa.[107] In this case the Court had to determine whether South African courts had jurisdiction to try the case of Wouter Basson, who was allegedly involved in acts of chemical and biological warfare. Although the case turned on domestic law, the Constitutional Court did refer to the customary nature of fundamental principles of international humanitarian law with reference to International Court of Justice (ICJ) and ICTY decisions. It described the apartheid government's extra-judicial killing of captives during the liberation struggle in Namibia as violating the minimal

101 UNGA Res 39 (1972) GAOR 39th Session, UN Doc A/RES/39/72 (1984) (confirming that apartheid is a threat to international peace and security).
102 International Convention on the Suppression and Punishment of the Crime of Apartheid (30 November 1973, UNGA Res 3068 (1973) GAOR 28th Session Supp30, UN Doc A/9030).
103 Relevant case-law already available at the time of the *AZAPO* decision included decisions of the Inter-American Commission of Human Rights involving Uruguay and Argentina; *Consuelo et al v Argentina* IAm Comm of HR (2 October 1992) Case 28/92 and; *Mendoza et al v Uruguay* IAm Comm of HR (4 October 1991) Case 29/92. *Velasquez Rodriguez v Honduras (Judgment)* IACHR (29 July 1988) Series C 4. and reported in 95 *International Law Reports* 259 (holding that a successor government was obliged to prosecute those members of the previous government responsible for human rights violations).
104 Sachs (n 88 above).
105 The Commission was founded through the Promotion of National Unity and Reconciliation Act 34 of 1995 http://www.justice.gov.za/legislation/acts/1995-034.pdf (accessed 20 September 2014).
106 Sachs (n 88 above).
107 *South Africa v Basson* 2005 (12) BCLR 1192 (CC).

standards of international humanitarian law which, according to the Advisory Opinion on the *Legality of the Threat or Use of Nuclear Weapons*,[108] constituted intransgressible principles of customary international law.[109] The Court further referred to the *Nicaragua*[110] and *Tadić* decisions[111] when underscoring that obligations under Common Article 3 of the 1949 Geneva Conventions have obtained customary status.[112] However, the Constitutional Court stopped short of determining the concrete implications of these obligations for South Africa in the particular case.

The most prominent reliance on customary law up to date was in a case decided by the South African Competition Appeals Court in 2002. In the *American Soda Ash* case,[113] the appellant faced a complaint of predatory conduct that contravened section 8 of the Competition Act 89 of 1998. The appellant, relying on a restrictive interpretation of section 3(1) of the Competition Act, argued that the dispute fell outside of the purview of the Act. Section 3(1) provided that the 'Act applies to all economic activity within, or having an effect within, the Republic'. According to the appellant, the word 'effect' in section 3(1) should be read to mean 'negative or deleterious effect' in as far as it concerned foreign based acts. The appellant based his argument on a customary international law argument pertaining to extra-territorial jurisdiction, according to which harm is an essential element of the 'effects doctrine'.

When deciding the issue, the Competition Appeals Court addressed the status of customary international law in the Republic explicitly. It first noted that section 1(2)(a) of the Competition Act provided that the Act must be interpreted in 'compliance with the international law obligations of the Republic'. Thereafter it confirmed that customary international law constituted municipal law in the domestic legal system, unless conflicting with legislation in accordance with section 232 of the Constitution. It further underscored that domestic legislation should be interpreted in accordance with international law where reasonable, in accordance with section 233 of the Constitution.[114]

Subsequently the Competition Appeals Court relied on ICJ practice and foreign case-law and legislation for clarifying the scope of the 'effects doctrine' in customary international law. This in turn was then used as a

108 *Legality of the Threat or Use of Nuclear Weapons (Advisory Opinion)* (8 July 1996) (1996) ICJ Reports 226.
109 *Basson* (n 107 above) para 174.
110 *Military and Paramilitary Activities in and against Nicaragua (Nicaragua v United States of America)* (Merits) (27 June 1986) (1986) ICJ Reports 14.
111 n 91 above.
112 Dugard (n 1 above) 466.
113 *American Soda Ash Corp CHC Global (Pty) Ltd v Competition Commission of South Africa* 2003 ZACAC 6, ILDC 493 (ZA 2002).
114 *American Soda Ash* (n 113 above) para 15.

guideline for interpreting the 'effects doctrine' in section 3(1) of the Competition Act, in accordance with section 233 of the Constitution.[115] The Competition Appeals Court cited the reference to the Permanent Court of International Justice (PCIJ) in the *Lotus* case[116] on the power of states to exercise jurisdiction over foreign acts having effects in their territory.[117] It also considered several US cases,[118] which the appellant relied on, as well as article 81 of the Treaty Establishing the European Community (EC Treaty),[119] which prohibited practices that might affect competition within the European common market. However, the Competition Appeals Court found that none of these sources supported the view that harm is an essential element of the 'effects doctrine'.

4 The role of the judiciary in the interpretation and application of international law

4.1 International (human rights) instruments guiding interpretation

Since its inception the Constitutional Court in particular has played a prominent role in the interpretation and application of international law within the domestic legal order. The Court has become known for its recourse to international human rights law as a guideline for interpretation when interpreting the Constitution, legislation and the common law. This development has its origin in section 39(1) of the Constitution, which determines that courts must consider international law when interpreting the Bill of Rights. Similarly, section 39(2) of the Constitution requires courts to promote the spirit of the Bill of Rights when interpreting the common law or legislation, while section 233 of the Constitution further requires an interpretation of legislation that is in conformity with international law, where reasonable.

Due to this mediating role of sections 39 and 233 of the Constitution, it is unlikely that any head-on collision between municipal and international law (whether treaty or custom) will occur.[120] The courts are

115 *American Soda Ash* (n 113 above) paras 18 - 21; D Tladi (2002) ILDC 493 (ZA).
116 *The Case of the SS Lotus* (*France v Turkey*) [1927] PCIJ Rep Series A No 10.
117 *American Soda Ash* (n 113 above) para 17.
118 *Lotus* (n 116 above); *American Banana Co v United Fruit Co* 213 US 347 (1909); *United States v Aluminium Co of America (Alcoa)* 148 F 2d 416 (1945); *Continental Co v Union Carbide* 370 US 690 (1962); *Timberlane Lumber Co v Bank of America* 549 F 2d 597 (1976); *Mannington Mills Inc v Congoleum Corp* 595 F2d 1287 (1979); *Matsushita v Zenith Radio* 475 US 574 (1986); *Hartford Fire Insurance Co v California* 509 US 764 (1993); *Metro Industries Inc v Sammi Corp* 82 F 3d 893 (1996); *United States v Nippon Paper Industries Co Ltd* 109 F 3d 1 (1997).
119 Treaty Establishing the European Community (Rome Treaty) (25 March 1957, 298 UNTS 11) art 81 (previously art 85).
120 Sachs (n 88 above); *Glenister* case (n 26 above) para 179.

therefore unlikely to be placed in a position in which they have to retreat behind the dualist veil (which the Constitutional dispensation formally provides for), in accordance with which the Constitution or a domestic statute trumps international law.

As far as international human rights law is concerned, the approach of the Constitutional Court has been very progressive. It draws on binding but as of yet unincorporated treaties, as well as on non-binding instruments as interpretive guidelines. However, the reliance on international treaties and other instruments in areas other than human rights occur less frequently. This was already illustrated (see 3 above) in connection with the limited impact that customary international law thus far has had as a guideline for interpretation. As indicated, this is mainly the result of the limited experience of South African litigators and judges with public international law outside the area of human rights law. A recent example where the Constitutional Court was guided by a decision of an international Tribunal in order to develop the common law concerns that of the *Government of the Republic of Zimbabwe v Louis Karel Fick.*[121] The implications of this case will be discussed in the chapter devoted to the status of decisions of international courts and tribunals in the domestic legal order (→ De Wet/International Decisions).

When resorting to international instruments in accordance with section 39(1) of the Constitution, the Constitutional Court reinforces its own position on a matter, as these instruments constitute a source of profound values that are compatible with the whole underlying core of the South African constitutional order.[122] However, a closer look at the Constitutional Court's practice reveals that the manner in which it resorts to non-binding international instruments is open to criticism. From the outset, the Constitutional Court regarded the interpretation clauses to refer to binding as well as non-binding international instruments.[123] These would include treaties that South Africa has not or cannot ratify (notably the Convention for the Protection of Human Rights and Fundamental Freedoms 1950[124]), as well as instruments that are by nature non-binding such as the Universal Declaration of Human Rights (UDHR); General Comments of United Nations Human Rights bodies; and resolutions of the General Assembly that are not meant for ratification.

121 *Government of the Republic of Zimbabwe v Louis Karel Fick and Others* 2013 (5) SA 325. For an earlier case in which the Constitutional Court used international law as a tool for interpreting the common law, *Carmichele v Minister of Safety and Security* 2001 (4) SA 938. Relying *inter alia* on the Convention on the Elimination of All forms of Discrimination against Women, the Court developed the law of delict to include a duty on the state to prohibit and prevent all gender-based discrimination that impairs the fundamental rights of women. N Botha 'The role of international law in the development of South African common law' (2001) 26 *South African Yearbook of International Law* 253, 259; Dugard (n 1 above) 46.

122 Sachs (n 88 above); *Glenister* case (n 26 above) para 192.

123 *S v Makwanyane* 1995 (3) SA 391 (CC).

124 European Convention on Human Rights (4 November 1950, 312 UNTS 221).

The choice of non-binding instruments sometimes appears inconsistent, with a tendency to rely on non-binding European instruments while excluding instruments that South Africa has ratified. This was particularly the case in the early years after the Constitutional Court's inception, as can be illustrated by the *Christian Education* decision.[125] It concerned the complaint of an American-based church group that established schools in South Africa during the 1980s on the principle that the Bible deemed corporal punishment as a necessary form of discipline for children.[126] The issue in question was whether the prohibition of corporal punishment in all schools, as prescribed by section 10 of the South African Schools Act 84 of 1996, violated the constitutional right to religious freedom of parents who, in accordance with their religious convictions, had consented to the corporal punishment of their children by teachers.[127]

While referencing applicable jurisprudence pertaining to the European Convention on Human Rights, the Constitutional Court made no mention of the African Charter on the Rights and Welfare of the Child 1999 (African Charter).[128] In the present context, articles XI(4) and XI(5) of this unmentioned Charter are of particular interest. Whereas the former guarantees the rights of parents to ensure the religious and moral education of the child in a manner consistent with the child's evolving capacities, the latter requires the state to ensure that parental or educational disciplinary measures conform to notions of humanity and inherent dignity. These two clauses would seem to illustrate the challenge that the Constitutional Court confronted in the *Christian Education* case, specifically, the reconciling of religious rights of parents and the protection of children against harm. By also referring to articles XI(4) and XI(5) in its judgment, the Court would have contributed to the development of an African regional human rights instrument and also strengthened the notion of human rights as an African value.[129]

The Court's affinity for the European Convention on Human Rights could be explained by the fact that the individual complaints procedure under it is elaborate and has produced an extensive jurisprudence to which common law-trained judges eagerly turn for guidance.[130] Since the complaints procedure of the African Charter and other African human rights instruments are not yet as well developed, the same judges (and litigators) tend to neglect these instruments.[131] Nonetheless, this should

125 *Christian Education South Africa v Minister of Education* 2000 (4) SA 757.
126 *Christian Education* (n 125 above) para 2.
127 Interim Constitution (n 4 above) chapter XV [1] and chapter XXX [1].
128 *Christian Education* (n 125 above) paras 43 - 45; African Charter on the Rights and Welfare of the Child (African Children's Charter) (11 July 1990, OAU Doc CAB/LEG/24.9/49) arts XI(4) and XI(5).
129 Declaration on the Rights and Welfare of the African Child (20 July 1979, AHG/St. 4 (XVI) Rev. 1).
130 C Heyns, 'The African regional human rights system: The African Charter' (2004) 108 *Pennsylvania State Law Review* 679.
131 Heyns (n 131 above) 694 - 695.

not lead to the neglect of regional human rights instruments to which South Africa is a party, nor of other African human rights instruments that could serve as guidance for interpretation. By relying on the European Convention on Human Rights to the exclusion of applicable African instruments, the Court can entrench the image of human rights as being a set of primarily Western values that are being imposed on African societies. It could also give the impression that the African human rights instruments are inferior to the other mentioned instruments.

These critical remarks are not directed at the fact that the Constitutional Court relies on non-binding international or European instruments when formulating its human rights jurisprudence, as the depth that this broad approach has contributed to its human rights jurisprudence is not disputed.[132]

However, the courts can benefit from a more rigid methodology that reflects a uniform and consistent strategy as to which international instruments to consider as guidelines for interpretation. Otherwise judges may be perceived as picking amongst those international human rights instruments that are closest to their own personal views and in accordance with the political mood of the day, as opposed to drawing from an international value system that is consonant with the South African constitutional order. In addition, there is the risk that African human rights instruments would be sidelined and the perception that human rights norms constitute a mere by-product of western imperialism would be (further) entrenched.

4.2 Deference to the Executive

Since the adoption of the new constitutional order in 1994, the courts have indicated on several occasions that the conduct of foreign relations is not – in principle – beyond judicial scrutiny. This is notably the case where such conduct has a direct impact on the fundamental rights of individuals with standing before the South African court in question.[133] However, the courts nonetheless grant significant deference to the executive in matters of

132 Some examples of decisions enriched by reference to international human rights instruments include *Government of South Africa v Grootboom* 2001 (1) SA 46; *Minister of Health v Treatment Action Campaign* 2002 (5) SA 721; *Mazibuko v City of Johannesburg* 2008 (4) All SA 471, *Fourie & Bonthuys, Lesbian and Gay Equality Project v Minister of Home Affairs* 2005 ZACC 19 ILDC.

133 *Kolbatschenko v King NO* 2001 (4) SA 336 (C); *Geuking v President of the RSA* 2003 (3) SA 34 (CC) para 27E. In this instance, no extradition treaty existed between South Africa and the state involved. The Court determined that that the President's consent to classify a particular individual as a 'person liable to be extradited' was a foreign policy decision, but one which was subject to limitations. These limitations were abuse of power by the President, or action which was contrary to the provisions of the Constitution. N Botha & M Oliver, 'Ten years of international law in the South African courts: Reviewing the past and assessing the future' (2004) 29 *South African Yearbook of International Law* 356 - 357; Dugard (n 1 above) 471.

foreign relations. This has been particularly visible in the area of diplomatic protection, where disagreement erupted in relation to the level of scrutiny that a court can apply in such instances.

The *Kaunda* case laid the foundation for a series of diplomatic protection cases and thus far the only one to have appeared before the Constitutional Court.[134] The case acknowledged a role for courts in issues of diplomatic protection, but with considerable deference toward the executive in relation to the type of action to be undertaken. The Constitutional Court was confronted with whether South Africa had to prevent the extradition of South African nationals from Zimbabwe to Equatorial Guinea, where they would face the death penalty for plotting a coup against the government. In answering this question in the negative, the Constitutional Court determined that no right to diplomatic protection existed under international law. South African citizens facing adverse state action in foreign countries were nonetheless entitled under section 3 of the Constitution to request protection from the government against acts that violated obligations. Similarly, the government had to consider such a request and its decisions in these matters were subject to constitutional control.[135]

However, courts had to acknowledge that diplomatic protection concerned an area with that the executive was better placed to deal with than the courts. Where, for example, the government refused to consider a legitimate request for diplomatic protection, or dealt with it irrationally or in bad faith, a court could require the government to deal with the matter properly. But in doing so a court had to respect the broad discretion of the executive, which was essentially responsible for determining the nature of the protection as an aspect of foreign policy.[136] The nature of the reaction called for government expertise and it would be inappropriate for a court to propose a different course of action.[137]

This position was subsequently followed by the Supreme Court of Appeal in the *Von Abo* case.[138] The case was marked by a long history of dismissive behaviour on the part of the government towards Von Abo's request for diplomatic protection, following the expropriation without compensation of his property by the Zimbabwean government. The

134 *Kaunda v President of the RSA* 2005 (4) SA 235 (CC) para 67.
135 *Kaunda* (n 134 above) para 67.
136 *Kaunda* (n 134 above) para 77, 80, 81. The principle that a court could not prescribe to government how to conduct foreign affairs and make diplomatic interventions was also applied by the SCA in *Van Zyl & Others v Government of the RSA & Others* 2008 (3) SA 294 (SCA). This case concerned the expropriation of property of a South African citizen by the Lesotho Government.
137 *Kaunda* (n 134 above) para 144. In this particular instance the South African High Commissioner had made representations to the Zimbabwean government and it was not established that the South African government had violated either international law or the Constitution.
138 *The Government of the Republic of South Africa v Von Abo* 2011(5) SA 262 (SCA).

undisputed reluctance of the government to respond to Mr Von Abo's request was rebuked by the Supreme Court of Appeal. It underscored that the government's response was inappropriate in as far as it did not provide Mr Von Abo or the courts with an honest and open disclosure of its policy, approach and action in relation to Mr Von Abo's request.[139] At the same time, however, the Court underscored that a right to have a request for diplomatic protection considered does not amount to a right to diplomatic protection as such, nor to a duty of government to provide a particular type of diplomatic protection.[140] The need for deference to the Executive in matters that involve relations with other states was therefore duly considered.

5 Assessment

In conclusion, it is fair to say that South Africa's track-record of receiving international law into the domestic legal order since the introduction of the new constitutional order in 1994 is mixed. On one hand, the Constitution of 1996 is very receptive to international law, notably as a guideline for interpretation. Also, the courts are keen to use international human rights instruments as a guideline for interpreting the Constitution, even though their methodology in this regard is open to criticism. Similarly, the executive follows the basic principles of the Vienna Convention when negotiating and executing treaties, despite the fact that South Africa is not a party to the Vienna Convention.

On the other hand, the courts remain reluctant to resort to international law as an instrument of interpretation in areas outside human rights law. Parliament's track-record in implementing non-self-executing and non-technical treaties is inconsistent. While the Rome Statute of the International Criminal Court was implemented within four years of its conclusion, the ICCPR and the WTO Agreement have still not been implemented, despite the fact that they have been ratified for more than a decade – to name but a few examples.

South Africa's inconsistent approach may relate to the fact that expertise in the field of public international law – in contrast to expertise pertaining to international human rights law – is limited across the country. Most judges, litigators and law-makers are not well versed in public international law, partly due to the fact the subject matter has traditionally been neglected at universities. This in turn is a remnant of the country's years of isolation and hostile attitude towards international law before 1994. Although some progress has been made in overcoming this attitude, the capacity deficit at universities in this area of law is still significant.

139 *Von Abo* (n 138 above) paras 39 - 40.
140 *Von Abo* (n 138 above) para 22.

The new constitutional order, notably through the work of the Constitutional Court, has laid important groundwork during the first decade of its existence for enhanced interaction between national and international human rights law. However, much work still needs to be done before this trend also becomes visible in the area of public international law proper. This reality poses a challenge to various sectors of the judicial profession, including the judiciary, the bar, legislature, and in particular the law faculties who produce the international lawyers of the future.

BIBLIOGRAPHY

De Wet, E (2008) 'The reception process in The Netherlands and Belgium' in Keller, H & Stone Sweet, A (eds) *A Europe of rights: The impact of the ECHR on national legal systems* Oxford University Press: Oxford/New York

De Wet, E 'South Africa' in Shelton, D (ed) (2011) *International law and domestic legal systems: Incorporation, transformation and persuasion* Oxford University Press: Oxford/New York

Du Plessis, M (4th edn, 2011) 'International criminal courts, the International Criminal Court, and South Africa's implementation of the Rome Statute' in Dugard, J *International Law: A South African perspective* Juta: Cape Town

Dugard, J 'South Africa' in Sloss, D (ed) (2009) *The role of domestic courts in treaty enforcement* Cambridge University Press: Cambridge/New York

Strydom, H & Huarka, T 'South Africa' in Gowlland-Debbas, V (ed) (2004) *National implementation of United Nations sanctions: A comparative study* Martinus Nijhoff: Leiden/Boston

6

INTERNATIONAL HUMAN RIGHTS LAW IN GERMANY

*Nicola Wenzel**

1 Introduction

Human rights play an essential role in the constitutional order of Germany. Articles 1 to 19 of the German Constitution (Basic Law) contain a catalogue of human rights (fundamental rights) that are binding on the legislature, the executive, and the judiciary (article 1(3) Basic Law).

Independent courts ensure the protection of these rights. Article 19(4) grants the right of recourse to courts to any person whose basic rights have been violated by public authorities. The right of recourse encompasses the right of individuals to seize the Federal Constitutional Court which, as the final arbiter, decides on the compatibility of acts by state authorities with fundamental rights.

This system of national human rights protection works well in practice and has great value in the eyes of German constituents. It has served as a model for other countries and is a good example for a successful legal export of human rights concepts.

The following contribution deals with the import of international human rights into the German legal system. It examines the significance of international human rights in the German fundamental-rights-centred legal system.

2 Relevant international law obligations

2.1 The development of international human rights law

International human rights law is a fairly recent development.[1] Traditionally, international law was understood as regulating relations

* Legal officer for the German Federal Ministry of Justice and Consumer Protection.

between states. Relations between states and individuals in contrast were considered to be part of the *domaine réservé* of states and therefore out of the reach of international law. Some international legal instruments were aimed at protecting individuals,[2] but individuals' legal position remained mediated by states. Individuals themselves were not recognised as right holders.

It is only under the impression of the barbarous acts committed by Nazi Germany 'which have outraged the conscience of mankind',[3] that this state-centred perception of international law changed. The Universal Declaration of Human Rights (Universal Declaration), adopted by the United Nations' General Assembly in 1948, embodied a new approach and can be considered the starting point for the development of an international law of human rights. For the first time, an international instrument recognised inalienable rights of individuals vis-à-vis their government. These rights include political as well as social and economic rights. In the following years, the non-binding Declaration was complemented by binding human rights treaties at UN level (→ 2.2.1). After the war, in addition, regional human rights systems emerged in Europe, the Americas and Africa (→ 2.2.1).

Today, the body of international human rights law is substantial and the era of basic standard-setting can be considered to be over. From time to time discussions resurge about the need for further human rights treaties on specific topics, most recently in relation to the rights of older persons. The main challenge for the international law of human rights, however, is to ensure compliance with existing standards.[4]

2.2 Sources of international human rights law

The international law of human rights is made up, first and foremost, of a number of treaties at the universal and regional level (→ 2.2.1). Customary human rights law (→ 2.2.2) and soft law (→ 2.2.3) also play a role. A specificity of international human rights law is the existence of elaborate compliance control mechanisms. The decisions, views, observations and

1 On the history of international human rights law see T Buergenthal 'Human rights' in R Wolfrum (ed) *Max Planck encyclopedia of public international law* (2013) paras 3ff.
2 For examples see Buergenthal (n 1 above) paras 4ff.
3 Universal Declaration of Human Rights (10 December 1948, 217 A (III)) Preamble.
4 G Staberock 'Domestic implementation' in Wolfrum (n 1 above) para 4.

recommendations adopted in this context may also be considered a source of international human rights law (→ 2.2.4).

2.2.1 International human rights treaties

Universal treaties

Together with the Universal Declaration, two UN treaties constitute the 'International Bill of Rights': the International Covenant on Civil and Political Rights (ICCPR)[5] and the International Covenant on Economic, Social and Cultural Rights (CESCR).[6] The Covenants are complemented by a number of specific treaties that either further specify certain rights (the Convention against Torture and other Cruel, Inhuman or Degrading Treatment or Punishment (CAT)[7] and the International Convention for the Protection of All Persons from Enforced Disappearance (CPED)),[8] aim to protect particularly vulnerable persons (the Convention on the Rights of the Child (CRC),[9] the Convention on the Rights of Persons with Disabilities (CRPD)[10] and the Convention on the Protection of the Rights of All Migrant Workers and Members of Their Families (CMW)),[11] or fight specific forms of discrimination (the Convention on the Elimination of All Forms of Racial Discrimination (CERD)[12] and the Convention on the Elimination of All Forms of Discrimination against Women (CEDAW)).[13] With the exception of CMW, Germany has ratified all of these treaties.[14]

5 International Covenant on Civil and Political Rights (ICCPR) (16 December 1966, 999 UNTS 171).

6 International Covenant on Economic, Social and Cultural Rights (CESCR) (16 December 1966, 999 UNTS 3).

7 Convention against Torture and other Cruel, Inhuman or Degrading Treatment or Punishment (CAT) (10 December 1984, 1465 UNTS 85).

8 International Convention for the Protection of All Persons from Enforced Disappearance (CPED) (20 December 2006, 2716 UNTS 3).

9 Convention on the Rights of the Child (CRC) (20 November 1989, 1577 UNTS 3).

10 Convention on the Rights of Persons with Disabilities (CRPD) (13 December 2006, 2515 UNTS 3).

11 Convention on the Protection of the Rights of All Migrant Workers and Members of Their Families (CMW) (18 December 1990, 2220 UNTS 3).

12 Convention on the Elimination of All Forms of Racial Discrimination (CERD) (7 March 1966, 660 UNTS 195).

13 Convention on the Elimination of All Forms of Discrimination against Women (CEDAW) (18 December 1979, 1249 UNTS 13).

14 ICCPR: ratified on 17 December 1973, entry into force on 23 March 1976 (Bundesgesetzblatt 1973 II 1533); CESCR: ratified on 17 December 1973, entry into force on 3 January 1976 (Bundesgesetzblatt 1976 II 428); CERD: ratified on 16 May 1969, entry into force on 15 June 1969 (Bundesgesetzblatt 1969 II 962); CEDAW: ratified on 9 July 1985, entry into force 9 August 1985 (Bundesgesetzblatt 1985 II 647); CAT: ratified on 1 October 1990, entry into force 31 October 1990 (Bundesgesetzblatt 1990 II 247); CRC: ratified on 6 March 1992, entry into force 5 April 1992 (Bundesgesetzblatt 1992 II 121); CRPD: ratified on 24 February 2009, entry into force 26 March 2009 (Bundesgesetzblatt 2009 II 812); CPED: ratified on 24 September 2009, entry into force 23 December 2010 (Bundesgesetzblatt 2009 II 932). For a list of

Regional treaties

At the regional level, human rights treaties have been adopted in particular under the auspices of the Council of Europe (CoE), the Organization of American States (OAS) and the African Union (AU) (→ Chenwi).[15] At the heart of each regional human rights system is a comprehensive human rights treaty, namely the European Convention for the Protection of Human Rights and Fundamental Freedoms (ECHR), the American Convention on Human Rights (ACHR) and the African Charter on Human and Peoples' Rights (AChHPR). Other regional treaties complement the rights contained in the ECHR, ACHR and AChHPR, within the Council of Europe *inter alia* the European Convention on the Prevention of Torture and Inhuman or Degrading Treatment or Punishment (CPT),[16] the European Social Charter (ESC)[17] and the Convention on Action against Trafficking in Human Beings.[18]

Germany is party to the ECHR and has ratified most of the additional protocols to the Convention. Exceptions are: Protocol 7,[19] which extends the list of rights protected under the Convention to include *inter alia* the right of aliens to procedural guarantees in the event of expulsion from the territory of a state, the right to appeal in criminal matters and the right not to be tried or punished twice; and Protocol 12[20] which provides for a general prohibition of discrimination. The recently adopted Protocol 15[21] has been signed and will probably be ratified soon. Protocol 16 has not been signed for the time being.[22] Both protocols do not contain additional substantive rights; they are part of the efforts to reform the European Court of Human Rights (ECtHR).[23] Germany has also ratified the above-

other human rights relevant treaties ratified by Germany see Core Document forming part of the reports of states parties – Germany, UN Doc HRI/CORE/1/Add.75/Rev.1 (2003) para 132.

15 Other regional organisations (in Europe the Organization for Security and Co-operation in Europe for example, for Africa see the chapter by Chenwi) are active in this field.

16 European Convention on the Prevention of Torture and Inhuman or Degrading Treatment or Punishment (CPT) (26 November 1987, ETS no 126).

17 European Social Charter (ESC) (18 October1961, ETS no 35).

18 Convention on Action against Trafficking in Human Beings (16 May 2005, ETS no 197).

19 Protocol 7 to the European Convention for the Protection of Human Rights and Fundamental Freedoms (22 November 1984, ETS no117).

20 Protocol 12 to the European Convention for the Protection of Human Rights and Fundamental Freedoms (4 November 2000, ETS no 177).

21 Protocol 15 to the European Convention for the Protection of Human Rights and Fundamental Freedoms (24 June 2013, ETS no 213).

22 Protocol 16 to the European Convention for the Protection of Human Rights and Fundamental Freedoms (2 October 2013, ETS no 214).

23 Protocol 16 (n 22 above) gives the ECtHR the competence to issue advisory opinions on request of the highest courts and tribunals of state parties and Protocol 15 (n 21 above) *inter alia* shortens the time limit within which an application must be made to the Court and adds a reference to the principle of subsidiarity and the doctrine of the margin of appreciation to the Preamble of the Convention.

mentioned CoE treaties.[24]

European Union

In the European Union, the Charter of Fundamental Rights[25] is the primary reference document for human rights protection.[26] In application of article 6(1) of the TEU, the Charter has the rank of primary Union law. It is legally binding primarily for EU institutions, bodies, offices and agencies (article 51, paragraph 1 of the EU Charter). But in certain circumstances, national authorities may also be bound by the Charter, namely in cases in which they implement Union law. The exact meaning of the implementation of Union law in this context is still unclear. In the Åkerberg judgment, the ECJ has recently suggested a broad view of the Charter's scope of application; but this remains controversial (→ Hestermeyer).[27]

Secondary European Union law has also become a source of human rights obligations for states. This is true in particular for instruments based on article 19 of the TFEU such as the Racial Equality Directive[28] and the Employment Equality Directive.[29]

2.2.2 Customary human rights obligations

In spite of difficulties in identifying customary law in the field of human rights,[30] there is agreement today that many of the rights contained in the Universal Declaration form part of customary international law.[31]

24 ESC: Bundesgesetzblatt 1965 II 1261 & 1122 (Germany has signed the revised ESC, but has not ratified it); Convention against Trafficking: Bundesgesetzblatt 2012 II 1107; CPT: Bundesgesetzblatt 1989 II 946.

25 Charter of Fundemental Rights of the European Union (30 March 2010, OJ C83/389). On the Charter see S Kadelbach 'Charter of fundamental rights of the European Union' in Wolfrum (n 1 above).

26 It will be complemented by the European Convention for the Protection of Human Rights and Fundemental Freedoms (ECHR) (4 November 1950, ETS 5) once the EU accedes to the ECHR (see the Draft Agreement on the Accession of the European Union to the Convention for the Protection of Human Rights and Fundamental Freedoms (47+1(2013)008rev2)). On the accession see J Polakiewicz 'EU law and the ECHR: Will the European Union's accession square the circle? The draft accession agreement of April 5, 2013' (2013) 13 *European Human Rights Law Review* 592.

27 C-617/10 Åkerberg Fransson ECJ (26 February 2013) para 17ff.

28 Council Directive 2000/43/EC of 29 June 2000 implementing the principle of equal treatment between persons irrespective of racial or ethnic origin [2000] OJ L180/22.

29 Council Directive 2000/78/EC of 27 November 2000 establishing a general framework for equal treatment in employment and occupation [2000] OJ L303/16.

30 On these difficulties see C Tomuschat *Human rights: Between idealism and realism* (2003) 37.

31 See HRC, General Comment 24, UN Doc CCPR/C/21/Rev.1/Add.6 para 8; ILA Committee on the Enforcement of Human Rights Law *Final Report on the status of the Universal Declaration of Human Rights in national and international law* (1994); RB Lillich 'The growing importance of customary international human rights law' (1995-1996) 25 *Georgia Journal of International and Comparative Law* 1, provides an overview of the different positions.

As Germany is state party to most international human rights conventions, customary human rights law does not play a substantial role in practice. Some authors, however, have relied on the status as customary law of many of the rights contained in human rights treaties to argue for a constitutional rank of these treaties in the German legal system (→ 4.1).

2.2.3 Soft law in the field of human rights

Soft law exists in the field of human rights in the form of numerous resolutions, recommendations and decisions by UN bodies or other international organisations such as the Council of Europe. Soft law by its nature is not binding on states. But it does have tremendous influence.[32] It can be used to interpret the meaning of binding treaties and can be an indicator for the existence of customary international law.[33]

2.2.4 Compliance control mechanisms as a specificity of international human rights law

A specificity of international human rights law is the existence of elaborate compliance control mechanisms at universal as well as at regional level.

Compliance control mechanisms at universal level

Compliance control mechanisms at universal level are either based directly on the UN Charter[34] or on treaties. Some mechanisms are of a political nature such as the Charter-based Universal Periodic Review carried out by the UN Human Rights Council, but most are legal mechanisms. All of the above-mentioned UN human rights treaties, for example, require states to submit periodical reports to a treaty body composed of experts which, in concluding observations or comments, sets out concerns regarding compliance.[35] Seven of these treaty bodies[36] may also consider complaints by individuals against those states that have accepted the individual complaint mechanism.[37] Although concluding observations and views

32 Tomuschat (n 30 above) 39.

33 On the legal effects of soft law see D Thürer 'Soft law' in Wolfrum (n 1 above) paras 26ff.

34 On the Charter-based compliance control see T Buergenthal 'Human rights' in Wolfrum (n 1 above) para 19.

35 ICCPR (n 5 above) art 40, CESCR (n 6 above) art 16, CPED (n 8 above) art 29, CRPD (n 10 above) art 35, CRC (n 9 above) art 44, CAT (n 7 above) art 19, CEDAW (n 13 above) art 18 & CERD (n 12 above) art 9.

36 For the CMW (n 11 above) the individual complaint mechanism has not yet entered into force.

37 Germany has accepted individual complaints for ICCPR (n 5 above) (25 August 1993), CEDAW (n 13 above) (15 January 2002), CRPD (n 10 above) (24 February 2009) and most recently CRC (n 9 above) (28 February 2013). For an overview of possibilities of individual complaints in the human rights system, see D Shelton 'Human rights, individual communications/complaints' in Wolfrum (n 1 above).

adopted by treaty bodies following an individual complaint are not binding on states,[38] they constitute an authoritative statement on the conformity of national law with treaty obligations and as such may not be easily disregarded.[39] The Human Rights Committee conceives the implementation of its views as part of the obligation of states in article 2, paragraph 3 of the ICCPR to provide an effective remedy for violations of the rights contained in the Covenant and emphasises that based on the principle of good faith in the observance of treaty obligations states have the duty to cooperate with the Committee.[40]

Germany regularly complies with its reporting obligations under the named treaties. It has accepted the possibility of individual complaints with regard to all treaties with the exception of the CESCR.[41] Individual complaints lodged against Germany have been rare.[42] Most applications are declared inadmissible and only four human rights violations have been found.[43] Fear of an important number of individual applications, however, is the reason for the delay in the ratification of the Optional Protocol to the CESCR in spite of Germany's strong involvement in the elaboration of the text. The executive's fears are a mass of individual applications with respect, in particular, to the prohibition of strikes by public servants in German law.[44] The Committee on Economic, Social and Cultural Rights has criticised Germany for a too extensive interpretation of 'the administration of the State' in article 8(2) of the CESCR and has recommended that Germany ensure that civil servants who do not provide essential services have the right to strike.[45] The ECtHR's jurisprudence points in the same direction. German law is currently undergoing change

38 T Buergenthal 'The UN Human Rights Committee' (2001) 5 *Max Planck Yearbook of International Law* 341397; C Tomuschat 'Human Rights Committee' in Wolfrum (n 1 above) para 14; D Kretzmer 'Human rights, state reports' in Wolfrum (n 1 above) para 28; D McGoldrick *The Human Rights Committee – Its role in the development of the ICCPR* (1994) 151; M Nowak *CCPR commentary* (2005) article 5 OP para 39.

39 Buergenthal (n 38 above) 397; Tomuschat (n 38 above) para 14; Staberock (n 4 above) paras 10 & 11.

40 General Comment 33 (2008) UN Doc CCPR/C/GC/33 paras 14 & 15.

41 ICCPR (n 5 above) (25 November 1993), CERD (n 12 above) (30 August 2001), CEDAW (n 13 above) (15 January 2002), CAT (19 October 2001) (n 7 above), CRPD (n 10 above) (24 February 2009), CPED (n 8 above) (26 June 2012) and most recently CRC (n 9 above) (28 February 2013).

42 Fewer than 25 decisions have been adopted following individual complaints lodged against Germany, most of them by CCPR.

43 *Abichou* CAT (27 June 2013) CAT/C/50/D/430/2010; *TBB-Turkish Union in Berlin/ Brandenburg* CERD (10 May 2013) CERD/C/82/D/48/2010; *M.G.* CCPR (23 July 2008) CCPR/C/93/D/1482/2006; *Gröninger* CRPD (4 April 2014) CRPD/C/11/D/ 2/2010.

44 Bundestagsdrucksache 17/9528 5.

45 CESR (24 September 2001) E/C.12/1/Add.68 paras 22 & 40; (12 July 2011) E/C.12/ DEU/CO/5 para 20.

in this respect. On the basis of the ECtHR's jurisprudence, the German Federal Administrative Court in a recent judgment has called on the legislator to bring German law in line with Convention standards.[46]

Compliance control mechanisms at the regional level

At the regional level, compliance control mechanisms are enhanced as all three regional systems have a human rights court that may issue final and binding decisions (the European Court of Human Rights, the African Court on Human and Peoples' Rights and the Inter-American Court of Human Rights). The Inter-American and the African system in addition have human rights commissions that investigate and screen claims of rights violations and also play a role in the court procedure.[47] In the Inter-American system, cases may only be brought before the IACtHR by the Inter-American Commission on Human Rights or states.[48] In the African system, access to the Court is open to the African Commission on Human and Peoples' Rights, states and African Inter-Governmental organisations and, in case the state against which the case is brought has made a separate declaration, NGO's with observer status before the ACommHPR as well as individuals.[49] In the European system, states and individuals may bring applications to the ECtHR.[50]

Germany as a state party to the ECHR comes under the jurisdiction of the ECtHR. In 2012, 1494 applications were lodged against Germany before the ECtHR. In the years from 1959 to 2010, about 99 per cent of applications lodged against Germany were declared inadmissible or were struck out of the list of cases. A judgment was only issued in 1 per cent of the filed cases.[51] Of these judgments 66 per cent found a Convention

46 Bundesverwaltungsgericht (27 February 2014) (2014) 67 *Neue Juristische Wochenschrift* 2218.

47 On the Inter-American Commission on Human Rights, see American Convention on Human Rights IACHR (22 November 1969) arts 34ff; for the mandate of the African Commission on Human and Peoples' rights, see African Charter on Human and Peoples' Rights (ACHPR) (Banjul Charter) (27 June 1981, CAB/LEG/67/3 rev. 5, 21 I.L.M. 58) art 45.

48 IACHR (n 47 above) art 61 para 1.

49 Protocol to the African Charter on Human and Peoples' Rights on the Establishment of an African Court on Human and Peoples' Rights (10 June 1998) art 5. Seven states have made a declaration under art 5 para 3, art 34 para 6 of the Protocol.

50 ECHR (n 26 above) arts 33 & 34.

51 ECtHR 'Statistics on judgments by state, 1959-2010'. http://www.echr.coe.int/Documents/Stats_violation_1959_2010_ENG.pdf (accessed 15 April 2015) 18. For the period from 1959 to 2013 this corresponds in numbers to 263 judgments, 173 thereof finding a Convention violation, 67 finding no violation, 10 friendly settlements or striking out judgments and 13 other judgments. See ECtHR 'Violations by article and by state, 1959-2013' http://www.echr.coe.int/Documents/Stats_violation_1959_2013_ENG.pdf (accessed 15 April 2015).

violation.[52] Over 50 per cent of judgments finding a Convention violation concerned the length of proceedings (article 6 of the ECHR). Ten per cent concerned the right to respect for private and family life (article 8), 9 per cent the right to liberty and security (article 5), 10 per cent the right to fair trial (article 6) and 20 per cent other rights.[53] The important number of applications concerning the length of proceedings is due to the fact that Germany did not have an effective remedy in place against excessive length of judicial proceedings. After a pilot judgment by the Court in 2010,[54] this situation was remedied by law in 2011 (→ 4.4.1). Subsequently, the Court declared new applications complaining about the length of judicial proceedings inadmissible for non-exhaustion of domestic remedies.[55] It is thus to be expected that the number of judgments against Germany that find Convention violations will decrease. In 2013, 6 judgments were issued in proceedings against Germany, 3 of them finding a Convention violation.[56]

In Germany, activities with respect to compliance control are centred in the Federal Ministry of Justice and Consumer Protection in the hands of the Commissioner for Human Rights Issues. The Commissioner is the agent of the Federal Government to the ECtHR and is also in charge of handling individual complaint proceedings before UN treaty bodies for the Federal Government. In addition, the Commissioner compiles many of the periodic reports that have to be submitted to the UN treaty bodies.

3 Germany's participation in international lawmaking

In the light of recent German history it is a declared aim of German foreign policy to actively further the development of international human rights law and to serve as role model in the implementation of existing standards. Germany thus participates actively in international law-making in the field of human rights. Recent examples of strong German involvement include the preparations for CRPD and the Optional Protocol to CESCR.

In the same vein, Germany strives to reduce the number of reservations and declarations with respect to human rights treaties. In 2010, a controversial declaration made upon ratification of CRC was withdrawn, according to which the rights contained in the CRC were not directly applicable in Germany (→ 4.2). Germany maintains reservations/

52 ECtHR (n 51 above) 11.
53 ECtHR (n 51 above) 4.
54 *Rumpf v Germany* App no 46344/06 (ECtHR, 2 September 2010).
55 For example *Schellmann and JSP Programmentwicklung GmbH & Co KG v Germany* App no 27366/07 (ECtHR, 10 July 2012).
56 *Glien v Germany* App no 7345/12 (ECtHR, 28 November 2013); *HW v Germany* App no 17167/11 (ECtHR, 19 September 2013); *BB and FB v Germany* App nos 18734/09 & 9424/11 (ECtHR, 14 March 2013).

declarations to CCPR[57] and its first protocol,[58] CEDAW,[59] CAT[60] and CPED[61] and to the first protocol to CRC.[62] Concerning the ECHR,

57 '(1) Articles 19, 21 and 22 in conjunction with article 2(1) of the Covenant shall be applied within the scope of article 16 of the Convention of 4 November 1950 for the Protection of Human Rights and Fundamental Freedoms. (2) Article 14(3)(d) of the Covenant shall be applied in such manner that it is for the court to decide whether an accused person held in custody has to appear in person at the hearing before the court of review (Revisionsgericht). (3) Article 14(5) of the Covenant shall be applied in such manner that: (a) A further appeal does not have to be instituted in all cases solely on the grounds the accused person having been acquitted by the lower court-was convicted for the first time in the proceedings concerned by the appellate court. (b) In the case of criminal offences of minor gravity the review by a higher tribunal of a decision not imposing imprisonment does not have to be admitted in all cases. (4) Article 15(1) of the Covenant shall be applied in such manner that when provision is made by law for the imposition of a lighter penalty the hitherto applicable law may for certain exceptional categories of cases remain applicable to criminal offences committed before the law was amended.'

58 'The Federal Republic of Germany formulates a reservation concerning article 5 paragraph 2(a) to the effect that the competence of the Committee shall not apply to communications (a) which have already been considered under another procedure of international investigation or settlement, or (b) by means of which a violation of rights is reprimanded having its origin in events occurring prior to the entry into force of the Optional Protocol for the Federal Republic of Germany (c) by means of which a violation of article 26 of the [said Covenant] is reprimanded, if and insofar as the reprimanded violation refers to rights other than those guaranteed under the aforementioned Covenant.'

59 Declaration: 'The right of peoples to self-determination, as enshrined in the Charter of the United Nations and in the International Covenants of 19 December 1966, applies to all peoples and not only to those living 'under alien and colonial domination and foreign occupation'. All peoples thus have the inalienable right freely to determine their political status and freely to pursue their economic, social and cultural development. The Federal Republic of Germany would be unable to recognize as legally valid an interpretation of the right to self-determination which contradicts the unequivocal wording of the Charter of the United Nations and of the two International Covenants of 19 December 1966 on Civil and Political Rights and on Economic, Social and Cultural Rights. It will interpret the 11th paragraph of the Preamble accordingly.'

60 Art 3 – 'This provision prohibits the transfer of a person directly to a State where this person is exposed to a concrete danger of being subjected to torture. In the opinion of the Federal Republic of Germany, article 3 as well as the other provisions of the Convention exclusively establish State obligations that are met by the Federal Republic of Germany in conformity with the provisions of its domestic law which is in accordance with the Convention.'

61 Declarations: 'Article 16 - The prohibition of return shall only apply if the person concerned faces a real risk of being subjected to enforced disappearance. Regarding Art. 17 (2) (f) - Under German law it is guaranteed that deprivation of liberty is only lawful if it has been ordered by a court or – in exceptional cases –subsequently authorized by a court. Article 104 para 2 of the Basic Law (Grundgesetz) expressly provides: 'Only a judge may rule upon the permissibility or continuation of any deprivation of liberty. If such a deprivation is not based on a judicial order, a judicial decision shall be obtained without delay'. Article 104 para 3 of the Basic Law provides that a person who has been provisionally arrested on suspicion of having committed a criminal offence 'shall be brought before a judge no later than the day following the arrest'. In the event that a person is being held arbitrarily in contravention of article 104 of the Basic Law, anyone can bring about a judicial decision leading to that person's release by applying to the competent Local Court for his/her immediate release. If the person concerned has been detained beyond the time limit permissible under the Basic Law, the court has to order that person's release pursuant to section 128 (2), first sentence, of the Code of Criminal Procedure (Strafprozessordnung, StPO). Article 17 para 3 – In the case of an involuntary placement of sick persons by a custodian or a person having power of attorney, the information required under letters (a) to (h) is known to the court which authorizes the placement. The court can

Germany does not have any reservations, but has made a number of declarations concerning certain additional protocols.[63]

4 Incorporation of international human rights obligations into the German legal order

4.1 Germany's mitigated dualism

Neither the ECHR nor the UN human rights treaties oblige states to accord

ascertain the information required under letters (a) to (h) at any time through the custodian or person having power of attorney; the information is then included in the case-file. This information is also to be regarded as records within the meaning of article 17 para 3. Regarding article 18 – Under German law, all persons with a legitimate interest are entitled to obtain information from the court files. The restrictions provided for in German law for the protection of the interests of the person concerned or for safeguarding the criminal proceedings are permissible pursuant to article 20 para 1 of the Convention. Regarding article 24 para 4 – It is clarified that the envisaged provision on reparation and compensation does not abrogate the principle of state immunity.'

62 Declaration: 'The Federal Republic of Germany declares that it considers a minimum age of 17 years to be binding for the voluntary recruitment of soldiers into its armed forces under the terms of article 3 paragraph 2 of the Optional Protocol. Persons under the age of 18 years shall be recruited into the armed forces solely for the purpose of commencing military training. The protection of voluntary recruits under the age of 18 years in connection with their decision to join the armed forces is ensured by the need to obtain the consent of their legal guardian and the indispensable requirement that they present an identification card or passport as a reliable proof of their age.'

63 First Protocol, declaration with respect to article 2 upon ratification: 'The Federal Republic of Germany adopts the opinion according to which the second sentence of article 2 of the (First) Protocol entails no obligation on the part of the State to finance schools of a religious or philosophical nature, or to assist in financing such schools, since this question, as confirmed by the concurring declaration of the Legal Committee of the Consultative Assembly and the Secretary General of the Council of Europe, lies outside the scope of the Convention for the Protection of Human Rights and Fundamental Freedoms and of its Protocol.'

Protocol no 6, declaration at time of ratification: 'In connection with the deposit of the instrument of ratification to Protocol No 6 of 28 April 1983 to the Convention for the Protection of Human Rights and Fundamental Freedoms concerning the Abolition of the Death Penalty I have the honour to declare on behalf of the Government of the Federal Republic of Germany that, in its view, the obligations deriving from Protocol no 6 are confined to the abolition of the death penalty within the Protocol's area of application in the respective State and that national non-criminal legislation is not affected. The Federal Republic of Germany has already met its obligations under the Protocol by means of article 102 of the Basic Law.'

Protocol no 7 at time of signature: '(1) By "criminal offence" and "offence" in articles 2 to 4 of the present Protocol, the Federal Republic of Germany understands only such acts as are criminal offences under its law. (2) The Federal Republic of Germany applies article 2(1) to convictions or sentences in the first instance only, it being possible to restrict review to errors in law and to hold such reviews in camera; in addition, it understands that the application of article 2.1 is not dependent on the written judgment of the previous instance being translated into a language other than the language used in court. (3) The Federal Republic of Germany understands the words "according to the law or the practice of the State concerned" to mean that article 3 refers only to the retrial provided for in sections 359 et seq. of the Code of Criminal Procedure. (cf *Strafprozessordnung*).'

a specific status to the treaties in their national law.[64] Nevertheless, UN treaty bodies have expressed the view that domestic law should ensure that UN treaties take precedence over ordinary laws.[65] The CRC has gone so far as to recommend that Germany consider the incorporation of CRC into the Basic Law.[66]

Customary human rights law is incorporated into the German legal system through article 25 of the Basic Law. Like all other international treaties, human rights treaties are incorporated into national law by a *Zustimmungsgesetz* (→ Vöneky/Wolfrum). As a consequence, they have the status of an ordinary federal law. They trump earlier federal laws and laws enacted by the *Länder*. In theory, however, higher-ranking law such as the Constitution as well as posterior law may deviate from the rights contained in these treaties. To avoid that consequence, several authors have argued for a supra-legislative or even constitutional rank of the ECHR in the German norm hierarchy,[67] but so far there is no consensus on this question and the Constitutional Court has explicitly declared that the ECHR does not have constitutional status.[68] It has, however, based on the openness of the German Constitution to international law, accepted for the first time in 1987 that the ECHR may be taken into account in the interpretation of the constitutional fundamental rights.[69]

The Constitutional Court clarified the significance of this jurisprudence in the *Görgülü* judgment in 2004.[70] In this case, the ECtHR had found a violation of article 8 of the ECHR because German courts had refused a natural father custody of and access rights to his child born out of wedlock which was in the care of foster parents.[71] The Strasbourg Court held that Germany was under an obligation to make it possible for the applicant at least to have access to his child. In further proceedings at

64 Staberock (n 4 above) para 20; P-M Dupuy 'International law and domestic (municipal) law' in Wolfrum (n 1 above) para 122. Seibert-Fohr argues for an obligation to provide the CCPR with constitutional rank, see A Seibert-Fohr 'Domestic implementation of the International Covenant on Civil and Political Rights pursuant to its article 2 para 2' (2001) *Max Planck Yearbook of United Nations Law* 399 439ff.

65 See for example CRC (31 January 2014) UN Doc CRC/C/DEU/CO/3-4 para 10.

66 CRC (26 February 2004) UN Doc CRC/C/15/Add. 226 para 10(a).

67 F Hoffmeister 'Die Europäische Menschenrechtskonvention als Grundrechtsverfassung und ihre Bedeutung in Deutschland' (2001) 40 *Der Staat* 349 367ff; JA Frowein 'Das Bundesverfassungsgericht und die Europäische Menschenrechtskonvention' in W Fürst et al (eds) *Festschrift für Wolfgang Zeidler* (1987) 1763 1768ff.

68 BVerfG Case 2 BvR 1481/04 (14 October 2004) 111 *Entscheidungen des Bundesverfassungsgerichts* 307, translation available http://www.bverfg.de/entscheidungen/rs20041014_2bvr148104en.html (accessed 15 April 2015) para 31.

69 BVerfG Case 2 BvR 589/79 *inter alia* (26 March 1987) (1987) 74 *Entscheidungen des Bundesverfassungsgerichts* 358 370.

70 BVerfG Case 2 BvR 1481/04 (n 68 above). On the judgment see F Hoffmeister 'Germany: Status of European Convention on Human Rights in domestic law' (2006) 4 *International Journal of Constitutional Law* 722; H Sauer 'Die neue Schlagkraft der gemeineuropäischen Grundrechtsjudikatur' (2005) 65 *Zeitschrift für ausländisches öffentliches Recht und Völkerrecht* 35.

71 *Görgülü v Germany* App no 74969/01 (ECtHR, 26 February 2004).

national level following the ECtHR judgment the Naumburg Court of Appeal revoked an interim measure by a lower court that had granted the applicant the right to see his son on a weekly basis for as long as proceedings remained pending. It considered that German courts were not bound by decisions of the ECtHR.[72] On the constitutional complaint of the applicant, the Constitutional Court quashed the decision of the Naumburg Court of Appeal. It confirmed that

> the guarantees of the Convention influence the interpretation of the fundamental rights and constitutional principles of the Basic Law. The text of the Convention and the case-law of the European Court of Human Rights serve, on the level of constitutional law, as guides to interpretation in determining the content and scope of fundamental rights and constitutional principles of the Basic Law ...

In practice this means that 'as long as applicable methodological standards leave scope for interpretation and weighing of interests, German courts must give precedence to interpretation in accordance with the Convention'.[73]

According to the Constitutional Court, all state authorities, including the courts, have a constitutional duty to take into account the Convention and relevant jurisprudence by the ECtHR. This obligation is based on article 1(2) together with article 59(2) of the Basic Law and thus is of constitutional nature. It is therefore possible, as recognised by the Constitutional Court for the first time in *Görgülü*, to base a constitutional complaint on the allegation that a state authority did not properly take into account an ECtHR judgment.[74]

The *Görgülü* judgment has been lauded as sending an important signal for a better implementation of the ECHR in Germany. This message has been blurred however by certain passages that emphasise the limits on the openness of the Basic Law to international law:

> The Basic Law aims to integrate Germany into the legal community of peaceful and free states, but does not waive the sovereignty contained in the last instance in the German constitution. There is therefore no contradiction with the aim of commitment to international law if the legislature, exceptionally, does not comply with the law of international agreements, provided this is the only way in which a violation of fundamental principles of the constitution can be averted.[75]

72 Oberlandesgericht Naumburg Case 14 WF 64/04 (30 Juni 2004) (2004) 31 *Europäische Grundrechte Zeitschrift* 598.
73 BVerfG Case 2 BvR 1481/04 (n 68 above) para 62.
74 BVerfG Case 2 BvR 1481/04 (n 68 above) para 63.
75 BVerfG Case 2 BvR 1481/04 (n 68 above) para 35.

Other passages emphasise the limits on the effects of international judgments by calling on courts to make sure that the incorporation of a judgment by the ECtHR does not violate constitutional law:

> German courts must give precedence to interpretation in accordance with the Convention. The situation is different only if observing the decision of the ECHR, for example because the facts on which it is based have changed, clearly violates statute law to the contrary or German constitutional provisions, in particular also the fundamental rights of third parties. 'Take into account' means taking notice of the Convention provision as interpreted by the ECHR and applying it to the case, provided the application does not violate prior-ranking law, in particular constitutional law.[76]

The strong wording used by the Court in this context was read by some as an invitation to open revolt against the Strasbourg court and as a reaction to the ECtHR's *von Hannover* judgment where the ECtHR differed from the opinion of the Federal Constitutional Court.[77] In a later judgment on preventive detention, however, the Constitutional Court, while reaffirming the principle of the German Constitution's last word, has used much less confrontational language and emphasised the idea of an open dialogue between itself and the ECtHR:

> The domestic effects of judgments by the ECtHR are not limited ... to a duty to take into account, for the Basic Law aims ... to avoid conflict between international obligations of the Federal Republic of Germany and national law. The openness of the Basic Law to international law thus expresses an understanding of sovereignty which not only opposes international and supranational integration; it presupposes and expects it. Against this background, the German Constitution's 'last word' does not exclude an international and European dialogue of courts but rather constitutes its normative foundation.[78]

76 BVerfG Case 2 BvR 1481/04 (n 68 above) para 62: '[...] German courts must give precedence to interpretation in accordance with the Convention. The situation is different only if observing the decision of the ECHR, for example because the facts on which it is based have changed, clearly violates statute law to the contrary or German constitutional provisions, in particular also the fundamental rights of third parties. "Take into account" means taking notice of the Convention provision as interpreted by the ECHR and applying it to the case, provided the application does not violate prior-ranking law, in particular constitutional law.'

77 See Hoffmeister (n 67 above) 729; E Lambert Abdelgawad & A Weber 'The reception process in France and Germany' in H Keller & A Stone Sweet (eds) *A Europe of rights* (2008) 137. This interpretation was dominant in newspaper articles on the decision, see the references in Sauer (n 70 above) 38 note 9.

78 BVerfG Case 2 BvR 2365/09 *inter alia* (4 May 2011) (2011) 128 *Entscheidungen des Bundesverfassungsgerichts* 326 para 89. On this judgment see U Volkmann 'Fremdbestimmung – Selbstbehauptung – Befreiung' (2001) 56 *JuristenZeitung* 836; M Payandeh & H Sauer 'Menschenrechtskonforme Auslegung als Verfassungsmehrwert: Konvergenzen von Grundgesetz und EMRK im Urteil des Bundesverfassungsgerichts zur Sicherungsverwahrung' (2012) 34 *Juristische Ausbildung* 289; A Zimmermann *Grundrechtsschutz zwischen Karlsruhe und Straßburg* (2012) 31ff; M Andenas & E Bjorge 'Preventive detention' (2011) 105 *American Journal of International Law* 768.

This case was particularly delicate: Prior to the ECtHR judgment the Constitutional Court had held that the legislation that eliminated a ten-year maximum period for preventive detention not only for the future but also for old cases was constitutional.[79] The ECtHR then held these same provisions to be incompatible with the ECHR. When seized with the question again after the ECtHR judgment, the Constitutional Court did not decline review on the basis of the principle of finality of Constitutional Court decisions, but held that ECtHR decision constituted legally relevant changes that allowed a new decision by the Constitutional Court. It then came to the conclusion that the legal provisions criticised by the ECtHR were incompatible with the German Constitution.

The Federal Constitutional Court has clarified in recent decisions that the principles developed in the *Görgüglü* decision also apply to other international human rights treaties.[80]

4.2 Legislative implementation

Where national law is incompatible with provisions of an international human rights treaty, national legislation is necessary to implement the treaty.[81] Implementing legislation may also be necessary if a treaty explicitly requires legislation (for example, specific criminal law provisions and remedies). Positive obligations inherent in human rights treaties may also trigger the need for legislation. Legislation that is adopted to implement a decision of a human rights treaty body will be dealt with separately (→ 4.4).

In Germany, when the executive proposes the law that allows ratification of an international treaty, it summarises the treaty concerned, explains how the provisions are implemented in German law and examines if German law is compatible with the treaty.[82] Legislative practice with respect to human rights treaties suggests that these are only ratified if the executive and the majority parties are convinced that national law conforms with the treaty and does not require changes. This conviction is sometimes held even in the face of broad opposition. Whereas the opposition parties and all experts consulted by Parliament for instance held that the ratification of the European Convention against Human Trafficking made legislative changes necessary, the majority maintained their conviction that domestic law was already consistent with

79 BVerfG Case 2 BvR 2029/01 (5 February 2004) (2004) 108 *Entscheidungen des Bundesverfassungsgerichts* 133.

80 For the CRPD BVerfG Case 2 BvR 882/08 (23 March 2011) (2011) 128 *Entscheidungen des Bundesverfassungsgerichts* 282 369 para 52. For the CRC see BVerwG Case 1 B 22.10 (10 February 2011).

81 On the need for implementing legislation see Staberock (n 4 above) paras 23 & 24.

82 See for example Bundestagsdrucksache 16/12592 for CPED.

the Convention and that the proposed changes were not mandatory, but would only further the realisation of Convention rights.[83]

In two cases (CRC and CAT), Germany has made a declaration to the effect that amendments of national law were not required to implement the treaty.[84] The declaration made upon ratification of CRC also stated that the Convention did not apply directly in Germany.[85] In spite of the Government's opinion that CRC standards were implemented in Germany and that no amendments or reforms were necessary,[86] the *Länder* feared that German courts would force implementing measures on them in certain cases and exerted pressure on the Federal Government to make the said declaration.[87] In 2010, the declaration was withdrawn.

Sometimes, the assessment whether legislative amendments are necessary changes over time as the example of CRPD shows: Whereas the executive initially was of the opinion that German law already fulfilled all of the requirements of the Convention,[88] it now recognises the need for further legislation. This is evident in the different action plans at federal and *Länder* level that contain ambitious goals and implementation measures. Several states have stated the need for an all-encompassing review of existing statutes, some have already conducted this review and the *Land* Berlin has asked the monitoring mechanism (→ 4.5.1) for a review of all state legislation as to its conformity with CRPD.[89] If the measures proposed in the different action plans are adopted, they will lead

83 See Bundestagsdrucksache 17/10165.

84 CAT: '[...] In the opinion of the Federal Republic of Germany, article 3 as well as the other provisions of the Convention exclusively establish State obligations that are met by the Federal Republic of Germany in conformity with the provisions of its domestic law which is in accordance with the Convention."; CRC: "[...] The Federal Republic of Germany also declares that domestically the Convention does not apply directly. It establishes state obligations under international law that the Federal Republic of Germany fulfils in accordance with its national law, which conforms with the Convention.'

85 The legal relevance of this declaration has been commented on divergently. Some authors consider the declaration to be irrelevant according to international law (RA Lorz & H Sauer 'Kinderrechte ohne Vorbehalt' (2011) 16 *MenschenRechtsMagazin* 5 6; A Lorz *Der Vorrang des Kindeswohls nach Art. 3 der UN-Kinderrechtskonvention in der deutschen Rechtsordnung* (2003) 25ff) Other qualify the declaration as a reservation (A Zimmermann 'Neuere Entwicklungen zum Verhältnis zwischen dem UN-Abkommen über die Rechte des Kindes und nationalem Familienrecht' (1996) *Praxis des internationalen Privat- und Verfahrensrechts* 167 173) that is incompatible with the Vienna Convention on the Law of Treaties (W Ullmann 'Verfassungs- und völkerrechtliche Widersprüche bei der Ratifikation der UNO-Kinderrechtskonvention' (1991) 38 *Zeitschrift für das gesamte Familienrecht* 898 899; J Wolf 'Ratifizierung unter Vorbehalten' (1991) 24 *Zeitschrift für Rechtspolitik* 374 378. See also E Peter 'Der Vorrang des Kindeswohls' (2005) 43 *Archiv des Völkerrechts* 257 261ff).

86 Bundestagsdrucksache 12/42, 32.

87 See Lorz & Sauer (n 85 above) 5.

88 Deutsches Institut für Menschenrechte 'Expertise für ein Artikelgesetz zur Umsetzung der UN-Behindertenrechtskonvention im Land Berlin' (2013) http://www.institut-fuer-menschenrechte.de/uploads/tx_commerce/Expertise_fuer_ein_Artikelgesetz_zur_Umsetzung_der_UN_Behindertenrechtskonvention_im_Land_Berlin_01.pdf (accessed 18 May 2015) 4.

89 Deutsches Institut für Menschenrechte (n 88 above) 5.

to substantive changes in German law. They imply for instance a major overhaul of the current education system. Insofar, the action plans are an encouraging sign for the willingness in Germany to adopt legislation to implement international human rights treaties even if this involves systemic changes and means breaking with traditions.

As noted before, Germany regularly complies with its reporting obligations under the different UN treaties and is in constant dialogue with the respective treaty bodies about necessary legislative amendments or desirable new legislation to further the realisation of treaty rights. Practice has shown, however, that the non-binding pronouncements by UN treaty bodies do not *per se* lead to the adoption of new legislation in Germany. New legislation is either passed when binding European Union law or binding pronouncements of the ECJ or the ECtHR oblige Germany to do so or when the social climate has developed in such a way that public opinion demands adoption of a specific law. A comprehensive anti-discrimination legislation covering in particular discrimination in the private sector for example had long been called for by CERD.[90] For years, there were discussions about the adoption of such a law, but it was only after binding EU legislation created the need for a law, that the Anti-Discrimination Act was adopted in 2006. This situation has been addressed by UN treaty bodies. CEDAW in particular has expressed concern that the Convention has not received the same degree of visibility and importance as regional legal instruments, particularly EU directives, and that it is not cited regularly as legal basis for legislation for the elimination of discrimination against women.[91] The legitimacy of this concern notwithstanding, it should not be inferred that recommendations are irrelevant for Germany. They serve as a basis for discussion, and are an important tool for NGOs active in the field to influence public opinion and exert pressure on the Government to initiate reform.[92]

4.3 The role of courts in the implementation of international law

For years, references to international human rights treaties by German courts were a rare occurrence.[93] This was due not only to a lack of knowledge on the part of judges but also to the conviction that the detailed human rights catalogue of the Basic Law already ensured such a strong human rights protection that it was not imaginable that international

90 See for example CERD (23 April 1997) UN Doc CERD/C/304/Add.24 para 20.
91 CEDAW (30 January 2004) UN Doc CEDAW/C/2004/I/CRP.3/add.6/Rev.1 para 26.
92 In this sense see Kretzmer (n 38 above) para 28.
93 B Simma et al 'The role of German courts in the enforcement of international human rights' in B Conforti & F Francioni (eds) *Enforcing international human rights in domestic courts* (1997) 71 72f. For the ECtHR see R Uerpmann *Die Europäische Menschenrechtskonvention und die deutsche Rechtsprechung* (1993).

instruments could go beyond that standard.[94] This changed in the middle of the 1990s. Since then, the number of references to the ECHR and the ECtHR has grown exponentially.[95] But not only the quantity, the quality of references has changed as well. Today, more and more courts rather than merely referring to the ECHR analyse the ECtHR's jurisprudence in detail and explain extensively how the jurisprudence is to be applied to the specific circumstances of the case.[96] Not in every case is the jurisprudence of the Court followed,[97] but in general the ECHR and the Court's jurisprudence do serve as a normative point of reference for German courts.[98]

The positive trend in the reference to the ECHR by German courts is not mirrored with respect to UN human rights treaties, however. As a matter of fact, UN human rights treaties are still rarely referred to by German courts.[99] There are exceptions[100] – the CRPD in particular has been referred to in a number of recent court decisions.[101] But very often, UN human rights treaties are not mentioned at all. Even courts that refer to the ECHR tend to ignore them. In the already mentioned proceedings on the right to strike for civil servants for instance, courts have extensively reviewed the ECtHR's jurisprudence on this question,[102] but have not even mentioned the CESCR, although the Committee on Economic, Social and Cultural Rights has repeatedly stated that the prohibition by Germany of strikes by public servants other than those who provide essential services is not compatible with article 8 of the CESCR.[103]

If UN human rights treaties are mentioned, courts often conclude that they are irrelevant for the case at hand. With regard to the CRPD courts have held, for example, that the federal *Zustimmungsgesetz* only

94 Simma et al (n 93 above) 107ff.

95 C Walter 'Nationale Durchsetzung' in R Grote & T Marauhn *EMRK/GG Konkordanzkommentar* (2013) para 3. See also Institut International des Droits de l'Homme *Die Rechtsprechung des Europäischen Gerichtshofs für Menschenrechte im Bundesgerichtshof und Bundesverfassungsgericht* (2012) http://www.iidh.org/upload/files/Bericht%20komplett%207.pdf (accessed 15 April 2015).

96 The Federal Constitutional Court has explicitly stated that ECtHR judgments have to be taken into account not only in the concrete case decided by the Court, but also in parallel cases, see BVerfG Case 2 BvR 2365/09 (n 78 above) para 89.

97 For a detailed analysis of the jurisprudence of federal courts see Walter (n 95 above) paras 8ff.

98 Walter (n 95 above) para 47.

99 This has been the object of criticism by UN treaty bodies, see for example CESCR (24 September 2001) UN Doc E/C.12/1/Add 68 para 13.

100 See for example BVerfG Case 1 BvL 10/10 & 1 BvL 2/11 (18 July 2012) (2012) 31 *Neue Zeitschrift für Verwaltungsrecht* 1024 1026; BVerwG Case 1 B 22.10 (n 80 above).

101 V Aichele 'Die UN-Behindertenrechtskonvention in der gerichtlichen Praxis' (2011) *Anwaltsblatt* 727 728ff. Most recently BAG Case 6 AZR 190/12 (19 December 2013) (2014) 69 *Arbeit und Arbeitsrecht* 112.

102 BVerwG Case (27 February 2014) (n 46 above); Oberverwaltungsgericht Nordrhein-Westfalen 3d A 317/11.0 (7 March 2012) (2012) 31 *Neue Zeitschrift für Verwaltungsrecht* 890; Verwaltungsgericht Düsseldorf Case 31 K 3904/10.0 (15 December 2010) (2011) 59 *Arbeit und Recht* 74.

103 CESCR (12 July 2011) UN Doc E/C.12/DEU/CO/5 para 20.

incorporates the parts of the treaty into German law that concern competencies of the federal state and that the *Länder* would need to adopt their own laws to incorporate the treaty into the law of the *Land*.[104] This jurisprudence has been the subject of critical reviews.[105] It has been held to be inconsistent with the jurisprudence of the German Constitutional Court. The *Zustimmungsgesetz* obliges all state authorities to apply the treaty irrespective of whether the federation or the *Länder* have jurisdiction in the areas covered by the treaty.[106] Who has jurisdiction only becomes relevant if legislation needs to be adopted to implement the treaty.

Another argument German courts often use to explain why a UN human rights treaty is irrelevant is the absence of directly applicable provisions. With reference to article 2 of the CESCR, some German courts have thus stated the view that the Covenant does not contain self-executing rights.[107] German administrative courts have denied the self-executing nature of CRPD provisions in view of article 4, paragraph 2 of the CRPD.[108] So far, superior courts have not answered this question authoritatively for these two treaties.[109] The restrictive position of courts with respect to direct application of treaties has been commented on critically. Most authors have argued that the question of direct application cannot be decided for a treaty as a whole but has to be examined on a case-by-case basis for each right separately.[110] The provisions that were the

104 See for example Hessischer Verwaltungsgerichtshof (12 November 2009) (2010) 23 *Neue Zeitschrift für Verwaltungsrecht Rechtsprechungs-Report* 602; Oberverwaltungsgericht Lüneburg Case 2 ME 278/10 (16 September 2010); BVerwG Case 6 B 52/09 (18 January 2010) para 8.

105 See for example Monitoring-Stelle zur UN-Behindertenrechtskonvention 'Stellung der Behindertenrechtskonvention innerhalb der deutschen Rechtsordnung und ihre Bedeutung für behördliche Verfahren und deren gerichtliche Überprüfung' (2010) http://www.institut-fuer-menschenrechte.de/uploads/tx_commerce/stellungnahme_der_monitoring_stelle_z_un_behindertenrechtskonvention_zur_stellung_der_behinder tenrechtskonvention_innerhalb_der_dt_rechtsordnung.pdf (accessed 15 April 2015) 10ff; V Aichele (n 101 above) 730 with further references; J von Bernstorff 'Anmerkung zur innerstaatlichen Anwendbarkeit ratifizierter Menschenrechtsverträge' (2011) *Recht der Jugend und des Bildungswesens* 203 206ff.

106 Von Bernstorff (n 105 above) 207. For a different opinion see U Fastenrath & T Groh 'Artikel 59' in Friauf & Höfling (eds) *Berliner Kommentar zum Grundgesetz* (2010) para 99; E Riedel 'Im Zweifel Inklusion: Zuweisung an eine Förderschule nach Inkrafttreten der BRK' (2010) 29 *Neue Zeitschrift für Verwaltungsrecht* 1346.

107 See for example Verwaltungsgerichtshof Baden-Württemberg Case 9 S 2163/90 (17 December 1991) (1993) *Zeitschrift für das gesamte Familienrecht* 828; Verwaltungsgerichtshof Baden-Württemberg Case 10 S 1666/90 (31 March 1992) (1993) 6 *Neue Zeitschrift für Verwaltungsrecht Rechtsprechungs-Report* 83; Verwaltungsgerichtshof Nordrhein-Westfalen Case 15 A 1596/07 (9 October 2007) (2007) 122 *Deutsches Verwaltungsblatt* 1442.

108 See for example Hessischer Verwaltungsgerichtshof Case 7 B 2763/09 (12 November 2009) (2010) 63 *Die öffentliche Verwaltung* 325.

109 See BVerwG Case 6 C 8.09 (15 December 2010) para 30 which does not answer the question of the self-executing nature of Covenant rights. But see BVerwG Case 1 B 22.10 (n 80 above) para 4 which recognises the direct applicability of the CRC.

110 Lorz & Sauer (n 85 above) 7; Simma et al (n 93 above) 86; Riedel (n 106 above) 1347.

object of the decisions are generally held to be self-executing.[111] In addition, it has been pointed out that direct application of a treaty and the use of a treaty in the interpretation of national law should be distinguished and that the latter application does not require the strict criteria for direct applicability to be fulfilled.[112]

Recent years have seen a positive trend in the number of references to the ECHR even if there is still room for improvement. UN human rights treaties in contrast play only a marginal role in German jurisprudence. The main reason for this situation certainly is the existence of the detailed human rights catalogue in the Basic Law. There is also still a lack of knowledge and expertise about international human rights treaties in German courts. Hopefully, this situation will improve. The executive in any case has deployed considerable efforts to make international human rights treaties more accessible (→ 4.5.3). In addition, *amicus curiae* briefs by the national human rights monitoring mechanisms seem to be an efficient way to draw the courts' attention to the significance of international human rights treaties for their proceedings (→ 4.5.1).

4.4 Implementation of decisions by international human rights treaty bodies

The following section examines how decisions of international human rights treaty bodies against Germany that find a human rights violation are implemented. The focus is on judgments by the ECtHR. So far, only four decisions by UN human rights treaty bodies have found a treaty violation by Germany. Although UN treaty bodies' decisions are non-binding, the German Government has made clear that Germany intends to cooperate with treaty bodies in the implementation of their decisions. This position has been followed through in the recent *TBB* case[113] even if strong reservations have been voiced with respect to the conclusions CERD has come to.[114]

If a ECtHR judgment affords just satisfaction (article 41 of the ECHR) to the applicant, Germany is bound by international law to pay the required sum to the applicant. This is done by the Federation's executive.

111 For art 24 CPED Monitoring-Stelle zur UN-Behindertenrechtskonvention (n 105 above); Von Bernstorff (n 105 above) 203; Riedel (n 106 above) 1347ff. See also P Masuch 'Die UN-Behindertenrechtskonvention anwenden!' in C Hohmann-Dennhardt et al (eds) *Festschrift für Renate Jaeger: Grundrechte und solidarität* (2011) 245.
112 Aichele (n 101 above) 730.
113 n 43 above.
114 See Bundestagsdrucksache 18/60 (18 November 2013) 3; M Payandeh 'Die Entscheidung des UN-Ausschusses gegen Rassendiskrminierung im Fall Sarrazin' (2013) 67 *JuristenZeitung* 980; C Tomuschat 'Der "Fall Sarrazin" vor dem UN-Rassendiskriminerungsausschuss' (2013) 40 *Europäische Grundrechtezeitschrift* 262.

In the relationship between the Federation and the *Länder*, the *Lastentragungsgesetz* determines how costs are to be divided.[115] If the Convention violation emanates from the sphere of a *Land*, the Federation may recover the sum from the *Land*.

Following a ECtHR judgment in which the ECtHR finds a Convention violation, the state has the obligation according to article 46 of the ECHR to put an end to the violation and make reparation for its consequences in such a way as to restore as far as possible the situation existing before the breach (*restitutio in integrum*).[116] The respondent state is free to choose the means by which it discharges the obligation. In a few cases, the Court has nevertheless ordered concrete measures to be taken by the state to fulfil its obligation under article 46.[117] To deal with repetitive cases, the Court has developed the pilot judgment technique.[118] The Court uses a pilot judgment to identify a structural problem in a state and order specific measures to be taken by the state to remedy the situation.

Whether legislation is required to put an end to the Convention violation and make reparation for its consequences depends on the nature of the violation. As a general rule, legislation will not be required if the violation is the result of the interpretation of a law that does not sufficiently take into account the ECHR. The judgment can then be implemented by interpreting the law in conformity with Convention standards.[119] If the law's wording itself clearly contravenes the Convention and does not give domestic courts the possibility to interpret the provision in conformity with the Convention, a legislative amendment becomes necessary.[120] In Germany, in addition, constitutional requirements have to be taken into account when deciding on the need to implement by legislation. Under German constitutional law, the principles of democracy and the rule of law require that the legislator itself enacts all provisions that are relevant for the realisation of fundamental rights and may not leave the determination of these provisions to the executive or the courts.[121] How detailed the legislator needs to be depends on how close the relevant cases are related to fundamental rights. In its decision on preventive detention for example,

115 On the Lastentragungsgesetz see N Wenzel 'Artikel 41' in U Karpenstein & FC Mayer *EMRK* (2012) 60.

116 J Meyer-Ladewig *EMRK* (2011) art 46 para 25.

117 See for example the above-mentioned *Görgülü* judgment (n 71 above) para 64. For other examples see M Breuer 'Artikel 46' in Karpenstein & Mayer (n 115 above) paras 9ff.

118 The technique was used for the first time by the Court in *Broniowski v Poland* App no 31443/96 (ECtHR Grand Chamber, 22 June 2004). On the pilot judgment technique see Breuer (n 117 above) paras 20ff; D Haider *The pilot-judgment procedure of the European Court of Human Rights* (2013).

119 Meyer-Ladewig (n 116 above) art 46 para 39.

120 C Grabenwarter & K Pabel *Europäische Menschenrechtskonvention* (2012) 104; Breuer (n 117 above) para 34; JA Frowein 'Artikel 46' in JA Frowein & W Peukert *Europäische Menschenrechtskonvention* (2009) para 7; Meyer-Ladewig (n 116 above) art 46 para 41.

121 BVerfG Case 1 BvR 402/87 (27 November 1990) (1991) 83 *Entscheidungen des Bundesverfassungsgerichts* 130 *(Josefine Mutzenbacher)* para 38.

the Constitutional Court has held that preventive detention has such repercussions on the right to personal freedom that legislation must determine all essential areas of executive and court action.[122]

4.4.1 Legislative implementation of decisions by a human rights treaty body

The German *Bundestag* has adopted a number of laws to implement decisions of the ECtHR. These include:[123]

- a law to strengthen the legal position of biological, non-legal fathers in the field of access and information rights;[124]
- an amendment of the Federal Hunting Act in order to allow property owners to oppose hunting on their premises for ethical reasons;[125]
- new rules on the execution of preventive detention orders and on the execution of prison sentences where preventive detention has been ordered or reserved;[126]
- an amendment of the Civil Code to allow fathers of children born out of wedlock to obtain joint parental custody without consent of the mother;[127]
- establishment of a legal remedy in the event of excessive length of judicial proceedings;[128]

122 BVerfG Case 2 BvR 2365/09 *inter alia* (n 78 above) para 110.

123 For examples see also Lambert Abdelgawad & Weber 'The reception process in France and Germany' in Keller & Stone Sweet (n 77 above) 133ff.

124 *Anayo v Germany* App no 20578/07 (ECtHR, 21 December 2010).

125 The Gesetz zur Änderung jagdrechtlicher Vorschriften (Bundesgesetzblatt 2013 I 1386) was adopted to implement *Herrmann v Germany* App no 9300/07 (ECtHR Grand Chamber, 26 June 2012). See action report of DD (2013)853 (12 July 2013) http://www.coe.int/t/dghl/monitoring/execution/Themes/Add_info/GER-ai_en.asp (accessed 15 April 2015).

126 The Gesetz zur Neuordnung der Sicherungsverwahrung und zu begleitenden Regelungen (Bundesgesetzblatt 2010 I 2300), the Gesetz zur Therapierung und Unterbringung psychisch gestörter Gewalttäter (Bundesgesetzblatt 2010 I 2300) and corresponding provisions at the level of the Länder (for an overview see action report DD (2013)1188 (26 September 2013) https://wcd.coe.int/com.instranet.InstraServlet?command=com.instranet.CmdBlobGet&InstranetImage=2391178&SecMode=1&DocId=2072220&Usage=2 (accessed 15 April 2015)) were adopted to implement *Mücke v Germany* App no 19359/04 (ECtHR, 17 December 2009) and 11 other judgments concerning the retroactive extension of preventive detention, or retroactive preventive detention orders.

127 *Zaunegger v Germany* App no 22028/04 (ECtHR, 3 December 2009).

128 The Gesetz über den Rechtsschutz bei überlangen Gerichtsverfahren und strafrechtlichen Ermittlungsverfahren (Bundesgesetzblatt 2011 I 2302) was adopted to implement *Sürmeli v Germany* App no 75529/01 (ECtHR Grand Chamber, 8 June 2006) and *Rumpf v Germany* (n 54 above).

- a law to eliminate the unequal treatment under the law of succession of children born outside marriage as compared with children born within marriage conveying in particular a statutory right of inheritance to children born outside of marriage in respect of their fathers and their parental relatives;[129]
- a law ensuring that in criminal proceedings, costs for an interpreter may only be imposed on the accused by the court if the accused incurred them unnecessarily by his own fault or in another culpable manner;[130] and
- an amendment of the Child Benefits Act to ensure foreigners with a temporary residence permit are entitled to child benefits.[131]

So far, all ECtHR judgments that necessitated legislation have been implemented. In some cases, this has been done reluctantly. The most blatant example is the law establishing a legal remedy in the event of excessive length of judicial proceedings. The law was only adopted after the Court issued its first and only pilot judgment against Germany. After the *Sürmeli* judgment in 2006 it was clear that a remedy was required in German law for cases in which judicial proceedings take too long.[132] A draft law had already been introduced in 2005, but the *Bundestag* refused to adopt the law and the draft was abandoned in 2007.[133] In March 2010, the Government introduced a new draft. In view of the long implementation period and the uncertainty about the fate of the new draft, however, the ECtHR issued a pilot judgment against Germany on 2 September 2010 and held that Germany must introduce without delay, and at the latest within one year from the date the judgment becomes final, a remedy in the national legal system in order to align it with Convention standards.[134] The pilot judgment was a strong blow as it was incompatible with Germany's commitment of being exemplary in the implementation of human rights standards. The judgment therefore became an important incentive to pass legislation which was finally done on 24 November 2011.

129 The Zweites Gesetz zur erbrechtlichen Gleichstellung nichtehelicher Kinder, zur Änderung der Zivilprozessordnung und der Abgabenordnung (Bundesgesetzblatt 2011 I 615) was adopted to implement *Brauer v Germany* App no 3545/04 (ECtHR, 28 May 2009).

130 Gesetz zur Regelung des Geschäftswerts bei land- oder forstwirtschaftlichen Betriebsübergaben und zur Änderung sonstiger kostenrechtlicher Vorschriften (Bundesgesetzblatt 1989 I 1082) art 2 was adopted to implement Öztürk v Germany App no 8544/79 (ECtHR, 21 February 1984).

131 The Gesetz zur Anspruchsberechtigung von Ausländern wegen Kindergeld, Erziehungsgeld und Unterhaltsvorschuss (Bundesgesetzblatt 2006 I 2915) was adopted to implement *Niedzwiecki v Germany* App no 58453/00 (ECtHR, 25 October 2005) and *Okpisz v Germany* App no 59140/00 (ECtHR, 25 October 2005).

132 In fact, it had been clear since the judgment issued against Poland in *Kudla v Poiland* App no 30210/96 (ECtHR Grand Chamber, 26 October 2000) that ECHR (n 26 above) art 13 requires States to provide for an effective remedy capable of affording redress for the unreasonable length of judicial proceedings.

133 On the history of the adoption of law establishing a legal remedy in the event of excessive length of judicial proceedings see C Steinbeiß-Winkelmann & G Ott *Rechtsschutz bei überlangen Gerichtsverfahren* (2012) Einführung paras 62ff.

134 *Rumpf v Germany* (n 54 above) para 73.

Reluctance of parliamentarians is particularly strong when the jurisprudence of the ECtHR differs from the Federal Constitutional Court's jurisprudence. In 2009, the judgments of the ECtHR holding that the German system of preventive detention was incompatible with the ECHR was met with outrage in Germany. Popular press raged about 'dangerous criminals having to be released',[135] and politicians stated that not the ECtHR but the German Constitutional Court was the leading authority in Germany and that the German Constitution must have the last word.[136] In the end, however, legislation was adopted.

4.4.2 Implementation of decisions by a human rights treaty body by the courts

An important obstacle to courts implementing decisions of human rights treaty bodies is the principle of finality of judgments. Although states are not obliged under the ECHR to provide for the possibility of reopening procedures,[137] the reopening of procedures is possible under German law following an ECtHR judgment. Since 1998, an ECtHR judgment is recognised as a reason allowing for the reopening of criminal procedures.[138] Since 2006, civil and all other kinds of court procedures may be reopened following an ECtHR judgment.[139] Reopening of procedures is only possible, however, with respect to the individual case decided by the ECtHR.[140] A reopening in similar cases is not possible. German law does not provide for the possibility of reopening procedures in case of a decision by a UN human rights treaty body either. An ECtHR judgment also has repercussions on the binding nature of judgments of the Federal Constitutional Court: The Constitutional Court has held that a ECtHR decision has the same effects as a legally relevant change of facts or law.[141] Lower courts may thus disregard the former decision of the

135 See heading of the daily newspaper 'Bild' of 12 July 2010: 'Diese Schwerverbrecher muss die Justiz laufen lassen.'

136 See for example statement by the Bavarian Minister of Justice Beate Merk in D Hipp 'Streit über Sicherungsverwahrung: Im Zweifel für die Dauerhaft' *Spiegel Online* (8 February 2011) http://www.spiegel.de/panorama/justiz/streit-ueber-sicherungs verwahrung-im-zweifel-fuer-die-dauerhaft-a-744298-7.html (accessed 15 April 2015).

137 Meyer-Ladewig (n 116 above) Artikel 46 para 28. For an obligation Frowein (n 120 above) para 15. The Council of Europe Committee of Ministers has invited states to provide for the possibility of re-examination of cases though, see Recommendation (2000) 2 of 19 January 2000.

138 Code of Criminal Procedure sec 359 no 6.

139 Code of Civil Procedure sec 580 no 8: 'An action for retrial of the case may be brought: ... 8. where the European Court of Human Rights has established that the European Convention for the Protection of Human Rights and Fundamental Freedoms or its protocols have been violated, and where the judgment is based on this violation.' This provision is applicable in other procedures as well. Their procedural codes refer to Code of Civil Procedure sec 580 no 8, see for example Arbeitsgerichtsgesetz sec 79 sentence 1 for labour court procedures, sec 179(1) Sozialgerichtsgesetz for social court procedures, Verwaltungsgerichtsordnung sec 163(1) for administrative court procedures.

140 Breuer (n 117 above) para 70.

141 BVerfG Case 2 BvR 2365/09 (n 78 above) para 82.

Constitutional Court[142] and the Constitutional Court may decide on the issue again.

Since the Federal Constitutional Court's judgments *Görgülü* and on preventive detention, the role of the courts in implementing ECtHR judgments has become clearer. Courts have to take the ECtHR decision into account, but the Constitutional Court has emphasised that they should not schematically apply it. This is particularly true in so-called multipolar fundamental rights situations in which the fundamental rights of two persons have to be weighed against each other.[143] Typical examples are family law cases such as the *Görgülü* case in which the right to family life of different family members are in conflict or press cases such as the *Von Hannover* case in which freedom of the press has to be balanced with freedom of expression. In those cases, the party that was not successful in the proceedings at national level brings the case to Strasbourg, but the other party that was successful in the proceedings at national level is not necessarily involved. It has the possibility, according to article 36, paragraph 2 of the ECHR, to participate in the proceedings as a third party, but this does not always happen. It is thus not guaranteed that its legal interests are properly represented at the level of the ECHR.

With regard to these cases, the Constitutional Court held:

> Precisely in cases in which national courts, as in private law, have to structure multipolar fundamental rights situations, it is always important that various subjective legal positions are sensitively weighed against each other, and if there is a change in the persons involved in the dispute or a change in the actual or legal circumstances, this weighing up may lead to a different result. There may therefore be constitutional problems if one of the subjects of fundamental rights in conflict with another obtains an ECHR judgment in his or her favour against the Federal Republic of Germany and German courts schematically apply this decision to the private-law relationship, with the result that the holder of fundamental rights who has 'lost' in this case and was possibly not involved in the proceedings at the ECHR would no longer be able to take an effective part in the proceedings as a party.[144]

The same concerns may be voiced with respect to decisions by UN treaty bodies. Contrary to the ECHR system, rules of procedure of UN treaty bodies do not provide for the possibility of third parties to participate in the proceedings before the UN human rights treaty body. This procedural inequality is enhanced – even if only in the perception of the party concerned – if the treaty body is a specialised one that does not decide on the basis of a comprehensive human rights treaty such as the ICCPR but on a treaty with a focus on a specific category of human rights (for example

142 See Kammergericht Berlin Case 9 W 128/04 (29 October 2004) (2005) 58 *Neue Juristische Wochenschrift* 605 606.
143 Critical Meyer-Ladewig (n 116 above) art 46 para 34.
144 BVerfG Case 2 BvR 1481/04 (n 74 above) para 50.

elimination of racial discrimination or elimination of discrimination against women).[145]

To ensure that both parties to a multipolar human rights situation are represented in the proceedings before the ECtHR, Germany has adopted two important measures. Very often, the other party of a multipolar human rights situation does not know that proceedings are pending in Strasbourg. It is not informed by the Court and thus cannot participate in the proceedings on the basis of article 36 of the ECHR. To minimise this obstacle, the Commissioner for Human Rights Issues at the Federal Ministry of Justice and Consumer Protection has developed the practice of informing the other party of a multipolar human rights situation about the pending proceedings and the possibility to participate in them.[146] As the legal aid scheme administered by the ECtHR only covers applicants, but not third parties, many third parties have not made use of this possibility in view of the costs involved. To overcome this obstacle, the German *Bundestag* has recently adopted a law on legal aid for third parties in proceedings before the ECtHR.[147]

4.5 Other means of implementation

4.5.1 National monitoring mechanisms

International law recommends and encourages the creation of independent national human rights institutions as a means to enhance compliance. Standards for such institutions are laid down in the UN principles relating to the Status of National Institutions (Paris Principles).[148] Recent human rights treaties go a step further and require the creation of specific national mechanisms for the implementation of the rights contained in the respective treaty.

The German Institute for Human Rights

The German Institute for Human Rights[149] was established in 2001 on the basis of a resolution of the German *Bundestag*. It operates in the legal form of a non-profit association and has been accredited with A-status according to the Paris Principles by the International Coordinating Committee. It is funded by the state, but acts independently. It has the task to promote and

145 See the criticism expressed with regard to the *TBB* decision by CERD (n 43 above).
146 See Wenzel (n 115 above) para 11.
147 Gesetz zur Einführung von Kostenhilfe für Drittbetroffene in Verfahren vor dem Europäischen Gerichtshof für Menschenrechte of 20 April 2013 (Bundesgesetzblatt 2013 I 829).
148 UNGA Res 48/134 (20 December 1993) UN Doc A/RES/48/134. See also Council of Europe Committee of Ministers Recommendation (97)14 (30 September 1997).
149 See the *Deutsches Institut für Menschenrechte* website for information available at http://www.institut-fuer-menschenrechte.de (accessed 15 April 2015).

protect human rights through information, documentation, research, human rights education, policy advice for representatives of politics and society, international cooperation with other national human rights institutions and human rights bodies of the EU, the CoE, the OSCE and the UN. It does not have a mandate to deal with individual cases, a fact that has been criticised by UN treaty bodies.[150] The International Coordinating Committee has in addition emphasised the need for a stronger legal basis for the Institute.[151] After long discussions and controversies, the basis has finally been laid for this recommendation to be followed in the near future.[152]

Treaty-based monitoring mechanisms

According to article 33, paragraph 2 of the CRPD, member states shall establish an independent mechanism to promote, protect and monitor implementation of the Convention. In 2009, a monitoring mechanism for CRPD was created within the German Institute of Human Rights.[153] The mechanism *inter alia* monitors the implementation measures adopted at the level of the federation and the *Länder*, gives *amicus curiae* statements in court cases that concern questions of fundamental importance to the implementation of CRPD, consults with organisations active in the field of rights of people with disabilities and gives expertise to state institutions on the implementation of the Convention.

According to article 17 of the Optional Protocol to the Convention against Torture (OPCAT), states shall establish an independent national preventive mechanism for the prevention of torture at the domestic level. At a minimum it shall have the power to examine the treatment of persons deprived of their liberty in places of detention regularly, make recommendations to the relevant authorities and submit proposals and observations concerning existing or draft legislation (article 20). As the vast majority of cases of deprivation of liberty in Germany fall within the competence of the *Länder*, a double structure was needed. The National Agency for the Prevention of Torture (*Nationale Stelle zur Verhütung von Folter*)[154] encompasses the Federal Agency for the Prevention of Torture (*Bundesstelle zur Verhütung von Folter*) and the Joint Commission for the Prevention of Torture (*Länderkommission zur Verhütung von Folter*). The

150 See for example CESCR (24 September 2001) UN Doc E/C.12/1/Add.68 para 12; CESCR (12 July 2011) UN Doc E/C.12/DEU/CO/5 para 8; CRC (31 January 2014) UN Doc CRC/C/DEU/CO/3-4 para 18.

151 International Coordinating Committee of National Institiutions for the Promation and Protection of Human Rights *Report and Recommendations of the Session of the Sub-Committee on Accreditation* (3-6 November 2008) http://nhri.ohchr.org/EN/AboutUs/ICCAccreditation/Pages/SCA-Reports.aspx (accessed 15 April 2015) 7.

152 Bundestagsdrucksache 18/4421 (24 March 2015).

153 Monitoring-Stelle zur UN-Behindertenrechtskonvention http://www.institut-fuer-menschenrechte.de/monitoring-stelle.html (accessed 15 April 2015).

154 http://www.nationale-stelle.de (accessed 15 April 2015).

Federal Agency was established by an Administrative Order of the Federal Ministry of Justice on 20 November 2008[155] and is responsible for deprivations of liberty under the jurisdiction of the Federation, namely at detention facilities of the Federal Armed Forces (*Bundeswehr*), the Federal Police (*Bundespolizei*) and customs authorities. The Joint Commission operates on the basis of a *Staatsvertrag* of 25 June 2009[156] and is responsible for deprivations of liberty under the jurisdiction of the *Länder*, namely at prisons, facilities of the state police, facilities for the detention of persons awaiting deportation, closed child and youth welfare facilities, homes for the elderly and long-term care homes. CAT has criticised the lack of sufficient staff, financial and technical resources.[157]

4.5.2 Human Rights impact assessment in the legislative process

Implementation of human rights treaties is likely to be greatly enhanced if the compliance of draft laws with international human rights is verified. UN treaty bodies have thus called on Germany to provide for a comprehensive and institutional human rights impact assessment in the legislative process.[158] The Council of Europe as well has recommended member states to ensure that there are appropriate and effective mechanisms in place at national level for systematically verifying the compliance of draft laws with the ECHR in the light of the case-law of the Court.[159]

Germany does not have a comprehensive pre-legislative scrutiny mechanism designed specifically to ensure the compliance of draft laws with international human rights. But draft legislation and regulations are generally reviewed by the Federal Ministry of Justice and Consumer Protection with respect to their compliance with higher-ranking law. This includes not only constitutional and European Union law, but also international law, in particular the UDHR and the ECHR.[160]

4.5.3 Accessibility

A major impediment to the implementation of international human rights in the domestic legal system is the lack of knowledge in the legal

155 Bundesanzeiger no 182 4277.
156 Reprinted *inter alia* in Gesetzblatt Baden-Württemberg of 7 December 2009 681.
157 CAT (12 December 2011) UN Doc CAT/C/DEU/CO/5 para 13. The German Institute for Human Rights has also called for reforms see P Follmar-Otto *Die Nationale Stelle zur Verhütung von Folter fortentwickeln!* (2013).
158 See for example CESCR (24 September 2001) UN Doc E/C.12/1/Add.68 para 14.
159 Committee of Ministers Recommendation (2004) 5 of 12 May 2004 on the verification of the compatibility of draft laws, existing laws and administrative practice with the standards laid down in the European Convention on Human Rights.
160 Federal Ministries' Joint Rules of Procedure (Gemeinsame Geschäftsordnung der Bundesministerien) art 46; Handbook of Legal Drafting (Handbuch der Rechtsförmlichkeit) Part A.3 sec 8.

community about these treaties.[161] In recent years, the German Government has enhanced its efforts to make international human rights, and in particular the ECHR, more accessible.[162] Decisions by the UN treaty bodies and the ECtHR issued against Germany, reports submitted by Germany to UN treaty bodies, and the corresponding concluding observations are translated and distributed to the ministries and courts and are accessible via the website of the Federal Ministry of Justice and Consumer Protection. In addition, the Federal Ministry of Justice and Consumer Protection publishes a yearly report on ECtHR jurisprudence in cases against Germany and the implementation of ECtHR jurisprudence in Germany[163] and another report on important ECtHR jurisprudence in cases against other states.

German-language literature on the ECHR has abounded in recent years. It includes, *inter alia*, two commentaries addressed to legal practitioners and a commentary comparing the ECHR guarantees with the fundamental rights of the German Constitution.

5 Conclusion

Fundamental rights form the core of the German legal system. This fundamentally informs the way international human rights are implemented in Germany. For a long time, international human rights lacked visibility at the domestic level. The legal community was not sufficiently aware of these instruments. But the main reason was the more or less outspoken conviction of courts and public authorities that the German Constitution provided such an expansive protection of fundamental rights that it could not be topped by any international instruments.

In the last two decades this perception has changed. The Federal Constitutional Court has laid the foundations for a better implementation of international human rights in national law. The ECHR in particular has thus become a point of reference for courts. Major judgments issued against Germany in recent years have been the object of extensive scientific analysis and political debate.

161 Tomuschat (n 30 above) 124. With respect to Germany in particular see CESCR (12 July 2011) UN Doc E/C.12/DEU/CO/5 para 7; CEDAW (12 Febraury 2009) UN Doc CEDAW/C/DEU/CO/6 para 22.

162 On these efforts see Lambert Abdelgawad & Weber 'The Reception Process in France and Germany' in Keller & Stone Sweet (n 77 above) 155.

163 This report is made by the executive to Parliament, see A Wittling-Vogel 'The role of the legislative branch in the implementation of the judgments of the European Court of Human Rights' in A Seibert-Fohr & ME Villiger (eds) *Judgments of the European Court of Human Rights – Effects and implementation* (2014).

UN human rights treaties still do not have the same degree of visibility and importance in Germany as the ECHR. The ICCPR in particular is overshadowed by the ECHR not only with respect to the number of individual applications but also with respect to references by German courts and legislative acts. This situation is unlikely to change. Whereas non-compliance with the ECHR and the ECtHR's jurisprudence engenders the risk of a binding ECtHR judgment against Germany, the HRC only issues non-binding views. In addition, the ECtHR's jurisprudence is more elaborate than that of the HRC not only because of the sheer number of judgments but also in view of their extensive reasoning. This facilitates implementation of the Convention guarantees. It is to be expected, however, that UN human rights treaties that focus on a specific aspect of human rights protection such as CRC and CRPD will gradually gain importance in Germany.

To ensure a better visibility of international human rights in Germany additional efforts in ensuring accessibility of international instruments and providing training to all relevant actors in the legal community are required. An additional promising tool is *amicus curiae* briefs by the national human rights monitoring mechanisms – so far they have proven to be very efficient in making courts aware of the existence of international human rights instruments and their requirements. Finally, even if the Federal Constitutional Court has found a way to ensure the precedence of international human rights treaties in the German legal system in spite of their rank as ordinary laws, the implementation of international human rights in Germany would be greatly enhanced if international human rights treaties would be accorded constitutional status. Unfortunately, however, this is not likely to happen in the near future.

BIBLIOGRAPHY

Breuer, M 'Artikel 46' in Karpenstein, U & Mayer, FC (2012) *EMRK* CH Beck: Munich

Buergenthal, T 'Human rights' in Wolfrum, R (ed) (2013) *Max Planck encyclopedia of public international law* Oxford University Press: Online

Dupuy, PM 'International law and domestic (municipal) law' in Wolfrum, R (ed) (2013) *Max Planck encyclopedia of public international law* Oxford University Press: Online

Follmar-Otto, P (2013) *Die Nationale Stelle zur Verhütung von Folter fortentwickeln*! Deutsches Institut für Menschenrechte: Berlin

Frowein, JA 'Artikel 46' in Frowein, JA & Peukert, W (2009) *Europäische Menschenrechtskonvention* NP Engel: Kehl am Rhein

Grabenwarter, C & Pabel, K (2012) *Europäische Menschenrechtskonvention* CH Beck: Munich

Lambert Abdelgawad, E & Weber, A 'The reception process in France and Germany' in Keller, H & Stone Sweet, A (eds) (2008) *A Europe of rights* Oxford University Press: Oxford/ New York

Lorz, A (2003) *Der Vorrang des Kindeswohls nach Art. 3 der UN-Kinderrechtskonvention in der deutschen Rechtsordnung* Arbeitsgemeinschaft für Jugendhilfe: Berlin

Masuch, P 'Die UN-Behindertenrechtskonvention anwenden!' in Hohmann-Dennhardt C; Masuch, P; Villiger, M (eds) (2011) *Festschrift für Renate Jaeger: Grundrechte und solidarität* NP Engel: Kehl am Rhein

McGoldrick, D (1994) *The Human Rights Committee – Its role in the development of the ICCPR* Clarendon Press: Oxford

Meyer-Ladewig, J (2011) *EMRK Europäische Menschenrechtskonvention* Nomos: Baden-Baden

Nowak, M (2005) *UN Covenant on Civil and Political Rights: CCPR commentary* NP Engel: Kiel am Rhein/ Starasbourg/ Arlington

Simma B; Khan, D-E; Zöckler, M & Geiger, R 'The role of German courts in the enforcement of international human rights' in Conforti, B & Francioni, F (eds) (1997) *Enforcing international human rights in domestic courts* Kluwer Law International: The Hague

Staberock, G 'Domestic implementation' in Wolfrum, R (2013) *Max Planck encyclopedia of public international law* Oxford University Press: Online

Steinbeiß-Winkelmann, C & Ott, G (2012) *Rechtsschutz bei überlangen Gerichtsverfahren* Luchterhand: Cologne

Thürer, D 'Soft law' in Wolfrum, R (ed) (2013) *Max Planck encyclopedia of public international law* Oxford University Press: Online

Tomuschat, C (2003) *Human rights: Between idealism and realism* Oxford University Press: Oxford/ New York

Uerpmann, R (1993) *Die Europäische Menschenrechtskonvention und die deutsche Rechtsprechung: Ein Beitrag zum Thema Völkerrecht und Landesrecht* Duncker & Humblot: Berlin

Wenzel, N 'Artikel 41' in Karpenstein U & Mayer, FC (2012) *EMRK* CH Beck: Munich

Wittling-Vogel, A 'The role of the legislative branch in the implementation of the judgments of the European Court of Human Rights' in Seibert-Fohr, A & Villiger, ME (eds) (2014) *Judgments of the European Court of Human Rights – Effects and implementation* Nomos: Baden-Baden

7

THE UNITED NATIONS CHARTER AND THE GERMAN LEGAL ORDER

*Mehrdad Payandeh**

1 Introduction: Implementing obligations, ensuring compliance and enabling participation

When Germany became a member state of the United Nations in 1973,[1] it entered into a set of international legal obligations under the United Nations Charter. Germany's membership in the United Nations, however, also raises questions under domestic law: First, there is the implementation of Germany's obligations under the United Nations Charter into domestic law. While most provisions of the Charter do not require such a transfer in the strict sense, implementation may be necessary – for example with regard to some Security Council resolutions – or may at least be desirable – for example with regard to the prohibition of the use of force – in order to effectively enforce the Charter provisions. Second, while many Charter provisions do not aim at domestic implementation, the domestic legal order needs to ensure that Germany can and does comply with its international obligations under the Charter. Third, the German legal order must enable Germany and the German state organs to actively participate in the work of the United Nations. Accordingly, the German constitutional order must, first of all, provide for the possibility of

* Junior Professor for Public Law and Public International Law at the Heinrich-Heine-University of Düsseldorf, Germany.

1 Gesetz zum Beitritt der Bundesrepublik Deutschland zur Charta der Vereinten Nationen of 6 June 1973 (Bundesgesetzblatt 1973 II 430); Bekanntmachung über das Inkrafttreten der Charta der Vereinten Nationen (Bundesgesetzblatt 1974 II 1397). The Federal Republic of Germany and the German Democratic Republic were accepted as the 133rd and 134th members of the United Nations on the same day. With the reunification of Germany, the German Democratic Republic ceased to exist, while the membership of the Federal Republic of Germany in international organisations remained untouched, see JA Frowein 'The reunification of Germany' (1992) 86 *American Journal of International Law* 152 157. For an overview over Germany's UN policy, see R Wolfrum 'Deutschland in den Vereinten Nationen' in J Isensee & P Kirchhof (eds) *Handbuch des Staatsrechts der Bundesrepublik Deutschland* vol X (3rd edn 2012) 555 paras 13 - 62.

Germany's accession to the United Nations Charter and integration into the UN system. Germany is, furthermore, required to participate in collective measures for the prevention and removal of threats to the peace,[2] and to engage in international cooperation.[3] While these obligations are framed in rather broad terms and do not oblige the member states to take any particular measures, they nevertheless demand that states are generally able and willing to cooperate and that they engage in the activities of the United Nations. The domestic legal order must ensure that such an engagement is possible.

2 Obligations under the United Nations Charter

Germany's membership in the United Nations entails a variety of international legal obligations.[4] They stem directly from the UN Charter as well as from measures taken by organs of the UN (→ 2.1). They are embodied in the Charter but may, at the same time, be recognised as customary international law or *jus cogens* (→ 2.2). They can be differentiated according to their content (→ 2.3) and with regard to their addressees (→ 2.4).

2.1 The Charter, resolutions and decisions of the International Court of Justice

As an international treaty the UN Charter is legally binding on its member states.[5] Beyond the obligations that are directly embodied in the UN Charter, member states may be bound by resolutions or decisions issued by the organs of the UN. However, with regard to the political organs of the UN, the UN Charter provides only for the binding nature of decisions of the Security Council.[6] By contrast, resolutions issued by the General Assembly are not legally binding, since the UN Charter only establishes a competence of the Assembly to make recommendations.[7] General

2 Charter of the United Nations (UN Charter) (26 June 1945, 1 UNTS XVI) art 1(1).
3 UN Charter (n 2 above) art 1(2) & (3).
4 Already before its formal accession to the UN in 1973, Germany had pledged to comply with the principles of the UN Charter. Against the background of its accession to NATO Germany declared on 3 October 1954: 'The German Federal Republic has agreed to conduct its policy in accordance with the principles of the Charter of the United Nations and accepts the obligations set forth in article 2 of the Charter', Bundestags-Drucksache 2/1061 (1954) 67.
5 UN Charter (n 2 above) art 2(2) reiterates and substantiates this obligation, providing that all member states 'shall fulfill in good faith the obligations assumed by them in accordance with the present Charter'.
6 According to UN Charter (n 2 above) art 25, the UN member states agree to accept and carry out the decisions of the Security Council in accordance with the Charter. Art 48 reaffirms this obligation with regard to decisions taken under Chapter VII of the Charter. On the binding nature of Security Council resolutions see A Peters 'Article 25' in B Simma et al (eds) *The Charter of the United Nations: A commentary*, vol I (3rd edn 2012) 787 paras 8 - 19; A Orakhelashvili *Collective security* (2011) 33 - 39.
7 See UN Charter (n 2 above) art 10 & Ch IV in general.

Assembly resolutions may, however, reflect existing rules of customary international law or contribute to the formation of new rules of customary international law.[8] Member states furthermore have to comply with decisions of the International Court of Justice in any case to which they are a party.[9]

2.2 Treaty law, customary international law and *jus cogens*

Notwithstanding its constitutional character,[10] the UN Charter is an international treaty. Accordingly, the general domestic implementation mechanisms designed to incorporate treaties apply to the UN Charter. At the same time, however, numerous substantive provisions of the UN Charter are recognised as customary international law,[11] in particular the prohibition of the use of force (article 2(4) of the UN Charter),[12] the right to self-defense (article 51 of the UN Charter),[13] the principle of non-intervention,[14] and the right to self-determination (article 1 of the UN Charter).[15] Moreover, many rules that can be derived from the principle of sovereign equality (article 2(1) of the UN Charter) are of a customary nature.[16]

While the content of these norms of customary international law might, as a matter of principle, differ from the content of the Charter norms, the Charter norms and their interpretation in the practice of states and UN organs will have an effect on the respective rule of customary international law.[17] From the perspective of international law such a parallel existence of a rule of international law, both as treaty law and customary international law, is primarily relevant with regard to states that

8 See eg M Shaw *International law* (6th edn 2008) 1212.

9 UN Charter (n 2 above) art 94(1); ICJ Statute (26 June 1945) art 59.

10 For a constitutionalist reading of the UN Charter, see B Fassbender *The United Nations Charter as the constitution of the international community* (2009); for a general analysis of constitutionalist approaches to international law see T Kleinlein *Konstitutionalisierung im Völkerrecht* (2012).

11 This possibility is explicitly envisaged in Vienna Convention on the Law of Treaties (23 May 1969, 1155 UNTS 331) art 38.

12 *Military and Paramilitary Activities in and against Nicaragua (Nicaragua v United States of America)* Merits Judgment ICJ (27 June 1986) (1986) ICJ Reports 14 paras 187 - 190.

13 *Nicaragua case* (n 12 above) paras 193 - 195.

14 *Nicaragua case* (n 12 above) para 202. While UN Charter (n 2 above) art 2(7) applies only to the organs of the UN, the general non-intervention principle as it is addressed to states can be derived from UN Charter art 2(1). See P Kunig 'Intervention, Prohibition of' in R Wolfrum (ed) *Max Planck encyclopedia of public international law* (2008) para 9.

15 R Wolfrum 'Article 1' in Simma et al (n 6 above) 107 para 4; for a more extensive discussion, see S Oeter 'Self-determination' in Simma et al (n 6 above) 313.

16 S Besson 'Sovereignty' in R Wolfrum (ed) *Max Planck encyclopedia of public international law* (2011) paras 86 - 89; see also *Jurisdictional Immunities of the State (Germany v Italy)* ICJ (3 February 2012) (2012) ICJ Reports 99 para 57.

17 See M Herdegen 'Article 25' in T Maunz & G Dürig (eds) *Grundgesetz, Kommentar* vol IV (2000) para 26; *Nicaragua* (n 12 above) para 181.

are not party to the UN Charter.[18] With the almost universal status of the UN Charter, the customary nature of Charter provisions has lost its significance.[19] However, since the German legal order provides for different rules regarding the domestic implementation of international treaties on the one hand and norms of customary international law on the other hand,[20] (→ Wolfrum, Hestermeyer & Vöneky) the distinction may be relevant from the perspective of domestic law.

It is furthermore maintained that some of the substantive principles laid down in the UN Charter constitute peremptory norms of international law (*jus cogens*).[21] The peremptory nature of, for example, the prohibition of the use of force[22] and the right to self-determination[23] are widely recognised. There is, however, no general consensus with regard to the legal consequences entailed by the qualification of an international rule as *jus cogens*.[24] While some authors hold the view that peremptory norms automatically unfold specific consequences within the domestic legal order,[25] this proposition is subject to serious challenges and has not yet found significant confirmation within legal practice.[26]

In light of the general indifference of international law towards its effects within the legal orders of the members states[27] as well as of the general reluctance in particular of the International Court of Justice to

18 On the relationship between the UN and non-member states see UN Charter (n 2 above) art 2(6); S Talmon 'Article 2(6)' in B Simma et al (n 6 above) 252.

19 The famous and controversial *Nicaragua* decision of the ICJ, however, shows that the customary nature of Charter rules can also be of relevance regarding the legal relationship between UN member states: Due to the so-called 'multilateral treaty reservation' of the United States, the ICJ was barred from deciding the case on the basis of the UN Charter. The Court held, however, that due to the customary nature of certain Charter provisions (in particular the prohibition of the use of force and the right to self-defense), it could decide the case on the basis of identical norms of customary international law. See *Military and Paramilitary Activities in and against Nicaragua (Nicaragua v United States of America)* Jurisdiction and Admissibility, Judgment, ICJ (26 November 1984) (1984) ICJ Reports 392 paras 67 - 73; *Nicaragua case* (n 12 above) paras 42 - 43 & 172 - 182.

20 While Basic Law art 59(2) is concerned with treaty law, customary international law is encompassed by Basic Law art 25.

21 See eg AL Paulus 'Article 2' in Simma et al (n 6 above) 121 para 24, holding that '[s]ome, if not most of the principles of Art. 2 may constitute *ius cogens*'.

22 C Gray 'The use of force and the international legal order' in MD Evans (ed) *International law* (3rd edn 2010) 615 617.

23 *Legal Consequences for States of the Continued Presence of South Africa in Namibia notwithstanding Security Council Resolution 276 (1970) Advisory Opinion, Separate Opinion Ammoun* ICJ (21 June 1971) (1971) ICJ Reports 16 67 & 89 - 90; A Orakhelashvili *Peremptory Norms in International Law* (2006) 51.

24 For an overview over the practice of international and domestic courts, see D Shelton 'International law and relative normativity' in Evans (n 22 above) 141 146ff.

25 See eg AA Cançado Trindade 'International law for humankind: Towards a new jus gentium (I)' (2006) 316 *Recueil des Cours* 9 341.

26 See E de Wet 'The prohibition of torture as an international norm of jus cogens and its implications for national and customary law' (2004) 15 *European Journal of International Law* 97 120f.; AL Paulus 'Jus cogens in a time of hegemony and fragmentation' (2005) 74 *Nordic Journal of International Law* 297 319ff.

27 K Kaiser 'Treaties, direct applicability' in R Wolfrum (ed) *Max Planck encyclopedia of public international law* (2013) para 6.

acknowledge far reaching legal consequences attributed to the concept of *jus cogens*,[28] a direct effect of peremptory norms within the domestic legal order cannot be assumed. It is therefore left to the domestic legal orders to determine whether the peremptory character of an international norm should lead to specific consequences under domestic law.[29] Accordingly, the German constitutional order does not have to but may attribute specific domestic consequences to *jus cogens* rules.

2.3 Obligations, rights and organisational provisions

The domestic implementation of international norms may also depend on the content of the respective rules. While some international norms are intended for domestic implementation and, for example, establish an obligation to enact legislation,[30] other international norms do not need to be transferred into the domestic legal order. The prohibition of the use of force, for example, requires states to abstain from threats and aggressive acts but does not necessarily require domestic implementation.

The UN Charter basically contains three different kinds of legal rules. First, many provisions provide for obligations of the member states. Amongst those rules are the general duty to fulfil their Charter obligations in good faith,[31] the obligation to settle disputes through peaceful means,[32] the prohibition of the use of force,[33] and the obligation to accept and carry out decisions of the Security Council[34] and to comply with the decisions of the International Court of Justice.[35] Second, the Charter provides for rights of its member states. The obligation to refrain from the threat or use of force is not only an obligation of states, but states also have a right against the threat or use of force by other states.[36] Similarly, the principle of sovereignty establishes different rights of states, for example, the rights

28 See *Jurisdictional Immunities case* (n 16 above) paras 89 & 92 - 97; GI Hernández *The International Court of Justice and the judicial function* (2014) 224ff.

29 Under the Federal Constitution of the Swiss Confederation (18 April 1999), for example, the violation of peremptory rules of international law is grounds for the Federal Assembly to declare a popular initiative to be void (art 139(3)), and revisions of the Constitution may not violate peremptory norms of international law (art 193(4) & art 194(2)).

30 See eg Convention on the Prevention and Punishment of the Crime of Genocide (9 December 1948, 78 UNTS 177) art 5; International Convention on the Elimination of All Forms of Racial Discrimination (21 December 1965, 660 UNTS 195) art 2(1)(d).

31 UN Charter (n 2 above) art 2(2).

32 UN Charter (n 2 above) arts 2(3) & 33(1).

33 UN Charter (n 2 above) art 2(4).

34 UN Charter (n 2 above) arts 25 & 48.

35 UN Charter (n 2 above) art 94(1).

36 Accordingly, the International Court of Justice held in its *Nicaragua* judgment that the United States had acted, 'against the Republic of Nicaragua, in breach of its obligation under customary international law not to use force against another State', see *Nicaragua case* (n 12 above) para 292.

under state immunity.[37] Moreover, states also have rights against the United Nations, such as the right of non-intervention into their domestic affairs[38] or the right to participate in the decision-making processes of the UN organs as provided for in the Charter. Third, the predominant number of Charter provisions is dedicated to the constitution and organisation of the organs of the United Nations, regulating their composition, decision-making processes and competences.[39] Other organisational provisions of the Charter encompass rules for membership in the United Nations[40] or regulate the relationship between the Charter and other rules of international law,[41] amendments to the Charter or its entry into force.[42]

While states are under an obligation to comply with every provision of the UN Charter, many Charter provisions are not suitable for domestic implementation. The numerous organisational provisions, for example, cannot be implemented domestically. Even with regard to the substantive obligations established under the Charter, there is no general duty to implement them into the domestic legal order[43] or to grant the Charter a specific status within the domestic hierarchy of norms.

2.4 States and individuals as addressees of United Nations law

Different rules for domestic implementation may also apply depending on the addressees of the Charter rules. The main addressees of the UN Charter are the member states and the organs of the United Nations. As far as the obligations under the UN Charter are suitable for domestic implementation, states can transfer their obligations into domestic law in order to ensure that their international obligations as subjects of international law are complied with by all state organs.

Different rules of implementation may apply when international legal obligations are addressed to individuals and private entities. While the UN Charter itself does not contain any direct obligations of individuals, individuals have come into the focus of the UN Security Council: The international criminal tribunals established by the Security Council operate under the assumption that the individual is responsible for crimes punishable under international criminal law.[44] However, since the

37 Accordingly, in its decision in the *Jurisdictional Immunities case* (n 16 above), the ICJ mentions the 'right to immunity' (paras 55, 56, 81, 106, 113) and holds that Italy 'violated its obligation to respect the immunity which the Federal Republic of Germany enjoys under international law' (para 139).
38 UN Charter (n 2 above) art 2(7).
39 See in particular UN Charter (n 2 above) Chs IV, V, VI, VII, X, XII, XIII, XIV & XV.
40 UN Charter (n 2 above) Ch II.
41 UN Charter (n 2 above) art 103.
42 UN Charter (n 2 above) Chs XVIII & XIX.
43 On the exception of UN Charter (n 2 above) arts 104 & 105 see below 3.2.1.
44 See Statute of the International Criminal Tribunal for the former Yugoslavia (ICTY Statute) (25 May 1993, UNSC 808/1993) art 6; Statute of the International Criminal Tribunal for Rwanda (ICTR Statute) (8 November 1994, UNSC S/RES/955) art 6.

criminal proceedings take place on the international plane and in front of international tribunals, those international rules addressing the individual do not need to be implemented into domestic law (→ Schmalenbach). Conversely the practice of the Security Council to target not only states but also individuals does not create individual obligations. The resolutions are addressed to the member states of the UN which are responsible for implementing the sanctions imposed by the Security Council. Individual obligations under international law are thereby not established. The domestic implementation of sanctions may, however, require addressing individuals and private entities, for example private banks that are capable of freezing the assets of blacklisted persons and entities.

3 Implementation of obligations under the United Nations Charter

3.1 The constitutional basis for Germany's participation in the United Nations

3.1.1 Application of general rules and absence of special rules

The German legal order does not only address the question of whether and how specific obligations under the UN Charter are implemented into the domestic legal order. It also provides a constitutional framework for Germany's participation in the United Nations. The Basic Law, however, does not contain any specific provisions that deal explicitly with the participation of Germany in the United Nations. Hence, the general constitutional provisions regarding Germany's involvement in international institutions and the relationship between the German legal order and international law apply: While article 59(2) of the Basic Law regulates the conclusion of international treaties in general, article 24 of the Basic Law contains provisions regarding Germany's participation in international organisations.[45] Article 24(2) of the Basic Law stipulates:

> With a view to maintaining peace, the Federation may enter into a system of mutual collective security; in doing so it shall consent to such limitations upon its sovereign powers as will bring about and secure a lasting peace in Europe and among the nations of the world.

45 Although Basic Law art 24 seems to be *lex specialis* with regard to the more general Basic Law art 59(2), the latter provision nevertheless finds application since the former does not contain any specific regulations regarding the conclusion of international treaties, see BVerfG Case 2 BvR 197/83 (22 October 1986) (1987) 73 *Entscheidungen des Bundesverfassungsgerichts* 339 367 & 375; BVerfG Case 2 BvE 6/99 (22 November 2001) (2002) 104 *Entscheidungen des Bundesverfassungsgerichts* 151 195; I Pernice 'Article 24' in H Dreier (ed) *Grundgesetz, Kommentar* vol II (2nd edn 2006) para 69; S Oeter 'Systeme kollektiver Sicherheit' in J Isensee & P Kirchhof (eds) *Handbuch des Staatsrechts der Bundesrepublik Deutschland* vol XI (3rd edn 2013) 619 631.

This constitutional provision was included in the Basic Law with a specific view towards the United Nations as the 'prototype' of a system of collective security.[46] It provides the constitutional foundation for Germany's participation in the United Nations.

Article 24(1) of the Basic Law, on the other hand, which allows for the transfer of sovereign powers to an international organisation, does not apply to the United Nations. The United Nations are not authorised to exercise sovereign power with direct effect in the domestic legal order of its member states as is envisaged in article 24(1) of the Basic Law.[47] Through its membership in the United Nations, the Federal Republic of Germany has rather entered into a framework of international legal obligations and thereby consented to limitations of its sovereign powers as provided for in article 24(2) of the Basic Law.

Since the Charter of the United Nations is a treaty regulating the political relations of the Federal Republic of Germany, the ratification of the Charter required the consent of the German Federal Parliament (Bundestag) and the Federal Assembly (Bundesrat) in the form of a federal law, according to article 59(2) of the Basic Law. With the law concerning the accession of Germany to the United Nations, the Bundestag and the Bundesrat have fulfilled the constitutional requirement for Germany's membership in the United Nations.

3.1.2 Allowing for dynamic development of the United Nations Charter

Just like the accession of Germany to the United Nations Charter required a federal law, any formal amendment of the Charter requires a renewal of parliamentary consent in the form of a federal law.[48] Due to the high requirements of articles 108 and 109 of the UN Charter, however, formal amendments or revisions of the UN Charter are rare.[49] In order to adapt the Charter regime to a global landscape that has undergone fundamental changes since the end of the Second World War and to meet global

46 BVerfG Case 2 BvE 3/92 et al (12 July 1994) (1994) 90 *Entscheidungen des Bundesverfassungsgerichts* 286 347ff; BVerfG Case 2 BvE 6/99 (n 45 above) 195; Pernice (n 45 above) para 54.

47 BVerfG Case 2 BvE 3/92 et al (n 46 above) 346 - 347; HD Jarass 'Article 24' in HD Jarass & B Pieroth (eds) *Grundgesetz, Kommentar* (12th edn 2012) para 5; Pernice (n 45 above) para 20; A Funke *Umsetzungsrecht* (2010) 44; JA Frowein 'Implementation of Security Council resolutions taken under Chapter VII in Germany' in V Gowlland-Debbas (ed) *United Nations sanctions and international law* (2001) 253 258; but see M Herdegen *Die Befugnisse des UN-Sicherheitsrates* (1998) 33 - 34; Herdegen (n 17 above) para 21 who argues in favour of the application of Basic Law art 24(1); see also Wolfrum (n 1 above) para 19.

48 See BVerfG Case 2 BvE 6/99 (n 45 above) 200.

49 The UN Charter has been formally amended three times, in order to increase the size of the Security Council and of the Economic and Social Council respectively. See T Rensmann 'Reform' in Simma et al (n 6 above) 25 para 14.

challenges that had not been envisaged by the Founders of the UN in 1945, the UN organs have therefore interpreted and applied the Charter provisions in a rather dynamic and flexible manner: The Security Council, most prominently, has expanded its range of action through an extensive interpretation of the term 'threat to the peace' in article 39 of the UN Charter, applying it increasingly to internal conflicts.[50] The Council has also resorted to a variety of measures under article 41 of the UN Charter, such as the creation of international criminal tribunals,[51] legislative action,[52] peacekeeping operations,[53] and the authorisation of the use of force in a manner not explicitly provided for in the Charter.[54]

While the legality of these developments has at times been cast into doubt,[55] they have generally been accepted by the UN member states. Furthermore, this dynamic and flexible interpretation of the UN Charter has been justified with reference to the role of the subsequent practice of the UN organs in interpreting the Charter,[56] as well as to systematic and functional methods of interpretation and to the principle of effectiveness (*effet utile*).[57] From the perspective of the domestic legal order, however, the question arises, whether this dynamic development of the United Nations is still covered by the parliamentary consent given to the UN Charter in 1973. In other words: does article 59(2) of the Basic Law require parliamentary consent only with regard to the conclusion and amendment of treaties or does it also apply to significant developments within a treaty regime that occur through interpretative development without formal amendment?

In the jurisprudence of the Constitutional Court of Germany, this question has been dealt with in the context of the integration of Germany in the European Union and with regard to Germany's membership in NATO. In the context of European integration, the Constitutional Court demands that the integration programme of the European Union must be sufficiently precise and that significant developments on the European level require parliamentary consent even when the EU treaties are not

50 C Gray 'The use of force and the international legal order' in MD Evans (ed) *International Law* (3rd edn 2010) 615 623.

51 W Sandholtz 'Creating authority by the council: The international criminal tribunals' in B Cronin & I Hurd (eds) *The UN Security Council and the politics of international authority* (2008) 131.

52 S Talmon 'The Security Council as world legislator' (2005) 99 *American Journal of International Law* 175.

53 M Bothe 'Peacekeeping' in Simma et al (n 6 above) 1171.

54 E de Wet *The Chapter VII powers of the United Nations Security Council* (2004) 256; M Payandeh 'The United Nations, military intervention, and regime change in Libya' (2012) 53 *Virginia Journal of International Law* 355 366ff.

55 See eg M Koskenniemi 'The police in the temple, order, justice and the UN: A dialectical view' (1995) 6 *European Journal of International Law* 325.

56 *Legal Consequences for States of the Continued Presence of South Africa in Namibia notwithstanding Security Council Resolution 276 (1970) Advisory Opinion* ICJ (21 June 1971) (1971) ICJ Reports 16, para 22; *Legality of the Use by a State of Nuclear Weapons in Armed Conflict Advisory Opinion* ICJ (8 July 1996) (1996) ICJ Reports 66, para 19.

57 S Kadelbach 'Interpretation' in Simma et al (n 6 above) 71 para 18.

formally amended.[58] However, this jurisprudence has to be seen against the background of the 'supranational' nature of EU law,[59] namely the competence of the EU to create legally binding law by way of majority vote that has direct effect[60] within the German legal order and takes priority over German law.[61] The constitutional standards developed by the Court in the context of European integration can therefore not be applied to the United Nations.

More insightful guidelines for the constitutional requirements for Germany's participation in the dynamic UN legal framework can be derived from the Constitutional Court's line of jurisprudence developed against the background of the significant changes in the security architecture of NATO.[62] When the German Parliament consented to the accession of Germany to the North Atlantic Treaty in 1955,[63] NATO was construed as a military alliance, determined to defend its member states against threats and attacks from the outside.[64] After the end of the Cold War, NATO significantly broadened its approach towards cooperation and security. Without formally amending the North Atlantic Treaty, the Heads of State and Government adopted the new Strategic Concepts of 1991[65] and 1999[66] respectively, thereby laying the ground for NATO's military involvement in the enforcement of UN Security Council resolutions, for example with regard to the embargo imposed on the Federal Republic of Yugoslavia,[67] the ban on military flights over Bosnia and Herzegovina,[68] and NATO's involvement in Kosovo and Afghanistan.

When the Constitutional Court was confronted with the question whether these developments were still covered by the parliamentary

58 BVerfG Case 2 BvE 2/08 et al (30 June 2009) (2010) 123 *Entscheidungen des Bundesverfassungsgerichts* 267 351 - 356 & 384 - 395; see already BVerfG Case 2 BvR 2194/92 et al (12 October 1993) (1994) 89 *Entscheidungen des Bundesverfassungsgerichts* 155 187f.

59 On the concept of supranational law see A Skordas 'Supranational law' in Wolfrum (n 16 above) paras 1 - 5.

60 See Treaty on the Functioning of the European Union (TFEU) (13 December 2007, 2008/C 115/01) art 288(2); ECJ Case 26/62 *Van Gend en Loos* [1963] ECR 1.

61 Case 6/64 *Costa v ENEL* [1964] ECR 585.

62 On the changing role of NATO see T Marauhn 'North Atlantic Treaty Organization' in Wolfrum (n 16 above) paras 1 - 13, 51 - 61.

63 Gesetz betreffend den Beitritt der Bundesrepublik Deutschland zum Brüsseler Vertrag und zum Nordatlantikvertrag of 24 March 1955 (Bundesgesetzblatt 1955 II 256).

64 See in particular North Atlantic Treaty (4 April 1949) arts 5 & 6.

65 NATO *New Strategic Concept* (7 and 8 November 1991) http://www.nato.int/cps/en/natolive/official_texts_23847.htm (accessed 2 March 2015).

66 NATO *The Alliance's Strategic Concept* (24 April 1999), http://www.nato.int/cps/en/natolive/official_texts_27433.htm (accessed 2 March 2015).

67 UNSC Res 713 (25 September 1991) UN Doc S/RES/713; UNSC Res 757 (30 May 1992) UN Doc S/RES/757.

68 UNSC Res 781 (9 October 1992) UN Doc S/RES/781; UNSC Res 816 (31 March 1993) UN Doc S/RES/816.

consent given to the NATO Treaty in 1955, the Court answered with a resounding yes. Building on its previous line of jurisprudence,[69] the Court adopted a formalist approach and held that article 59(2) of the Basic Law required parliamentary consent only with regard to the conclusion or formal amendment of an international treaty.[70] According to the Court, the constitutional requirement of parliamentary consent could not be extended to substantive modifications of a treaty brought along through dynamic interpretation or through subsequent state practice, as long as those developments took place – according to the intention of the parties to the treaty – within the already established treaty regime. The scope of consent given by Parliament would only be exceeded, when the subsequent development went beyond the 'programme of integration'[71] of the treaty, in the sense that it would be incompatible with 'fundamental structural decisions' embodied in the treaty.[72]

The Court did not only develop rather restrictive standards. It also applied these standards in a restrictive manner: The Court held that the expansion of NATO's range of action to crisis response operations of potentially global reach did not exceed the programme of integration as it was embodied in the NATO Treaty.[73] The Court upheld this conclusion with regard to the NATO-led ISAF operation in Afghanistan.[74]

Against the background of the Constitutional Court's line of jurisprudence with regard to NATO, there can hardly be any doubt that the parliamentary consent given to the UN Charter in 1973 encompasses the developments that took place in the United Nations, in particular after the end of the Cold War. The UN Charter is even more open for dynamic interpretation and for adaptation to change without formal amendment than the NATO Treaty. With regard to the United Nations' broad commitment to the maintenance of international peace and security and in

69 BVerfG Case 2 BvR 1107/77 et al (23 June 1981) (1982) 58 *Entscheidungen des Bundesverfassungsgerichts* 1; BVerfG Case 2 BvE 13/83 (18 December 1984) (1985) 68 *Entscheidungen des Bundesverfassungsgerichts* 1.

70 BVerfG Case 2 BvE 3/92 et al (n 46 above) 361ff. The decision was taken with the smallest margin possible (4:4). It was, however, confirmed in BVerfG Case 2 BvE 6/99 (n 45 above) 199 - 206; BVerfG Case 2 BvE 2/07 (3 July 2007) (2008) 118 *Entscheidungen des Bundesverfassungsgerichts* 244 263 - 270; BVerfG Case 2 BvE 1/03 (07 May 2008) (2009) 121 *Entscheidungen des Bundesverfassungsgerichts* 135 157 - 158.

71 Critical with regard to the conception of a 'programme' embodied in a treaty M Nettesheim 'Article 59' in Maunz & Dürig (n 17 above) para 135.

72 BVerfG Case 2 BvR 1107/77 et al (n 69 above) 37 - 38; BVerfG Case 2 BvE 13/83 (n 69 above) 98 - 99; BVerfG Case 2 BvE 6/99 (n 45 above) 209 - 210.

73 BVerfG Case 2 BvE 6/99 (n 45 above) 210 - 212. In light of NATO's construction as a defensive alliance with a regional focus on the European and transatlantic region, it seems, however, highly doubtful whether this expansion of NATO's field of action to out of area operations is still covered by the North Atlantic Treaty's programme of integration and compatible with its fundamental structural decisions. For a critical assessment of this holding, see H Sauer 'Die NATO und das Verfassungsrecht: neues Konzept – alte Fragen' (2002) 62 *Zeitschrift für ausländisches öffentliches Recht und Völkerrecht* 317 333f & 339ff.

74 BVerfG Case 2 BvE 2/07 (3 July 2007) (2008) 118 *Entscheidungen des Bundesverfassungsgerichts* 244 263 - 270.

light of the open-textured character of the Security Council's powers under Chapter, innovative developments such as peacekeeping,[75] the establishment of ad hoc criminal tribunals,[76] or the authorisation of the use of force through the Security Council do not go beyond the integration programme of the UN Charter or run counter to fundamental structural decisions embodied in the Charter. Moreover, Germany ratified the UN Charter only in 1973, when the general tendency to apply the Charter in a dynamic and functional way was already apparent and, for example, peacekeeping operations were already a well-established part of UN practice.[77] In conclusion, the jurisprudence of the Constitutional Court allows that dynamic developments within the United Nations system are encompassed by the consent given by the German Parliament to the UN Charter and hence constitutionally legitimised.

3.2 Implementation of specific provisions of the United Nations Charter

3.2.1 Implementation in general

Through the ratification of the UN Charter on the basis of a federal law according to article 59(2) of the Basic Law, the UN Charter has become part of the German legal order (→ Wolfrum, Hestermeyer & Vöneky).[78] Within the hierarchy of the domestic legal order, the Charter is therefore attributed the rank of a federal law. All German state organs are thereby bound by the provisions of the Charter and prohibited from violating it. Nevertheless, the question arises whether specific provisions of the Charter require domestic implementation in the sense of an incorporation of international rules into domestic law. Such an incorporation is required when international norms are intended to have a specific effect within the domestic legal order but cannot be regarded as self-executing. The UN Charter, however, does not contain many obligations that require such a transfer: The organisational rules of the Charter are not suitable for domestic regulation. And the Charter's obligations on member states regulate primarily their international conduct with regard to other states and to the UN and are therefore also not intended to have any domestic effect.

75 See S Vöneky & R Wolfrum 'Die Reform der Friedensmissionen der Vereinten Nationen und ihre Umsetzung nach deutschem Verfassungsrecht' (2002) 62 *Zeitschrift für ausländisches öffentliches Recht und Völkerrecht* 569 600f.

76 Herdegen (n 47 above) 34 - 35. The German legislature has, furthermore, passed federal laws with regard to its obligations towards the tribunals, thereby explicitly consenting to these obligations, see below 3.3.2.

77 This is also emphasised by the Constitutional Court, see BVerfG Case 2 BvE 3/92 et al (n 46 above) 379.

78 Funke (n 47 above) 270 - 271. The formal law required under Basic Law art 59(2) has a dual function: It allows the Federal Government to enter into treaty obligations and grants the Federal President the power to ratify the treaty and it transfers the treaty provisions into the German legal order.

Articles 104 and 105 of the Charter are an exception to this rule and require domestic implementation. According to article 104 of the UN Charter, the UN shall enjoy legal capacity within the territory of its member states as far as this may be necessary for the exercise of its functions and the fulfilment of its purposes.[79] Article 105 of the UN Charter furthermore holds that the UN shall enjoy privileges and immunities within the member states. The Convention on the Privileges and Immunities of the United Nations of 1946[80] and the Convention on the Privileges and Immunities of the Specialized Agencies of 1947[81] substantiate these provisions of the Charter (→ Tladi).[82]

In accordance with the general indifference of international law towards the modalities of its domestic implementation, the UN Charter as well as the conventions leave the question of how these obligations are implemented in the domestic legal orders to the discretion of the member states.[83] In Germany, the ratification of the UN Charter and of the conventions have implemented these provisions into domestic law in the status of a federal law. No further act of implementation by the German parliament, for example, in the form of a specific federal act, is required. Within the German legal order, the UN therefore enjoys legal capacity, and privileges and immunities are granted.[84] As a result, the UN can rely directly on these rights and privileges in front of German courts and agencies.

3.2.2 Implementation of the prohibition of the use of force

Through the ratification of the UN Charter, the prohibition of the use of force under article 2(4) of the Charter has become part of the domestic law

79 On the legal personality of the UN under international law, see *Reparation for injuries suffered in the service of the United Nations* Advisory Opinion ICJ (11 April 1949) (1949) ICJ Reports 174.

80 Convention on the Privileges and Immunities of the United Nations (13 February 1946, 1 UNTS 15). Germany has signed and ratified this Convention, see Gesetz zu dem Übereinkommen vom 13. Februar 1946 über die Vorrechte und Immunitäten der Vereinen Nationen of 16 August 1980 (Bundesgesetzblatt 1980 II 941). Even before its membership in the United Nations, Germany had enacted a decree recognising the juridical personality of the UN, see AR Ziegler 'Article 104' in B Simma et al (n 6 above) 2138 para 6.

81 Convention on the Privileges and Immunities of the Specialized Agencies (21 November 1947, 33 UNTS 261). See Gesetz über den Beitritt der Bundesrepublik Deutschland zum Abkommen über die Vorrechte und Befreiungen der Sonderorganisationen der Vereinten Nationen of 22 June 1954 (Bundesgesetzblatt 1954 II 639).

82 UN Charter (n 2 above) arts 104 & 105.

83 According to sec 34 of the Final Article of the 1946 Convention, however, every member state has to be in a position under its own law to give effect to the terms of the Convention.

84 The German Courts Constitution Act of 27 January 1877 (Reichsgesetzblatt 1877 41) sec 20(2) affirms, in a declaratory manner, that German courts are without jurisdiction insofar as exemptions on the basis of international agreements apply. See W Zimmermann 'Section 20 GVG' in W Krüger & T Rauscher (eds) *Münchener Kommentar zur Zivilprozessordnung* vol 3 (4th edn 2013) para 16.

of Germany in the rank of a federal law (→ Wolfrum, Hestermeyer & Vöneky).[85] A higher rank is, however, attributed to the prohibition of the use of force through the recognition of its customary nature, due to article 25 of the Basic Law.[86] According to article 25 of the Basic Law, the prohibition of the use of force thereby has a rank higher than other federal laws but lower than the federal Constitution (→ Wolfrum, Hestermeyer & Vöneky). While technically it is not the Charter provision but a norm of customary international law that is incorporated through article 25 of the Basic Law, this differentiation is without practical relevance due to the identical content of article 2(4) of the UN Charter and the customary prohibition of the use of force.

The recognition of the *jus cogens* character of the prohibition of the use of force, on the other hand, does not influence the domestic status of article 2(4) UN Charter. Since *jus cogens* norms are generally also norms of customary international law,[87] there is no added value in the generally accepted proposition[88] that article 25 of the Basic Law also encompasses *jus cogens* norms.[89] While some authors maintain the view that *jus cogens* norms are endowed with constitutional rank or even with a rank higher than the Constitution,[90] there is no indication in the Basic Law to support this position.[91]

In the context of the prohibition of the use of force, however, the German Constitution encompasses a specific provision in article 26(1) which reads:

> Acts tending to and undertaken with intent to disturb the peaceful relations between nations, especially to prepare for a war of aggression, shall be unconstitutional. They shall be made a criminal offence.

Article 26(1) of the Basic Law is but one expression of the general commitment of Germany to peace as it is recognised as a fundamental constitutional principle underlying the Basic Law.[92] While the provision does not explicitly refer to international concepts of peace and the prohibition of the use of force, it is intended to synchronise the

85 See Basic Law art 59(2).

86 See BVerfG Case 2 BvE 6/99 (n 45 above) 212; BVerfG Case 2 BvE 2/07 (n 74 above) 270 - 271.

87 H Thirlway 'The sources of international law' in MD Evans (ed) *International law* (3rd edn 2010) 95 119.

88 See eg BVerfG Case 2 BvR 955/00 et al (26 October 2004) (2005) 112 *Entscheidungen des Bundesverfassungsgerichts* 1 27.

89 C Hillgruber 'Article 25' in B Schmidt-Bleibtreu, H Hofmann & A Hopfauf (eds) *Grundgesetz, Kommentar* (12th edn 2011) para 11; M Herdegen 'Review of the Security Council by National Courts: A Constitutional Perspective' in E de Wet & A Nollkaemper (eds) *Review of the Security Council by member states* (2003) 77 82f.

90 See I Pernice 'Article 25' in Dreier (n 45 above) para 25.

91 See Herdegen (n 17 above) para 42.

92 See BVerfG Case 2 BvE 2/08 et al (n 58 above) 346; A Proelß 'Das Friedensgebot des Grundgesetzes' in J Isensee & P Kirchhof (eds) *Handbuch des Staatsrechts der Bundesrepublik Deutschland* vol XI (3rd edn 2013) 63.

constitutional prohibition with the international rules on the use of force. All violations of the prohibition of the use of force under article 2(4) of the UN Charter therefore fall within the scope of article 26(1) Basic Law.[93] The wording 'war of aggression' was explicitly chosen in order to distinguish internationally prohibited military acts from legitimate acts of self-defense permitted under international law. Accordingly, all other constitutional provisions that refer to the concept of defense, such as article 115a(1) and article 87a of the Basic Law in particular, have to be read within their international context: The German Constitution does not allow the use of military force contrary to the international legal framework established by the UN Charter.[94]

While article 26(1) of the Basic Law has to be seen and interpreted in the context of the prohibition of the use of force, it goes beyond Germany's obligations under international law. While article 2(4) of the UN Charter outlaws only the actual threat or use of force, the constitutional prohibition applies to acts undertaken in preparation of illegal uses of force, provided they are carried out with the intention to disturb the peaceful relations between nations.[95] Article 26(1) therefore encompasses, for example, armament measures taken with a view to the illegal use of force or pro-war propaganda.[96] While the prohibition of the use of force under international law applies only to states,[97] article 26(1) of the Basic Law addresses state organs as well as individuals and private entities.[98] The provision therefore bans all acts that could potentially disturb the peaceful relations between nations, regardless of whether Germany would be responsible for those acts under international law.[99]

According to article 26(1) of the Basic Law the acts encompassed shall be made a criminal offence. The provision thereby establishes a constitutional obligation of the legislature to enact criminal laws, an obligation which the German legislature has only partially fulfilled through sections 80 and 80a of the Criminal Code, which encompass the preparation of and the incitement to wars of aggression, provided that

93 M Herdegen 'Article 26' in Maunz & Dürig (n 17 above) paras 4 &14; Proelß (n 92 above) para 25; for a more restrictive reading see C Hillgruber 'Article 26' in Schmidt-Bleibtreu et al (n 89 above) para 4.

94 C Tomuschat 'Staatsrechtliche Entscheidung für die internationale Offenheit' in J Isensee & P Kirchhof (eds) *Handbuch des Staatsrechts der Bundesrepublik Deutschland* vol XI (3rd edn 2013) 3 para 41.

95 I Pernice 'Article 26' in Dreier (n 45 above) para 17; Federal Administrative Court Case 2 WD 12/04 (21 June 2005) (2006) 59 *Neue Juristische Wochenschrift* 77 81.

96 R Streinz 'Article 26' in M Sachs (ed) *Grundgesetz, Kommentar* (7th edn 2014) para 21; U Fink 'Article 26' in H von Mangoldt, F Klein & C Starck (eds) *Grundgesetz, Kommentar* vol II (6th edn 2010) para 40.

97 A Randelzhofer & O Dörr 'Article 2(4)' in Simma (n 6 above) 200 para 29.

98 Federal Administrative Court Case 1 C 61/76 (23 June 1981) (1982) 35 *Neue Juristische Wochenschrift* 194 - 195; Streinz (n 96 above) para 22.

99 Beyond the symbolic nature of art 26 its legal implications are rather limited and do not go beyond the legal consequences the German legal order attributes to illegal acts in general, see Hillgruber (n 93 above) para 9.

Germany is meant to participate and that the danger of German participation is created.[100]

The German constitutional order does not only provide for the possibility of Germany's participation in the United Nations, but also for its membership in NATO. However, even with regard to the membership in NATO, the German constitutional order ensures that the international legal framework for the use of force as it is established under the UN Charter may not be violated. According to the Constitutional Court, article 24(2) of the Basic Law provides the constitutional basis for Germany's membership in NATO.[101] This constitutional provision allows for the integration of Germany into a system of collective security only 'with a view to maintaining peace'. As a result, the Constitutional Court emphasises that NATO can only be considered to fall within the scope of article 24(2) of the Basic Law if and as long as it is strictly committed to maintaining peace.[102]

In subsequent decisions, the Constitutional Court has further substantiated this holding and brought the rather vague constitutional requirement of 'maintaining peace' in close alignment with the UN Charter: With regard to NATO's new Strategic Concept of 1999, the Court held that the organisation's continuous commitment to maintaining peace was beyond question, in particular because the Concept allowed for military involvement only in accordance with international law, thereby subjecting NATO to the requirements for the use of force under the UN Charter.[103] Against the background of the NATO-led ISAF operation in Afghanistan, the Constitutional Court confirmed NATO's commitment to maintaining peace, *inter alia* referring to the authorisation of the ISAF operation through the Security Council under Chapter of the UN Charter.[104] Although the Constitutional Court emphasises that it will not generally scrutinise whether every NATO operation is in accordance with international law, since only a general and systemic deviation from the parliamentary approved programme of integration is constitutionally relevant, the Court's line of jurisprudence nevertheless contributes to aligning NATO's activities with the UN system of collective security.

100 See Proelß (n 92 above) para 28. The Criminal Code's phrasing that only wars of aggression that involve German participation are encompassed is more restrictive than the constitutional provision. Other criminal laws, such as the Code of Crimes against International Law, supplement the Criminal Code. Basic Law art 26(2) further supplements the prohibition of art 26(1), stipulating that weapons designed for warfare may be manufactured, transported or marketed only with the permission of the Federal Government.

101 BVerfG Case 2 BvE 3/92 et al (n 46 above) 350 - 351; BVerfG Case 2 BvE 6/99 (n 45 above) 209.

102 BVerfG Case 2 BvE 3/92 et al (n 46 above) 349. In BVerfG Case 2 BvE 6/99 (n 45 above) 212 the Court explicitly confirmed its competence to review whether NATO fulfills this requirement and acts within the scope of the parliamentary authorisation.

103 BVerfG Case 2 BvE 6/99 (n 45 above) 212 - 213.

104 BVerfG Case 2 BvE 2/07 (n 74 above) 270 - 276.

In conclusion, the international prohibition of the use of force is fully implemented in German constitutional law through article 59(2) and article 25 of the Basic Law. Article 26 of the Basic Law aims at effectively preventing acts of aggression and other acts that could disturb the peaceful relations between nations. Also, article 24(2) of the Basic Law, in the interpretation of the Constitutional Court, ensures that Germany participates in regional systems of collective security such as NATO only as long as they generally operate within the legal framework of the UN Charter.

3.3 Implementation of Security Council resolutions

3.3.1 The need for implementation

Unlike most provisions of the UN Charter, resolutions of the Security Council may require implementation within the domestic legal orders of the member states, depending on their regulatory content: Resolutions that authorise the use of force, for example, do not entail the need for such implementation, since they are only meant to have a legal effect on the international level, regarding the relationship between states.[105] Other resolutions explicitly aim at evoking legal effects within the domestic legal orders:[106] The Security Council explicitly demanded domestic measures of the member states in order to comply with their obligation to cooperate with the International Criminal Tribunal for the Former Yugoslavia,[107] and required member states to criminalise and prohibit the financing of terrorist acts.[108] Moreover, domestic implementation is required in order to give effect to resolutions through which the Security Council imposes sanctions on states or individuals.[109]

In general, however, resolutions of the Security Council are deemed to not unfold direct effect within the German legal order.[110] Therefore, resolutions need to be implemented into domestic law through legislative

105 They may, however, raise the question whether the domestic legal order provides a sufficient legal framework for the participation of Germany in UN mandated or authorised operations, see below 3.5.
106 See Funke (n 47 above) 246 - 258.
107 UNSC Res 827 (25 May 1993) UN Doc S/RES/827 para 4.
108 UNSC Res 1373 (28 September 2001) UN Doc S/RES/1373 para 1.
109 On the binding nature of sanctions imposed by the Security Council under UN Charter art 41 see N Krisch 'Article 41' in Simma et al (n 6 above) 1305 paras 9 - 10.
110 See the statement of the German government with regard to the draft of the German Foreign Trade Law (Außenwirtschaftsgesetz) Bundestags-Drucksache 3/1285 (1959) 237; BGH Case 1 Str 700/94 (21 April 1995) 41 *Entscheidungen des Bundesgerichtshofes in Strafsachen* 127 129; B Fassbender 'Art. 19 Abs. 4 GG als Garantie innerstaatlichen Rechtsschutzes gegen Individualsanktionen des UN-Sicherheitsrates' (2007) 132 *Archiv des öffentlichen Rechts* 257 265; Frowein (n 47 above) 259; but see also Herdegen (n 47 above) 32 - 37.

or administrative measures before domestic bodies, such as administrative agencies or courts, can apply them.[111] This prevailing view, which is in accordance with the general practice of most states,[112] is based on the general premise that – unlike the law of the European Union – international law does not regulate its effects within the states' legal orders.[113] Resolutions of the Security Council are not of a supranational nature. Neither the UN Charter, nor the Security Council demand that resolutions are attributed direct effect within the domestic legal order.[114]

Whether resolutions have direct effect within the domestic legal order is therefore left to the decision of the member states. Against this background, it is argued that Security Council resolutions are not directly applicable since the member states have not transferred sovereign rights to the Security Council in a manner that would enable the Council to pass resolutions with such a direct effect.[115] This reasoning, however, confuses the question of whether the Security Council has the power to make decisions with direct effect with the question of whether the domestic legal order attributes direct effect to resolutions. While the UN Charter does not contain any indication that the Security Council would possess such a supranational competence, this does not preclude that resolutions can be granted direct effect under domestic law, in accordance with the general requirements the German legal order establishes for the direct effect of international legal norms, namely that the norm is suitable and sufficiently precise for direct applicability.[116]

Against this background, it seems, in general, possible to attribute direct effect to at least some Security Council resolutions.[117] Regularly, however, significant reasons will argue against the direct applicability of Security Council resolutions. Firstly, Security Council resolutions are

111 On the concept of direct applicability see Peters (n 6 above) para 45; H Sauer *Staatsrecht III* (2nd edn 2013) 82 - 91.

112 J Polakiewicz 'International Law and Domestic (Municipal) Law, Law and Decisions of International Organizations and Courts' in Wolfrum (n 16 above) para 18; HK Ress *Das Handelsembargo* (2000) 78; V Gowlland-Debbas 'Concluding Remarks' in V Gowlland-Debbas (ed) *National implementation of United Nations Sanctions* (2004) 643 644.

113 Kaiser (n 27 above) para 6.

114 Nettesheim (n 71 above) para 194; Funke (n 47 above) 270; C Porteila 'National Implementation of United Nations sanctions' (Winter 2009-10) *International Journal* 13 18; A Pellet & A Miron 'Sanctions' in Wolfrum (n 16 above) para 45. See also Joined Cases C-402/05 P & C-415/05 *Kadi and Al Barakaat v Council and Commission* [2008] ECR I-6351, para 298; *Nada v Switzerland* App No 10593/08 (ECtHR, 12 September 2012) para 176.

115 Frowein (n 47 above) 258; N Weiß *Kompetenzlehre internationaler Organisationen* (2009) 185; O Rojahn 'Article 24' in I v Münch & P Kunig (eds) *Grundgesetz, Kommentar* vol 1 (6th edn 2012) para 55.

116 On these requirements see Kaiser (n 27 above) paras 9 - 20; for a modification of these requirements in light of the special nature of Security Council resolutions see Peters (n 6 above) para 47.

117 See Peters (n 6 above) para 53; but see also Nettesheim (n 71 above) para 195 (arguing that the German legal order does not attribute direct effect to secondary acts of international organisations).

generally addressed to states only, thereby excluding their direct application with regard to individuals and private entities.[118] Effective implementation of Security Council resolutions may, however, also require obligating private entities to comply with resolutions, for example, private banks to freeze the accounts of alleged terrorists, or private companies to respect the terms of a trade embargo. Secondly, numerous Security Council resolutions explicitly require their domestic implementation through legislative or administrative measures, as is, for example, the case with regard to the obligations established under Resolution 1373 (2001) or, more recently Resolution 2178 (2014). Thirdly, resolutions that are intended to have an effect within the domestic legal order will regularly restrict the rights of individuals or private entities. Under domestic law, such restrictions require a sufficiently clear legal basis, and it is doubtful whether the resolution itself – in conjunction with the law concerning the accession of Germany to the United Nations – can be regarded as fulfilling this requirement.[119]

In conclusion, resolutions of the Security Council therefore need to be implemented under German law, provided that their regulatory content or their effective enforcement requires them to unfold legal effects within the domestic legal order. Germany has taken different legislative measures in order to comply with this obligation.

3.3.2 Implementation of resolutions establishing ad hoc tribunals

The international criminal tribunals established by the Security Council with regard to the former Yugoslavia[120] and Rwanda[121] depend on the effective cooperation with states, for example, with regard to the arrest of suspects and their surrender to the tribunals, measures of investigation and prosecution in general, or the execution of judgments.[122] The Security Council therefore established a general obligation of member states to cooperate with the tribunals.[123] The statutes of the tribunals substantiate this obligation, providing for an obligation of states to comply with requests for assistance and orders of the tribunals[124] and to respect the primacy of the tribunals' jurisdiction.[125]

118 Even individual-oriented sanctions of the Security Council are, in general, addressed to states. Only exceptionally has the Security Council directly addressed non-state entities, see eg the address to the 'Afghan faction known as the Taliban' in UNSC Res 1267 (15 October 1999) UN Doc S/RES/1267 paras 1f.
119 See Peters (n 6 above) para 51.
120 UNSC Res 827 (n 107 above).
121 UNSC Res 955 (8 November 1994) UN Doc S/RES/955.
122 See in general MC Bassiouni *Introduction to International Criminal Law* (2nd edn 2003) 22 - 26.
123 UNSC Res 827 (n 107 above) para 4; UNSC Res 955 (n 121 above) para 2.
124 See ICTY Statute (n 44 above) art 29; ICTR Statute (n 44 above) art 28. Moreover, the Prosecutor may seek the assistance of state organs, see ICTY Statute (n 44 above) art 18(2); ICTR Statute (n 44 above) art 17(2).
125 ICTY Statute (n 44 above) art 9; ICTR Statute (n 44 above) art 8.

Germany has implemented these obligations and created the legal framework for cooperation with the tribunals through two almost identical federal laws which were passed to fulfil Germany's obligations under the Security Council resolutions and to ensure that state organs comply with those obligations (→ Schmalenbach).[126] At the request of the tribunals, criminal proceedings in Germany have to be transferred to the tribunals,[127] German state organs are required to arrest and transfer suspects to the tribunals upon request,[128] and are obliged to cooperate in general.[129] Moreover, a constitutional amendment of article 16(2) of the Basic Law provides for the possibility to extradite German nationals to the international tribunals.[130]

3.3.3 Implementation of legislative resolutions

The most obvious requirement for domestic implementation is established through the legislative resolutions of the Security Council, Resolution 1373 (2001) regarding the prevention and suppression of the financing of terrorist acts,[131] as well as Resolution 1540 (2004) regarding the non-proliferation of weapons of mass destruction[132] and the most recent Resolution 2178 (2014) on foreign terrorist fighters.[133] While Germany could, in part, rely on previously enacted legislation, the resolutions also obliged Germany to amend or change established legislation.[134]

Security Council Resolution 1373 (2001) obliges member states to criminalise and prohibit the financing of terrorist acts and explicitly demands that member states establish terrorist acts as serious criminal offences in their domestic law.[135] The German legal order already encompassed criminal offences as required by the resolution, in particular

126 Gesetz über die Zusammenarbeit mit dem Internationalen Strafgerichtshof für das ehemalige Jugoslawien of 10 April 1995 (Bundesgesetzblatt 1995 I 485) sec 1; Gesetz über die Zusammenarbeit mit dem Internationalen Strafgerichtshof für Ruanda of 4 May 1998 (Bundesgesetzblatt 1998 I 843) sec 1. For an overview see JA Frowein & N Krisch 'Germany' in Gowlland-Debbas (n 112 above) 233 239 & 258ff for a comprehensive analysis, see K Ambos *Internationales Strafrecht* (3rd edn 2011) paras 62 - 102.

127 Sec 2 of the respective laws.

128 Sec 3 of the respective laws.

129 Secs 4 & 5 of the respective laws.

130 While the Constitution was amended with a view to the German ratification of the Rome Statute establishing the International Criminal Court, it applies also with regard to the tribunals established by the Security Council, see A Zimmermann 'Die Auslieferung Deutscher an Staaten der Europäischen Union und internationale Strafgerichtshöfe' (2001) *Juristenzeitung* 233.

131 UNSC Res 1373 (n 108 above).

132 UNSC Res 1540 (28 April 2004) UN Doc S/RES/1540.

133 UNSC Res 2178 (24 September 2014) UN Doc S/RES/2178.

134 On the legality of the legislative practice of the Security Council see eg M Happold 'Security Council Resolution 1373 and the constitution of the United Nations' (2003) 16 *Leiden Journal of International Law* 593 (arguing that the Security Council acted ultra vires); Talmon (n 52 above) 175 (arguing that legislative measures are within the scope of the competences of the Council).

135 UNSC Res 1373 (n 108 above) paras 1(b) & 2(e).

Section 89a of the German Criminal Code on the preparation of a serious violent offence endangering the state, Section 129a of the German Criminal Code on the formation of terrorist organisations, but also the criminal offence of participation in terrorist acts that are criminal offences by themselves.[136] In order to fully comply with its obligations under Resolution 1373, the German legislature furthermore enacted numerous legislative changes focusing on combatting international terrorism.[137]

Similarly, Security Council Resolution 1540 (2004) requires member states to enact legislation in order to prohibit non-state actors 'to manufacture, acquire, possess, develop, transport, transfer or use nuclear, chemical or biological weapons and their means of delivery'.[138] Again, Germany did not implement this obligation through a separate law, but could rely on already existing legal acts, such as the War Weapons Control Act of 1961.[139]

Passed against the background of the Islamic State's growing influence, in particular in Syria and in Iraq, Security Council Resolution 2178 (2014) obliges member states to prevent the movement of terrorists across borders and to criminalise the travel or attempt to travel as well as aiding or abetting such actions.[140] In light of the already far-reaching anti-terrorism laws in Germany, it is subject to debate whether this resolution actually required further implementing legislation.[141] In April 2015, the German Parliament nevertheless passed a law further criminalising the travel or attempt to travel of potential terrorists as well as the financing of terrorism.[142]

136 See Germany *Report to the Security Council Committee established pursuant to Resolution 1373 (2001) concerning Counter-Terrorism* UN Doc S/2002/11, 5.

137 Gesetz zur Bekämpfung des internationalen Terrorismus of 9 January 2002 (Bundesgesetzblatt 2002 I 361). While the governmental explanatory statement to the draft legislation refers to the implementation of Resolution 1373 (2001) in numerous instances (see Entwurf eines Gesetzes zur Bekämpfung des internationalen Terrorismus (8 November 2001) Bundestags-Drucksache 14/7386 (2001) 35), the law goes beyond what was required under the Resolution, see Frowein & Krisch (n 126 above) 239 & 254 - 255.

138 UNSC Res 1540 (n 132 above) para 2.

139 See Note verbale dated 26 October 2004 from the Permanent Mission of Germany to the United Nations addressed to the Chairman of the Committee (2 November 2004) UN Doc S/AC.44/2004/(02)/20; and the list provided by Germany in its response to the Secretariat of the 1540 Committee by the Permanent Mission of the Federal Republic of Germany to the United Nations in New York (26 May 2010) Pol 555.33, Note No 210/2010 http://www.un.org/en/sc/1540 (accessed 2 March 2015).

140 UNSC Res 2178 (n 133 above) para 6.

141 See M Payandeh 'Globale Anti-Terrorgesetzgebung: Die deutsche Rechtsordnung im Sog des UN-Sicherheitsrats?' (2014) *Zeitschrift für Rechtspolitik* 241.

142 See Entwurf eines Gesetzes zur Änderung der Verfolgung der Vorbereitung von schweren staatsgefährdenden Gewalttaten of 24 February 2015 (Bundestags-Drucksache 18/4087).

3.3.4 Implementation of resolutions imposing sanctions

Since the end of the Cold War, the Security Council has made increasing use of its power to impose sanctions under article 41 of the UN Charter.[143] Sanctions against states can encompass a variety of measures, including arms embargos, comprehensive trade restrictions, or restraints on air traffic. Moreover, the Council has enacted 'targeted sanctions' against individuals and private entities, in the form of asset freezes and travel bans.[144] The effective implementation of these sanctions regularly requires member states to take action under their domestic legal regimes.

With regard to different mechanisms of implementation, three kinds of sanctions imposed by the Security Council can be distinguished: First, the Security Council can impose sanctions against states. After the Iraqi invasion of Kuwait in 1990, for example, the Security Council enacted comprehensive sanctions against Iraq, including a trade and weapons embargo as well as the freezing of Iraqi financial assets.[145] Second, the Security Council can impose sanctions on individuals and private entities, listing the targeted persons directly or through a sanctions committee established by the Council. This approach has been taken, most prominently, against Osama bin Laden, the Taliban and members of Al-Qaida, initially imposed through Security Council Resolution 1267 (1999) and further developed through subsequent resolutions.[146] Third, the Security Council can impose sanctions against individuals without identifying the targeted persons, leaving it to the member states to determine which persons or entities fall within the scope of the sanctions. The Council has resorted to this approach through Resolution 1373 (2001), according to which the member states have to freeze the assets of persons suspected to be involved in terrorist acts.[147]

As a member state of the United Nations, Germany has an obligation to implement resolutions of the Security Council under article 25 of the UN Charter and, with regard to resolutions adopted under Chapter, article 48 of the UN Charter. Within the context of the European Union, however, sanctions are primarily implemented through the EU and not directly through the German legal order.

143 See V Gowlland-Debbas 'Sanctions regimes under article 41 of the United Nations Charter' in Gowlland-Debbas (n 112 above) 3 6ff.
144 See Krisch (n 109 above) paras 15 - 18.
145 UNSC Res 661 (6 August 1990) UN Doc S/RES/661 paras 2 - 4.
146 UNSC Res 1267 (n 118 above) also established the so-called Al-Qaida and Taliban Sanctions Committee, which in 2011 was divided into one committee concerned with Al-Qaida (UNSC Res 1989 (17 June 2011) UN Doc S/RES/1989) and one committee dealing with the Taliban (UNSC Res 1988 (17 June 2011) UN Doc S/RES/1988).
147 UNSC Res 1373 (n 108 above) para 1(c).

Implementation through the European Union

The European Union is not a member of the United Nations. It is therefore not directly bound by the UN Charter and does not have an obligation to implement Security Council resolutions.[148] The Court of Justice of the European Union, nevertheless, recognises a general obligation of the EU to respect international law and the United Nations in particular[149] and emphasises that the EU may generally not impede the performance of the obligations of the member states under the UN Charter.[150]

Against this background, the Treaty of Lisbon contains rather comprehensive competences of the EU with regard to the implementation of sanctions imposed by the Security Council. Article 215(1) of the TFEU constitutes the key provision, dealing with economic sanctions (restrictive measures) imposed against third states. Article 215(2) of the TFEU, moreover, explicitly provides a competence of the EU for sanctions against individuals and private entities.[151] Under article 215 of the TFEU, Security Council resolutions are implemented in a two-step process. Action under article 215 of the TFEU first requires a unanimously adopted decision by the Council of the European Union within the context of the Common Foreign and Security Policy (CFSP). The Council can then take the necessary measures with a qualified majority on a joint proposal from the High Representative of the Union for Foreign Affairs and Security Policy and the Commission. The Council regularly implements the CFSP decision through a regulation which, according to its nature as a binding legal act that is directly applicable in the member states,[152] serves as the domestic legal basis for the implementation of the sanctions imposed by the Security Council.[153]

The sanctions regime established by the Security Council with regard to Osama bin Laden, the Taliban and members of Al-Qaida, for example, has been implemented by the EU through a Council Common Position that referred to the Security Council Resolution, stipulated that action was necessary, and that financial assets of the individuals and entities as envisaged by the Security Council will be frozen.[154] This Common

148 Case T-315/01 *Kadi v Council and Commission* [2005] ECR II-3649 para 192; HJ Cremer 'Article 215' in C Calliess & M Ruffert (eds) *EUV/AEUV, Kommentar* (4th edn 2011) para 9; M Payandeh & H Sauer 'European Union: UN sanctions and EU fundamental rights' (2009) 7 *International Journal of Constitutional Law* 306 311.

149 *Kadi case* (n 114 above) paras 291 - 297.

150 *Kadi case (CFI)* (n 148 above) para 197.

151 Before the Treaty of Lisbon entered into force, sanctions against individuals were enacted on the basis of arts 60, 301 & 308 of the Treaty establishing the European Community, an approach that was upheld by the Court of Justice of the European Union, see *Kadi case* (n 114 above) paras 158 - 236.

152 TFEU (n 60 above) art 288(2).

153 See Funke (n 47 above) 264 & 266 - 267.

154 Common Position 1999/727/CFSP of 16 November 1999 OJ L294/1; later replaced by Common Position 2002/402/CFSP of 29 May 2002 OJ L139/4; amended by

Position was then implemented through a Council regulation that substantiated these obligations and included, as an annex, a list of persons and entities that the sanctions regime should apply to, in accordance with the determinations made by the Security Council sanctions committee.[155] Amendments to the list of targeted persons and entities made by the Security Council sanctions committee are transposed into the EU legal order through regulations adopted by the European Commission.[156] In general, the EU legal order therefore provides for an almost automatic adoption of the listings undertaken by the Security Council and its sanctions committee into EU law and thereby into the legal orders of the EU member states.[157]

Implementation through German law

As long as Security Council sanctions are implemented through the European Union, no additional implementation measures are required under German law. EU regulations are directly applicable within the domestic legal order, thereby providing a sufficient legal basis to directly bind state organs, individuals, and private entities. However, even in light of its far-reaching competences, the EU may not be competent with regard to every measure envisioned by the Security Council. When the Security Council in 2003, for example, ordered member states to not only freeze Iraqi funds but to transfer them to the Development Fund for Iraq,[158] this obligation was not implemented through the EU but through the member states.[159] In the field covered by article 215 of the TFEU, however, the European Union has an exclusive competence,[160] thereby generally barring independent measures by the member states.[161] German

Common Position 2003/140/CFSP of 28 February 2003 OJ L53/62 and Council Decision 2011/487/CFSP of 2 August 2011 OJ L199/73.

155 Council Regulation (EC) No 337/2000 of 16 February 2000 OJ L43/1; later replaced by Council Regulation (EC) No 467/2001 of 9 March 2001 OJ L67/1; and then Council Regulation (EC) No 881/2002 of 29 May 2002 OJ L139/9.

156 See Council Regulation (EC) No 881/2002 of 29 May 2002 OJ L139/9 art 7.

157 Apart from TFEU (n 60 above) art 215, TFEU art 75 contains a specific EU competence with regard to preventing and combatting terrorism. Unlike TFEU art 215, TFEU art 75 does not require a unanimously adopted decision by the Council as a prerequisite for further action but provides for the application of the ordinary legislative procedure, thereby requiring that measures are adopted jointly by the European Parliament and the Council (TFEU art 289(1)) whereas under TFEU art 215 the European Parliament is merely informed of the measures adopted by the Council. According to the Court of Justice of the European Union, TFEU art 75 does, however, not exclude the application of TFEU art 215, see Case C-130/10 *European Parliament v Council* [19 July 2012] paras 50 - 66. Therefore TFEU art 215 will continue to provide the most important legal basis for EU measures implementing sanctions imposed by the UN Security Council, even with regard to terrorism.

158 UNSC Res 1483 (22 May 2003) UN Doc S/RES/1483 para 23.

159 See Council Regulation (EC) No 1210/2003 of 8 July 2003 OJ L 169/6, para 5; Funke (n 47 above) 275.

160 Cremer (n 148 above) para 29; J Kokott 'Article 215 TFEU' in R Streinz (ed) *EUV/AEUV, Kommentar* (2nd edn 2012) para 7.

161 TFEU (n 60 above) art 2(1).

implementing measures may, however, be required and admissible in case the EU does not take action.[162]

Under German law, sanctions imposed by the Security Council are implemented through the Foreign Trade Act[163] and the Foreign Trade Regulation.[164] Section 4(2) of the Foreign Trade Act provides for the possibility of restricting foreign trade if Germany is required to implement such restrictions under EU law or under a Security Council resolution. The specific restrictions are enumerated in the Foreign Trade Regulation, adopted by the Federal Government.[165] In case immediate action is required, the Federal Minister of Economics can impose provisional restrictions through an executive order.[166]

Specific forms of sanctions can, furthermore, be implemented through different means. With regard to restrictions on arms trade, for example, the general rules of the law concerning military arms trade apply.[167] According to this law, the trade of military arms requires specific authorisation. The German authorities can therefore implement an arms embargo imposed by the Security Council through denying such authorisation.[168] Similarly, travel restrictions can be implemented through denying visas to persons listed by the Security Council.[169]

Administratively, sanctions imposed by the Security Council are implemented and enforced through different governmental agencies. With regard to restrictions on foreign trade the Federal Office of Economics and Export Control (BAFA) is tasked with overseeing and enforcing the rules of export control. With regard to financial sanctions, the central bank of Germany (Deutsche Bundesbank) is the competent domestic authority, providing information on existing sanctions or granting exceptions to the restrictions, as provided for in the decisions of the Security Council.

162 Funke (n 47 above) 268; Fassbender (n 110 above) 273; for a skeptical view, see PJ Kuijper, 'Implementation of Binding Security Council Resolutions by the EU/EC' in E de Wet & A Nollkaemper (eds) *Review of the Security Council by Member States* (2003) 39 40ff. On the applicability of TFEU art 347, see Cremer (n 148 above) para 29; R Arnold & E Meindl 'Außenhandelsrecht' in M Dauses (ed) *Handbuch des EU-Wirtschaftsrechts* (2013) para 119. On the applicability of TFEU art 351 to Germany's obligations under the UN Charter, see *Kadi case (CFI)* (n 148 above) para 187.

163 Außenwirtschaftsgesetz of 6 June 2013 (Bundesgesetzblatt 2013 I 1482).

164 Außenwirtschaftsverordnung of 2 August 2013 (Bundesgesetzblatt 2013 I 2865).

165 See Foreign Trade Regulation secs 74 - 77. Violations of these restrictions may be punishable offenses, see Foreign Trade Act secs 17 - 19; Foreign Trade Regulation secs 80 - 82.

166 Foreign Trade Act secs 6 & 13(2)(2)(2).

167 Gesetz über die Kontrolle von Kriegswaffen of 22 November 1990 (Bundesgetzblatt 1990 I 2506).

168 Frowein & Krisch (n 126 above) 237.

169 Frowein & Krisch (n 126 above) 237.

Fundamental rights and implementation

The most significant and controversial obstacle to implementing Security Council resolutions that impose individual sanctions against alleged terrorists is the question of whether – in the absence of effective means of judicial or administrative review on the international level – domestic or regional courts may review the compatibility of these sanctions with human rights guarantees. With regard to the implementation of sanctions in Germany, the question has most prominently been dealt with by the Court of Justice of the European Union in the *Kadi* case.[170] In 2005, the General Court (then called the Court of First Instance) held that EU regulations which implement Security Council resolutions could, in general, not be subject to judicial review.[171] Upon appeal, the Court of Justice (ECJ) rejected this proposition and emphasised its responsibility to review the lawfulness of all EU legal acts.[172] Since the listing procedure of the UN Sanctions Committee provided neither for a communication of the reasons for listing a person, nor for any means of administrative or judicial review, the ECJ found a violation of the right to be heard, of the right to an effective remedy and of the right to property.[173] This approach of the ECJ has been confirmed in subsequent decisions.[174] And in the most recent *Kadi* decision, the ECJ held that while the listed suspect had received sufficient information on the grounds of his listing in order to satisfy his rights of defense and his right to judicial review, there had not been produced sufficient information or evidence with regard to his involvement in terrorist activities that would justify the adoption of restrictive measures against him.[175]

While the ECJ therefore recognises improvements within the UN Sanctions Committee's listing procedure, it nevertheless continues to review whether EU legal acts that implement Security Council resolutions are in accordance with the fundamental rights guarantees of the EU legal order. However, the ECJ also indicated, already in the first *Kadi* decision, its willingness to refrain from such a review, provided that a sufficient level of rights protection is guaranteed within the UN system.[176]

170 For a current overview over the proceedings see CA Feinäugle 'Case note' (2013) 107 *American Journal of International Law* 878 - 881. In October 2012 the Sanctions Committee removed Mr Kadi from its list, see UN Press Release (5 October 2012) UN Doc SC/10785.

171 *Kadi case (CFI)* (n 148 above). The Court held, however, that it could review indirectly whether Security Council resolutions are in accordance with peremptory norms of international law (*jus cogens*) but found that the sanctions practice did not violate any of these 'higher rules of public international law'.

172 *Kadi case* (n 114 above) paras 278 - 326.

173 *Kadi case* (n 114 above) paras 333 - 371.

174 Case T-85/09 *Kadi v Commission* [2010] ECR II-5177; Joined Cases C-399/06 P & C-403/06 P, *Hassan v Council* [2009] ECR I-11393.

175 Joined Cases C-548/10 P, C-539/10 P & C-595/10 P *Commission v Kadi* [18 July 2013].

176 For this reading of the decision see Payandeh & Sauer (n 148 above) 314; see also J Kokott and C Sobotta 'The Kadi Case – Constitutional core values and international law – Finding the balance?' (2012) 23 *European Journal of International Law* 1015.

German courts have, until now, not yet had the chance or seized the opportunity to rule on the legality of the UN sanctions regime.[177] Nevertheless, a preliminary and cautious assessment of how the German Constitutional Court would decide a case involving the UN sanctions regime is possible in light of the Court's jurisprudence with regard to the European Union and international law in general. In its jurisprudence, the Court routinely refers to the openness of the German constitutional order towards international law (*Völkerrechtsfreundlichkeit*)[178] and towards European Union law (*Europarechtsfreundlichkeit*)[179] – constitutional principles the Court operationalises in order to avoid conflicts with international law and EU law. At the same time, however, the Court emphasises the limits of these principles: According to the well known *Solange* jurisprudence, the Constitutional Court will refrain from reviewing whether legal acts of the EU are compatible with the fundamental rights guarantees of the German Constitution only as long as the EU and the ECJ in particular protect fundamental rights to a degree essentially equivalent to the level of fundamental rights protection under the Basic Law.[180] Against this background, the Constitutional Court will, on the one hand, take Germany's obligations under the UN Charter and the importance of the UN system and its functioning for the international community seriously. On the other hand, the Court will only be willing to refrain from reviewing whether UN mandated sanctions are compatible with the fundamental rights of the German Constitution if and as long as a sufficient level of individual rights protection is guaranteed either within the EU system or within the United Nations.[181] Notwithstanding some improvements and positive developments (→ Tladi), the UN system of targeted sanctions does, at this point, lack such a sufficient level of fundamental rights protection against the listing of terrorist suspects.[182] On the basis of its previous jurisprudence, it can therefore be assumed, that the Constitutional Court would not refrain from reviewing whether UN mandated sanctions are in conformity with the fundamental rights guarantees of the German Constitution. As soon as sufficient means of

177 In one of the few pertinent cases before German courts, the Administrative Court of Munich rejected the petition of the applicant to suspend the proceedings and to refer the case to the Constitutional Court for a ruling on the constitutionality of the sanctions regime. The Administrative Court rather emphasised that the applicant had to seek legal remedies against the listing primarily within the EU system of judicial protection and that the EU courts had demonstrated that they ensure a sufficient level of fundamental rights protection against the listing procedure. See Administrative Court of Munich Case M 17 K 07.452 (13 December 2007).

178 See in particular BVerfG Case 2 BvR 1481/04 (14 October 2004) (2005) 111 *Entscheidungen des Bundesverfassungsgerichts* 307 317f.

179 See in particular BVerfG Case 2 BvE 2/08 et al (n 58 above) 346 - 347.

180 BVerfG Case 2 BvR 197/83 (n 45 above) 387; for a summary and evaluation of this line of jurisprudence see M Payandeh 'Constitutional review of EU law after Honeywell: Contextualising the relationship between the German Constitutional Court and the EU Court of Justice' (2011) 48 *Common Market Law Review* 9 13f.

181 For a similar assessment, see Fassbender (n 110 above) 257.

182 See eg A Ciampi 'Security Council targeted sanctions and human rights' in B Fassbender (ed) *Securing human rights? Achievements and challenges of the UN Security Council* (2011) 98.

legal protection are established at the UN level, however, the Court would be more willing to defer to the UN organs.

This general approach of the Constitutional Court is, moreover, in accordance with the position of the European Court of Human Rights with regard to the obligations of the member states of the European Convention on Human Rights under international law and under the UN Charter in particular: In the *Bosphorus* case, the Strasbourg Court held that when states implement obligations flowing from their membership in an international organisation, the compatibility of these implementing measures with the European Convention can be presumed, as long as the organisation protects fundamental rights in a manner which can be considered to be at least equivalent to that of the Convention.[183] In a recent decision[184] regarding the Iraq sanctions regime established by the Security Council,[185] the European Court of Human Rights, however, held that due to the lack of legal protection within the UN sanctions regime, the *Bosphorus* presumption did not apply and concluded that Switzerland had violated its obligations under the European Convention on Human Rights.[186]

In conclusion, European courts have challenged the compatibility of UN imposed sanctions on individuals with fundamental rights guarantees, and it can be presumed that the German Constitutional Court would adopt a similar approach. As long as the United Nations do not guarantee a sufficient level of human rights protection against the listing of individuals, a comprehensive implementation of these sanctions within the European Union and Germany cannot be guaranteed.

3.4 Consideration of United Nations soft law

Resolutions adopted by the UN General Assembly are not legally binding, they can therefore not be implemented into the German legal order in a strict sense. General Assembly resolutions can, nevertheless, be regarded

183 *Bosphorus Hava Yollari v Ireland* App no 45036/98 (ECtHR, 30 June 2005) paras 154 - 155.

184 Previously, the European Court of Human Rights had avoided ruling on the relationship between Security Council resolutions and the European Convention on Human Rights: In the 2011 *Al-Jedda* decision, the Court resorted to the presumption that 'the Security Council does not intend to impose any obligation on Member States to breach fundamental principles of human rights', see *Al-Jedda v United Kingdom* App no 27021/08 (ECtHR, 7 July 2011) para 102. And in the 2012 *Nada* decision the Court found that Switzerland, when implementing a Security Council resolution, had not used all the latitude it enjoyed under the resolution, see *Nada case* (n 114 above) para 180.

185 UNSC Res 1483 (n 158 above).

186 *Al-Dulimi et Montana v Switzerland* App no 5809/08 (ECtHR, 26 November 2013) paras 114 - 121. While the case does not deal with the sanctions regime established under UNSC Res 1267 (n 118 above), the Court explicitly holds that the 1267 sanctions regime does not guarantee the minimum standard of human rights protection, see para 119.

as authoritative statements of existing customary international law, indicate customary international law in the making, or even 'crystallize' emerging customary international law.[187] Against this background, and in light of the contribution of domestic legal orders and domestic courts to the formation and identification of customary international law in general,[188] the question whether and how domestic legal orders recognise the normative significance of General Assembly resolutions gains importance.

The German legal order does not explicitly attribute significance to resolutions of the General Assembly or other kinds of United Nations soft law. The jurisprudence of German courts, and of the Constitutional Court in particular, nevertheless exhibits considerable openness towards General Assembly resolutions. The Constitutional Court, for example, repeatedly and routinely refers to the Universal Declaration of Human Rights as a subsidiary means of interpretation with regard to the open-textured constitutional rights of the Basic Law.[189] The Court furthermore refers to the International Law Commission's Draft Articles on State Responsibility as they were adopted by the General Assembly, thereby confirming and reinforcing the claim that the draft embodies existing customary international law.[190] In a similar vein, the Court has relied on the Friendly Relations Declaration,[191] on resolutions interpreting the term genocide,[192] or on principles adopted by the General Assembly with regard to mental health issues.[193] While these references to resolutions of the General Assembly may not have far-reaching legal significance in the particular cases, the continuous affirmative reference to the resolutions can be understood as a recognition of the authoritative voice of the General Assembly within the international community.

187 E Klein & S Schmahl 'Article 10' in Simma et al (n 6 above) para 51.

188 See eg A Tzanakopoulos 'Domestic courts in international law: the international judicial function of national courts' (2011) 34 *Loyola of Los Angeles International & Comparative Law Review* 133 154ff.

189 See eg BVerfG Case 2 BvR 61/96 (12 May 1998) (1998) 51 *Neue Juristische Wochenschrift* 2587 2589; BVerfG Case 2 BvR 2560/95 (7 April 1998) (1998) 51 *Neue Juristische Wochenschrift* 2585; BVerfG Case 1 BvL 4/54 (17 January 1957) (1957) 6 *Entscheidungen des Bundesverfassungsgerichts* 55 73; on the reception of the Universal Declaration through the German constitutional order in general see T Rensmann *Wertordnung und Verfassung* (2007).

190 See eg BVerfG Case 2 BvR 2660/06 (13 August 2013) para 43; BVerfG, Case 2 BvM 1/03 et al (8 May 2007) (2008) 118 *Entscheidungen des Bundesverfassungsgerichts* 124 136 - 137; BVerfG Case 2 BvR 955/00 (26 October 2004) (2005) 24 *Neue Zeitschrift für Verwaltungsrecht* 560 563f - 564; BVerfG Case 2 BvR 1379/01 (28 June 2004) (2004) 57 *Neue Juristische Wochenschrift* 3257 3258.

191 BVerfG Case 2 BvR 955/00 et al (n 88 above) 36.

192 BVerfG Case 2 BvR 1290/99 (12 December 2000) (2001) 51 *Neue Juristische Wochenschrift* 1848 1852.

193 BVerfG Case 2 BvR 882/09 (23 March 2011) (2012) 128 *Entscheidungen des Bundesverfassungsgerichts* 282 308, 310, 313 - 315.

3.5 Enabling participation in the United Nations system of collective security

The UN system of collective security, as it is established by the UN Charter and substantiated and further developed through the practice of the Security Council, envisions different mechanisms in order to maintain peace and security: the institutionally safeguarded obligation of member states to settle their disputes peacefully, the Security Council's enforcement mechanisms under Chapter of the Charter, as well as the multi-facetted peacekeeping practice. All these measures require that the member states not only comply with but actively support actions taken by the United Nations. While the UN Charter does not establish obligations of member states to participate in any particular measure,[194] article 2(5) UN Charter establishes a general obligation to support the UN. And although the obligation to provide forces depends on the conclusion of special agreements between the member states and the Security Council,[195] member states are under a general, albeit weak, obligation to participate in carrying out measures decided upon by the Security Council and to mutually assist each other while doing so.[196]

While the UN Charter therefore does not establish any concrete obligations that would require domestic implementation, effective participation in undertakings mandated by the UN nevertheless necessitates a domestic legal framework that enables a member state to contribute to the activities of the United Nations. The German legal order, however, does not provide for any concrete procedures or substantive standards with regard to Germany's participation in the UN. The decision of whether and how Germany participates in and contributes to the activities of the United Nations is rather left to the political discretion of the Federal Government in cooperation with Parliament.[197]

Of specific concern is, however, the question of whether and how Germany can participate militarily in the context of the United Nations system of collective security. While the German Constitution prohibits any action that would violate the UN Charter's prohibition against the use of force (→ 3.2.2), it is potentially open towards military involvement in accordance with the UN Charter: military participation in UN

194 Vöneky & Wolfrum (n 75 above) 595.

195 UN Charter (n 2 above) art 43. On the lack of implementation of the mechanism envisioned by UN Charter arts 43 & 47, see N Krisch 'Article 43' in Simma et al (n 6 above) paras 9 - 13.

196 UN Charter (n 2 above) arts 48 & 49.

197 Basic Law art 32(1) establishes a federal competence with regard to foreign relations. And while foreign relations traditionally fall within the scope of the competences of the executive, the Constitutional Court emphasises that under the German Constitution the executive and parliament are required to work together in the field of foreign relations, see BVerfG Case 2 BvE 6/99 (n 45 above) 210; BVerfG Case 2 BvE 1/03 (n 70 above) 162.

peacekeeping operations, UN Security Council mandated use of force, as well as acts of individual or collective self-defense under article 51 of the UN Charter.

According to article 87a(2) of the Basic Law, the primary constitutional provision with regard to the use of military force, '[a]part from defense, the Armed Forces may be employed only to the extent expressly permitted by the Basic Law'. While the first part of this provision generally allows for military measures in accordance with article 51 of the UN Charter,[198] the second part requires an explicit constitutional authorisation for military engagement beyond measures of self-defense. Accepted at face value, this constitutional provision could be interpreted as excluding involvement of German armed forces in Security Council mandated military measures and peacekeeping operations, since such measures cannot be understood as defense[199] and the German Constitution does not contain any explicit authorisation for participation in Chapter measures. Accordingly, it was, for a long time, subject to controversial debate whether such involvement of Germany would only be admissible after a constitutional amendment.[200] In 1994 the Constitutional Court held in a landmark decision that article 24(2) of the Basic Law, which allows for Germany's integration into the collective security system of the United Nations, constitutes the constitutional authorisation for the deployment of armed forces in the context of and in accordance with the rules of the UN.[201] According to the Constitutional Court, however, the deployment of armed forces in a particular case requires the prior consent of Parliament.[202]

This line of jurisprudence of the Constitutional Court enables Germany to effectively participate in Security Council mandated operations. The Court recognises a general constitutional authorisation for Germany's participation in military measures under the auspices of the Security Council, both, with regard to peacekeeping operations as well as with regard to military engagement on the basis of an authorisation of the Council under Chapter.[203] Moreover, this jurisprudence ensures that German armed forces are deployed only in accordance with the rules of the UN Charter: The participation of the German military in a manner incompatible with the UN Charter is therefore not only prohibited due to

198 V Epping 'Article 87a' in V Epping & C Hillgruber (eds) *Grundgesetz, Kommentar* (2nd edn 2013) para 6.
199 B Pieroth 'Article 87a' in Jarass & Pieroth (n 47 above) para 9a.
200 See Tomuschat (n 94 above) para 40.
201 BVerfG Case 2 BvE 3/92 et al (n 46 above) 345 - 357. Accordingly, the Constitutional Court regarded Germany's participation in the peacekeeping operation UNOSOM II to be in accordance with the Constitution, see BVerfG (as above) 351 - 353. The Court has confirmed this holding subsequently, see BVerfG Case 2 BvE 1/03 (n 70 above) 157.
202 BVerfG Case 2 BvE 3/92 et al (n 46 above) 381 - 390; BVerfG Case 2 BvE 1/03 (n 70 above) 153 - 170.
203 Vöneky & Wolfrum (n 75 above) 595.

the constitutional implementation of the prohibition of the use of force,[204] but also because such a deployment would not be authorised under article 87a(2) of the Basic Law (→ 3.2.2).

3.6 Germany and the International Court of Justice

The German legal order, furthermore, allows for effective participation in the dispute-settlement mechanism of the International Court of Justice (→ Herdegen). According to article 24(3) of the Basic Law, 'the Federation shall accede to agreements providing for general, comprehensive and compulsory international arbitration'. While this provision does not establish a concrete obligation of Germany to recognise the compulsory jurisdiction of the ICJ,[205] it nevertheless reflects the significance the German legal order attributes to the international judiciary and international dispute-settlement mechanisms. In accordance with this constitutional commitment to the international judiciary, Germany has accepted the compulsory jurisdiction of the ICJ with a declaration of 1 May 2008.[206]

This positive openness of the German legal order towards the international judiciary also applies to the implementation of ICJ decisions. Since the obligation of Germany to comply with decisions of the ICJ in any case to which Germany is a party is established in the Charter and the ICJ Statute,[207] it is transformed into the domestic legal order through the federal law with which Germany acceded to the UN. Going beyond the obligation to implement decisions of the ICJ in cases to which Germany is a party, the Constitutional Court furthermore recognises an obligation of all state organs to take into consideration the jurisprudence of the ICJ in general when applying international law.[208]

The German constitutional order, as it is interpreted and applied by the Constitutional Court, thereby enables and encourages the participation of Germany within the United Nations judiciary and provides a legal framework for state organs to comply with and to implement the decisions and jurisprudence of the Court.

204 Basic Law arts 25 & 26.

205 Jarass (n 47 above) para 25; for the opposing view, see CD Classen 'Article 24' in von Mangoldt et al (n 96 above) para 100.

206 See CJ Tams & A Zimmermann '[T]he federation shall accede to agreements providing for general, comprehensive and compulsory international arbitration' (2009) 52 *German Yearbook of International Law* 391.

207 UN Charter (n 2 above) art 94(1); ICJ Statute (n 9 above) art 59.

208 BVerfG Case 2 BvR 2115/01 et al (19 September 2006) (2007) 60 *Neue Juristische Wochenschrift* 499; for a critical view, see KF Gärditz 'The Vienna Convention on Consular Relations case – German Federal Constitutional Court decision on failure to provide consular notification' (2007) 101 *American Journal of International Law* 627; for an affirmative view, see M Payandeh 'Die verfassungsrechtliche Stärkung der internationalen Gerichtsbarkeit: Zur Bindung deutscher Gerichte an Entscheidungen des Internationalen Gerichtshofs' (2007) 45 *Archiv des Völkerrechts* 244.

4 Conclusion

At first glance, the German legal order does not exhibit a particular sensitivity with regard to the United Nations and the obligations of Germany under the UN Charter: The constitutional order does not contain any provisions explicitly mentioning the United Nations. UN law is not automatically implemented into the domestic legal order, nor is it, in general, considered to have direct effect. Within the hierarchy of norms, UN law ranks below the Constitution. The domestic legal order does not stipulate any obligations of Germany to participate in UN peacekeeping or peace enforcement measures, but leaves participation to the discretion of the political organs. On close inspection, however, the German legal order provides for the comprehensive implementation of Germany's obligations under the UN Charter. The Charter provisions are part of the German legal order and, as far as required, transferred into German law. The constitutional order pays specific attention to the prohibition of the use of force, implementing it with a rank between the Constitution and other federal law, establishing rules that aim at the effective enforcement of the provision, and ensuring that military measures of Germany comply with the Charter framework on the use of force, even when German forces are deployed within the regional context of NATO. Furthermore, the Constitutional Court's jurisprudence constitutionally legitimises the dynamic practice of the UN organs and of the Security Council in particular, and allows for the participation of Germany within Security Council mandated or authorised operations. Sanctions that are imposed by the Security Council are effectively implemented either through the European Union or through the German legal order. While the German legal order therefore lacks specific constitutional or statutory provisions particularly dedicated to the United Nations, it nevertheless provides a legal framework which enables Germany's full participation in the activities of the UN and ensures that all state organs comply with Germany's obligations under the UN Charter.

BIBLIOGRAPHY

Ambos, K (3rd edn 2011) *Internationales Strafrecht* CH Beck: Munich

Arnold, R & Meindl, E (2013) 'Außenhandelsrecht' in Dauses, M (ed) *Handbuch des EU-Wirtschaftsrechts* CH Beck: Munich

B Pieroth 'Article 87a' in Jarass, HD & Pieroth, B (eds) (12th edn 2012) *Grundgesetz, Kommentar* CH Beck: Munich

Besson, S 'Sovereignty' in Wolfrum, R (ed) (2011) *Max Planck encyclopedia of public international law* Oxford University Press: Online

Bothe, M 'Peacekeeping' in Simma, B; Khan, DE; Nolte, G & Paulus, A (eds) (vol I, 3rd edn, 2012) *The Charter of the United Nations: A commentary* Oxford University Press: Oxford

CD Classen 'Article 24' in von Mangoldt, H; Klein, F & Starck, C (eds) (vol II, 6th edn 2010) *Kommentar zum Grundgesetz* Vahlen: Munich

Ciampi, A 'Security Council targeted sanctions and human rights' in Fassbender, B (ed) (2011) *Securing human rights? Achievements and challenges of the UN Security Council* Oxford University Press: New York

Cremer, HJ 'Article 215' in Calliess, C & Ruffert, M (eds) (4th edn 2011) *EUV/ AEUV, Kommentar* CH Beck: Munich

De Wet, E (2004) *The Chapter VII powers of the United Nations Security Council* Hart Publishing: Oxford/Portland

Epping, V 'Article 87a' in Epping, V & Hillgruber, C (eds) (2nd edn 2013) *Grundgesetz, Kommentar* CH Beck: Munich

Fassbender, B (2009) *The United Nations Charter as the constitution of the international community* Martinus Nijhoff: Leiden/Boston

Fink, U 'Article 26' in von Mangoldt, H; Klein, F & Starck, C (eds) (vol II, 6th edn 2010) *Kommentar zum Grundgesetz* Vahlen: Munich

Frowein, JA & Krisch, N 'Germany' in Gowlland-Debbas, V (ed) (2004) *National implementation of United Nations sanctions: A comparative study* Martinus Nijhoff: The Hague/Leiden

Frowein, JA 'Implementation of Security Council Resolutions taken under Chapter VII in Germany' in Gowlland-Debbas, V (ed) (2001) *United Nations sanctions and international law* Kluwer Law International: The Hague

Funke, A *Umsetzungsrecht* (2010) Mohr Siebeck: Tübingen

Gowlland-Debas, V 'Concluding Remarks' in Gowlland-Debbas, V (ed) (2004) *National implementation of United Nations sanctions: A comparative study* Martinus Nijhoff: The Hague/Leiden

Gowlland-Debas, V 'Sanctions regimes under article 41 of the United Nations Charter' in Gowlland-Debbas, V (ed) (2004) *National implementation of United Nations sanctions: A comparative study* Martinus Nijhoff: The Hague/Leiden

Gray, C 'The use of force and the international legal order' in Evans, MD (ed) (3rd edn 2010) *International law* Oxford University Press: Oxford/New York

Gray, C 'The use of force and the international legal order' in MD Evans (ed) (3rd edn 2010) *International Law* Oxford University Press: Oxford/New York

Herdegen, M (1998) *Die Befugnisse des UN-Sicherheitsrates* CF Müller: Heidelberg

Herdegen, M 'Article 25' in Maunz, T & Dürig, G (eds) (vol IV, 2000) *Grundgesetz, Kommentar* CH Beck: Munich

Herdegen, M 'Article 26' in Maunz, T & Dürig, G (eds) (vol IV, 2000) *Grundgesetz, Kommentar* CH Beck: Munich

Herdegen, M 'Review of the Security Council by National Courts: A Constitutional Perspective' in de Wet, E & Nollkaemper, A (eds) (2003) *Review of the Security Council by member states* Intersentia: Antwerp

Hernández, GI (2014) *The International Court of Justice and the judicial function* Oxford University Press: Oxford/New York
Hillgruber, C 'Article 25' in Schmidt-Bleibtreu B, Hofmann, H & Hopfauf, A (eds) (12th edn 2011) *Grundgesetz, Kommentar* Heymanns: Cologne
Hillgruber, C 'Article 26' in Schmidt-Bleibtreu B, Hofmann, H & Hopfauf, A (eds) (12th edn 2011) *Grundgesetz, Kommentar* Heymanns: Cologne
Jarass, HD 'Article 24' in Jarass, HD & Pieroth, B (eds) (12th edn 2012) *Grundgesetz, Kommentar* CH Beck: Munich
Jarass, HD 'Article 24' in Jarass, HD & Pieroth, B (eds) (12th edn 2012)*Grundgesetz, Kommentar* CH Beck: Munich
Kadelbach, S 'Interpretation' in Simma, B; Khan, DE; Nolte, G & Paulus, A (eds) (vol I, 3rd edn, 2012) *The Charter of the United Nations: A commentary* Oxford University Press: Oxford
Kaiser, K 'Treaties, direct applicability' in R Wolfrum (ed) (2013) *Max Planck encyclopedia of public international law* Oxford University Press: Oxford
Klein, E & Schmahl, S 'Article 10' in Simma, B; Khan, DE; Nolte, G & Paulus, A (eds) (vol I, 3rd edn, 2012) *The Charter of the United Nations: A commentary* Oxford University Press: Oxford
Kleinlein, T (2012) *Konstitutionalisierung im Völkerrecht* Springer: Berlin
Kokott, J 'Article 215 TFEU' in Streinz, R (ed) (2nd edn 2012) *EUV/AEUV, Kommentar* CH Beck: Munich
Krisch, N 'Article 41' in Simma, B; Khan, DE; Nolte, G & Paulus, A (eds) (vol I, 3rd edn, 2012) *The Charter of the United Nations: A commentary* Oxford University Press: Oxford
Krisch, N 'Article 43' in Simma, B; Khan, DE; Nolte, G & Paulus, A (eds) (vol I, 3rd edn, 2012) *The Charter of the United Nations: A commentary* Oxford University Press: Oxford
Kuijper, PJ 'Implementation of Binding Security Council Resolutions by the EU/EC' in de Wet, E & Nollkaemper, A (eds) (2003) *Review of the Security Council by Member States* Intersentia: Antwerp
Kunig, P 'Intervention, Prohibition of' in Wolfrum, R (ed) (2008) *Max Planck encyclopedia of public international law* Oxford University Press: Online
Marauhn, T 'North Atlantic Treaty Organization' in Wolfrum, R (ed) (2011) *Max Planck encyclopedia of public international law* Oxford University Press: Oxford
Nettesheim, M 'Article 59' in Herdegen, M 'Article 25' in Maunz, T & Dürig, G (eds) (vol IV, 2000) *Grundgesetz, Kommentar* CH Beck: Munich
Oeter, S 'Self-determination' in Simma, B; Khan, DE; Nolte, G & Paulus, A (eds) (vol I, 3rd edn, 2012) *The Charter of the United Nations: A commentary* Oxford University Press: Oxford
Oeter, S 'Systeme kollektiver Sicherheit' in Isensee J & Kirchhof, P (eds) (vol XI, 3rd edn 2013) *Handbuch des Staatsrechts der Bundesrepublik Deutschland* CF Müller: Heidelberg
Orakhelashvili, A (2006) *Peremptory norms in international law* Oxford University Press: New York
Orakhelashvili, A (2011) *Collective security* Oxford University Press: Oxford
Paulus, AL 'Article 2' in Simma, B; Khan, DE; Nolte, G & Paulus, A (eds) (vol I, 3rd edn, 2012) *The Charter of the United Nations: A commentary* Oxford University Press, Oxford
Pellet, A & Miron, A 'Sanctions' in Wolfrum, R (ed) (2011) *Max Planck encyclopedia of public international law* Oxford University Press: Online
Pernice, I 'Article 24' in Dreier, H (ed) (vol II, 2nd edn 2006) *Grundgesetz, Kommentar* Mohr Siebeck: Tübingen
Pernice, I 'Article 25' in Dreier, H (ed) (vol II, 2nd edn 2006) *Grundgesetz, Kommentar* Mohr Siebeck: Tübingen

Pernice, I 'Article 26' in Dreier, H (ed) (vol II, 2nd edn 2006) *Grundgesetz, Kommentar* Mohr Siebeck: Tübingen

Peters, A 'Article 25' in Simma, B; Khan, DE; Nolte, G & Paulus, A (eds) (vol I, 3rd edn, 2012) *The Charter of the United Nations: A commentary* Oxford University Press: Oxford

Polakiewicz, J 'International Law and Domestic (Municipal) Law, Law and Decisions of International Organizations and Courts' in Wolfrum, R (ed) (2008) *Max Planck encyclopedia of public international law* Oxford University Press: Online

Proelß, A 'Das Friedensgebot des Grundgesetzes' in Isensee, J & Kirchhof, P (eds) *Handbuch des Staatsrechts der Bundesrepublik Deutschland* (vol XI, 3rd edn 2013) CF Müller: Heidelberg

Randelzhofer, A & Dörr, O 'Article 2(4)' in Simma, B; Khan, DE; Nolte, G & Paulus, A (eds) (vol I, 3rd edn, 2012) *The Charter of the United Nations: A commentary* Oxford University Press: Oxford

Rensmann, T 'Reform' in Simma, B; Khan, DE; Nolte, G & Paulus, A (eds) (vol I, 3rd edn, 2012) *The Charter of the United Nations: A commentary* Oxford University Press: Oxford

Ress, HK (2000) *Das Handelsembargo: Volker-, Europa- und Aussenwirtschaftsrechtliche Rahmenbedingungen, Praxis und Entschadigung* Springer: Berlin

Rojahn, O 'Article 24' in Münch, I & Kunig, P (eds) (vol 1, 6th edn 2012) *Grundgesetz, Kommentar* CH Beck: Munich

Sandholtz, W 'Creating authority by the council: The international criminal tribunals' in Cronin, B & Hurd, I (eds) (2008) *The UN Security Council and the politics of international authority* Routledge: London/New York

Sauer, H (2nd edn 2013) *Staatsrecht III* CH Beck: Munich

Shaw, M (6th edn 2008) *International law* Cambridge University Press: Cambridge

Shelton, D 'International law and relative normativity' in Evans, MD (ed) (3rd edn 2010) *International law* Oxford University Press: Oxford/New York

Skordas, A 'Supranational Law' in Wolfrum, R (ed) (2011) *Max Planck encyclopedia of public international law* Oxford University Press: Online

Streinz, R 'Article 26' in Sachs, M (ed) (6th edn 2011) *Grundgesetz, Kommentar* CH Beck: Germany

Talmon, S 'Article 2(6)' in Simma, B; Khan, DE; Nolte, G & Paulus, A (eds) (vol I, 3rd edn, 2012) *The Charter of the United Nations: A commentary* Oxford University Press: Oxford

Tomuschat, C 'Staatsrechtliche Entscheidung für die internationale Offenheit' in Isensee, J & Kirchhof, P (eds) (vol XI, 3rd edn 2013) *Handbuch des Staatsrechts der Bundesrepublik Deutschland* CF Müller: Heidelberg

Weiß, N (2009) *Kompetenzlehre internationaler Organisationen* Springer: Berlin

Wolfrum, R 'Article 1' in Simma, B; Khan, DE; Nolte, G & Paulus, A (eds) (vol I, 3rd edn, 2012) *The Charter of the United Nations: A commentary* Oxford University Press: Oxford

Wolfrum, R 'Deutschland in den Vereinten Nationen' in Isensee, J & Kirchhof, P (eds) (vol X, 3rd edn 2012) *Handbuch des Staatsrechts der Bundesrepublik Deutschland* CF Müller: Heidelberg

8

THE UNITED NATIONS CHARTER AND THE SOUTH AFRICAN LEGAL ORDER

*Dire Tladi**

1 Introduction

While both South Africa and Germany have played prominent roles in the foundational years of the United Nations (hereinafter the UN), these roles have been sharply divergent. South Africa is a founding member of the UN, having signed the Declaration by United Nations of 1942.[1] However, South Africa has had a sharply unsettled relationship with the world body, which has often affected the manner and extent of South Africa's implementation of obligations flowing from the UN Charter.

South Africa was not only a passive participant in the creation of the United Nations. It's Prime Minister at the time, Jan Smuts, was an instrumental participant in the creation of the United Nations and seen by some as one of the architects of the United Nations Charter.[2] He presided over the Commission on the General Assembly in the elaboration of the Charter and is credited with drafting its preamble.[3] However, for fifty years of the UN's existence after the initial honeymoon period, this relationship

* Fellow at the Institute of International and Comparative Law in Africa and Professor of International Law at the Faculty of Law, University of Pretoria. He is also a member of the United Nations International Law Commission and Special Adviser to the South African Minister of International Relations and Cooperation.

1 Article 3 of the Charter of the United Nations (The UN Charter) (26 June 1945, 1 UNTS XVI) provides that the 'original members of the United Nations shall be the States which, having participated in the United Nations Conference on International Organization at San Francisco, or having signed the Declaration by United Nations of January 1, 1942, sign the present Charter and ratify it in accordance with article 110.' South Africa signed the Declaration by United Nations and participated in the San Francisco Conference. See generally J Shearer *Against the world: South Africa and human rights at the United Nations 1945-1961* (2011) especially at 7ff

2 See eg J Barber & J Barret *South Africa's foreign policy: The search for status and security, 1945-1988* (1990) 17.

3 Barber & Barret (n 2 above) 17. See also C Heyns 'The Preamble of the United Nations Charter: The contribution of Jan Smuts' (1995) 7 *African Journal of International and Comparative Law* 329.

has been tumultuous and controversial.[4] From South Africa's perspective during those years, the United Nations had sought to interfere in its domestic affairs and had 'made concerted efforts to isolate South Africa in practically every field of human endeavour from the rest of the international community'.[5] The other perspective, however, is that it was successive South African governments, through their racist policies that stigmatised South Africa, that turned it into a pariah state and led to its isolation by the UN.[6] Ironically, it was, *inter alia,* Smuts' preamble, and its reaffirmation of 'faith in fundamental human rights, in the dignity and worth of the human person' which were used to champion the fight against apartheid in the United Nations.[7] The first UN action against the apartheid policies of South Africa was a General Assembly resolution in 1946.[8] UN actions against South Africa, which lasted until the end of apartheid in the early 1990s, are too numerous to recount but include General Assembly resolutions,[9] Security Council resolutions,[10] an unsuccessful International Court of Justice (hereinafter the ICJ) application,[11] an Advisory Opinion by the ICJ[12] and even the adoption of

4 See J Cassette 'United Nations observer mission in South Africa – A significant event' (1992) 18 *South African Yearbook of International Law* 1 3.

5 JC Heunis *United Nations versus South Africa: A legal assessment of United Nations – and United Nations related activities in respect of South Africa* (1986) 1. See also eg the statement by the then Minister of Defence, Mr PW Botha, before the House of Assembly on 24 January 1977 in which he said, describing the isolationist UN policy: 'Surely we are dealing with extreme hypocrisy here' cited in DJ van Vuuren 'South Africa's foreign policy and international practice during 1997 as reflected mainly in speeches, statements and replies by the Government in Parliament' (1977) 3 *South African Yearbook of International Law* 258.

6 Cassette (n 4 above) 3.

7 Barber & Barret (n 2 above) 17.

8 See GA Res. 44(I), initiated by India, on the treatment by South Africa of Indians. See for discussion Shearer (n 1 above) 24 - 27.

9 In addition to the example listed above see GA Resolution 616(VII), titled 'The question of race conflict in South Africa resulting from the policies of *Apartheid* of the Government of the Union of South Africa', which was the first General Assembly resolution on the broader question of apartheid. The focus on the General Assembly on South Africa and its apartheid policies is reflected in Heunis's lament: 'In 1981 South Africa was attacked during the course of 62 of the 109 plenary meetings, whereas 353 plenary speeches dealt with South Africa ... The 36th session adopted 45 resolutions which attacked South Africa directly ... Among these were 16 core resolutions on *apartheid* ... In addition more than 20 other resolutions adopted on recommendation of the Main Committees [were adopted]'. See Heunis (n 5 above) 2ff.

10 In the first UN Security Council resolution on South Africa and Apartheid, UNSC Resolution 134 (1960), adopted in 1960 after the Sharpeville Massacre, the Council deplored 'the policies and actions of the Government of the Union of South Africa' and called upon the Government of the Union of South Africa to initiate measures aimed at bringing about racial harmony based on equality.' Subsequent to Resolution 134 (1960) the Council adopted several other resolutions including the first mandatory sanctions resolution, UN Security Council resolution 418 (1977). See for discussion of UN Security Council resolutions on South Africa Cassette (n 4 above) at 5ff.

11 *South West Africa Cases (Ethiopia v South Africa; Liberia v South Africa) Second Phase* (18 July 1966) (1996) ICJ Reports 6.

12 *Legal Consequences for States of the Continued Presence of South Africa in Namibia Notwithstanding Security Council Resolution 276 Advisory Opinion* (21 June 1971) (1971) ICJ Reports 16.

the Apartheid Convention directed against South Africa and its policies.[13]

In recent years, after the end of apartheid, South Africa has taken on an ever-increasing role at the United Nations, although even this has not been without its controversies.[14] During this period, South Africa has served twice as a non-permanent member of the Security Council, three times on the Human Rights Council, is at the forefront of the UN Security Council reform discussions and is seen as a front-runner for a permanent seat on the Security Council in the improbable event that Security Council reform were to take place – incidentally on the latter issue, South Africa and Germany find themselves on similar side of the United Nations isle and very often as partners. During this same period, however, South Africa has often been severely criticised for some of its positions in the UN, particularly during its stints on the Security Council.[15] Particular criticism has been reserved for South Africa's vote (and explanation of vote) in the situation in Myanmar as well as its criticism of the manner in which Security Council resolution 1973, which led to the demise of Gaddafi and his regime, was implemented.[16]

The relationship between South Africa and the United Nations over the years has influenced both the willingness and the ability of South Africa to implement its UN obligations. In the past, given the acrimonious relationship between South Africa and the United Nations, South Africa often chose not to implement its obligations under the UN Charter. However, the re-emergence of South Africa as a respected member of the international community has created an incentive for and an expectation on South Africa to implement fully its international obligations, in particular those under the Charter. In this chapter, I assess the extent to which South Africa has been successful in the implementation of its UN obligations, focusing on the challenges and opportunities. Whether the legal environment is conducive for implementation is, of course, a key indicator in such an assessment. The assessment is undertaken with a dual

13 International Convention on the Suppression and Punishment of the Crime of Apartheid (30 November 1973, A/RES/3068(XXVIII)) See for a discussion of the Convention, in defence of South Africa's policies, H Booysen 'Convention on the Crime of Apartheid' (1976) 2 *South African Yearbook of International Law* 56.

14 See for a discussion of South Africa's foreign policy under the spotlight N Valji & D Tladi 'South Africa's foreign policy: Between idealism and the realpolitik of being an emerging power' *OpenDemocracy* 19 June 2013 http://www.opendemocracy.net (on file with author).

15 See Valji & Tladi (n 14 above). See also for example, J Dugard 'The future of international law: A human rights perspective – with some comments on the Leiden School of International Law' (2007) 20 *Leiden Journal of International Law* 729. See for appraisals of the criticism D Tladi 'South African lawyers, values and the new vision of international law: The road to perdition is paved with laudable goals' (2008) 33 *South African Yearbook of International Law* 167; D Tladi 'Strict positivism, moral arguments, human rights and the Security Council: South Africa and the Myanmar vote' (2008) 1 *African Human Rights Law Journal* 23.

16 See Valji & Tladi (n 14 above). See also C Petré 'South Africa's Janus-faced foreign policy' *ThinkAfricaPress* 8 December 2011 http://thinkafricapress.com/south-africa/janus-faced-foreign-policy (accessed on 9 May 2015).

purpose in mind. First, to test the assumption that South Africa's record of implementation of international law is 'at times meagre'. The second purpose is to provide, to the extent that there are gaps in South Africa's implementation of its obligation under the UN Charter, recommendations on improving the record. I begin in the next section by providing a descriptive overview of the obligations under the UN Charter. Having provided an overview of the UN obligations, I move to an assessment of the implementation of these obligations in the South African legal system before offering some concluding remarks.

2 Obligations under the Charter of the UN

2.1 General

The UN Charter is a treaty, and comprises of a myriad of rights and obligations. In the accompanying chapter on German implementation of UN obligations, Payandeh observes that the Charter contains different rules, and that not all of them are obligations, for example, the rights of states against non-intervention by the United Nations and the constitutional arrangements such as the decision-making processes of the organisation (→ Payandeh). Moreover, even where obligations can be identified, not all of them are susceptible to domestic implementation strictly speaking. Some of the obligations in the Charter, for example, are purely interstate obligations, that is, enforceable only, or principally, between states on the international plane and not subject to domestic implementation. The prohibition on the threat or use of force, arguably a norm of *jus cogens* under the Charter, is one such obligation.[17] Similarly, the obligation to settle disputes peacefully, provided in article 2(3) and article 33 of the Charter, is applicable between states on the international plane. These obligations are not, by their nature, susceptible to domestic implementation. This is not to say that domestic law cannot provide for them, for surely it can, particularly in order to empower the executive to perform. The South African Constitution, for example, provides that the primary objective of the South African defence is 'to defend and protect the Republic of South Africa ... in accordance with the Constitution and the principles of international law regulating the use of force'.[18] The 'principles of international law' regulating the use of force include article 2(4) of the Charter.[19] While it would also be possible to argue that the

17 n 1 above, art 2(4). On its status as a norm of *jus cogens,* see *Military and Paramilitary Activities in and Against Nicaragua (Nicaragua v United States)* ICJ (27 June 1986) (1986) ICJ Reports 14 para 190 where the Court referred to the fact that the prohibition on the use of force is often referred to by states as being 'a fundamental or cardinal principle of [customary international] law' and that the International Law Commission has identified it as a 'conspicuous example of a rule of customary international law having the character of *jus cogens*'.

18 The Constitution of the Republic of South Africa, 1996, sec 200(2).

19 *Military and Paramilitary Activities case* (n 17 above) at paras 175ff.

prohibition on the use force is implemented by virtue of section 232 of the Constitution which provides that customary international law is law in South Africa, this would not, strictly speaking be an implementation of UN obligations but rather a co-existing obligations flowing from a separate source of international law.[20] More importantly, neither the application of section 232 of the Constitution to the use of force or even the constitutional provision providing for the defence of South Africa in accordance with international law principles on the use of force are really 'domestic implementation'. Rather, they affirm the existence of the obligation to be complied with on the international plane. These obligations, and other similarly interstate obligations, are therefore not addressed in this chapter.

Chapter of the UN Charter, on the other hand, contains obligations which are, by their nature, susceptible to domestic implementation. Article 55 of the Charter provides that the United Nations shall promote, *inter alia,* higher living standards, full employment, conditions of economic and social development and universal respect for human rights and fundamental freedoms for all. Member states also themselves pledge to 'take joint and separate action' to achieve these objectives.[21] While these obligations, on a purely literal reading, do not impose any clear obligations, a purposive and evolutive interpretation reveals concrete obligations.[22] Moreover, these obligations have, over time, been fleshed out through various other international instruments, particularly as the Universal Declaration of Human Rights, the International Covenant on Civil and Political Rights and the International Covenant on Economic, Social and Cultural Rights. While these obligations of the Charter, and the international instruments giving them flesh, are intended for domestic implementation, they are more appropriately covered elsewhere in this volume and will also not be discussed further in this chapter (→ Chenwi).

The Charter also has obligations on compliance with the decisions of some of its principal organs, in particular the Security Council and the International Court of Justice. Binding decisions of the Security Council, currently the basis of the most important and topical UN obligations for domestic implementation, are discussed in some detail in paragraph 2.3 below. With regards to International Court of Justice, member states are obliged to 'comply with the decisions of the International Court of Justice *in any case to which it is party*'.[23] While it is conceivable that some judgments of the International Court of Justice, in cases to which South Africa is a party, could require domestic implementation, this would be no different than for any other case of domestic implementation brought on by the

20 As above.
21 UN Charter (n 1 above) art 56
22 Vienna Convention on the Law of Treaties (The Vienna Convention) (23 May 1969, 1155 UNTS 331) art 31 provides the general rule of interpretation, which includes not only the ordinary meaning of the text, but also context, object and purpose as well subsequent agreements and subsequent practice.
23 UN Charter (n 1 above) art 94(1).

necessity of complying with decisions of another judicial or quasi-judicial body, for example, the African Court of Human and Peoples' Rights. Moreover, South Africa's reticence for judicial settlement of disputes, preferring amicable solutions even where it has a strong legal case, makes the possibility of the need for implementation of decisions of the International Court of Justice remote. Speaking on the occasion of the commemoration of the hundredth anniversary of the Peace Palace, on the subject of peace and justice, the then Deputy Minister of International Relations and Cooperation, Mr Ebrahim Ebrahim, asserted South Africa's support for peaceful settlement of disputes.[24] In direct response to South Africa's reluctance to accept the compulsory jurisdiction of the International Court of Justice, the Deputy Minister then made the following observation:

> South Africa is committed to [the idea of peaceful settlement of disputes] and whether through the judicial settlement of disputes or through other equally peaceful means such as consultations, we will ensure that our disputes are resolved [peacefully] ... it is important to emphasise that the acceptance of the compulsory jurisdiction of the International Court ... should not be equated with support for justice, the respect for the rule of law and the promotion of justice as it as possible to achieve justice, the rule of law through means other contentious proceedings.[25]

It is also worth pointing out that non-binding instruments emanating from the United Nations, such as General Assembly resolutions, are not binding. As such they do not create obligations to be implemented. While General Assembly resolutions may be legally significant through, for example, their role as reflecting customary international law or even contributing to its formation, they themselves cannot be implemented. Their relevance in domestic law is largely for interpretative purposes (→ De Wet/Introduction).[26] Since they are not, as such, subject to implementation, non-binding instruments of the United Nations are not considered.

24 Speech by Mr Ebrahim Ismail Ebrahim, Deputy Minister of International Relations and Cooperation, South Africa, 'On peace and justice: commemorating 100 years of the Peace Palace' 29 August 2013, the University of Pretoria.

25 As above.

26 See also E de Wet 'South Africa' in D Shelton (ed) *International law and domestic legal systems: incorporation, transformation and persuasion* (2011) 588. For examples of South African case law relying on UN non-binding instruments see also *S v Williams and Others* 1995 (2) SACR 251 (CC). See also *Fuel Retailers Association of Southern Africa v Director-General Environmental Management, Department of Agriculture, Conservation and Environment, Mpumalanga Province, and Others* 2007 (6) SA 4 (CC) where the Court refers, *inter alia,* to the 1986 Declaration on the Right to Development adopted by General Assembly Resolution 41/128, the 1972 Stockholm Declaration on the Human Rights, the 1992 Rio Declaration on Environment and Development and the Johannesburg Declaration on Sustainable Development. See also *Carmichele v Minister of Safety and Security and Another* 2001 (4) SA 928 (CC) para 72, where the Court relied on the *United Nations Guidelines on the Role of Prosecutors.*

2.2 Immunities of the United Nations

Members of the United Nations have several obligations towards the United Nations intended to allow the organisation to perform its functions. Some of these are obligations that require domestic application while others do not require domestic application. An example of the latter type of obligation is the obligation to pay assessed contributions.[27] An example of an organisational obligation requiring domestic implementation includes the obligation to ensure legal capacity of the organisation 'for the necessary exercise of its functions'.[28] The obligation to provide immunities to the organisation is perhaps the most important organisational obligation towards the UN requiring domestic implementation. The Charter provides that the UN 'shall enjoy in the territory of its Members such privileges and immunities as are necessary for the fulfilment of its purposes'.[29] Additionally the Charter provides that representatives of the members of the UN and the UN's officials 'shall similarly enjoy such privileges and immunities as are necessary for the independent exercise of their functions' related to the United Nations.[30]

Although the obligations seem sufficiently clear, the Charter makes provision for the conclusion of further conventions 'with a view to determining the details of the' immunities provided for in the Charter.[31] The creation of various Specialised Agencies of the United Nations, programmes and other entities related to the UN, so-called UN-family, has also resulted in the need for further UN immunities-related rules. Examples of UN Agencies, autonomous international organisations linked to the United Nations through special agreements and created to achieve UN objectives, include the International Monetary Fund, the World Bank Group, the World Health Organisation and the World Tourism Organisation amongst many others. Examples of UN entities that are not Specialised Agencies include United Nation Environment Programme (hereinafter the UNEP), United Nations Development Programme (hereinafter the UNDP) and the United Nations Populations Fund (hereinafter UNFPA). In recognition of the various types of entities that fall within the UN family and which require immunities and pursuant to the call for the further convention, the United Nations adopted two separate conventions, namely the 1946 Convention on the Privileges and Immunities of the United Nations (hereinafter the 1946 Convention) and the 1947 Convention on the Privileges and Immunities of Specialised Agencies (hereinafter the 1947 Convention).

27 UN Charter (n 1 above) art 17(2).
28 UN Charter (n 1 above) art 104.
29 n 1 above, art 105(1).
30 n 1 above, art 105(2).
31 n 1 above, art 105(3).

The 1946 Convention provides for the legal personality (termed juridical personality) of the United Nations and its programmes and identifies its specific competencies.[32] It applies to the United Nations and its constituent organs such as the UNDP, UNEP and UNFPA. It provides, in elaborate detail, for the immunity of the United Nations, its property and assets 'from every form of legal process'.[33] The 1946 Convention also provides for the inviolability of UN premises and its documents.[34] In addition to immunity, the 1946 Convention provides for privileges in the form of exemption from taxes and custom duties for the United Nations.[35] In addition to the immunities of the organisation itself, the 1946 Convention also provides for the immunities and privileges of the officials of the United Nations[36] and experts on mission being persons not employed by the UN but performing missions for the UN.[37] With respect to officials of the UN, whether the immunity to be provided is 'absolute' or 'functional' depends on the rank of the officials, with 'the Secretary-General and all Assistant Secretaries-General' having immunity similar to those of 'diplomatic envoys', that is, absolute immunity.[38] Experts on mission are only accorded such immunities 'as are necessary for the independent exercise of their functions', that is, functional immunity.[39] The 1947 Convention follows closely the 1946 Convention, applying its provisions to Specialised Agencies.

Immunities serve as exceptions to domestic jurisdiction and, for that reason, require domestic implementation. In a dualist country such as South Africa, the international law obligations to respect the immunity of the United Nations and its officials could not be complied with in the absence of implementing legislation. Similarly, privileges, particularly the tax exemption, serve as exceptions to the applicability of domestic tax laws and must accordingly also be implemented domestically. Thus, in addition to the conventional rules as contained in the Charter, the 1946 Convention and the 1947 Convention, domestic implementation is required to give effect to the immunities and privileges. How South Africa implements the obligations to provide for immunities and privileges of the United Nations and its officials, is considered in section 3.1 below.

32 Convention on the Privileges and Immunities of the United Nations (The 1946 Convention) (13 February 1946, 1 UNTS 15) art 1.
33 1946 Convention (n 32 above) art II sec 2.
34 n 32 above, art II secs 3 & 4.
35 1946 Convention (n 32 above) art II sec 7.
36 n 32 above, art V.
37 See the 1946 Convention (n 32 above) art VI.
38 See the 1946 Convention (n 32 above) sec 18. Presumably, the Deputy Secretary-General and all Under-Secretary-Generals, being of higher rank than the Assistant Secretary-General, will have similar immunity under the 1946 Convention.
39 1946 Convention (n 32 above) art VI sec 22.

2.3 Obligation to comply with UN Security Council decisions

The extensive powers bestowed on the Security Council by the UN Charter in relation to its 'primary responsibility for the maintenance of international peace and security' have generated significant debate.[40] The Council, in carrying out its responsibilities, does so on behalf of the members of the UN.[41] The members of the UN in turn 'agree to accept and carry out the decisions of the Security Council in accordance with the ... Charter'.[42] There is thus a positive obligation on South Africa to carry out the decisions of the UN Security Council. Whether the duty to carry out the decisions of the Security Council requires domestic implementation is dependent on number of factors, including whether the particular resolution is a binding resolution and, if it is a binding resolution, what type of obligations are imposed by the resolution. These questions determine not only whether domestic implementation is required, but also the nature of the domestic implementation. It is apposite to point out that under South Africa law, Security Council resolutions requiring domestic implementation cannot have direct effect.[43]

As to the first question, that is, whether the particular resolution is a binding resolution, there has been some debate as to whether the injunction to 'accept and carry out the decisions of the Security Council' applies to all decisions of the Security Council or only to decisions of the Security Council adopted under Chapter of the Charter.[44] This is a key question because, depending on the answer, the duty to implement obligations could be applied to a narrower or wider range of decisions. In addition to resolutions, whether Chapter or not, the Council also adopts other decisions notably Presidential Statements and Press Statements. There is also the less formal 'elements of the press' which are not recorded. All of these are, without question, 'decisions' of the Council requiring agreement of the members of the Security – indeed, in terms of

40 See generally E de Wet *The Chapter VII powers of the Security Council* (2004). See also S Talmon 'The Security Council as world legislature' (2005) 99 *American Journal of International Law* 175.

41 UN Charter (n 1 above) art 24.

42 n 1 above, art 25.

43 See E de Wet 'South Africa' in D Shelton (ed) (n 26 above). Compare A Peters 'Article 25' in B Simma et al (eds) *The Charter of the United Nations: A commentary: Volume I* (3rd edn 2012) 804.

44 Peters (n 43 above) 793ff; R Higgins 'The Advisory Opinion on Namibia: Which UN Resolutions are binding under article 25 of the Charter?' (1972) 21 *Comparative and International Law Quarterly* 273, 275. See also De Wet (n 40 above) 37ff. It is interesting to note that on the UN's website, the question whether all Security Council resolutions are binding is raised as a 'Frequently Asked Question', but no answer is provided. Instead, the website ambivalently states that how 'this issue has been addressed in the Council can be found in the Repertoire [of Practice of the Security Council]'.

the practice of the Security Council decisions other than resolutions require unanimity.[45]

The injunction for members of the United Nations to comply with the decisions of the Security Council in article 25 refers to 'decisions of the Security' and not 'Chapter decisions of the Security Council', suggesting perhaps that the obligation to 'accept and carry out', and hence to implement domestically where necessary, persists whether the decision is contained in a Chapter resolution, other resolution, a Presidential Statement or Statement of the Press.[46] However, it should be noted that Chapter, the other chapter under which the Council acts,[47] does not make provision for binding decisions but only for recommendations.[48] Moreover, an overview of the documents of the Security Council suggests that the Security Council itself deems Chapter as binding resolutions while other outcomes are not binding. The Council does not, as a practice, make decisions which, by their language, bind member states in resolutions or decisions not categorised as Chapter.[49] For example, while 16th Supplement of the Repertoire of the Practice of the Security Council notes that a President Statement 'explicitly invoked article 25', nothing in the Presidential Statement itself creates an obligation on member states.[50] The Presidential Statement in question, for example,

45 Although the UN Charter (n 1 above) art 27(3) provides that '*Decisions* of the Security Council ... shall be by an affirmative vote of nine members', in practice this has only been applied to resolutions with other decisions adopted strictly by consensus.

46 See eg A Peters (n 43 above) 793ff; Higgins (n 44 above) 275. These views are often based on a dicta from the International Court of Justice Advisory Opinion in *Legal Consequences for States of the Continued Presence of South Africa in Namibia (South West Africa) Notwithstanding Security Council Resolution 276* (21 June 1971) (1971) ICJ Reports where the Court, at para 113, stated that the view that article 25 applies only to Chapter VII has finds does not find support in the Charter since *inter alia* it is not placed in Chapter VII.

47 Technically the Council can also make decisions under Chapter VIII. However, resolutions that could potentially fall under Chapter VIII, have to date been institutional resolutions related to the relationship between Security Council and regional organisations and not purporting to create obligations on Member States.

48 See the UN Charter (n 1 above) arts 36, 37 and 38. The theoretical possibility of a decision to investigate a dispute leading to a duty to 'accept and carry' on the part of member states, particularly in relation to access, is discussed in several works, including Peters (n 43 above) at 794. However, a 'decision' to institute a an investigate cannot itself carry an substantive obligations and to attempts to salvage binding character of Chapter VI on the basis of article 34 seems awkward at best. See De Wet (n 40 above) 40, who refers to the 'practical unimportance of article 34 resolutions'.

49 This conclusion is consistent with the *Namibia Opinion* (n 46 above) para 114, where the Court cautioned that the 'language of a resolution should be careful analysed before a conclusion can be made as to its binding nature' noting that the question whether the power to issue a decision under article 25 has been exercised should is a matter of interpretation. Although Jost Delbrück, in the first and second editions of Simma's Commentary to the Charter, also rejects the view that article 25 applies only to Chapter VII resolutions, he does conclude that it is necessary to determine the binding nature of the resolution from an interpretation of the language. Thus resolutions that are couched in non-mandatory terms would not create the duty to 'accept and carry out'. See J Delbrück 'Article 25' in B Simma (ed) *The Charter of the United Nations: A commentary* (1994) 410, 411 & 413.

50 Part V of the Repertoire of the practice of the Security Council, 16th Supplement (2008-2009) 12.

'calls upon' members to 'make efforts' towards cooperation in the areas concerned, 'recalls' obligations, stresses certain things, emphasises others but never decides on any obligations for member states.[51] The legal duty to 'accept and carry out' the decisions of the Security Council, and the legal duty to implement them when necessary, consequently arises only in practice in relation to Chapter resolutions.

Even if a decision of the Security Council is binding, whether there is duty 'accept and carry out' such a decision will also be dependent upon whether such a decision is lawful or not – the famous legal limits debate.[52] The basic premise around which the debate is centred proceeds from article 103 of the Charter, which creates supremacy for UN Charter obligations over other treaty obligations. From this premise, since UN Charter obligations, including binding decisions of the Security Council, are superior to the other rules of international law, binding the decisions of the Council do not have to be consistent with such other international law rules.[53] The generally accepted view, however, is that while Council decisions do not have to be consistent with general international law, the Council is bound by *jus cogens* and the purposes and principles of the UN as contained in Chapter of the Charter.[54] However, given the amorphous nature of both principles and purposes and *jus cogens,* these doctrinal limits may be of limited practical effect.[55] What is likely to serve as a constraining factor on Security Council decisions-making is 'national level repudiation', that is, the national system failing to implement a Security Council resolution not on account of the decision being contrary to international law but rather due to inconsistency with domestic constitutional requirements (or in the case of the EU, regional requirements).[56] Nonetheless, a determination by a state (whether the judiciary or the executive), that a decision of the Security Council is invalid, because it is inconsistent with *jus cogens* or the purposes and principles of the Charter, may well lead to national level repudiation in the form of unwillingness or even legal inability to implement such decisions domestically. The identification of the limits on the powers of the Security Council, and whether a particular decision to be implemented is consistent with such limits, is therefore important from the perspective of implementation.

51 See S/PRST/2008/43 on the 'Maintenance of international peace and security' adopted on 19 November 2008. See for similar discussion Chapter VII of the Repertoire of Practice of the Security Council, 15th Supplement 63.

52 See generally De Wet (n 40 above) and Peters (n 43 above).

53 In the *Namibia Opinion* (n 46 above) the Court certainly appears to adopt the approach that there is only a duty to 'accept and carry out' decisions of the Council if they are taken in 'accordance with the' Charter (para 115).

54 See D Tladi 'Reflections on the rule of law in international law: The Security Council, international law and the limits of power' (2006) 31 *South African Yearbook of International Law* 231.

55 D Tladi & G Taylor 'On the Al Qaida/Taliban sanctions regime: Due process and sunsetting' (2011) 10 *Chinese Journal of International Law* 771, 776.

56 Tladi & Taylor (n 55 above) 777. See C Forcese & K Roach 'Limping into the future: The UN 1267 terrorism listing at the crossroads' (2010) 42 *George Washington International Law Review* 217 261.

The other factor identified as relevant in determining the scope of the legal obligation to implement is the nature of the decision. The nature of measures that the Council can adopt are numerous, ranging from the authorisation to engage in acts which would, but for the authorisation, be inconsistent with rules,[57] to authorising the deployment of peacekeepers and the creation of international tribunals,[58] to less intrusive measures such as calling upon a party to a conflict to cooperate with international bodies.[59] However, the measure most resorted to, and coincidentally, the measure most requiring domestic implementation, is the imposition of sanctions. The Security Council has, in recent times, preferred targeted sanctions over country sanctions. There are two main types of sanctions regimes employed by the Security Council, namely country-specific sanctions regimes and counter terrorism regimes. The main counter terrorism sanctions regimes are contained in resolutions 1373 and 1267/1989. Examples of country specific regimes include the Liberia sanctions regime,[60] Libya sanctions regime,[61] the Sudan sanctions regime,[62] and the Afghanistan sanctions.[63] In addition, the Security Council has also established regimes to counter the proliferation of weapons of mass destruction. These include the 1540 regime, which requires states to prevent the attainment of weapons of mass destruction by non-state actors.[64]

Typically, Security Council sanctions regimes, whether country specific or counter- terrorism, have three elements. The first element typically contained in such resolutions is an arms embargo, that is, there is an obligation on member states of the UN to prevent the sale of arms to listed individuals and entities. The second element typically found in sanctions regimes is a travel ban, that is, an obligation to ensure that listed individuals do not travel. Finally, and perhaps most intrusively, Security Council sanctions regimes typically require member states to freeze the assets of the listed individuals or entities. In addition, Security Council resolution 1373, a more general terrorism-related resolution, provides an obligation on states to prevent, suppress and criminalise the wilful financing of terrorism.[65] In recent years, the UN sanctions regime has come under pressure from academic literature and domestic and regional

57 These include the authorisation to use of force eg UN SC Res 1973 (2011) authorising the use of force in Libya and the authorisation to enter Somali territorial waters in the fight against piracy off the coast of Somalia in UN SC Res 1816 (2008).
58 ICTY, ICTR and RM resolutions.
59 See eg UN SC Res 2131 (2013) on the situation in Middle East (Syria) para 4.
60 Established by UN SC Res 1521 (2003).
61 Established by UN SC Res 1970 (2011).
62 Established by UN SC Res 1591 (2005).
63 Established by UN SC Res 1988 (2011). Originally the Afghanistan sanctions regime was part of the Al Qaida regime.
64 See eg UN SC Res 1540 (2004) paras 1 - 3.
65 UN SC Res 1373 (2001) para 1.

courts for lack of due process, in particular the listing and delisting procedures.[66] In summary the concerns relate to the lack of information relating to the reasons for listing as well as the lack of an effective remedy in cases of alleged unjustified listing. While these concerns have been raised with respect to the Al Qaida (1267) sanctions regime, the issues raised can apply equally to other sanctions regimes.

To the extent that the concerns can be expressed in terms of the inconsistency of the decisions with the constraints placed by international law, then the duty to 'accept and carry out' would theoretically fall away. If such a determination were to be made by the judiciary of the state in which implementation should take place, national-level repudiation may take place through a legal inability to implement domestically. The *Kadi* saga, discussed by Payandeh, is perhaps the best example of a national, or in that case regional, level repudiation with the potential for non-implementation (→ Payandeh).[67] *Kadi,* however, was not about the consistency of Security Council decisions with *jus cogens* or the principles and purposes of the Charter, but rather the consistency of the decisions with fundamental rights under EU Law. Thus, national-level repudiation becomes possible even for decisions taken 'in accordance with the' Charter and for which there is duty to 'accept and carry out'.

In response to the spectre of national level repudiation, the Council has sought to improve the due process standards of the sanctions regime, in particular the Al Qaida regime with a view to promoting implementation in domestic law. The first element for improving the Al Qaida listing process was the requirement that a 'statement of case' be provided before an individual or entity can be listed.[68] A second element, which applied to all sanctions regime and not only the Al Qaida sanctions, relates to the institution of the Focal Point, mandated to receive the delisting requirements.[69] Without a doubt, the most far-reaching changes to the Al Qaida sanctions regime have related to the creation of the Office of the Ombudsperson and subsequent expansion of the role of the Ombudsperson.[70] The Office of the Ombudsperson was created in 2009 to replace, for the purposes of the 1267 regime, the focal point.[71] While the Ombudsperson has the power to receive requests for de-listing, evaluate the case for de-listing and make recommendations (referred to as observations) to the Sanctions Committee on the de-listing of an entity or individual, this was still not seen as sufficient to address the due process concerns because the process remained essentially diplomatic and not a

66 Tladi & Taylor (n 55 above) 775 - 780.
67 ECJ Case C-584/10 P, C-593/10 P and C-595/10 P *Kadi v Commission and joined cases* [2013].
68 UN SC Res 1617 (2005) para 5. The 'statement of case', however, remains vague and would not satisfy an evidentiary burden.
69 See UN SC Res 1730 (2006).
70 Tladi & Taylor (n 55 above) para 36 .
71 UN SC Res 1904 (2009).

judicial (or quasi-judicial), that is, because the Ombudsperson did not have decision-making powers, process could not be said to include an independent arbiter to determine the validity or not of the continued listing. Under the 'sun-set clause' of Resolution 1989, the recommendations of the Ombudsperson can only be reversed by a unanimous decision of the sanctions committee.[72] Even with these attempts at placating those arguing for greater due process, this author has questioned whether the introduction of the sun-set clauses is sufficient to address the due process concerns associated with the 1267/1989 regime.[73]

3 The implementation of UN obligations in South Africa: Challenges and prospects

3.1 Implementation of the UN immunities-related obligations

As a member of the UN and party to the UN Charter and agreements on immunities in respect of the UN and its Specialised Agencies, South Africa is under an international law obligation to grant immunities to the UN and its officials as well as entities related to the UN and their personnel. This international law obligation, stemming as it does from treaty law, requires implementing legislation in terms of section 231(4) of the Constitution of the Republic of South Africa, 1996 (→ De Wet/Introduction). South African courts have, to date, avoided the vexed question of what, in the context of the Constitution, is meant by 'self-executing'.[74] It is fortunately unnecessary to consider whether any the provisions on immunities in the Charter or any of the provisions in the various agreements are self-executing because the obligations on immunities have been incorporated into domestic law.

The Diplomatic Immunities and Privileges Act (hereinafter the Act),[75] explicitly incorporates the 1946 and 1947 Conventions into South African law. The Act provides that the 1946 and 1947 Conventions, the Vienna Convention on Diplomatic Relations and the Vienna Convention on

72 For a detailed discussion of the Resolution 1989 see Tladi & Taylor (n 55 above) paras 32 - 43. It is important to emphasise, however, that any member of the sanctions committee could escalate an issue of delisting to the Security Council, where any recommendation of the Ombudsperson can be overturned by a veto of a Permanent member of the Security Council.

73 See Tladi & Taylor (n 55 above) 788. Similarly, the *Kadi Grand Chamber* (n 67 above) held at para 133, 'despite the improvements added, in particular after the adoption of the contested regulation, the procedure for delisting and *ex officio* re-examination at UN level they do not provide the person ... the guarantee of effective judicial protection.'

74 See N Botha 'Justice Sachs and the Use of International Law by the Constitutional Court: Equity or Expediency?' (2010) 25 *SA Public Law* 235 246ff.

75 Diplomatic and Privileges Act 37 of 2001 (as amended) ('The Act').

Consular Relations, all of which are reproduced in Schedules to the Act, 'have the force of law in the Republic'.[76] Although, the provisions of the Charter on immunities are themselves not incorporated into domestic law, since the 1946 and 1947 Conventions respectively give effect to the provisions of the Charter on immunities, the substance of the Charter provisions can be deemed to be incorporated and are part of South African law. Although the law relating to immunities has been incorporated into South Africa, conflicts between domestic law and immunities and privileges sometimes create complications.

Under the 1946 and 1947 Conventions, officials of the United Nations and its Specialised Agencies respectively, are 'exempt from taxation on the salaries and emoluments paid' by the UN and its Specialised Agencies.[77] It is the UN or the Specialised Agencies that determine the categories of persons entitled to the enumerated immunities and privileges.[78] The practice of the UN is to categorise all professional staff members, that is, P1 to P5, Directors and above, as 'officials' for the purposes of immunities irrespective of nationality. Under South African legislation, however, South African nationals serving in South Africa are not exempt from taxation even if employed by the UN or one of its Specialised Agencies.[79] While the Income Tax Act makes provision for exemption from income tax for persons serving in missions, this exemption does not extend to nationals.[80] South Africa is therefore prevented under the Income Tax Act to provide tax exemption to South Africa nationals serving as officials of the United Nations or its Specialised Agencies. This contradiction is resolved through a cumbersome administrative off-set arrangement. Under this system, South African officials employed by a UN entity have an amount deducted from their salary (referred to as a United Nations fee) in lieu of tax, which amount is paid over to the treasury but then off-set against South Africa's assessed contribution to the organisation. In short, the system, in a round-about way, provides de facto exemption from taxation for South African nationals employed by UN entities. While the system in place seems to work, it is rather cumbersome and much easier ways exist to ensure implementation. It is not clear for example, since the

76 n 75 above, sec 2. See also sec 5 of the Act which deals with immunities of the United Nations and its Specialised Agencies. Sec 5(1) provides simply that the 1946 Convention 'applies to the United Nations and its officials in the Republic' while Section 5(2) provides similarly that the Convention on the Privileges and Immunities of the Specialized Agencies (the 1947 Convention) (21 November 1947) 'applies to the specialised and its officials in the Republic.'

77 n 32 above, art V section 18(b); & n 76 above, art VI sec 19(b).

78 See the 1946 Convention (n 32 above) art V section 17 and the 1947 Convention (n 76 above) art VI sec 18.

79 The Value-Added Tax Act 89 of 1991 sec 68(2) and the Income Tax Act 58 of 1962 sec 10.

80 Income Tax Act (n 79 above) sec 10(1)(c)(iii). It is noteworthy that the Vienna Convention on Diplomatic Relations, while providing for exemption from taxation, excludes from the scope of the exemption persons who are 'nationals of or permanent resident in the receiving state'. See the Vienna Convention on Diplomatic Relations (18 April 1961, 500 UNTS 95) art 33(2)(a).

1946 and 1947 are law in South Africa, why the various rules of the interpretation of statutes are not applied in a way in a way to ensure consistency. An even more definitive solution would be to amend the Income Tax Act to create necessary exemption.

In addition to issues of compatibility between the obligation to provide for immunities and privileges, on the one hand, and domestic law, on the other, interpretative questions concerning the scope of the obligations have also arisen. In 2011, a dismissed employee of the UNFPA filed a complaint against the Commission for Conciliation Mediation and Arbitration (hereinafter the CCMA), a statutory body created to conciliate, mediate and arbitrate labour disputes, for unfair labour practice after she was dismissed, allegedly in violation of the South African labour requirements. The UN requested the Government of the Republic of South Africa to 'take steps' to prevent what would amount to a violation of the immunities under the 1946 Convention. These steps, the UN argued, should include providing legal representation for the UN.[81] However, it is not the practice of South Africa, nor did South Africa accept it as a legal obligation under the 1946 Convention, to provide legal representation in the case of suit against a person or entity entitled to immunities. Rather the Act requires the Director-General of the Foreign Ministry to issue an executive certificate to the relevant court or tribunal confirming that the relevant entity or person enjoys immunity.[82] Moreover, the Act provides for criminal sanctions punishable by three years or a fine against anyone for any person, including a party, the attorney, or officer of the court, who initiates or executes legal process against anyone with immunity. This, South Africa argued, was sufficient to implement its legal obligations. After lengthy diplomatic debate, it was agreed that the Foreign Ministry would send a communication to the CCMA informing it of the status of the UNFPA and making the CCMA aware of the criminal sanctions that could be imposed for continuation of the legal process against the UNFPA.

It appears therefore, at least with respect to the immunities, that South Africa has been able to implement its UN obligations. The few challenges that have arisen, whether as a result of conflict of domestic law and the immunities and privileges or differing interpretation of the South Africa's obligation by the South African and UN authorities have, to date, been resolved amicably.

81 This particular assertion, according to the United Nations Legal Office, was based on the advisory opinion on the *Differences Relating to Immunity from Legal Process of a Special Rapporteur of the Commission of Human Rights* (29 April 1999) (1999) ICJ Reports 62, 4; where the International Court of Justice held that there was an obligation 'to convey that finding [concerning the immunities] to the national courts concerned'.

82 n 75 above, sec 9(3). In response to the UN's legal argument, South Africa argued that the provision of an executive certificate is sufficient to meet the requirement in the Advisory opinion *Differences Relating to Immunity from Legal Process of a Special Rapporteur of the Commission of Human Rights* (n 81 above).

3.2 Implementation of UNSC obligations

While the obligations of South Africa to provide for immunities and privileges of the UN are implemented domestically by means of a single piece of legislation, there is no equivalent comprehensive legislation on the implementation of Security Council obligations. Although Parliament passed legislation on the application of Security Council resolutions, the Act never entered into force.[83] Thus, UN Security Council decisions are currently implemented through different, theme specific, legislative enactments.

The primary legislative tool for the implementation of the terrorism-related Security Council resolutions is the Protection of Constitutional Democracy Against Terrorism and Related Activities Act (hereinafter the POCDATARA).[84] The POCDATARA was adopted to give effect to the obligations of South Africa under, *inter alia,* UN Security Council resolutions. The purpose of the POCDATARA, for example, is defined as, *inter alia,* 'to provide for a mechanism to comply with United Nations Security Council Resolutions, which are binding on member States'.[85] The POCDATARA makes it a criminal offence to engage in terrorist or related activities, including activities related to the financing of terrorism as is required by Security Council resolution 1373.[86] The jurisdiction by South African courts over terrorism-related offences is broad and includes acts not perpetrated in the territory of South Africa.[87]

The POCDATARA also makes provision for the freezing of assets as required by UN Security Council sanctions regimes.[88] The assets freeze

83 Application of Resolutions of the Security Council of the United Nations Act 172 of 1993. Under section 5 the Act would 'come into operation on a date fixed by the State President by proclamation in the Gazette.' The President never made the required proclamation because it was felt that the Act would not pass constitutional muster. According to H Strydom 'South Africa and Namibia: Part I: South Africa' in V Gowlland-Debbas (ed) *National implementation of United Nations sanctions: A comparative study* (2004) 433, an act 'in which legislative measures [could be achieved through] executive sleight of hand [was] unlikely to pass constitutional muster.'

84 Protection of Constitutional Democracy against Terrorism and Related Activities Act 33 of 2004 (POCDATARA). See for discussion De Wet (n 26 above) 576.

85 The preamble specifically refers to UN SC Res 1373 as well as other 'resolutions under Chapter VI1 of the United Nations Charter, requiring Member States to combat terrorist and related activities, including taking effective measures to prevent and combat the financing of terrorist and related activities, and the freezing of funds, assets or economic resources of persons who commit terrorist and related activities.'

86 n 84 above, sec 1 & 2. In addition POCDATARA enumerates other terrorist related activities, including hijacking-related offences (sec 9 and sec 10), hostage taking (sec 7) and explosives-related offences.

87 See POCDATARA (n 84 above) sec 15. The first basis of jurisdiction, in sec 15(1), is where a person accused of terrorism-related is 'arrested in the territory of the Republic' irrespective of where the offence was allegedly committed. The second basis of jurisdiction, in sec15(2), is where there is a connection between, on the one hand, the place where the offence was allegedly committed, the person allegedly committing the offence, the place was the damaged was caused or the persons who were harmed by the activities and, on the other hand, the Republic of South Africa.

88 n 84 above, sec 25.

provisions under the POCDATARA, however, can only be invoked in relation to terrorism sanctions regime and not country specific regimes. The assets freeze under the Libya or the DRC sanctions regime, for example, cannot be implemented in terms of the POCDATARA. The POCDATARA permits a High Court to make an order freezing the assets of a person or entity where such a person or entity 'has committed, attempted to commit, or participated' in the commission of acts of terror,[89] or where such a person or entity is 'identified in a notice issued by the President under section 25'.[90] Section 25 in turn, provides that the President must give 'notice that the Security Council of the United Nations, under Chapter of the Charter of the United Nations, has identified a specific entity as being' involved in terrorist activities or as an entity or person against whom members of the United Nations are obliged to take measures specified in terrorism-related resolutions.[91] The provisions of the POCDATARA with respect to freezing are complemented by the surveillance provisions of the Financial Intelligence Centre Act.[92] It is important to note, however, that any notice by the President, does not, in and of itself, have legal consequences. Rather the notice must be tabled before Parliament which must consider the notice and make any decision that it deems it necessary.[93] Moreover, the freezing of assets takes place on the basis of an order by a High Court in terms of section 23. Because the freezing order takes place by means of a court order, which is subject to the normal court processes, including challenge by affected persons, the criticisms surrounding due process that have been directed at the Al Qaida regime are less likely to arise.[94]

POCDATARA is an exemplary implementation of the terrorism resolutions of the Security Council, especially as pertains to the obligations to freeze assets and to criminalise. In its report on South Africa, subsequent to its country visit in 2011, the Analytical Support and Sanctions Monitoring Team of the Al Qaida sanctions regime (hereinafter the Monitoring Team) concluded that 'the South African authorities have made commendable effort to fulfil their obligations'.[95] Similarly, while a survey conducted by the Counter-Terrorism Executive Directorate, the entity charged with the monitoring the implementation of resolution 1373, found areas of concern, notably with regards to the potential vulnerabilities in regulating non-profit organisations in South Africa,[96] on specific questions relating to the adequacy of the legal framework, the analysis

89 n 84 above, sec 23(1)(a).
90 n 84 above, sec 23(1)(b).
91 POCDATARA (n 84 above) sec 25.
92 See Financial Intelligence Centre Act 39 of 2001, especially sec 28A.
93 POCDATARA (n 84 above) sec 26.
94 In this regard, De Wet (n 26 above) 576 states that the implementation of the measures under POCDATARA are made subject to 'domestic control'.
95 Analytical Support and Sanctions Monitoring Team *Report on visit to Pretoria, South Africa, 11-12 May 2011* MT/TRAVEL/2011/16a (on file with the author) para 2.
96 UN Counter-Terrorism Executive Directorate *Overview of implementation assessment: South Africa, April 2013* (on file with the author).

consistently found that POCDATARA either fully complied with the obligations or largely complied.[97] This does not mean that there are no legal gaps with the implementation of the sanctions regime. To date, South Africa has had to implement 1267 sanctions against only one individual, Ali Bakr Tantoush, a Libyan national residing in South Africa, who appears not to have any assets that can be frozen and so is largely unaffected by the sanctions imposed. If Tantoush were to challenge the asset freeze, given the basis of his listing, namely mere association with groups suspected of being terrorist, it is possible that a South African court could overturn the freezing order. This could result in the inability to continue implementing the obligations under the 1267 and the potential for national-level repudiation. On the other hand, given the improvement to the Al Qaida Sanctions, it is *possible* that South African courts may require the exhaustion of the procedures under the UNSC Resolution 1989, before considering there to be violation of due process rights.

While POCDATARA makes provision for an assets freeze it does have two limitations. The first limitation, as already mentioned, is that POCDATARA only applies to measures in respect of terrorism-related resolutions. Country-specific obligations flowing from other Security Council resolutions are thus dealt with under a catalogue of unrelated pieces of legislation. Secondly, POCDATARA makes provision for an assets freeze and criminal sanctions for terrorism-related offences but does not cover other measures such as arms embargos and travel bans, even with respect to terrorism-related obligations.[98] For these other measures, implementation has to take place through the same fragmented legislative framework that is applicable to non-terrorism-related resolutions. An arms embargo, for example, *could* be implemented through the National Conventional Arms Control[99] and the Firearms Control Act.[100] The Firearms Control Act provides that a person may not possess a firearm unless they are in possession of a license.[101] Although section 9 of the Firearms Control Act provides the National Police Commissioner with the power to decline an application for a certificate of competence, which is a

97 UN Counter-Terrorism Executive Directorate *Detailed Implementation Survey: South Africa, April 2013* (on file with the author). For example, on whether there has been sufficient criminalisation, the survey responds 'yes'; on whether every aspect of terrorist financing is covered, the survey responds 'yes'; on whether the collection of funds is criminalised independently of the provision of funds, the survey responds 'yes'; and on whether the state has sufficient legal measures to freeze assets the survey responds 'yes'. Indeed of the first eleven question, the survey responds 'no' to only one question, namely whether the state has to date frozen any assets. Needless to say that question is not a normative that goes to the legal framework but rather empirical question.

98 Although the Financial Intelligence Centre Act 38 of 2001 sec 34 provides that the Financial Intelligence Centre 'may direct [an] institution ... not to proceed with the carrying out of ... [certain] proposed transactions', such an order is limited to five days. In any event, it is not contemplated that this provision could be applied to a person merely by virtue of being listed in, for example, a country specific sanctions list.

99 National Conventional Arms Control Act 41 of 2002.

100 Firearms Arms Control Act 60 of 2000.

101 Firearms Control Act (n 100 above) sec 4.

condition for obtaining a license, listing by a sanctions committee of the Security Council is not ground for refusal.[102] Similarly, travel bans *could* be enforced through the Immigration Act.[103] In the application of the power to grant or refuse entry into South Africa,[104] South African authorities check against the Security Council sanctions lists.[105] The Passports and Travel Documents Act also provides an avenue for implementation of travel bans, particularly in relation to South Africans.[106]

It appears from the above, that through a network of unrelated legislation, South Africa *could* be in a position to implement the various obligations flowing from UN Security Council resolution. Nonetheless, the status quo is also unsatisfactory for a number of reasons. First, as already mentioned, there is no provision for assets freeze outside of the terrorism context.[107] Second, in most instances there are gaps in the legislation that could be applied to implement the Security Council obligations. Third, the implementation of many of the obligations, because it is not expressly provided, is dependent on strained interpretation which is susceptible to legal challenge. Finally, even apart from the legal gaps, it is desirable to have a comprehensive piece of legislation to deal with the implementation of Security Council obligations. For all these reasons, the South African government has been actively engaged in a process to elaborate legislation to comprehensively provide for the implementation of Security Council obligations.

Since the 1993 Act, which never entered into force, was adopted there have been various drafts of a bill to implement Security Council obligations with the most recent attempt beginning in 2012. Perhaps the

102 The grounds in section 9 generally relate to the commission of crimes or the mental state of a person. Since listing does not depend on commission of a crime, most of the grounds would be inapplicable. There is, however, a broad requirement of being 'fit and proper' which could potentially be used decline a certificate on the basis of listing. Whether such a generous interpretation of 'fit and proper person' would be meet constitutional muster remains to be seen.

103 Immigration Act 13 of 2002.

104 The Immigration Act (n 103 above) sec 9(4) read with sec 11.

105 See Analytical Support and Sanctions Monitoring Team (n 95 above) para 11.

106 See especially sec 4(1) of the South African Passports and Travel Documents Act 4 of 1994 which permits the Minister of Home Affairs to make regulations on a number of issues including 'endorsements on South African passports', 'restrictions' and 'the circumstances under which the issue of a South African passport or travel document may be refused'.

107 While provisions of the Financial Intelligence Centre Act (n 98 above) this is probably not sufficient to effect a freeze on the assets. The recent high profile case concerning Libyan assets in South Africa is are reflective of this difficulty. See The Sunday Independent 'UN, SA rRow over Gaddafi aAssets' available at http://www. safpi.org/news/article/2013/un-sa-row-over-gaddafi-assetshttp://www.safpi.org/news/article/2013/un-sa-row-over-gaddafi-assets (last accessed 6 January 2013). See also Annex IV Final report of the Panel of Experts established pursuant to Resolution 1973 (2011) concerning Libya S/2013/99 where the South Africa is red-listed for non-responsiveness to questions about the freezing of Libyan assets under UN SC Res 1970.

most controversial aspect that the drafters of any legislation will need to address is the question of the judicial review of any listing. It is foreseen that the Bill will provide for the taking of measures (arms embargo, travel ban and assets freeze) on the decision of the court on the application of the Directorate of Public Prosecutions. The primary question is whether an individual can challenge the taking of measures on the grounds that there is no evidence of wrongdoing. An affirmative answer could place South Africa at odds with Security Council sanctions regime, which are deemed by the Security Council to be 'preventative and not putative' and thus should not require proof of wrongdoing.[108] An answer in the negative, however, could be challenged as unconstitutional as it would imply the violation of rights, including the rights to property and dignity, without justification. To date South Africa has not had to deal with the fallout from the lack of comprehensive legislation[109] largely because no South African and only one person living in South Africa finds themselves on a sanctions list. This, however, may change in the future[110] and the sooner South Africa adopts the comprehensive sanctions list the better.

The implementation of the 1540 regime, however, does not suffer from similar deficiency. The implementation of 1540 regime is done principally through the Non-Proliferation of Weapons of Mass Destruction Act, with the criminal sanctions being imposed through POCDATARA.[111] The Act provides for the Minister of Trade to provide, by notice in Government Gazette, the overall policy of South Africa with respect to, *inter alia,* the prevention of the proliferation of weapons of mass destruction.[112] By its own account, South Africa appears to be successfully implementing the obligations under Resolution 1540.[113]

108 Preamble of UNSC Resolution 1989 (2011).

109 Except perhaps with regards to Libya.

110 In late 2012 the 1970 Committee made enquiries about a South Africa citizen, a Daleen Sanders, in connection with assistance offered to Saif Gaddafi. She was subsequently listed by the US Government. See http://www.treasury.gov/press-center/press-releases/Pages/tg1742.aspx (last accessed 13 May 2015).

111 See especially the Non-Proliferation of Weapons of Mass Destruction Act 87 of 1993 sec 2.

112 The Non-Proliferation of Weapons of Mass Destruction Act (n 111 above) sec 2(1)(d) - (g). The specific prohibition are detailed in Government Notice No 712 of 8 June 2004.

113 Letter from South Africa to the Chair of the 1540 Committee, dated 14 December 2007, responding to the 1540 Matrix for compliance. In its comprehensive overview of implementation, the Group of Experts of the 1540 Committee stated that while compliance in Africa was poor, the 'notable exceptions are performance by one State in Southern Africa, rated very high, and the Northern African states, rated average.' See *Comprehensive Review on the State of Implementation of Resolution 1540* (2004), Background Paper Prepared by the 1540 Committee of Experts According to the Document for Modalities for the Conduct of a Comprehensive Review (S/2009/170): Specific Element C (Conduct of Regional Analysis of Implementation, with Some Examples of National and Regional Experience) http://www.un.org/en/sc/1540/comprehensive-review/open-meetings.shtml (last accessed 13 May 2015).

4 Conclusion

In general South Africa's legislative framework for implementing UN obligations is commendable. The obligations to provide for and respect the immunities of the United Nations, its officials, its Specialised Agencies and their officials have been implemented in accordance with the Diplomatic Immunities Act and Privileges Act which incorporates, in full, the relevant treaties detailing the obligations of the UN and its Specialised Agencies.

Where there are some challenges, although even these ought not to be overstated, is with respect to the implementation of Security Council obligations. The primary challenge is the lack of a comprehensive statute to implement binding UN Security Council decisions. Although to date this has not resulted in many cases of non-compliance, this state of affairs could change if more South Africans or persons with connections to South Africa are listed on Security Council sanctions lists. The current endeavour to elaborate legislation to implement the obligations of South Africa under Security Council resolutions is therefore to welcome. However, in elaborating this legislation, it should be recalled that the Constitution is the supreme law of the land, and any legislation must be consistent with it, even if this requires it to fall short of the Security Council requirements.

BIBLIOGRAPHY

Barber, J & Barret, J (1990) *South Africa's foreign policy: The search for status and security, 1945-1988* Cambridge University Press: Cambridge

De Wet, E (2004) *The Chapter VII powers of the Security Council* Hart Publishing: Oxford/Portland

De Wet, E 'South Africa' in Shelton, D (ed) (2011) *International law and domestic legal systems: incorporation, transformation and persuasion* Oxford University Press: Oxford/New York

Delbrück, J 'Article 25' in Simma,B (ed) (1994) *The Charter of the United Nations: A commentary* Oxford University Press: Oxford/New York

Heunis, JC (1986) *United Nations versus South Africa: A legal assessment of United Nations – and United Nations related activities in respect of South Africa* Lex Patria: Johannesburg

Peters, A 'Article 25' in Simma, B; Khan, DE; Nolte, G & Paulus, A (eds) (3rd edn 2012) *The Charter of the United Nations: A commentary* Oxford University Press: Oxford/New York

Shearer, J (2011) *Against the world: South Africa and human rights at the United Nations 1945-1961* UNISA Press: Pretoria

Permissions

All chapters in this book were first published in TIILGSA, by Pretoria University Law Press (PULP); hereby published with permission under the Creative Commons Attribution License or equivalent. Every chapter published in this book has been scrutinized by our experts. Their significance has been extensively debated. The topics covered herein carry significant findings which will fuel the growth of the discipline. They may even be implemented as practical applications or may be referred to as a beginning point for another development.

The contributors of this book come from diverse backgrounds, making this book a truly international effort. This book will bring forth new frontiers with its revolutionizing research information and detailed analysis of the nascent developments around the world.

We would like to thank all the contributing authors for lending their expertise to make the book truly unique. They have played a crucial role in the development of this book. Without their invaluable contributions this book wouldn't have been possible. They have made vital efforts to compile up to date information on the varied aspects of this subject to make this book a valuable addition to the collection of many professionals and students.

This book was conceptualized with the vision of imparting up-to-date information and advanced data in this field. To ensure the same, a matchless editorial board was set up. Every individual on the board went through rigorous rounds of assessment to prove their worth. After which they invested a large part of their time researching and compiling the most relevant data for our readers.

The editorial board has been involved in producing this book since its inception. They have spent rigorous hours researching and exploring the diverse topics which have resulted in the successful publishing of this book. They have passed on their knowledge of decades through this book. To expedite this challenging task, the publisher supported the team at every step. A small team of assistant editors was also appointed to further simplify the editing procedure and attain best results for the readers.

Apart from the editorial board, the designing team has also invested a significant amount of their time in understanding the subject and creating the most relevant covers. They scrutinized every image to scout for the most suitable representation of the subject and create an appropriate cover for the book.

The publishing team has been an ardent support to the editorial, designing and production team. Their endless efforts to recruit the best for this project, has resulted in the accomplishment of this book. They are a veteran in the field of academics and their pool of knowledge is as vast as their experience in printing. Their expertise and guidance has proved useful at every step. Their uncompromising quality standards have made this book an exceptional effort. Their encouragement from time to time has been an inspiration for everyone.

The publisher and the editorial board hope that this book will prove to be a valuable piece of knowledge for researchers, students, practitioners and scholars across the globe.

List of Contributors

Engela C Schlemmer
Professor of law at the University of the Witwatersrand, Johannesburg, South Africa

Wolfgang Durner
Professor of Public Law at Bonn University, Germany and Director of the Bonn Institute for Water Law

Rüdiger Wolfrum
Director emeritus of the Max Planck Institute for Comparative Public Law and International Law, Heidelberg, Germany and Co-Director of the Max Planck Foundation for International Peace and the Rule of Law

Holger Hestermeyer
Reader at the Dickson Poon School of Law at Kings College London, United Kingdom

Silja Vöneky
Co-Director of the Institute for Public Law and Professor of Public International Law and Ethics of Law at the University of Freiburg, Germany

Lisa Chamberlain
Deputy Director, Centre for Applied Legal Studies (CALS) and Senior Lecturer, School of Law, University of the Witwatersrand (Wits), Johannesburg, South Africa

Tumai Murombo
Director and Associate Professor of Law, Mandela Institute, School of Law, University of the Witwatersrand, Johannesburg, South Africa

Erika de Wet
The contribution is based on E de Wet 'South Africa' in D Shelton (ed) International law and domestic legal systems: Incorporation, transformation and persuasion (2011) 567 - 593

Nicola Wenzel
Legal officer for the German Federal Ministry of Justice and Consumer Protection

Mehrdad Payandeh
Junior Professor for Public Law and Public International Law at the Heinrich-Heine-University of Düsseldorf, Germany

Dire Tladi
Fellow at the Institute of International and Comparative Law in Africa and Professor of International Law at the Faculty of Law, University of Pretoria

Index

CPSIA information can be obtained
at www.ICGtesting.com
Printed in the USA
LVHW082311100122
708212LV00001B/21

9 781639 873265